Tell My Beloved

*Words of Hope and Encouragement for
All God's Children for All God's Creation*

VICKIE L. BROOKS

Copyright © 2018 Vickie L. Brooks.

All rights reserved. No part of this book may be used or reproduced by any means, graphic, electronic, or mechanical, including photocopying, recording, taping or by any information storage retrieval system without the written permission of the author except in the case of brief quotations embodied in critical articles and reviews.

WestBow Press books may be ordered through booksellers or by contacting:

WestBow Press
A Division of Thomas Nelson & Zondervan
1663 Liberty Drive
Bloomington, IN 47403
www.westbowpress.com
1 (866) 928-1240

Because of the dynamic nature of the Internet, any web addresses or links contained in this book may have changed since publication and may no longer be valid. The views expressed in this work are solely those of the author and do not necessarily reflect the views of the publisher, and the publisher hereby disclaims any responsibility for them.

Any people depicted in stock imagery provided by Getty Images are models, and such images are being used for illustrative purposes only.
Certain stock imagery © Getty Images.

ISBN: 978-1-9736-3690-8 (sc)
ISBN: 978-1-9736-3689-2 (hc)
ISBN: 978-1-9736-3691-5 (e)

Library of Congress Control Number: 2018909819

Print information available on the last page.

WestBow Press rev. date: 8/27/2018

Scripture quotations marked HCSB are taken from the Holman Christian Standard Bible®, Copyright © 1999, 2000, 2002, 2003, 2009 by Holman Bible Publishers. Used by permission. Holman Christian Standard Bible®, Holman CSB®, and HCSB® are federally registered trademarks of Holman Bible Publishers.

Scripture quotations marked (NLT) are taken from the Holy Bible, New Living Translation, copyright © 1996, 2004, 2007 by Tyndale House Foundation. Used by permission of Tyndale House Publishers, Inc., Carol Stream, Illinois 60188. All rights reserved.

THE HOLY BIBLE, NEW INTERNATIONAL VERSION®, NIV® Copyright © 1973, 1978, 1984, 2011 by Biblica, Inc.® Used by permission. All rights reserved worldwide.

Scripture taken from the Amplified Bible, Copyright © 1954, 1958, 1962, 1964, 1965, 1987 by The Lockman Foundation. Used with permission.

Scripture taken from the NEW AMERICAN STANDARD BIBLE®, Copyright © 1960, 1962, 1963, 1968, 1971, 1972, 1973, 1975, 1977, 1995 by The Lockman Foundation. Used by permission.

Scripture quotations are from the ESV® Bible (The Holy Bible, English Standard Version®), copyright © 2001 by Crossway, a publishing ministry of Good News Publishers. Used by permission. All rights reserved.

Scripture taken from the New Century Version®. Copyright © 2005 by Thomas Nelson. Used by permission. All rights reserved.

Scripture taken from The One New Man Bible, copyright © 2011 William J. Morford. Used by permission of True Potential Publishing, Inc.

Scripture taken from the New King James Version®. Copyright © 1982 by Thomas Nelson. Used by permission. All rights reserved.

I dedicate this book to you, the reader—every one of you. May this journal encourage you to seek the Lord your God with all your heart, strength, mind, and soul. May you be encouraged to love one another as Jesus Christ loves us.

Together, we are on a journey. It is often a hard and dangerous journey that requires much work, discerning diligence, and bravery. But step by step, God will lead us as we follow Him.

Thanks and Appreciation

First, I thank the Lord Jesus Christ, who has loved me and watched over me my whole life even when I did not know, recognize, or acknowledge Him. Thank You, Lord, for drawing me to Yourself with Your kindness and goodness. May my life and the words in this journal reveal Your love and kindness for all Your creation and draw us ever closer to You.

I give thanks and honor to my loving husband, who through all our years together has provided for our family and stood faithfully dedicated to our maturing in the grace and knowledge of Jesus Christ. Your consistent pursuit of excellence in all things has kept us in His care. Thank you for encouraging me and our children to grasp the vision of our calling and destiny to serve God and others.

My appreciation, thanks, and honor also go to our extended family and friends and even those we have yet to meet and get to know. We are brothers and sisters on this life's journey. Thank you for the kindness and goodness you have shown us.

Special Acknowledgments

We thank also Debbie and Lance Haluka and Sean Rathbun for allowing us to use some of their amazing photos depicting the beauty and significance of God's creation.

Thanks and appreciation also to all the folks at WestBow Press who skillfully and with sensitivity carried the manuscript of *Tell My Beloved* and brought it through to publication.

What Are Words of Hope and Encouragement?

Words of hope and encouragement are not just feel-good, warm-and-fuzzy, temporary bandages for your soul. Rather, words of hope and encouragement speak energizing life into your heart and spirit. They give you perspective and understanding and clarify what is true and good. These discerning truths give you a foundation for making wise decisions and choices.

Sprinkled here and there embedded in the words of hope and encouragement are golden nuggets of correction, discipline, and warning as would come from loving parents who are directing and training their children. I am still learning to calm down, drop my defensive posturing, and receive instruction and correction with grace and wisdom. Lord, help me see things through Your eyes, hear them with Your ears, and understand them with Your heart.

Words of hope and encouragement for all God's creation tell us God has made a provision for the restoration of whatever has been marred by sin and blackened and cheapened by our failures. The angels announced the beginning of restoration. Peace, wholeness, radiant beauty and joy—God has made available to us His restoration and redemption plan!

Do not our hearts cry out for relief from the pain and dysfunctions we endure on this earth in its present fallen condition? Do we have a certain feeling, a knowing in our hearts that it wasn't meant to be like this? Yes, God has placed in our hearts an awareness that life was meant to be blessed and good in every way. You and I have an innate desire for restoration, renewal, and redemption.

All of God's children and His creation eagerly await the fulfillment of His redemption for us!

Ways to Use This Book

1. Read it prayerfully as a devotional.
2. Use it to study the Bible: look up, study, and meditate on the scriptures listed. Answer the questions in the Selected Scripture Reading sections. Unless noted otherwise, scriptures are from the New King James Version.
3. Using a concordance or other Bible study resources that can be found online; do related topical and word studies.
4. Answer the question: In light of the scriptures, how might God be leading me to think and live differently?
5. Do additional research on the scriptures listed by using different translations, commentaries, and study Bibles.
6. Respond to the discourses and Bible verses by writing your own prayers to God. You may wish to keep a journal.
7. Identify scriptural principles that help define a Christian worldview on hot-button cultural issues.

Introduction and Important Clarification

Each of the 225 numbered narratives in *Tell My Beloved* is written as though God is speaking to you and me—rephrasing, applying the principles, and highlighting what He has spoken to us in the past through the scriptures. Number 226 is a prayer.

I want to make an important statement and clarification. The Bible alone is the accepted and canonized representation of God's messages to mankind. Factual yet powerfully poetic, the scriptures answer our basic questions about life, God, and ourselves. The Bible alone is to be trusted to give us the balanced and solid foundation we must have to foster overcoming faith in our increasingly confusing world.

Tell My Beloved comprises 225 short essays I journaled. It is creative writing based on the principles and truths in the Bible. The essays have distinct and recognizable biblical phrases and principles that express what I feel God said to us in the Bible and continues to speak to us. Nothing new—just saying the same things in new ways that catch our attention and make us think.

Imagine sitting under God's heaven on His majestic earth alone with Him. Your heart desires to know Him, who created you. What is the purpose and meaning of life? How do I fit in? What am I meant to be? All these things and more are racing through your mind. Your emotions are flooded with a deep yearning to know God and make sense of everything swirling around you.

You set your intentions on not just any god, concept, or teaching. Rather, you position yourself before Him, the Creator of heaven and earth, the universe, and Creator of you and me. You cry out, "God, I want to know You!" And with your heart, you begin to listen.

Contents

1. Tell My Beloved 1
2. Take Time to Be with Me 2
3. Rest in Me 3
4. I Shall Move the Mountains 5
5. The Place of Obedience 6
6. Come Up Higher 8
7. You Are Building Your Testimony Every Day 9
8. I Am Gathering My Sheep to Myself 12
9. Your Names Are Written in the Lamb's Book of Life 13
10. Behold, I Come Quickly 14
11. Reach Out with My Grace 15
12. I Am Searching for My Beloved 17
13. Listen to My Holy Spirit 18
14. This Is a Season of Restoration 20
15. It Is Time to Prepare 22
16. A Word for the Musicians 23
17. Pray for All These 25
18. The Rest You Are Seeking 26
19. Give Me All Your Hurts and Disappointments 28
20. Prepare Your Hearts 29
21. Then I Shall Lead You 30
22. And I See You 32
23. The Lord Has Heard 33
24. In My Presence You Will Overcome 35
25. You Are My Treasure 36
26. I Am Coming with a Mighty Cleansing 37
27. Walk in Holiness 39
28. Hear My Voice to Your Heart 40

29. Embrace the Wind of My Holy Spirit 42
30. Keep Praying 44
31. You Are Called to Stand in the Gap 45
32. An Everlasting Love 46
33. Your Heart Is My Treasure 48
34. I Am Your Strength and Joy 49
35. The Bread of Life 51
36. Cry Out to the Lord Your God 52
37. You Are My Testimony upon the Earth 54
38. The Secret Place of Worship 55
39. Allow My Spirit and My Truth to Cleanse and Purify 57
40. Follow Me 58
41. In Your Hearts Leave the World 59
42. Put On Tender Mercies 61
43. Before the Throne of God 63
44. Let Faith Well Up in Your Heart 65
45. Hear the Sound of the Trumpet 66
46. Dig Up the Uncultivated Ground 67
47. Living Water in a Dry and Thirsty Land 69
48. I Shall Restore My Church 71
49. Washed Pure to Move Forward 72
50. Great Joy in the Kingdom 73
51. Your Heart Will See and Understand 75
52. Will You Answer My Call to Your Heart? 76
53. The Perfect Gift 78
54. You Shall Walk in Newness of Life and Great Joy 79
55. I Give You Grace 81
56. Stand Still and See the Salvation God Has Prepared 82
57. I Am Restoring What Has Been Lost and Stolen 83
58. My Disciples 85
59. If My People 86
60. Walking in Obedience 87
61. Trust Me to Carry the Heavy Burdens 89
62. Wait upon Me 91
63. My Love Will Bring Healing to Your Soul 92
64. There Is No Other Name 94
65. Be Faithful in Intercession 95

66. Let Go of Past Wounds and Hurts 96
67. Prophecies Given Long Ago Are Soon to Be Fulfilled 98
68. Stand with Israel and You Will Be Blessed 99
69. Listen to My Holy Spirit as I Speak to Your Heart 101
70. My Love Will Lift You Up on Eagles' Wings 103
71. I Have a People 104
72. Come to Me for Healing and Restoration 105
73. Receive from Me What Your Heart Seeks 107
74. You Are My Child, and I Love You 108
75. I Have Plans for You, and They Are Good 109
76. Seek Me and You Will Find Me 111
77. For the Beauty in My People 112
78. I Have Called You to Be Peacemakers 113
79. Lay Up Treasures in Heaven 115
80. Let Me Be Your Refuge 117
81. I Have Made Preparations for You 119
82. Repent and Cleanse Your Hearts 121
83. Awaken and Arise 124
84. I Delight in Communing with You 125
85. The Sounds of Worship 126
86. Remain under My Wings 127
87. Look Ahead 129
88. I Am with You to Lead You 130
89. I Give You This Warning and This Charge 132
90. When My Righteous Ones Cry Out to Me 133
91. Consecrate Your Heart and Receive from Me 134
92. Will You Be Found Faithful? 135
93. Know That I Am with You 137
94. Be Wise and Gracious 138
95. My Gift to You 140
96. A Holy Nation Set Apart, Consecrated 141
97. Shall I Not Do a Great Work? 142
98. Have Faith and Do Not Lose Hope 144
99. Refreshed by My Spirit 145
100. Lift Up the Name and Love of Jesus 147
101. See What I Am Doing among You 149
102. I Make Clean What Is Mine 150

103. Shine and Be My Light ... 152
104. Choose Wisely ... 153
105. Hunger and Thirst ... 154
106. My Love Gives Wisdom and Grace ... 156
107. Rejoice, My Beloved ... 157
108. I Will Speak to Your Heart ... 158
109. The Time Is Short ... 160
110. No Longer Tossed About ... 161
111. Righteousness Shall Take Root in the Earth ... 162
112. Do Not Harden Your Hearts ... 164
113. That Only I Can Give You ... 165
114. You Are Precious ... 168
115. You Will Know Which Path to Take ... 170
116. Come and Work with Me ... 171
117. This Is a Good Time ... 172
118. Must Birth It by Prayer ... 174
119. Decide Whom You Will Serve ... 175
120. Put On White Garments ... 177
121. Grace to Overcome All Things ... 178
122. Restoration for My People ... 180
123. I Will Teach You ... 181
124. My Peace in Turbulent Storms ... 183
125. According to Kingdom Principles ... 185
126. Build Your House upon the Rock ... 187
127. Love and Honor One Another ... 188
128. Give No Place to Evil ... 191
129. You Are My Living Church ... 193
130. Come Closer to My Heart ... 194
131. Created to Be Clothed in My Light ... 196
132. Take My Yoke ... 197
133. Written in My Word ... 199
134. America, Repent ... 200
135. That I May Impart to You ... 204
136. Lifted Up in Purity and Righteousness ... 206
137. A Higher Way ... 207
138. Faith Works by Love ... 208
139. Come, My Beloved, and Follow Me ... 210

140. You Shall Come Forth............................211
141. I Will Welcome You Home 212
142. Will You Walk with Me?..........................214
143. I Am Calling My People to Walk in Holiness 217
144. Then Shall Your Light Shine 219
145. Come Out of Your Complacency..................221
146. Grow in Grace..................................222
147. Call unto Me with a Heart of Repentance..........223
148. Know the Foundations of Your Faith...............225
149. Be a Source of Strength.........................226
150. I Will Open Your Eyes to Hope...................228
151. Ask Me for Eye Salve 229
152. I Will Lead You Safely and Triumphantly 231
153. Come into Alignment...........................233
154. Trust Me to Do a Good Work 234
155. Clothe Yourselves in My Humility 236
156. Soften Your Hearts.............................237
157. The Windows of Heaven's Blessings................238
158. All the Nations Will Know 240
159. With Meekness and Humility....................242
160. Let Go of the Sins of Previous Generations 244
161. The Holy Spirit Will Witness to the Truth 246
162. No Compromise or Confusion Shall Blind Your Eyes 247
163. Your Bridegroom Comes 249
164. You Will Understand My Words because You Know Me.....250
165. The Secret Place of Intimacy and Communion 252
166. Come, All You Saints 253
167. Come Out from among the Spirit of Babylon 255
168. I Am Calling to My People.......................257
169. A Living Sanctuary..............................258
170. That You May Walk above the Confusion 260
171. It Is with Your Heart............................262
172. Will You Stand for Truth?........................263
173. Into These Times of Shaking and Storms...........264
174. Look to Me and See............................266
175. Welcome My Correction 268
176. Wisdom, Insight, and Diligence Are Required 269

177. Embrace Instruction in Righteousness 271
178. I Am the Good Shepherd 272
179. Understanding and Wisdom Will Be Your Companions 275
180. I Desire to Comfort and Protect My People 276
181. Walk with Me and You Will Walk in My Glory 277
182. Know the Plans I Have for You Are Good 279
183. The Time Appointed for Salvation 280
184. I Have a Calling and a Purpose for Each of My Children 281
185. Remain in Communion with Me 283
186. Be Merciful and Gracious to One Another 284
187. For My Shepherds 286
188. All the Issues of Life 288
189. My Kingdom Is Not of This World 289
190. Guard Your Heart and Your Thoughts 291
191. As You Wait Patiently 292
192. Only Remain Faithful 293
193. You Are Created in My Image 295
194. Take on My Nature and You Will See Clearly 296
195. The Simplicity of the Gospel 297
196. I Will Be All Things to You 299
197. Listen with Your Heart and Hear Me Calling 300
198. Surrender to Me and Receive from Me 302
199. I Will Feed You with Manna from Heaven and Water from
     the Rock 303
200. Come, Return to the Lord Your God 304
201. Move Forward with Me 306
202. The Key to Restoration 307
203. Do Not Refuse the Blessings I Have for You by Entertaining
     Evil 308
204. Live My Word and You Will Not Be Taken In by
     Lawlessness and Deceptions 309
205. I Am the Resurrection 311
206. Both Male and Female 312
207. Set Yourselves Apart to Honor Me 313
208. In Times of Great Spiritual Conflict 315
209. Fear Not 316
210. The Coming Beauty 317

211. Sorrow Shall Be Turned into Rejoicing 319
212. My Plans and Purposes for You 320
213. I Have a Covenant with Those Whose Hearts Belong to Me ..322
214. Have Confidence in My Love for You 323
215. Choose Life That You May Live 325
216. Remember 326
217. And You Will See 327
218. Have Courage 329
219. Restoration Is a Process 330
220. Build Eternal Treasures with Great Joy..................331
221. Peoples and Nations, Come 333
222. Drink of the Living Waters 334
223. I Am Here to Comfort You 335
224. Your Fulfilled Redemption Is Drawing Near 337
225. Every One of My Children.............................338
226. My Prayer to You, O My God 339

1. Tell My Beloved

If I were to ask God, "Lord, what would you say to Your people today?" what would He say? What follows in the numbered narratives is my interpretation of what God would say based on my understanding of the Bible.

Speak to My bride and tell her I love her. Tell My beloved bride I am coming soon to fulfill her complete redemption. She shall be revealed. She shall be clothed in glory. She will be beautiful and held in awe and respect.

Tell My bride to see what I am doing and prepare herself. I am doing a quick work among My people. If you procrastinate, if you disregard and treat lightly My call to you to put oil in your lamps and trim your wicks, you will not be prepared. You will not be ready.

Know that the plans I have for you are good and will bring peace and understanding to you. I desire to bless your going out and your coming in. I desire to bless everything you set your hands to.

These are perilous times. There are many deceptions and great evils—darkness in the hearts of mankind. Yet I say to you, put oil—the oil of My Holy Spirit—into your heart and trim your wicks—increase your understanding of My Word so you will be a light of God's glory to this generation.

I am coming soon to all the nations and will take My bride. She shall be ready, and I will present her to the Father.

Selected Scripture Reading

1. Isa. 62:5b—"And as the bridegroom rejoices over the bride, so shall your God rejoice over you." Some Old and New Testament scriptures use the marriage relationship to describe God's love for us and the love He desires we have for Him. See Isa. 54:5; Hos. 2:19–20; John 15:13–14; Eph. 5:25b–27.

2. Matt. 25:1–13—This passage uses the allegory of preparing for a wedding to teach that the church is to prepare herself for the Lord's return. See 1 Thess. 4:14–18; Rev. 19:7.
3. John 14:15–16:33—In these verses, Jesus explained that if we believe and love Him, we will follow His teachings carefully to prepare for His return. He explained that God would send us His Holy Spirit to teach and comfort us and be an indwelling presence and gift of peace. John 15 is an allegorical teaching about staying connected to God; it is about the critical importance of a branch being attached to the vine to receive sustenance and bear fruit.
4. Phil. 2:12–16—"Therefore, my beloved ... work out your own salvation with fear and trembling; for it is God who works in you both to will and to do for His good pleasure. Do all things without complaining and disputing, that you may become blameless and harmless, children of God without fault in the midst of a crooked and perverse generation, among whom you shine as lights in the world, holding fast the word of life." In Acts 24:15–16, the apostle Paul affirmed his hope in the resurrection of all people and stated that he wanted to live with a clear conscience before God and men.
5. Ps. 22:27—"All the ends of the world shall remember and turn to the LORD... For the kingdom is the LORD's and He rules over the nations." See Isa. 61:11; Pss. 72:11, 9:17; Matt. 25:31–32; Rev. 1:5.

2. Take Time to Be with Me

Listen to the Lord your God. Listen. Take time to be with Me. Take time to learn to know My voice. Listen.

Quiet your spirit. Put away and shut out all the clamor surrounding you. I speak softly. I speak gently.

Selected Scripture Reading

1. Rev. 3:20 (HCSB)—"Listen! I stand at the door [of your heart] and knock." Many scriptures tell us to pay attention to what God is speaking to our hearts. See Ps. 78:1; Prov. 8:4; 2 Chron. 20:15; Isa. 51:4; Mark 7:14; John 10:29.

2. Ps. 95:1–11—"Oh Come, let us sing to the LORD ... Let us kneel before the LORD our maker, for He is our God, and we are the sheep of His hand. Today if you will hear His voice; do not harden your hearts, as in the rebellion." It takes time to listen and develop relationships with people and with God. We want to spend time with those we love. See Ps. 111:2; Isa. 51:4; 2 Tim. 2:15. If we spend time with them, we will get to know them better. It is also good for our bodies, souls, and spirits to have a day of rest and time to recover from our scheduled busyness—a time to reflect on the bigger picture and our relationship with our Creator.
3. Matt. 13:3–23; Luke 8:4–15—Jesus told a parable about a sower; some of the seed fell by the wayside, and some fell on rocks. Birds ate some, and so on. Jesus explained to His disciples why He was speaking in story form. To comprehend what Jesus was saying in the story, we have to understand what the real points of the story are because they are hidden in the allegory. His disciples asked Him to explain the parable, and He did. In the same way, we have to seek to find Him.
4. Pss. 46:10, 90:12, 131:1–2; Prov. 10:19, 18:15, 29:11; 1 Tim. 4:7; James 1:19–20—These passages instruct us on what our attitude and position need to be while listening.
5. 1 Tim. 6:20–21a—"Guard what was committed to your trust, avoiding the profane and idle babblings and contradictions of what is falsely called knowledge—by professing it some have strayed concerning the faith." We must disregard the clamoring distractions.
6. 1 Kings 19:12—"And after the earthquake a fire; but the Lord was not in the fire; and after the fire a still small voice." To our hearts, God most often speaks softly and gently.
7. John 10:27—"My sheep hear My voice, and I know them, and they follow Me."
8. Heb. 2:1—"Therefore we must give the more earnest heed to the things we have heard, lest we drift away."

3. Rest in Me

My people who are watching for Me—My people who are waiting for My return—My people who are looking up shall be fully prepared. You shall be full of the Holy Spirit, ready for everything in your future.

You need not fear. You shall be ready. You shall be prepared. Rest in Me. Seek Me. Spend time alone with Me. Learn to know My voice and walk with Me. You shall be ready.

Selected Scripture Reading

1. Luke 12:37, 40; 1 Thess. 5:5—tell us that believers who are eagerly anticipating Jesus Christ's return are very blessed because they are spiritually alert and keenly aware of the struggle between good and evil. They will be living in light of eternal values and perspectives.
2. Ezek. 11:19 (NLT)—"And I will give them singleness of heart and put a new spirit within them. I will take away their stony, stubborn heart and give them a tender, responsive heart." God promises those who follow Him that they shall be blessed by His Spirit. See Jer. 24:7; Ezek. 33:14; Pss. 23, 27:4, 29:11. Ps. 149:4 and Acts 2:37–39 indicate that the humble will receive the message of salvation.
3. John 10:27–28—"My sheep hear My voice, and I know them, and they follow Me, And I give them eternal life, and they shall never perish; neither shall anyone snatch them out of My hand." Genuine love for God means we seek to please Him in all we think and do.
4. Acts 1:8—"But you shall receive power when the Holy Spirit has come upon you; and you shall be witnesses to Me in Jerusalem, and in all Judea and Samaria, and to the end of the earth." Shortly before His ascension into heaven, Jesus told His followers that He would be leaving soon but they would be baptized with the Holy Spirit to empower them to be His witnesses and to live overcoming lives. See Luke 24:36–53.
5. Acts 2:37–39, Acts; 1 Cor. 12–14; Rom. 12; Eph. 4—The scriptures and His Holy Spirit are available to prepare our hearts and minds to lead overcoming lives on earth and be prepared for eternity. However, we have to give consistent and diligent attention to understanding spiritual truths and obedience.
6. Matt. 11:29–30—"Take My yoke upon you and learn from Me, for I am gentle and lowly in heart, and you will find rest for your souls. For My yoke is easy and My burden is light." In contrast to the heavy burdens of legalism and works that religious regulations impose on people, Jesus said that following Him would be a comfortable fit and

bring rest to our souls. Note the character qualities highlighted in this verse: teachable, humble, gentle, obedient, and peaceful.
7. Gal. 5:22–23—"But the fruit of the Spirit is love, joy, peace, longsuffering, kindness, goodness, faithfulness, gentleness, self-control. Against such there is no law. And those who are Christ's have crucified the flesh with its passions and desires. If we live in the Spirit, let us also walk in the Spirit."

4. I Shall Move the Mountains

As you lift up the name of Jesus, as you pray, as you seek My face, as you humble yourselves and call on Me, as you turn from your wicked ways and walk before Me in righteousness, I shall hear from heaven and answer your prayers. I shall move the mountains. I shall influence the nations and heal your land.

Do not be weary in well doing. Continue in prayer. Continue in praise and thanksgiving. Rejoice. Believe and faint not. Continue and be strengthened. Hold fast to what is pure. Hold fast to your faith.

Selected Scripture Reading

1. Isa. 11, 12—Isa. 11 is a beautiful prophecy about the coming Messiah bringing the peace of righteousness. Isaiah 12 is a hymn of thanksgiving for God's provision of peace through salvation. Verse 2 reads, "Behold, God is my salvation." Verse 3 reads, "Therefore with joy you will draw water From the wells of salvation." In *Strong's Hebrew and Chaldee Dictionary* no. 3444, the word *salvation* is "Yeshuah."
2. Acts 3, 4—In Acts 3, God's Spirit used Peter and John to heal a lame man. Because of this miracle, the people listened to Peter as he explained that the power to heal physically and spiritually came through believing that Jesus Christ was the Son of God. Verse 19 shows what "believing" means: "Repent therefore and be converted, that your sins may be blotted out, so that times of refreshing may come from the presence of the Lord." The religious authorities disliked that Peter and John were preaching about Jesus and teaching

the resurrection of the dead, so they arrested them. Nevertheless, over 5,000 people heard and believed the message.

Later, as Peter and John were interrogated and commanded not to preach or teach about Jesus, Peter answered that the lame man had been healed physically by the name of Jesus Christ of Nazareth and that there was not "salvation in any other, for there is no other name under heaven given among men by which we must be saved" (Acts 4:12). Read the entire passage for additional information. See Rom. 5:8–9, 10:9–1; Eph. 1:7–8.

3. 2 Chron. 7:14—"If My people who are called by My name will humble themselves, and pray and seek My face, and turn from their wicked ways, then I will hear from heaven, and will forgive their sin and heal their land." See Isa. 55:6–7; Jer. 18:7–10; Joel 2:12–13, 15; Luke 3:8; 1 Thess. 5:12–24, which teach that repentance and turning away from sin brings restoration.

4. "Mountains" have many symbolic meanings in the Bible. Here are a few: things we put our trust in (Ps. 11:1, 121:1); actual and symbolic references to places of worship, of God, or idolatrous worship (Num. 22:41; 1 Kings 11:7; Gen. 22:2; Judg. 6:26; Ps. 68:16); immoveable power or strength (Ps. 36:6); powers and authorities used to highlight spiritual principles (Ps. 72:1–4a, 11; Eph. 6:12); and a person's position or standing (Ps. 30:6–7a); obstacles (Isa. 49:11; Zech. 4:7). Matthew 21:18–46 and Mark 11:20–26 illustrate that unfruitfulness is an obstacle. In these verses, it may be implied that a religious spirit and attitude created unbelief and unfruitfulness causing many to reject the Messiah.

5. The Place of Obedience

I am calling you to obedience. The place of obedience is a place of protection. The place of obedience is a place of peace. The place of obedience is a place of refuge, and strength. The place of obedience is a place of hope and great joy.

I am calling you to obedience. In obedience you will overcome. In obedience you will walk through closed doors and hearts will be moved.

In obedience, you will hear My voice. In obedience, you will fulfill your destiny.

Walk in the way of righteousness so your faith will increase.

Selected Scripture Reading

1. Ps. 27:5—"For in the time of trouble He shall hide me in His pavilion; in the secret place of His tabernacle He shall hide me; He shall set me high upon a Rock." Psalm 27 is a magnificent declaration of faith in God. It says we have nothing to fear no matter what happens. Even in the midst of great difficulty, we can be "in the presence of the Lord" knowing that on earth and in eternity, we will see the Lord's goodness. Psalm 16:8–9 gives a key to being confident in God's protection.
2. Ps. 46:1–2—"God is our refuge and strength, a very present help in trouble. Therefore we will not fear, even though the earth be removed and the mountains be carried into the midst of the sea." Revelation 6:14 and 16:20 speak of every mountain being moved.
3. Deut. 5:29—"Oh that they had such a heart in them that they would fear Me and always keep all My commandments, that it might be well with them and with their children forever." See 2 Chron. 16:9a about God looking for people to bless.
4. Ex. 19:5–6; Ezek. 18:21; Gal. 6:1; James 1:25; John 4:36, 14:23; Matt. 7:24–25 confirm that the reward of obedience is blessing and protection from eternal destruction.
5. Acts 6:5–7:60—This is the story of Stephen, a man full of faith and the Holy Spirit. He spoke publicly about Jesus being the Messiah. God confirmed his testimony with signs and wonders. Because he spoke by the Spirit and wisdom of God—proving by the Old Testament scriptures that God was putting into place a new covenant (Acts 7:37–53)—the religious leaders plotted his death. As he was being stoned, Stephen saw in the heavens the glory of God and Jesus at His right hand. The cloaks of those killing Stephen were laid at the feet of a young man named Saul who heard Stephen pray, "Lord Jesus, receive my Spirit. Lord, do not charge them with this sin." Saul, who had been hunting down the believers (8:3) and persecuting them,

was later converted (Acts 9) and preached Christ with eloquence and power (9:22, 13:13–49). Saul became known as the apostle Paul (13:9). This story is one of ultimate sacrificial obedience and blessing.

6. Come Up Higher

The songs you have sung are My words of comfort to you. My Word warns you of things to come—wars, rumors of war, pestilences, droughts, floods, persecutions, and earthquakes. Be comforted and know that I walk with you through these things.

I am there with you. Be not offended or fearful. Lean on Me. I have come that you might have life more abundantly, rising above everything on earth. Look up. Rise up. Come up higher.

Biblical Insights from Psalms

Psalms is a compilation of 150 hymns—spiritual songs—written by Moses, David, the Levitical singing clans of Korah and Asaph, King David's choir master (1 Chron. 16:4–7), Solomon, and others. These songs have been used throughout the centuries in congregational and personal worship. See Eph. 5:19–21.

The New Testament quotes from Psalms more than any other Old Testament books (more than a hundred times). For example, in Matthew 7:23, Jesus said, "And then I will declare to them, 'I never knew you; depart from Me, you who practice lawlessness!'" What Jesus said was a quote from Psalm 6:8—"Depart from me, all you workers of iniquity."

The word *psalms* in Hebrew is *tehillim*, "praises." The Greek word used is *psalmoi* and means the sounds of harp strings indicating songs to be accompanied by stringed instruments (1 Chron. 16:42). The psalms were written in Hebrew poem form. In English poetry, the rhyming of words is paramount, while in Hebrew, parallel thoughts characterize poetic form. These are usually expressed in groups of two or three short sentences or phrases.

Psalms and Proverbs make extensive use of the parallel form of writing. There are three basic types of parallelism: the two sentences say the same thing just in a different way, the second elaborating on the previous; the sentences contrast two different types of people, ways of acting, things, etc. showing opposites; and comparing two things often using the phrase "better than" as wisdom is better than foolishness. Understanding the Hebrew poetic style helps us grasp the meaning.

Typical themes of the psalms are

1. praises to God,
2. God's working throughout history,
3. God's deliverance and salvation of His people often recounting actual events in Israel's history,
4. teaching God's attributes and principles of mercy, love, kindness, etc.,
5. acknowledging great personal and national difficulties or failures with honest emotions (laments); then often as the psalm progresses, the psalmist hears from God or states God's perspective bringing emotions under the lordship of God,
6. identifying and lamenting the destructiveness of sin, even God's abhorrence of sin and wickedness,
7. stating God's righteous judgment of the unrepentant and that vengeance belongs to God; in the end, God's justice will prevail also over the nations, and
8. seventeen psalms speak of the Messiah.

7. You Are Building Your Testimony Every Day

My children, My children, listen carefully to My words. In the scriptures, you read, "They overcame by the words of their testimony."0

Every day, you are building your testimony. Let the thoughts you think, the words you speak, and your very being speak of Me. I desire for My Spirit to flow through you to bring life to a hurting and lost world.

Listen carefully. I have come to bring you life and life more abundantly. The words I speak to you are Spirit; they are life.

Remain in Me and your joy will be great.

Selected Scripture Reading

1. Isa. 43:10–12—"You are My witnesses, says the LORD, and My servant whom I have chosen, that you may know and believe Me, and understand that I am He. Before Me there was no God formed, nor shall there be after Me. I, even I, am the LORD. And besides Me there is no savior. I have declared and saved ... and there was no foreign god among you; therefore you are my witnesses, says the LORD that I am God." These statements are confirmed in Luke 24:48; Acts 1:8, 2:32, 5:3; 1 Thess. 2:10.
2. Mal. 3:16—"Then those who feared the LORD spoke to one another, and the LORD listened and heard them; so a book of remembrance was written before Him for those who fear the LORD and who meditate on His name. They shall be Mine, says the LORD of hosts, on the day that I make them My jewels. And I will spare them as a man spares his own son who serves him."
3. Titus 3:8–9—"This is a faithful saying, and these things I want you to affirm constantly that those who have believe in God should be careful to maintain good works. These things are good and profitable to men. But avoid foolish disputes."
4. Matt. 28:18–20—"And Jesus came and spoke to them, saying, All authority has been given to Me in heaven and on earth. Go therefore and make disciples of all the nations, baptizing them in the name of the Father and of the Son and of the Holy Spirit, teaching them to observe all things that I have commanded you; and lo, I am with you always, even to the end of the age. Amen." Witnessing and making disciples is the believer's task.
5. John 6:63 (Jesus speaking)—"It is the Spirit who gives life; the flesh profits nothing. The words that I speak to you, are spirit, and they are life." See 1 Peter 4:7–11.
6. Rev. 12:11—"And they overcame him [the accuser of the brethren] by the blood of the Lamb and by the word of their testimony, and they did not love their lives to the death."

8. I Am Gathering My Sheep to Myself

The last days are indeed troubling and confusing. Many voices are speaking. Let not your hearts be dismayed or troubled. I am the Lord your God. I watch over you to carefully perform every good work in your life. Trust Me.

Know this and keep this before you: I love you enough to give My only Son for your redemption and salvation. You shall not be lost. You shall be saved. I am gathering My sheep to Myself. Learn to know My voice. Spend time with Me. I will comfort you. I will strengthen you. I will prepare you.

In the world, you will have tribulation and trials, but be of good heart. Listen to My words and you will overcome. My peace I give to you. Your reward is sure.

Selected Scripture Reading

1. Ps. 27:4—"One thing I have desired of the LORD, that will I seek: That I may dwell in the house of the LORD all the days of my life, to behold the beauty of the LORD and to inquire in His temple. For in the time of trouble He shall hide me in His pavilion; in the secret place of His tabernacle He shall hide me; He shall set me high upon a rock." When our hearts are determined to seek and follow God, we will know He will take care of us even in the last days. We shall have confidence and strength based on our personal relationship with Him knowing our eternal lives are safe in Him.

2. Acts 2:1–2:47—the Day of Pentecost (in Hebrew, *Shavuot*/Feast of Weeks/*Yom Hubikkurim*/Day of First Fruits of the Summer Wheat Crop) was one of the three feasts God required the nation to come together to celebrate. See Ex. 23:14–17, 34:22; Deut. 16:10–16; 2 Chron. 8:13.

    In about AD 30, the Holy Spirit came into the room where 120 believers were gathered just as Jesus had promised in Luke 24:49 and Acts 1:4–8. This event of the first spiritual harvest of souls into the church coincided with the Hebrew celebration of *shavuot*, which marked the beginning of the summer wheat harvest.

    In Acts 2:14, Peter spoke to the large crowd who had observed

the coming of the Holy Spirit and told them what was happening and what it meant. He quoted from Joel 2 about the new covenant God was making with humanity. The term "last days" implies that the last days began on the Day of Pentecost. Hebrews 1:1–2, 14 indicate that the last days refer to the church age, the time of "the summer harvest of souls." Accordingly, now is the time to receive God's invitation of salvation.
3. 2 Tim. 3:1–5; 2 Peter 2:1–3, 3:3–4; Matt. 24; Luke 21—These scriptures are about the last days.
4. Rom. 8:38–39; Phil. 1:6—Nothing can separate us from God; as long as we remain in Him, He will continue to do good works in us.

9. Your Names Are Written in the Lamb's Book of Life

My beloved children, hear My words to you. You are Mine, and I will keep you. You are My inheritance.

Trials and tribulations are coming over the earth. Continue to sing and worship Me and you will overcome. You will rise above all that is going on around you.

Praise. Worship. Surrender yourselves to My Spirit so the majesty of salvation, the majesty of redemption through the blood of Jesus Christ, may be released in power.

Look not to the right. Look not to the left. Look unto Me. Rejoice. Again, I say to you, rejoice. Your names are written in the Lamb's Book of Life.

Selected Scripture Reading

1. Ps. 2:7–8—"I will declare the decree: The LORD has said to Me [Jesus], You are My Son, Today I have begotten You, Ask of Me, and I will give You the nations for Your inheritance, And the ends of the earth for Your possession." God, the Lord, was speaking prophetically to His Son, Jesus. This verse from Psalms is quoted in Acts 13:33 and Hebrews 1:5, 5:5.
2. John 17:6–26—Jesus was praying for His disciples in verses 6–19. He said that He had manifested God's name to those the Father had given Him and that they had received in their hearts the teachings

He had given them. Jesus said that He had told them what the Father had directed Him to say and that the people had believed Him. He prayed that though they would be surrounded by worldly influences, they would have unity in their faith in God.

He prayed that the believers would have in their hearts the same joy that was in Him—joy that came from being united in spirit with our heavenly Father. In verses 14–16, acknowledging the destructive works of the evil one to destroy faith, truth, and genuine unity, Jesus prayed that God would keep the believers safe "in the world." In verse 17, Jesus established that God's truths would work sanctification in the lives of those who believe and make their salvation sure. He specified in verse 20 that His prayers applied to all believers. Praying again for unity in verses 21–26, He spoke of being made perfect by God's love with the result being a glorious testimony to the world that God existed and was in the hearts of mankind.

3. Rev. 3:5—"He who overcomes shall be clothed in white garments, and I will not blot out his name from the Book of Life; but I will confess his name before My Father and before His angels." See Dan. 12:1–4; Luke 10:20; Rev. 20:12, 21:27.

10. Behold, I Come Quickly

The time is short. Behold, I come quickly. Do what I have commanded and released you to do. I am with you to be a bright light in a dark world.

Know that My love and words will keep you safe. They will prepare you to do the work I have set before you. Fear not. Rejoice in My words and My love.

You are My children. You are the sheep of My pasture. You are the saints of the Most High. You are the bride of the Messiah—the Messiah who is the King of Kings and Lord of Lords. Prepare yourselves.

Selected Scripture Reading

1. Rom. 13:11–12—"And do this, knowing the time, that now it is high time to awake out of sleep; for now our salvation is nearer than when we first believed. The night is far spent … let us cast off the works

of darkness, and let us put on the armor of light." See context about how to cast off the works of darkness and put on the armor of light.
2. Matt. 28:18–20—"And Jesus came and spoke to them, saying 'All authority has been given to Me in heaven and on earth. Go therefore and make disciples of all the nations, baptizing them in the name of the Father and of the Son and of the Holy Spirit, teaching them to observe all things that I have commanded you; and lo, I am with you always, even to the end of the age.'" Jesus made it clear God gave Him the authority to speak God's words to the people and to be the sacrificial Lamb for the sins of the people, which would open the doors to salvation for humanity. For additional scriptures on Jesus's authority and mission, see Dan. 7:13; John 12:49, 14:10; Luke 1:32, 4:32, 36, 9:1, 10:19; John 17:1–4; Acts 2:29–36; Eph. 1:20–21; Phil. 2:5–11; Heb. 1:1–4.
3. John 7:17—Those who are sincere and intentional in seeking God will recognize that the doctrine and teachings of Jesus are from God. See Matt. 4:17–19; Acts 14:37; 2 Cor. 4:6–7; Rom. 13:9–10; 1 John 3:16–23; John 15:4–8; Matt. 5:1–7:29.
4. Ps. 23:1; Isa. 40:11; Ezek. 34:1–31; Matt. 9:36; Mark 6:34; Heb. 13:20; 1 Peter 2:25, 5:4; Rev. 7:17—These are some verses that use sheep and shepherd metaphors to teach spiritual concepts.
5. Dan. 7:18—"But the saints of the Most High shall receive the kingdom, and possess the kingdom forever, even forever and ever." See Matt. 5:5; Rev. 1:5–7, 19:16.
6. Isa. 62:5; Matt. 9:15, 25:1–13; John 3:29; Rom. 7:4; 2 Cor. 11:2; Eph. 5:22–32; Rev. 19:7, 21:2, Rev. 22:17—These verses use bride, bridegroom, and marriage metaphors to teach spiritual truths.
7. Rev. 1:5–7—"And from Jesus Christ, the faithful witness, the firstborn from the dead, and the ruler over the kings of the earth. To Him who loved us and washed us from our sins in His own blood."
8. Rev. 19:16—"And He has on His robe and on His thigh a name written: KING OF KINGS AND LORD OF LORDS."

11. Reach Out with My Grace

My children, let My glory shine through you. Let My love shine through you. Let My grace shine through you.

Through you, the world will see and know that I am. Let your light shine before others that they may see the power of the Almighty God. Goodness, kindness, meekness, gentleness.

Reach out in My love. Reach out in My goodness and kindness. Reach out with My grace and see My power.

Selected Scripture Reading

1. Ex. 33:18–19—Moses asked God to show him His glory. God said He would cause His goodness to pass before Moses, He would proclaim the name of the Lord before Moses, and He would be gracious and compassionate to people. These verses give a definition of the glory of God, which can be overwhelming for mankind as is demonstrated in subsequent verses.

    There is a particular phrase used in Exodus 33:20, where God said, "You cannot see My face." A very similar phrase is used in 1 John 4:12: "No one has seen God at any time." As in Exodus and in 1 John 4:7–20, seeing God is connected to recognizing and receiving His goodness and love. The glory of God shines through us as we love others with the love of God.

    Additional verses on God's glory are Deut. 7:8; Jer. 31:3; Ps. 89:1–4, 117; Haggai 2:9; John 3:16; Acts 15:14-17, 19:10; Rom. 5:8; Eph. 2:4–10; James 5:7; 1 John 3:1, 4:7–19.

    Furthermore, as point number 2 above connects the glory of God to the name of the Lord, 1 John 4:15, 5:1 also stress believing in the name of Jesus, God's Messiah. Throughout 1 John, we see the same three points as in Exodus 33:18–19. John encourages us to stay true to reflecting God's glory and not fall into the deceptions of the last days by loving the world (1 John 2:15–23).

2. Dan. 12:3—"Those who are wise shall shine like the brightness of the firmament, and those who turn many to righteousness like the stars forever and ever."

3. 2 Cor. 3:18 (NLT)—"So all of us who have had that veil removed can see and reflect the glory of the Lord. And the Lord—who is the Spirit—makes us more and more like Him as we are changed into His glorious image." See Isa. 43:10.

4. Matt. 5:16 (Jesus speaking)—"Let your light so shine before men, that they may see your good works and glorify your Father in heaven. See Eph. 5:8–14; 1 Peter 4:7–11 for how we let our light shine before others so they may see God at work in us."
5. Gal. 5:22–24—"But the fruit of the Spirit is love, joy, peace, longsuffering, kindness, goodness, faithfulness, gentleness, self-control. Against such there is no law. And those who are Christ's have crucified the flesh with its passions and desires."
6. Isa. 40:31—"But those who wait on the LORD shall renew their strength; They shall mount up with wings like eagles, They shall run and not be weary, They shall walk and not faint."

12. I Am Searching for My Beloved

I am going to and fro over the whole earth looking—searching for a people who will worship Me with their whole heart—who will give to Me their lives, worship, and love. I am searching for My bride—My beloved—My chosen.

Open your hearts to Me completely that I may fill you with My love. I am going to and fro searching for those who will purify themselves by allowing Me to fill them with My love.

Selected Scripture Reading

1. 2 Chron. 16:9a—"For the eyes of the LORD run to and fro throughout the whole earth, to show Himself strong on behalf of those whose heart is loyal to Him." John 14:21 says Jesus will manifest Himself to those who love and follow Him.
2. Ps. 34:15—"The eyes of the LORD are on the righteous, And His ears are open to their cry." Psalms 14:2, 53:2 describe God looking down from heaven to see if there are people who are seeking Him and looking for understanding.
3. 1 Peter 2:25—"For you were like sheep going astray but have now returned to the Shepherd and Overseer of your souls." See the parable of the lost sheep in Matt. 18:10; Luke 15:1-7.

4. Ps. 95:6–7—"Oh come, let us worship and bow down; Let us kneel before the LORD our Maker. For He is our God, And we are the people of His pasture, And the sheep of His hand." Psalm 95 begins with a resounding call to worship and states the magnificence of God. God gives a warning to not harden our hearts lest we miss the rest He has for us. Psalm 96 expands the theme of declaring God's glory among the nations but also warns that God is coming to judge the earth.
5. John 4:23—"But the hour is coming, and now is, when the true worshipers will worship the Father in spirit and truth; for the Father is seeking such to worship Him."
6. Matt. 22:37–40—"Jesus replied, You must love the LORD your God with all your heart, all your soul, and all your mind. This is the first and greatest commandment. A second is equally important: Love your neighbor as yourself. The entire law and all the demands of the prophets are based on these commandments."
7. 1 Peter 1:22–23—"Since you have purified your souls in obeying the truth through the Spirit in sincere love of the brethren, love one another fervently with a pure heart, Having been born again, not of corruptible seed but incorruptible, through the word of God which lives and abides forever."
8. 2 Cor. 13:11—"Finally, brethren, farewell. Become complete. Be of good comfort, be of one mind, live in peace; and the God of love and peace be with you."

13. Listen to My Holy Spirit

My children often give up in prayer just before the answer is dispatched from heaven—the answer that directs their words in prayer—the answer that gives understanding, hope, and peace to their hearts—the answer that builds faith.

Don't doubt. Pray and believe. Listen. Still your hearts. Listen to My Holy Spirit and I will direct you.

There will be times of great travail and groanings as in the spirit you give birth to answered prayers. There will be times of quiet supplication where you grasp the mind of Christ interceding for one another and the kingdom of God.

There will be times of rejoicing and great thanksgiving in your spirit because you will know you have touched the hem of My garment and know we have met. I have heard you, and you have heard Me.

Selected Scripture Reading

1. Ps. 4:3–4; Prov. 8:33; Dan. 9–10; 1 Tim. 1:18; Luke 11:1–13, 18:1–8; Matt. 6:1–34, 11:3–6; Mark 5:25–34; James 1:5–8; Gal. 5:6; Eph. 6:10–18; 1 Thess. 5:16–22; 1 John 3:21–23, 5:14–15; Rom. 8:26–28, 15:13; John 16:13; Phil. 2:3–5—These passages teach many principles about prayer such as

   1. attitude of humility
   2. asking God for wisdom
   3. praying in agreement with prophetic insights (Dan. 9; 1 Tim. 1:18)
   4. recognizing God as Lord with full sovereignty
   5. praying in harmony with God's will
   6. acknowledging God as the source of everything
   7. walking in total forgiveness toward others and self
   8. recognizing our limitations therefore seeking God's help and protection
   9. being persistent in prayer without trusting in vain repetitions or shouting
   10. worry indicates doubt and fear, which frustrates or negates God's blessings
   11. some delays are divine
   12. faith works by love
   13. having a clear conscience and right relationship with God allows us to trust Him unequivocally
   14. sometimes when we don't know what to pray, the Holy Spirit prays through us
   15. prayer is spiritual warfare

2. 1 Thess. 5:16–22—"Rejoice always, Pray without ceasing. In everything give thanks; for this is the will of God in Christ Jesus

for you. Do not quench the Spirit. Do not despise prophecies. Test all things; hold fast what is good. Abstain from every form of evil."
3. Some hindrances to answered prayer: disobedience (Deut. 1:45), secret sin (Ps. 66:18), indifference (Prov. 1:28), neglect of mercy (Prov. 21:13), despising God's teachings (Prov. 28:9), unrepentant guilt of shedding blood (Isa. 1:15), iniquity (Isa. 50:2; Mic. 3:4), stubbornness (Zech. 7:13), instability, indecisiveness, double mindedness (James 1:6–7; Mark 11:23), and self-indulgence (James 4:3).
4. Matt. 9:20–22, 14:36; Mark 5:25–34, 6:56; Luke 8:43–44—These passages refer to "touching the hem of the garment." The Hebrew word *tsitsit* (tassels, Num. 15:37–41) was translated into the Greek word *kraspedon* (hem). The tassels on the four corners of the outer cloak, garment, or prayer shawl—*talit*—were to remind one of God's commands and promises and are therefore symbolic of His Word and power.

14. This Is a Season of Restoration

This is the season of restoration. This is the time of coming before Me to receive restoration. I have plans for you, and they are good—plans of blessing, plans of hope, and plans of overcoming. Come before Me with your whole heart.

Grasp My love and promises. I will not leave you or forsake you. This is the time for you to see the restoration of My church, the restoration of My people. Look up—your redemption is near.

Families. Come before Me and pray for your families that they may be restored to peace and harmony. There is much work to do in My kingdom. Each one has a job and a place in My kingdom.

Selected Scripture Reading

1. Pss. 6, 32, 38, 51, 102, 130, 143 are known as the seven psalms of repentance. They have themes such as praying for faith in times of distress, rejoicing in God's forgiveness, requesting mercy when

feeling chastised for sins, feeling utterly discouraged and in need of God's perspective, waiting patiently until God sets things in order, and praying for guidance, deliverance, and help.

Psalm 51 is considered King David's psalm of repentance after the prophet Nathan confronted him for having committed adultery with Bathsheba and causing Uriah's death. Undoubtedly, one reason the scriptures call David "a man after God's own heart" is that he was humble enough to repent openly and seek a restored relationship with God (1 Sam. 13:14; Acts 13:22).

2. Jer. 3:14–15—The Lord called the backsliders to return to Him. God said that if they returned, He would give them shepherds who knew Him and would teach them with knowledge and understanding. Hebrews 3:6 and Luke 16:10 indicate the necessity of personal responsibility and following through.

3. Mal. 5:5—"Behold, I will send you Elijah the prophet before the coming of the great and dreadful day of the LORD: And he will turn the hearts of the fathers to the children, And the hearts of the children to their fathers." This message of restoration was repeated by the angel of the Lord that appeared to Zacharias, the father of John the Baptist, telling him about his son who was to be born (Luke 1:11–17). God was saying that the new covenant/gospel of salvation was a message of restoration.

4. Pss. 19, 119; John 8:32—These explain in detail that the key to restoration is understanding and following the teachings in the Bible. Words such as *statutes, teaching, commandments, instruction, testimony, law, judgments, precepts, word, truth,* and *ordinances* are used interchangeably to define the essential guidelines for living a successful and blessed life.

5. Eph. 5 25–27—"Husbands, love your wives, just as Christ also loved the church and gave Himself for her, That He might sanctify and cleanse her with the washing of water by the word, That He might present her to Himself a glorious church, not having spot or wrinkle or any such thing, but that she should be holy and without blemish." Love is the spiritual component that empowers genuine restoration. See 1 Thess. 3:12–13.

15. It Is Time to Prepare

My children, it is time to prepare yourselves to meet Me in the air. There will be a catching up to the throne of God.

I am preparing a people to move forward in the power of the Holy Spirit. Do not underestimate My grace and power to move among you. You will build a church by the power of God.

Selected Scripture Reading

1. 1 Thess. 4:16–18—"For the Lord Himself will descend from heaven with a shout, with the voice of an archangel, and with the trumpet of God. And the dead in Christ will rise first. Then we who are alive and remain shall be caught up together with them in the clouds to meet the Lord in the air. And thus we shall always be with the Lord. Therefore comfort one another with these words."
2. Matt. 24:31—"And He will send His angels with a great sound of a trumpet, and they will gather together His elect from the four winds, from one end of heaven to the other." See Matt. 24:3–51; Mark 13:3–37; Luke 21:7–38 for information on the signs of the end of the age. There are precise descriptions of the unfolding challenges facing humanity and instructions on how to prepare your heart. For example, don't be drawn into a self-indulgent or emotionally charged mind-set and thus miss seeing the spiritual significance of events taking place.
3. Matt. 25:1–46—This passage includes the parable of the wise and foolish virgins (those who prepared and those who didn't), the parable of the talents (comparison of wise and unwise stewardship of time, resources, and talents), and the parable of the sheep and goats (defining the test of obedience in loving and caring for others' physical and spiritual needs).
4. Acts 2:16–21—This was Peter's sermon on the day of Pentecost, which marked the beginning of the church age. He quoted from the Old Testament prophet Joel. Verses 17–18 speak of God pouring His Spirit out on all mankind so we may better know and serve Him. Verses 19–21 describe the day of the Lord and are similar to Matthew 24:29–31. Compare these verses with descriptions of the day of the Lord in Joel 2 and Revelation 6:12–17.

5. 1 Thess. 5:1–23—"For you yourselves know perfectly that the day of the Lord so comes as a thief in the night ... Therefore let us not sleep, as others do, but let us watch and be sober... putting on the breastplate of faith and love, and as a helmet the hope of salvation. For God did not appoint us to wrath, but to obtain salvation through our Lord Jesus Christ. Be at peace among yourselves. In everything give thanks ... Do not quench the Spirit. Do not despise prophecies. Test all things; hold fast what is good. Abstain from every form of evil. Now may the God of peace Himself sanctify you completely; and may your whole spirit, soul, and body be preserved blameless at the coming of our Lord Jesus Christ."
6. Ps. 127:1—"Unless the LORD builds the house, they labor in vain who build it; unless the LORD guards the city, the watchman stays awake in vain." See Eph. 2:13–22.

16. A Word for the Musicians

I will anoint your music for I have given you a voice to declare My mercy and power. Your music and songs will deliver the captives and be an anointing to release the Holy Spirit to minister to the hearts and souls of My people.

God is calling the musicians of His church to hear His voice, be wrapped in His presence, and release the gifts He gives them to be life-giving waters, washing and refreshing the bride of Christ. This washing and refreshing is an essential preparation for the bride to make herself ready for the appearance of the Bridegroom.

Bathe in, soak in the presence of God. Let your worship create an atmosphere for the power of God to work–building faith, and washing away doubt. Give yourself to the Holy Spirit to minister to the hurting and confused. Your music given by the Holy Spirit will bring healing, reconciliation, and restoration.

I have called you forth as musicians, singers, psalmists, and readers of the Word. My Spirit is in and on you to minister in knowledge and power. You are to call forth the body of Christ and prepare them to receive My Word to their hearts. Anointed music will bring them with thanksgiving into My courts. Anointed music will impart grace and deliverance.

Come together in unity, each of you esteeming one another more highly than yourself. In humility, give honor to the King of Kings and Lord of Lords. My power will be released to work among the body and even to call the unsaved to enter the kingdom of God.

Rejoice. This is your calling. This is your ministry. I have given you these gifts for such a time as this.

Selected Scripture Reading

1. Ps. 150:1–6 (NIV)—"Praise the LORD! Praise God in His sanctuary; Praise Him in His mighty firmament! Praise Him for His mighty acts; Praise Him according to His excellent greatness! Praise Him with the sound of the trumpet; Praise Him with the lute and harp! Praise Him with the timbrel and dance; Praise Him with stringed instruments and flutes! Praise Him with loud cymbals; Praise Him with clashing cymbals! Let everything that has breath praise the LORD. Praise the LORD!"
2. 2 Chron. 21:21–22; Neh. 12; Acts 10:30, 12:5–11, 16:25—These are examples of strategic praise and worship.
3. Eph. 5:18b–21—"Be filled with the Spirit, speaking to one another in psalms and hymns and spiritual songs, singing and making melody in your heart to the Lord, giving thanks always for all things to God

the Father in the name of our Lord Jesus Christ, submitting to one another in the fear of God."

17. Pray for All These

Be strong and of good courage, My children. An attack is coming, and there will be much fear and confusion, but do not be afraid. It will not be devastation. What the enemy has meant for harm will be turned around and used for good, for benefit.

Let love reign. Overcome evil with good. Sing and rejoice. For God has given you weapons of warfare that are far greater than any weapons created by mankind. Put on the belt of truth and the breastplate of righteousness. Take up the helmet of salvation, the shield of faith, and the sword of the Spirit. With these, you shall quench all the enemy's fiery darts. With these, you shall overcome and sing the victor's song.

This attack is a spiritual attack. It is designed to destroy your conscience and awareness of sin. But Satan has overplayed his hand and will expose great evil. The foundations of faith remaining in this land will awaken to do battle with the forces of the occult and witchcraft.

Awaken, My people. Put on the garments of praise and righteousness. Separate yourselves from unrighteousness. Cleanse yourselves. Purify your hearts. No longer accept the bondages of Egypt. Awaken to the freedoms of holiness.

Love one another as I have loved you. As My Son, Jesus, gave His life for you, sacrifice your lives for one another. Love your brothers and sisters, love your wives and husbands, love your children, love your parents, love your friends, and love your enemies. Pray for all these that I may come and rain righteousness upon you and your land.

Selected Scripture Reading

1. Deut. 31:6—"Be strong and of good courage, do not fear nor be afraid of them; for the LORD your God, He is the One who goes with you. He will not leave you nor forsake you."
2. 1 Tim. 4:1–11—"Now the Spirit expressly says that in the latter times some will depart from the faith, giving heed to deceiving spirits and

doctrines of demons, Speaking lies in hypocrisy, having their own conscience seared with a hot iron."
3. 1 Cor. 15:34—"Awake to righteousness, and do not sin; for some do not have the knowledge of God. I speak this to your shame." See Ezek. 22 for a list of sins that bring judgment.
4. Ex. 3:8, 32:1–35—God told Moses in Ex. 3:8 that He would take His people out of Egypt, and we see in Ex. 32 that it would also be necessary to take Egypt out of the people. The many lessons they would learn on their wilderness journey exemplify the same lessons we must learn.
5. Hos. 10:12—"Sow for yourselves righteousness; reap in mercy; Break up your fallow ground, For it is time to seek the LORD, Till He comes and rains righteousness on you."

18. The Rest You Are Seeking

A righteous person's steps are ordered by the Lord. Come before Me in the righteousness of Christ and I will direct your steps and light the path for you to follow. Draw near Me and I will draw near you.

Give your heart to Me and I will release My words and My Spirit to your heart. Know that I love you and that the plans I have for you are good. Come to Me and you will not walk in darkness, nor will you walk in confusion. Come to Me and you will walk in the light. My light gives hope. My light gives wisdom, knowledge of salvation, and peace.

Do not seek the peace of the world. The peace the world gives is no peace at all. Cleanse yourselves and receive the peace your Father in heaven prepared for you by the sacrifice of His Son, Jesus Christ. His peace is an everlasting peace and full of life. Come to Me and I will give you the rest you are seeking. Come, says the Lord your God.

Selected Scripture Reading

1. Pss. 18:36, 37:23–24, 40:1–3; Prov. 4:12, 16:9, 20:24; Jer. 10:23— These passages speak of the "steps of a man" and "steps of a good man." Some of principles expressed in these scriptures.

1. God works through circumstances to help things go well for us.
2. God directs the path and steps of those who desire to do right, and even if they fail or "fall down," God will help them get things in order again.
3. When we cry out to God for help, He will bring us through the difficulties we have gotten ourselves in, and as long as we continue to seek Him, He will establish blessings in our lives.
4. When we make our choices based on God's wisdom, our steps will not be hindered
5. We may have our own ideas about what we should be doing, but if we commit all things to Him, He will see things turn out the way they should (also Rom. 8:28).
6. It is not always possible to understand everything that happens to us in this life.
7. By themselves, people simply do not have enough wisdom and knowledge to always know what the right decision is.

2. Pss. 5:8, 23:2, 25:9, 48:14, 73:24, 143:10; Prov. 3:5–12; James 4:8—These passages encourage us to seek a relationship with God and His help in making decisions.
3. Jer. 23:5–6; Hab. 2:4; Acts 2:37–38; Rom. 6:23, 10:1–13; 1 Cor. 2:30–31; Heb. 11; Phil. 1:9–11, 3:9—These verses help to define the righteousness of Christ. Romans 1:16–17 summarizes this: "For I am not ashamed of the gospel of Christ, for it is the power of God to salvation for everyone who believes, for the Jew first and also for the Greek [Gentile]. For in it the righteousness of God is revealed from faith to faith; as it is written, 'The just shall live by faith'"—a quote from Habakkuk 2:4. The apostle Paul taught in Ephesians 5:1–17 how to live following Jesus's teachings.
4. John 8:12—-"Then Jesus spoke to them again, saying, 'I am the light of the world. He who follows Me shall not walk in darkness, but have the light of life.'"
5. John 14:27 (Jesus speaking)—"Peace I leave with you, My peace I give to you; not as the world gives do I give to you. Let not your heart be troubled, neither let it be afraid."

19. Give Me All Your Hurts and Disappointments

I, the Lord your God, delight in restoring the brokenhearted. You are my treasure, and I will restore the pieces you thought had been lost forever. Come to Me with all your being. I will restore your heart.

Give Me all your hurts and disappointments and My Spirit will work great grace in your heart. You will see and know the glory of God. I am preparing great miracles to reveal My love and presence among My people. I walk in the midst of your praise and worship.

Selected Scripture Reading

1. Some words that fit into the same category as "brokenhearted" are *depressed, mournful, forlorn, despair, sorrowful, hopeless, despondent, worried, anxious, broken-spirited, disheartened, wretched, miserable, disconsolate,* and *greatly discouraged.* In Proverbs 13:12, we read, "Hope postponed grieves the heart." Most often, our feelings can be observed as described in Proverbs 15:13—"A Warm, smiling face reveals a joy-filled heart, but heartache crushes the spirit and darkens the appearance." Our emotions alter our countenance and may affect us physically. Proverbs 17:22 reads, "A joy-filled heart is curative balm, but a broken spirit hurts all the way to the bone." Sometimes, we can be so discouraged that we despair of life: Job 10:1 reads, "I hate my life, so I will unload the full weight of my grievance against God." Job had suffered great business and personal losses—the deaths of his children and workers—and even his health was gone. The book of Job is a study in why bad things happen to good people and makes it clear we have an accuser who says we will serve God only when things go our way. But God says, "No, My people will love me 'in sickness and in health, for richer, for poorer.'"

    When love is the preeminent force in the universe, the testimony of our love must also include enduring through to the victory and blessing. This kind of love is based upon a trust of God's faithfulness to bring ultimate good in the end.

2. Luke 4:18 (Jesus quoting Isa. 61:1–2a)—"The Spirit of the LORD is upon Me, Because He has anointed Me to preach the gospel to the poor; He has sent me to heal the brokenhearted, to proclaim liberty

to the captives and recovery of sight to the blind, to set at liberty those who are oppressed, to proclaim the acceptable year of the LORD." Jesus stood up in the synagogue and read this passage from Isaiah. He was announcing He was the Messiah who brought spiritual healing and eternal life to us all. Read in the Gospels what Jesus taught and did among the people. The church is to carry forward the love and truths of the gospel by stepping boldly into the throne of grace, where we can find help (Heb. 4:14–16).
3. Ps. 100:4; 2 Chron. 5:13, 20:22; Luke 19:37; Acts 2:47; Heb. 13:15—These are a few scriptures about praise and worship.

20. Prepare Your Hearts

Prepare your hearts, My beloved, to receive My love. I sent My Son into the world as a sacrifice to redeem the hurting and lost. Believe in My Son because He is the testimony of My love for you. Believe and you will be saved.

The love I have for you is pure, holy, and righteous. I discipline you in love. I care for you in love.

I prepare a place for you that I may receive you into My kingdom and presence. Prepare your hearts, My beloved children. Prepare your hearts.

Selected Scripture Reading

1. Hos. 10:12—God uses poetic language to call Israel to repentance; He compares uncultivated ground to hardened hearts: "Sow for yourselves righteousness, Reap in mercy; Break up your fallow [uncultivated] ground, For it is time to seek the LORD." Repentance requires changing our thinking about ourselves, sin, and our being accountable to God. Repentance is how we prepare our hearts to receive God's love. See Judg. 10:15–16; Hos. 14:2; Prov. 3:11–12; Isa. 1:16–20, 55:7; Dan. 4:34; Matt. 3:2, 8; Mark 1:4; Luke 24:47; Acts 3:19, 10:42–43, 17:29–31, 20:21; Rom. 2:1–16; 2 Cor. 7:9–10; 2 Peter 3:9. Sometimes, difficulties or afflictions help prepare our hearts for repentance; Psalm 119:67 reads, "Before I was afflicted I went astray, But now I keep Your word."

2. Deut. 7:8—"But because the LORD loves you, and because He would keep the oath which He swore to your fathers, the LORD has brought you out with a mighty hand, and redeemed you." See Jer. 31:3, Pss. 78:38, 86:15, 146:8; John 3:16, 16:27.
3. Rom. 5:8; Gal. 5:7–14; Eph. 2:4–10; John 3:1–23—These are more readings on God's love.
4. Heb. 11:6—This verse describes the kind of faith that pleases God.
5. Rom. 10:9–13—"That if you confess with your mouth the Lord Jesus and believe in your heart that God has raised Him from the dead, you will be saved. For with the heart one believes unto righteousness, and with the mouth confession is made unto salvation… For whoever calls on the name of the LORD shall be saved."
6. John 14:1–3—We love to be with those we love and who love us. Peter asked in John 13:37 if he could go with Jesus. Jesus replied that He was going to be with the Father: "I am going to make arrangements for your arrival. I will be there to greet you personally and welcome you home, where we will be together." (Voice). See 1 Cor. 15:50–58; 1 Thess. 4:13–18.
7. John 15:1–17—These verses speak directly as well as in poetic style about God's pure and holy love for us. They also tell us how we can live out that same righteous and pure love in our lives toward others as we abide in Christ's love and commandments. Verse 12 reads, "This is My commandment, that you love one another as I have loved you."

21. Then I Shall Lead You

Seek Me and you shall find Me. I give My grace to those who seek Me. These are times and times are coming that try mankind's hearts and souls, but it must be so. Nevertheless, when the Son of Man comes, will He find faith on the earth?

Let not your heart be overcome with trouble; believe in Him who gave His life for you that your soul would not die. Believe in Jesus Christ and you shall have eternal life. Follow Him. Learn of Him. Obey His commandments and you shall have life abundantly.

I have loved you and given you My Son. You must be obedient to do those things I have commanded you—obedient with all your heart, strength, and mind. Then I shall lead you, and you shall not be afraid of the pestilence, wars or rumors of wars, disasters, or signs in the heavens. Fear shall not overcome you for I shall be your peace. You will hear My voice and be strong. I love you. I will not forsake you. You are My beloved.

Selected Scripture Reading

1. Deut. 4:29–31—"But from there [a place of being surrounded by an idolatrous culture and a backslidden condition] you will seek the LORD your God, and you will find Him if you seek Him with all your heart and with all your soul. When you are in distress and all these things come upon you in the latter days, when you turn to the LORD your God and obey His voice (for the LORD your God is a merciful God), He will not forsake you." God promises that even if we live in a wicked and idolatrous culture, if we will consistently seek Him—that is, search out His truths and walk in His divine love—He will show us what to do, where to go, and how to live (John 10:9–10).
2. Isa. 7:14—"Therefore the Lord Himself will give you a sign: Behold, the virgin shall conceive and bear a Son, and shall call His name Immanuel." This is one of the more than three hundred prophecies written in the Old Testament about the Messiah. The OT was completed some 450 years before Jesus was born. Among other details, the prophecies include specifics of His deity (Isa. 9:6; Titus 2:13; Rev. 12:5), nationality (Gen. 22:18; Matt. 1:1; Luke 3:34; Acts 3:25), birthplace (Mic. 5:2; Matt. 2:1), time of His appearance (Dan. 9:25; Luke 2:1–7), tribe (Gen. 49:10; Luke 3:33), family (Isa. 11:1; Matt. 1:1, 6) and humanity (Gen. 3:15; Luke 2:7; Gal. 4:4).
3. Isa. 9:6—"For unto us a Child is born, Unto us a Son is given; and the government will be upon His shoulder and His name will be called Wonderful, Counselor, Mighty God, Everlasting Father, Prince of Peace." Other verses deal with the Messiah and His Mission; see Isa. 61; Luke 4:16–21; Matt. 1–3; Luke 1–3; John 1:1–36; Rom. 8:1–17; Heb. 2:1–18; 1 Tim. 3:16.
4. Luke 18:8b—"Nevertheless, when the Son of Man comes, will He really find faith on the earth?" Matt. 3:8, 7:21–29; John 16:33; 2

Cor. 9:8; Phil. 1:6; 1 Tim. 1:19–20; Heb. 3–4, 10:35–39; James 1:22; Rev. 2–3 indicate faith and believing means not only giving mental agreement but also heartfelt, lifestyle, and action behaviors.

22. And I See You

I am seeking for the genuine, for the real—for the pure in heart. I am seeking for those servants. I am seeking for those friends of God.

I see your love. I see your devotion. I hear the cry of your heart. Faint not. Hold fast to the good. I am coming soon. I will deliver you from the hands of the enemy.

Your righteousness is of the righteousness of Christ, and I see you.

Selected Scripture Reading

1. Matt. 5:8 (Voice)—"Blessed are those who are pure in heart—they will see God." Matthew 5–7 is a report of what Jesus taught in the Sermon on the Mount. He began with a group of sayings (many of which appear in similar form in the Old and New Testaments) called the beatitudes or "blessedness." These sayings identify character qualities of people God calls blessed.

   1. those who recognize their need for God (Ps. 116)
   2. the contrite and repentant (2 Chron. 7:14; Isa. 57:15; Acts 2:38)
   3. the meek (Zeph. 2:3, 3:12; Ps. 149:4; Gal. 5:23)
   4. those who are hungry for a relationship with God (2 Chron. 15:15; Pss. 27:4–8, 63:1; Acts 17:11)
   5. the merciful and compassionate (Isa. 58; Pss. 41, 112)
   6. those who seek to live righteously (Isa. 33:15–16)
   7. those who are peacemakers (Ps. 133; Prov. 12:20; Rom. 14:19)
   8. those who are persecuted because they do what is right (Ps. 119:137–144)
   9. those who are persecuted because they believe in and follow the teachings of Christ (Ps. 119:86; Isa. 53:5; Matt. 19:29; 1 Cor. 4:10; 1 Peter 4:14).

God calls those people who endeavor to live out His teachings His servants, even friends (Matt. 24:44–45; James 2:22–24; John 15:12–17).

2. 1 Chron. 28:9; Jer. 32:19; Pss. 11:4, 34, 44:20–21; Nah. 1:7; 2 Tim. 2:19—God searches out, knows, and tests the thoughts and intents of our hearts; thus, He knows those who love and honor truth, justice, mercy, grace, patience, wisdom, love, and all His ways.
3. Ps. 34:6—"This poor man cried out, and the LORD heard him, and saved him out of all his troubles." See Gal. 6:9; 2 Cor. 4:16–17.
4. Rom. 1:16–17—"For I am not ashamed of the gospel of Christ, for it is the power of God to salvation for everyone who believes, for the Jew first and also for the Greek. For in it the righteousness of God is revealed from faith to faith; as it is written, 'The just shall live by faith'" (Hab. 2:4).
5. Ps. 17:15—"As for me, I will see Your face in righteousness; I shall be satisfied when I awake in Your likeness."
6. Ps. 18:19 (Voice)—"He set me down in a safe place; He saved me to His delight; He took joy in me."

23. The Lord Has Heard

I have heard the cries of My people. I have called you to be a witness to the nations, and I have placed the nations at your doorstep.

Allow My love to flow through you—for My love will release My power and you will be a witness to the nations.

Selected Scripture Reading

1. Pss. 5:1–3, 6:8–9, 10:17, 34:15, 94; 2 Sam. 22:7; 2 Chron. 6–7; Isa. 59; Jer. 18:8; 1 John 5:14–17—These verses affirm that God hears the prayers of those who cry out to Him.
2. Ex. 22:30; Ps. 126:5–6; Luke 18:1, 21:36; John 17; Acts 28:8; Eph. 6:18; Col. 1:9–12, 4:2; James 5:13–18; Rom. 15:30; Phil. 1:9; 1 Thess. 5:17; 1 Tim. 2:8—We are encouraged and admonished to pray for one another for blessings, salvation, and peace with God. Abraham

interceded for his nephew's family living in the wicked city of Sodom (Gen. 13:13, 18:16–33). Moses interceded for Israel (Ex. 32:11–14; Ps. 106:23). Esther interceded for the Jewish nation to save them from extinction. When Nehemiah learned of Jerusalem lying in ruins, he wept, prayed, and prepared his heart to be used by God (Neh. 1:4–11). Daniel repented on behalf of his people and interceded for their restoration (Dan. 9). Jesus prayed for Himself, His disciples, and all future believers (John 17). Stephen prayed for those who stoned him and forgave them (Acts 7). Peter and John prayed for the Samaritans to receive the Holy Spirit (Acts 8:14–17).

3. John 4:35b–36—"Behold, I say to you, lift up your eyes and look at the fields, for they are already white for harvest! And he who reaps received wages and gathers fruit for eternal life, that both he who sows and he who reaps may rejoice together."

4. Ps. 2:7–8—"I will declare the decree: The LORD has said to Me, 'You are My Son, Today I have begotten You. Ask of Me, and I will give You The nations for Your inheritance, And the ends of the earth for Your possession.'" See Rev. 11:15.

5. Isa. 43:10–12—"You are My witnesses, says the LORD, And My servant whom I have chosen, That you may know and believe Me, And understand that I am He. Before Me there was no God formed, Nor shall there be after Me. I, even I, am the LORD, And besides Me there is no savior. I have declared and saved ... And there was no foreign god among you; Therefore you are My witnesses, Says the LORD, that I am God." See Pss. 107:2, 145:10–11; Matt. 10:18–20; Luke 8:39; 2 Cor. 3:2; Rev. 12:11.

6. Acts 1:8—"But you shall receive power when the Holy Spirit has come upon you; and you shall be witnesses to Me in Jerusalem, and in all Judea and Samaria, and to the end of the earth." The gift of the Holy Spirit in the life of the believer empowers one to witness and minister God's love to others as well as to be a comforter, teacher, and guide. Like all gifts, the gift of the Holy Spirit must be wisely stewarded.

7. Matt. 28:18b–20—Jesus gave us the command to share the gospel with all nations.

24. In My Presence You Will Overcome

My children, My dearly beloved, I am calling you to Myself.

Lay aside all those things that separate you from Me, says the Lord your God. I am calling you up higher. I am calling you to Myself, to walk in My presence—to walk in My freedom and power.

There is a power to overcome in My presence. In My presence, you will overcome all fears, all hindrances. Come to Me, says the Lord your God. I am calling you to Myself.

Selected Scripture Reading

1. Isa. 45:22, 55:1; Matt. 11:28–30; Acts 2:37–39—God is speaking to all people to come to Him.
2. Isa. 59:1–2—"Behold, the LORD's hand is not shortened, that it cannot save; nor His ear heavy, that it cannot hear. But your iniquities have separated you from your God; And your sins have hidden His face from you, so that He will not hear." Our sinful condition separates us from God, but our coming to Him in humble repentance restores our relationship with Him.
3. Heb. 12:1—"Therefore we also, since we are surrounded by so great a cloud of witnesses, let us lay aside every weight, and the sin which so easily snares us, and let us run with endurance the race that is set before us."
4. Ps. 78—This psalm teaches every generation has a moral obligation to the next generation.
5. Gen. 4:7–11, 6:5, 7:1–12; Ex. 33:3; Deut. 23:14; Isa. 64:7; Jer. 2:19, 5:24–25; Pss. 66:18, 107:17; Prov. 13:15; Hos. 5:4; Ezek. 14:13; Matt. 18:21–35; John 9:31; Rom. 2:9, 3:9–18; James 5:1; 1 Peter 2:11; Col. 1:9–11, 21; James 5:16—Sins or wrongdoings have all sorts of repercussions and consequences.
6. Ex. 7:1–7; Deut. 6:16; Matt. 12:38–42—It appears that contentiously demanding that God do something as a sign He is among us is a presumptuous sin that does not please Him. An accusing attitude can be detected; it is not evidence of humbly desiring to please God.

7. Isa. 5:20; Neh. 13:26; Mal. 2:17; Rom. 1—The sustained embracing of sinful attitudes and behaviors results in confusion—a lack of discerning between good and evil. This applies to cultures as well as individuals. See Matt. 12:36–37, 15:10–19; Acts 19:18–19; Gal. 5:19–21; Eph. 5:3; 1 Peter 2:1, 4:3; Rev. 9:20–21.
8. Ps. 16:11—"You will show me the path of life; in Your presence is fullness of joy; at Your right hand are pleasures forevermore."
9. Rev. 22:17—"And the Spirit and the bride say, 'Come!' And let him who hears say, 'Come!' And let him who thirsts come, whoever desires, let him take the water of life freely."

25. You Are My Treasure

I have a word for you, My children. I see your love. You are giving yourself to Me, allowing My Word to wash over you and cleanse and refresh you. I want you to know I rejoice in you. You are My delight. Rejoice and celebrate in My love. Know that you are My treasure and I am among you.

Yes, there are trials and afflictions. Come up higher and see these as stepping stones of growing in grace and power in My Holy Spirit. Let My Word and My love flow through you and you will be victorious.

Let My love be perfected in you.

Selected Scripture Reading

1. Deut. 14:2—"For you are a holy people to the LORD your God, and the LORD has chosen you to be a people for Himself, a special treasure above all the peoples who are on the face of the earth." Eph. 1:4; James 2:5; 2 Tim. 2:10–13; Heb. 10:35–39; 1 Peter 1:1–9; 2:4–9; 2 Peter 3:17; Jude 5–23; Col. 1:9–11, 22–23; Deut. 7:1–8; Ex. 19:1–6; 1 Tim. 1:19–20; Rev. 3:4 appear to indicate that just as a bride and groom come together voluntarily to unite their lives, so do people voluntarily choose to respond to God's invitation to be part of His special treasure—a redeemed people who receive salvation and eternal life.
2. 1 Cor. 8:3 (AMP)—"But if one loves God truly [with affectionate reverence, prompt obedience, and grateful recognition of His

blessing], he is known by God [recognized as worthy of His intimacy and love, and he is owned by Him]." See also 2 Tim. 2:19.
3. Heb. 4:12 (AMP)—"For the Word that God speaks is alive and full of power [making it active, operative, energizing, and effective]; it is sharper than any two-edged sword, penetrating to the dividing line of the breath of life (soul) and the [immortal] spirit, and of joints and marrow [of the deepest parts of our nature], exposing and sifting and analyzing and judging the very thoughts and purposes of the heart."
4. Pss. 19:1–14, 46:4, 101:3; Isa. 34:16, 55:1–13; Joel 3:18; Matt. 7:24–29; John 4:10, 5:39–40, 7:37–39, 17:17; Titus 1:9; 2 Tim. 2:15, 3:16; Acts 17:11; Rom. 4:23–24, 15:4; 1 Peter 1:22–23; Eph. 5:26; Rev. 7:16–19, 22:17—We cannot live without water, so pure, life-giving water is a suitable metaphor for the Word of God. The scriptures wash over us and refresh us. Jesus said that we are sanctified as we embrace God's truths in our hearts.
5. John 15:9–11—"As the Father loved Me, I also have loved you; abide in My love. If you keep My commandments, you will abide in My love, just as I have kept My Father's commandments and abide in His love. These things have I spoken to you, that My joy may remain in you, and that your joy may be full."

26. I Am Coming with a Mighty Cleansing

My people have been and are being poisoned in body, soul, and spirit. Many are weak and sick. But I am coming with a mighty cleansing and washing of My Holy Spirit.

There will be revelations and understandings of truth and righteousness, and they will know how to live. I will reveal My glory among My people, and it will bless the nations. I am the Lord, your most high God.

Selected Scripture Reading

1. Ex. 15:26; Deut. 30:15–16; Pss. 4:4–5, 41:4, 84:11, 107:17; 1 Cor. 11:27–32; Mic. 6:13; Jer. 30:17; 3 John 1:2; Prov. 4:20–27, 8:34, 15, 17:22; Hab. 2:1; Matt. 10:7–8; Mark 16:20; John 14:12; James

2:14–22; Col. 2:6–7; Eph. 4:7, 25–26, 28–32, 5:10–11; 1 Peter 1:13–17; Phil. 4:4–13—God desires we live in good physical, emotional, and spiritual health with the primary importance on spiritual health—salvation and deliverance from the bondages of sin with the reward of eternal life. Revelation 21:1–22:5 describes humanity's future redemption.

   Scriptures confirm that the lifestyle choices we make as well as the thoughts we allow to take root in our hearts have life-altering effects on our entire beings now and eternally. Therefore, through His Word, God teaches and admonishes us about what is truth and how to think and live. God often uses natural things in our everyday lives such as food, bread, water, light, darkness, wind, plants, trees, growth, sheep, shepherds, etc. as metaphors to teach spiritual truths. Proverbs is one of the three wisdom books of the Bible and also uses poetic descriptions. Many times, Jesus taught spiritual truths using parables and stories. Those genuinely desiring to find the truth will take time to prayerfully consider the symbolic meaning of the metaphors, similes, parables, and stories. See Ps. 78:1–4; Matt. 13:34–35, 13:45–46.

2. Isa. 1:4–19—"Alas, sinful nation, a people laden with iniquity ... They have forsaken the LORD... Why should you be stricken again? ... The whole head is sick, and the whole heart faints. From the sole of the foot even to the head, There is no soundness in it ... Wash yourselves, make yourselves clean; put away the evil of your doings from before My eyes. Cease to do evil, learn to do good; seek justice. Rebuke the oppressor; defend the fatherless, plead for the widow ... If you are willing and obedient, you shall eat the good of the land." See Hos. 6:1; Isa. 53:5–6; 1 Peter 2:21–25.

3. Isa. 60:1–3—"Arise, shine; for your light has come ... The LORD will arise over you, and His glory will be seen upon you, The Gentiles shall come to your light, and kings to the brightness of your rising."

4. Rom. 12:9–21—These verses give practice advice on how to love others well even when they are not lovable. For a better understanding, read these verses in multiple translations; Voice reads, "Love others well, and don't hide behind a mask; love authentically. Despise evil; pursue what is good as if your life depends on it. Live in true devotion."

27. Walk in Holiness

I am the Lord your God, and I am in your midst.

My children, I have robes of white—robes of righteousness—bright, shining, and glowing with My majesty and glory. Wear your robes of salvation and righteousness knowing that you are fully accepted by Me. I purchased your salvation—your robes of righteousness—with My blood and sacrifice.

I am returning soon. Prepare your hearts. Walk in holiness and righteousness that My glory be revealed among you.

Biblical Insights on God's Presence

God's presence is often described "in the midst of"—God appeared to Moses in a flame of fire from the midst of a bush (Ex. 3:2–4). God stretched out His hand and struck Egypt, doing wonders of plagues in the midst of Egypt so Pharaoh would know God existed and allow the Israelites to leave Egypt (Ex. 3:20, 8:22; Deut. 11:3; Ps. 135:9). The glory of the Lord rested on Mount Sinai, and God called to Moses out of the midst of a cloud. (Ex. 24:16).

After the idolatrous golden calf incident, God was angry with the Israelites and called them a stiff-necked people. He threatened to come into their midst and destroy them (Ex. 33:3). The Lord spoke to Moses out of the midst of the fire (Deut. 4:36, 5:24).

On several occasions, God was spoken of as dwelling in the midst of the Israelite camp. The people were warned to keep all contagions and contamination out of the camp because the Lord dwelt in their midst (Num. 5:2–4, 35:34). Deuteronomy 23:14 reads, "For the LORD your God walks in the midst of your camp to deliver you and give your enemies over to you; therefore your camp shall be holy that He may see no unclean thing among you and turn away from you."

Here, we can see the spiritual lesson that whatever defiles us separates us from God's presence and blessing. This principle is evident in the story of Israel's defeat at Ai in Joshua 7. The proverbial "sin in the camp" was disobedience, greed, and deception by Achan.

Recorded in Acts 5:1–11 during the founding of the early church is the story of Ananias and Sapphira. They could have been honest about how much money they had sold their property for and rightfully retained a portion for themselves. Instead, they conspired to lie; they said they were giving all the money to the church. God's glory and presence was powerful in the early church (Acts 5:12–16), and He evidently wanted the people to understand the importance of "purity in the camp."

God revealed their deception to Peter, who told them, "You have not lied to men but to God." Upon hearing God's judgment against them, they fell dead. This may seem like harsh judgment to us and even out of character with mercy and grace, but we must bow to God's sovereignty and take His call to purity and holiness seriously and cast away lying and deception. See 1 John 1:9; Rom. 11:22; 1 Peter 1:13–19.

The beauty and freedom that purity brings are depicted as "robes of righteousness for the overcomers" (Isa. 61:10; Rev. 3:5; 19:8). See Rom. 5:8–9 about how God purchased them for us. Wearing the robes of righteousness from Jesus, we can be safe in God's presence.

28. Hear My Voice to Your Heart

As I begin to move among My people with a fresh wind, Satan will manifest in protest. He will incite backbiting, accusations, and slander as he is flushed out. Tell My church to overcome evil with good. Overcome lies with truth. Overcome hate with love. Overcome jealousy with generosity and compassion. Overcome fears with love and willing obedience. Turn from every sin and follow My words and you will walk in powerful confidence.

These are going be unusual times, and you must be able to hear My voice to your heart. Get away from the confusion and voices of the world. Separate yourself and come into My presence so you will hear from Me receive wisdom and life. Then you will know what to do and where to go and be prepared to speak My words.

Biblical Insights from the Book of Ezekiel

Like Daniel and Revelation, there is much imagery and symbolism in the book of Ezekiel. Ezekiel was a prophet from the priestly line who was deported to Babylon in 597 BC. He lived with the Jewish exiles near the Tigris and Euphrates Rivers. From about 593 to 588 BC (chapters 1–24), Ezekiel preached to the demoralized exiles and those remaining in Jerusalem explaining how their individual sins had collectively resulted in God's judgment against their nation.

He warned about the guilt of the people and the future destruction of Jerusalem, which occurred in 587 BC. Chapter 22 specifies the sins that caused the nation to lose God's protection and fall under judgment.

- violence and killing the innocent
- idolatry, even setting up idols in one's heart (Ezek. 14)
- power struggles
- disrespect for parents and those in authority
- oppression of the less fortunate
- despising what is holy and good
- not observing God's Sabbaths/times of physical and spiritual rest
- slanderous attacks on each other
- lewdness
- pornography
- sexual immorality including incest, homosexuality, bestiality, fornication, and adultery
- lack of proper regard and respect for women
- loan sharks/greedy business practices
- unscrupulous business activities
- extortion
- governmental corruption
- religious leaders manipulating and twisting God's commands and principles thereby confusing good and evil
- false prophets leading people astray
- crimes including theft
- corrupt judicial system with people being denied justice

Ezekiel was bold enough to proclaim that the people's sins were the cause of the destruction of their nation. The discipline was severe, but never again would Israel practice gross idolatry.

God also gave Ezekiel a vision of the future—an incredible vision of Israel's restoration—a new move of God's Spirit would breathe new life into the nation (chapters 33–48). It is understood that this prophecy was fulfilled in 538 BC, when Cyrus the Great made provision for the first exiles to return to Jerusalem. Spiritual restoration is pictured in the allegory of God's Spirit breathing into dry bones in chapter 37. Sometimes, prophetic words have more than one interpretation and application: near and far in time or specific and broad in scope. Many principles of restoration can be gleaned from the allegories and words in Ezekiel.

29. Embrace the Wind of My Holy Spirit

The Lord speaks to the hearts of His children: Brace for the wind, My children. Brace for the wind of My Holy Spirit.

I am coming with a mighty, cleansing, rushing wind, and all the things of this world—of the flesh—will be blown away, all the human pride and foolishness, all the human attempts to create and control. The works of the flesh shall not stand before a holy God. I will blow them away.

But the same wind that destroys and cleanses will lift up My children. You will rise above all the circumstances, and trials, and tribulations. My glory shall be revealed in power and the beauty of holiness.

Brace for the wind of My Holy Spirit. Rejoice and sing. You have prayed and cried for this work of the Holy Spirit. Embrace the wind of My Holy Spirit says the Lord.

Selected Scripture Reading

1. Ps. 135:5–7—"For I know that the LORD is great, And our Lord is above all gods. Whatever the LORD pleases He does in Heaven and in earth ... He causes the vapors to ascend from the ends of the earth; He makes lightning for the rain; He brings the wind out of His treasuries." God is majestic, in the natural and in the spiritual.
2. Ezek. 37:9–10—"Also He said to me, prophesy to the breath, prophesy, son of man, and say to the breath, 'Thus says the Lord GOD: Come from the four winds, O breath, and breathe on these slain, that they may live.'" As in Genesis 2:7, when God created mankind, here, God breathed life into Israel and restored the nation.
3. Isa. 30:28—The imagery in this verse varies slightly in different translations. However, all describe God's breath as a winnowing wind and rushing waters sifting the proud nations and making all their efforts futile and hopeless.
4. 1 Chron. 16:29; 2 Chron. 20:21; Pss. 29:2, 96:9—These verses speak in harmony about giving honor, praise, and glory to the Lord by worshipping Him "in the beauty of holiness." The definition of holiness is embodied in God's attributes and character; He is the ultimate manifestation of love, truth, mercy, grace, justice, goodness, purity, integrity, and righteousness, and we see the humility of a servant's heart in the plan of redemption for mankind specifically in the life of His Son, Jesus Christ, the Lamb of God (John 1:29; Heb. 1:1–3; Matt. 20:28; Luke 4:18, 22:25–27; Phil. 2:5–8; Rom. 8:29–32; Acts 10:43).
5. Ex. 15:11; 1 Sam. 2:2; Rev. 5:4—These passages declare God alone is holy, but many scriptures such as 1 Peter 1:13–2:3 (quoting Lev. 20:26) instruct us to be holy in all our attitudes and conduct. In simple terms, we are holy when we endeavor to live by God's Spirit—His character qualities in our lives. We then reflect Him, and that honors Him while bringing blessings for us and others. See Eph. 1:4; Heb. 12:3–11; Phil. 3:9.

30. Keep Praying

The United States is like a tree that will be cut down to its roots. Yet from those roots, it shall grow again, and it shall be good. Once more, it shall give testimony to Jesus Christ as Lord and Savior. She shall be hated by other nations that seek to defy the Most High, but she shall be loved by the Lord.

Pray for her. She is facing her darkest days and great perils. Pray that the Lord of the Harvest sends an army of intercessors to stand in the gap and defeat Satan's attempts to steal the heart of your nation.

This—to intercede for your land—is not easy. You must persevere and listen to the Holy Spirit praying in His power and unction. Do not give up. Breakthrough comes when it looks hopeless and very dark before sunrise.

Remember My words to you. It will look hopeless, but keep praying; press in all the more. If My people do this, they will give birth to a miracle.

Selected Scripture Reading

1. "Trees, vines, vineyards, plants, fruit, and flowers" in their various conditions as well as "planting, growing, root out, pull/pluck up, and cut down" are used to provide many descriptive images of life's situations, safety, shelter, prosperity, health, strength, power, fruitfulness or lack thereof, nourishment, wisdom, the righteous and upright, sinners, realized hopes, encouraging words, the rewards of work, idols, nations, eunuchs, Gentiles, and Israel. Therefore, it is imperative to look at the context in which the imagery appears to grasp the intended meaning. For example, Proverbs 11:30 reads, "The fruit of the righteous is a tree of life, And he who wins souls is wise." Because the righteous understand the importance of knowing God, they will share God's words with others so they also may know Him.
2. Pss. 2:8, 9:5–20, 86:9; Prov. 14:34; 2 Chron. 7:14; Isa. 24:5, 26:2, 60:12, 61:11; Jer. 45:4; Amos 9:8; Hos. 4:1–3; Zech. 14:16; Matt. 25:31–21—From these scriptures, we see that God holds nations and their people accountable.
3. Ezek. 14:13—"When a land sins against Me by persistent unfaithfulness, I will stretch out My hand against it; I will cut off its

supply of bread, send famine on it, and cut off man and beast from it." See Deut. 8:10–20, 32; Pss. 33:8–10, 47:8, 102:15; Jer. 12:17, 17:4; Obad. 1:16.
4. Deut. 8:5; 2 Chron. 7:14; Ps. 81:8–16, 106:43–48; Isa. 61:11; Jer. 2:22–23, 29:10–14; Ezek. 11:14–20; Zech. 2:11, 8:14–15; Zeph. 2:3, 3:8b; Heb. 12:3–11—In these verses, we see God's discipline is designed to bring us to repentance and a restored, blessed relationship with Him. See Ps. 119:67.
5. Isa. 6:13b—"As a terebinth tree or an oak, Whose stump remains when it is cut down, So the holy seed shall be its stump." See Job 14:7–9.

31. You Are Called to Stand in the Gap

I speak to you, My children. Listen carefully. Pray. Intercede and give thanks to the Lord your God for all those in positions of authority. Pray that your leaders be the servants of the most high God as they were called to be so all may lead peaceable lives with all godliness and reverence holding fast to the commandments and precepts of God.

Stand in the gap, My people, and hold up the hands of your leaders and hold up the hands of those I am calling to be your leaders as they are facing problems that are insurmountable without My intervention. You are called to stand in the gap, My beloved. Do the works I have called you to do.

The hour is near. I am coming for My bride. I am eager to receive you to Myself, My bride and My beloved. I love you with an everlasting love. Prepare your hearts to be lifted up into My presence. Humble yourselves to be lifted up into glory.

We shall soon go together to the marriage supper of the Lamb. Be ready, My beloved. I am coming soon. Be ready.

Selected Scripture Reading

1. Isa. 58; Luke 18:9–14—These verses teach that through humility and repentance, we come before God in worship and prayer. God detests self-righteousness, religious talk, and trusting in our own works and

comparing ourselves to others. He calls us to stop our hypocrisy, live genuinely, and love Him and others. See James 5:7–16.
2. Luke 18:1–8—This is the story of a widow persistently going before an uncaring judge to seek justice in a case. Her persistence caused the judge to act. Jesus contrasted the unwilling judge with our heavenly Father, who will at the appointed time bring justice to His own and all the earth. We are called to remain steadfast in our trusting, prayers, and faith in God to bring justice as we wait patiently for that time. See Heb. 10:35–39.
3. 1 Tim. 2:1—"Therefore I exhort first of all that supplications, prayers, intercessions, and giving of thanks be made for all men, for kings and all who are in authority, that we may lead a quiet and peaceable life in all godliness and reverence. For this is good and acceptable in the sight of God our Savior." See Eph. 6:18; 1 Peter 2:13–17.
4. Ps. 106:23—"Therefore He said that He would destroy them, had not Moses His chosen one stood before Him in the breach, to turn away His wrath." Here are a few examples of leaders who "stood in the gap" praying for their people.

- Moses interceded for his people (Deut. 9:26; Ex. 32:11–14).
- Daniel prayed for the return of the exiles after reading Jeremiah's prophecies about why the nation seventy years earlier had been defeated and carried in exile to Babylon and after reading about the future restoration of Israel to the land (Dan. 9:3–20).
- Nehemiah prayed and worked to rebuild the walls of Jerusalem (Neh. 1:4–11).
- Jesus prayed for Himself, for His disciples, and for you and me (John 17).

See also Matt. 5:13–16; 1 Peter 3:8–12.

32. An Everlasting Love

You are My beloved. You are My chosen. I love you with an everlasting love. Tenderly, I seek you to spend time with Me.

Come away, My beloved, and spend time with Me and you will find times of refreshing. I long to draw you to Myself so My love will fill you. You have been hurt and wounded.

Come to Me and you will be healed. Find the peace you are longing for in Me—in My presence—says the Lord.

Selected Scripture Reading

1. Jer. 31:3—"The LORD has appeared of old to me, saying: 'Yes, I have loved you with an everlasting love; Therefore with loving kindness I have drawn you'" (spoken to the faithful remnant of Israel, ca. 606 BC. See Rom. 9:27–11:36). God established the first covenant with Abraham and his descendants—the nation of Israel—as we read about in Gen. 12 (ca. 1921 BC). About 470 years later (ca. 1451 BC), Moses spoke to the Israelites at the close of their forty years of wandering in the wilderness—a journey during which they learned about themselves and God.

    In Deuteronomy 8:2, Moses told the people something that applies to us today: "And you shall remember that the LORD your God led you all the way these forty years in the wilderness, to humble you and test you, to know what was in your heart, whether you would keep His commandments or not." The Israelites were about to enter a new phase of their walk with God, and Moses was reviewing the critical importance of loving and obeying God, who had chosen them to be His people so they would fulfill their destiny.

    In Genesis 12:3, 17:7, we read that all the families of the earth would be blessed through what God would do with Abraham's descendants. Because of the testimony of the Israelites, we Gentiles have the opportunity to know almighty God and the salvation He has made possible. See Ps. 22:27; Gen. 22:18; Isa. 45:22, 49:6, 60:3; Jer. 16:19; Dan. 7:14; Mal. 1:11; Matt. 12:18–21; John 1:1–17; Acts 13:44–48; Rom. 5:8; 9:25–26; Hebrews; 1 John 3:1.
2. Ps. 108:5–6 (Voice)—"O God, that You would be lifted up above the heavens in the hearts of Your people until the whole earth knows Your glory."
3. Isa. 61:1—"The Spirit of the Lord GOD is upon Me, because the LORD has anointed Me to preach good tidings to the poor; He has sent Me to heal the brokenhearted, To proclaim liberty to the

captives, And the opening of the prison to those who are bound." Jesus quoted this verse when He read the scripture in the synagogue (Luke 4:16–21).
4. Acts 3:19—"Repent therefore and be converted, that your sins may be blotted out, so that times of refreshing may come from the presence of the Lord." See Pss. 4:3, 51.
5. Ps. 16:11—"You will show me the path of life; In Your presence is fullness of joy; At Your right hand are pleasures forevermore."

33. Your Heart Is My Treasure

Call upon Me and I will answer you. Your heart is My treasure. I love you and desire to meet every need of your heart. Come to Me with all your concerns, with all your burdens. Come unto Me and I will give you the rest and peace you are crying out for.

Do not go to the wolves in sheep's clothing but come before the Lord your God. Seek Me. Seek My truth. Seek My ways and you shall live, says the Lord your God. I love you. I love you. I love you.

Selected Scripture Reading

1. Ps. 86:7; Joel 2:32; Acts 2:5, 21, 4:12, 10:34; Rom. 10:11–13; Rev. 22:17—God hears us when we humbly cry out to Him.
2. Ps. 116:13—"I will take up the cup of salvation, and call upon the name of the LORD." Many verses in the Old and New Testaments instruct us to call out to God as well as give examples. The story of the prophet Elijah on Mount Carmel is one of the more dramatic. Israel's extremely wicked leaders, Ahab and Jezebel, had led the nation astray even into idolatry. Elijah was moved to challenge the 450 prophets of the false god Baal to a showdown. In 1 Kings 18:24, we read that after the sacrifices were laid on their respective altars, Elijah said to the false prophets, "Then you call on the name of your gods, and I will call on the name of the LORD; and the God who answers by fire, He is God." Despite the hours of yelling and self-flagellation, nothing happened on Baal's altars. Then Elijah built an altar, placed the sacrifice on it, had water poured on it, and called on the Lord God

to answer by consuming the sacrifice with fire as a confirmation that He was God and that all the people were to turn their hearts back to Him and follow His commands and teachings.

It is a story of great victory, yet it is also a story of gut-wrenching challenge and hardship. More scriptures deal with the importance of turning away from false gods, witchcraft, and occult practices. See Ex. 23:32–33; Lev. 19:31; Deut. 18:9–14; 1 Chron. 16:26; 1 Sam. 15:22–23; 2 Kings 9:22b; 1 Chron. 10:13; Isa. 2:8, 8:19, 47:9; Dan. 5:4; Hos. 2:16–18; Mic. 5:12–14; Acts 8:4–23, 16:16–18, 17:16–34, 19:18–20; Gal. 5:20; Rev. 9:21.
3. Ex. 19:5–6—"Now therefore, if you will indeed obey My voice and keep My covenant, then you shall be a special treasure to Me above all people ... And you shall be to Me a kingdom of priests and a holy nation." See Matt. 13:44; 1 Peter 2:4–10; Titus 2:11–14.
4. Matt. 11:20–30—Jesus had performed many miracles in the cities of Korazin and Bethsaida, yet the people did not repent. In verse 25, Jesus praised the Father for hiding spiritual truths from the self-righteous and proud while revealing them to those hungry for truth. Understanding and living Jesus's teachings will give rest to our souls.
5. Matt. 7:15—"Beware of false prophets who come disguised as harmless sheep but are really vicious wolves." See 1 Peter 2–3; 1 Tim. 1:3–8, 6:3–11; 2 Tim. 2:14–3:17.
6. John 16:27—"For the Father Himself loves you, because you have loved Me, and have believed that I came forth from God." See John 3:16, 8:31–32; Rom. 8:38–39.

34. I Am Your Strength and Joy

My children, I speak these words of comfort to you so you may receive My peace.

I am planning something very big. The world has never seen anything like this before. Mankind will see the power and fury of a mighty God. Do not fear. I am here with you and will protect My own. Many will run to and fro looking for peace, but My peace shall be in you.

You do not need to look to the right or left for help because I am your help. I will not leave you or forsake you. I shall lift you up on eagles' wings.

You shall run and not be weary. You shall walk and not faint. For I am your strength and I am your joy.

I say again to you. You do not need to look to the right or left for help, for I am your help. I will not leave you or forsake you. I shall lift you up on eagles' wings. You shall run and not be weary. You shall walk and not faint. For I am your strength and I am your joy.

Rest in Me. Look to Me for your peace.

Selected Scripture Reading

1. John 16:33—"These things I have spoken to you, that in Me you may have peace. In the world you will have tribulation; but be of good cheer, I have overcome the world."
2. Ps. 47:2–3—"For the LORD Most High is awesome; He is a great King over all the earth. He will subdue the peoples under us, and the nations under our feet." The prophet Joel was the first to speak of the day of the Lord (ca. 835–805 BC). This phrase is used many times in the Old and New Testaments and appears to indicate the time when God's mercy for mankind will end and His acts of judgment begin. See Amos 5:18; Isa. 2:12, 13:6, 9, 34:8; Zeph. 1:7–8, 14, 18, 2:2–3; Jer. 46:10; Lam. 2:22; Ezek. 13:5, 30:3; Obad. 1:15; Zech. 14:1; Mal. 4:5; Acts 2:20; 1 Cor. 5:5; 2 Cor. 1:14; 1 Thess. 5:2; 2 Peter 3:10). A few verses about the end of the wicked are Pss. 37, 73; Matt. 13:24–30, 13:36–43; Phil. 3:18–19; 1 Peter 4:17–19; 2 Peter 2:17; Jude 13; Rev. 20:11–15, 21:8. For info on the signs of the end times, see Matt. 24; Mark 13; Luke 21.
3. Ps. 83:1–18—"Do not keep silent, O God! Do not hold Your peace … For behold, Your enemies make a tumult; And those who hate You have lifted up their head. They have taken crafty counsel against Your people … They have said, "Come, and let us cut them off from being a nation, that the name of Israel may be remembered no more." … O my God, make them like the whirling dust … So pursue them with Your tempest … That they may seek Your name O LORD … That they may know that You, whose name alone is the LORD, are the Most High over all the earth." See Zech. 14:9; Rev. 11:15. It appears Psalm 83 may speak of a time when nations conspire against Israel.

4. Isa. 40:28–31—"Have you not known? Have you not heard? The everlasting God, the LORD, the Creator of the ends of the earth, neither faints nor is weary ... But those who wait on the LORD shall renew their strength; They shall mount up with wings like eagles, They shall run and not be weary, They shall walk and not faint." See Pss. 29:11, 50:15, 119:64–68.

35. The Bread of Life

Does not My Word say He who has begun a good work in you will continue it through to completion until the day of Jesus Christ?

Shall I not do this work before you—before your eyes for all the world to see? Behold, I am coming quickly, and My reward is with Me. Only persevere, hold fast to what I have given you until I return. Hold fast to your faith.

You shall be fed with the finest of wheat. With honey from the rock I shall satisfy you. My words in your heart—they are wheat; they are honey. My words in your heart shall give you strength. My words in your heart shall give you peace.

My dear children, I plead with you. Hide My words in your heart that you may learn to hear and recognize My voice. Hide My words in your heart. Walk with Me and I shall walk with you, says the Lord your God. Come to Me and receive the Bread of Life.

Selected Scripture Reading

1. Phil. 1:6—"He who has begun a good work in you will complete it until the day of Jesus Christ." See also Col. 1:23.
2. John 6:22–68—Jesus used the metaphor of eating and drinking for natural nourishment to teach the spiritual principle that taking His teachings into our hearts will give us spiritual life.
3. Ps. 81:16—"He would have fed them also with the finest of wheat; And with honey from the rock I would have satisfied you." Psalm 81 is a shorter version of the Song of Moses (Deut. 32:1–47), a call to repentance that God directed Moses to write saying He knew after

Moses's death that the Israelites would rebel and break covenant with Him.

God told Moses that He wanted the song to be written down and taught to adults and children throughout the generations to remind them of who they were and how they had forsaken God. Verses 36–39 say God will judge His people but also have compassion on them and heal them. In the process of delivering and restoring Israel, God would "render vengeance to My enemies, And repay those who hate Me" (v. 41). Deuteronomy 32:43 speaks of the Gentiles rejoicing with the Israelites because of God's ultimate justice: "He will provide atonement for His land and His people." The Song of Moses and its shorter version, Psalm 81, summarize the journey Israel and we take when we do not hold fast to God's words.

4. John 14:23—"Jesus answered and said to him, 'If anyone loves Me, he will keep My word; and My Father will love him, and We will come to him and make Our home with him.'"
5. Ps. 119:10–11—"With my whole heart I have sought You; Oh, let me not wander from Your commandments! Your word I have hidden in my heart, that I might not sin against You."
6. 1 Tim. 4:13—"Until I come, give attention to the public reading of Scripture, to exhortation and teaching." See Rev. 22:12.

36. Cry Out to the Lord Your God

My children, My precious children, by the Holy Spirit, the Lord your God warns you that great storms are forming over the seas and and over the seas of mankind. These storms will bring great destruction, death, and chaos.

But I say to you, My people, arise and do battle in the spiritual. Come together in unity, laying aside every sin and burdensome weight. Cry out to the Lord your God for mercy for your land. Cry out to the Lord your God for deliverance. Cry out to the Lord your God for truth and honesty to be established over the land and over the waters. I am your only hope says the Lord your God.

Again I say to you, pray for truth and honesty to be established in the hearts of your people that your land may be spared. I will call some to come forth and speak the truth. Pray for them. Pray for your leaders and those in authority that they will love the truth and honor Me with all humility and grace.

The storms shall come. Be there ahead of them with Me, and I shall deliver you, says the Lord your God.

Selected Scripture Reading

1. Rom. 8:12–16 (NIV)—"Therefore, brothers, we have an obligation—but it is not to the sinful nature, to live according to it. For if you live according to the sinful nature, you will die; but if by the Spirit you put to death the misdeeds of the body, you will live, because those who are led by the Spirit of God are sons of God ... The Spirit himself testifies with our spirit that we are God's children." Regardless of what happens in life, we are obligated to act with integrity and wisdom according to God's principles.
2. Gen. 6:9–9:17; Heb. 11:7—"Storms" of evil and wickedness had been raging over the earth (Gen. 6:1–5). Noah and his family had weathered those cultural storms because "Noah walked with God" (Gen. 6:9). Because of Noah's relationship with God, he heard His warning and understood what to do.
3. Pss. 37:11, 133:1–3, 149:4; Zeph. 2:3; Matt. 5:5; Rom. 15:5–6; Eph. 4:2–16; Col. 3:9–16; Phil. 2:1–4; 2 Tim. 2:24–26; James 3:13–16—Developing the character qualities of love, respect, humility, grace, wisdom, truthfulness, patience, and being teachable are prerequisites for unity in the body of Christ. Consider reading and studying Psalm 40; Hebrews 10:5–9, and 1 Peter 5:5–11 in light of the importance of maintaining godly character qualities while realizing we are in spiritual warfare against such things as pride, greed, arrogance, fear, perversion, immorality, dissimulation, lying, rebellion, and so on.
4. Luke 21:7–36—"And there will be great earthquakes ... and great signs from the heavens ... You will be brought before kings and rulers for My name's sake. But it will turn out for you as an occasion for testimony ... By your patience possess your souls ... Watch therefore, and pray always that you may be counted worthy to escape all these things that will come to pass, and to stand before the Son of Man."

37. You Are My Testimony upon the Earth

My children, you are my ambassadors. You are my witnesses—my testimony upon the earth to speak and live the words of salvation and eternal life. I have called you to be salt and light to your generation.

Do not take your calling lightly. Seek Me. Let My words burn in your hearts and My wisdom fill your very being. I move and act by the Spirit and power of wisdom.

I desire truth and holiness in your inward parts. Seek My truth and wisdom and you will live as salt and light. Your joy will be great because My Spirit and My power will be released among you. Great will be your joy.

I am coming soon for My children. Prepare your hearts, My beloved. Let there be great rejoicing.

Selected Scripture Reading

1. Isa. 43:10—"You are My witnesses, says the LORD, and My servant whom I have chosen that you may know and believe Me, and understand that I am He, Before Me there was no God formed, nor shall there be after Me. I even I, am the LORD, and besides Me there is no savior ... Therefore you are My witnesses, says the LORD, that I am God."
2. 1 Chron. 16:7–36; Ezra 8:22; Neh. 5:9; Pss. 26:7, 60:4, 107:1–3, 119:172; Isa. 12:4; Mal. 3:16; Matt. 10:18–20; Mark 5:19; Luke 8:39; Acts 1:8, 2:4, 4:20, 5:32, 18:9–10, 22:12–16, 26:22; 2 Cor. 3:3, 4:1–18; Eph. 5:15–21; 2 Tim. 1:8; 1 Peter 3:15; Titus 2:15; Rev. 12:11—Like Isa. 43:10, these scriptures expand our understanding of what it means to be a witness for God and share our testimony with others. Clearly, witnesses are to be well informed about the facts, to speak truthfully with humility and wisdom, to be aware of their limitations, and to be sensitive about the appropriate time to speak.
3. Ex. 20:1–17; Deut. 5:1–22; 1 Tim. 1:5–11; Matt. 5:17; John 13:34–35; Rom. 8:4—God gave the Ten Commandments and old covenant teachings to show mankind the basics for honoring Him and respecting one another. Galatians 3:19–25 explains that the "Law" was given as a schoolmaster/tutor/guardian to make mankind aware of our sins and need for a Mediator between God and us.

Though it is natural for us to slide down into trusting in legalisms, ceremonies, and sacrifices, even King David understood the more important meanings of the symbolism and rules. He wrote in Ps. 40:6–10 that God was not pleased with our legalistic attempts at holiness and righteousness; rather, He desired hearts full of love and obedient devotion. In Ps. 51:5–6, David acknowledged that we were born with a carnal nature subject to sin but that we could overcome that by a desire and diligence in seeking God's truths and wisdom with the help of His Holy Spirit. See Isa. 11:1–5; Eph. 1:15–23.
4. Luke 24:32—"And they said to one another, 'Did not our heart burn within us while He talked with us on the road, and while He opened the Scriptures to us?'"

38. The Secret Place of Worship

My beloved, I see your hearts. I receive your worship. You delight My heart. You are My children. I watch over you with a Father's great love. You are My treasure. You are My delight. I am pleased with you, and your ways are ever before Me.

Call out to Me in the secret place of worship—where your heart is fully open to Me. There you will find Me. I am calling to My beloved bride. Prepare yourself. Make ready your bridal attire. I am returning to take you home with Me to be with Me forever. I love you, My children.

Biblical Insights from 2 Kings 21–22

In 2 Kings 21 is the account of King Manasseh. He was undoubtedly a powerful man and looked good in others' eyes, but what did God see? In 1 Samuel 16:7, we read, "For the LORD does not see as man sees; for man looks at the outward appearance, but the LORD looks at the heart." See 1 Kings 8:61; Prov. 11:20.

Manasseh, king of Judah around 698 BC, was an example of a leader with a perverse heart; 2 Kings 21 records that he reigned in Jerusalem for fifty-five years and followed the forbidden, wicked, idolatrous, and occult practices of the neighboring cultures; constructed temples to Baal; built altars for the worship of the sun, moon, and stars; had idols built; practiced child sacrifice; practiced sorcery and divination; consulted mediums and spiritists; and placed a carved Asherah (the image of a Canaanite fertility goddess of Assyrian origin) pole in the temple of the Lord.

God's blessings for the Israelite nation were conditional upon their remaining loyal to Him (2 Kings 21:8). Verse 9 states that the people did not heed God's warning and that Manasseh led them astray into evil and idolatry thus incurring loss of God's protection and His anger. After Manasseh died, his son, Amon, who was also wicked, reigned for two years before Amon's son, Josiah, became king.

In 2 Kings 22:2, Josiah "did what was right in the sight of the LORD." As a godly leader, he

1. directed that the temple of the Lord be repaired, symbolizing returning to the Lord God,
2. after the book of the Law was discovered in the temple, instructed the priests to inquire of the Lord, which they did by speaking with a prophetess of the Lord, Huldah (2 Kings 22:13–20),
3. gathered the elders, priests, prophets, and people in Jerusalem and read to them "all the words of the Book of the Covenant" (23:2),
4. led the people in renewing their covenant with almighty God (2 Kings 23:3),
5. directed the removal and destruction of all idolatrous articles of worship,
6. removed the idolatrous priests and occult practitioners. (2 Kings 23:5 20, 24), and
7. destroyed places of idol worship and child sacrifice (23:6–19).

Scripture commends Josiah saying he "turned to the LORD with all his heart, with all his soul, and with all his might." John 4:23–24 and Galatians 5:16–6:10 reflect the grace and purity of the new covenant worship of God. See Ps. 31:19–20 about being hidden in the secret place of God's presence.

39. Allow My Spirit and My Truth to Cleanse and Purify

Come to Me all you who are burdened with worry and the cares of this life. Come to Me and you will find peace for your souls. In the world are many trials and tribulations. I say to you, overcome the world.

Come to Me and allow My Spirit and My truth to cleanse and purify your life. Then My love, even faith, will flow through you in increasing measure. This world offers many enticing counterfeits. You cannot embrace both the counterfeit and the genuine at the same time and overcome the world. Walk away from the counterfeit. Walk away from the sins that separate you from Me.

Come to Me. Seek My truth. Seek My ways and you will overcome. Your joy and peace will be great. I love you, my treasure. Come to Me with all your heart.

Selected Scripture Reading

1. Gen. 7:1, 18:19; Isa. 1:18, 30:15, 45:22, 55:1–11, 59:2; Jer. 30:2, 35:15; Ezek. 33:11; Hos. 6:1; Matt. 11:28–30, 22:1–14, 28:19–20; Luke 14:17; John 6:44–45, 14:6–7, 17:17; Acts 2:37–39; 1 Cor. 2:4–5; 2 Cor. 5:20; Eph. 2:11–16; 2 Tim. 4:1–5; Rev. 3:20; 22:17—God calls us to come to Him by His Spirit, His servants, and His written Word.
2. Deut. 10:12–16; 1 Sam. 15:22; Ps. 51:16; Eccl. 12:13; Isa. 58; Hos. 6:6; Mic. 6:8; Zech. 7:1–14; Matt. 5:20, 18:3; 22:36–40; Mark 12:30–34; Luke 13:2, 18: 9–14; John 3:5, 4:24; 6:44–45, 8:24; Rom. 13:8–10, 14:17; 1 Cor. 1:26–30, 7:19, 8:8; James 1:21–27; Heb. 9:16–28, 11:6, 12:14; 2 Tim. 2; 1 Peter 1:22–23—These are a few of the scriptures that give a definition of true religion and worship of God. Notice the flow of harmony from the Old Testament to the New Testament clarifying that outward manifestations of worship, piety, ceremonies, or traditions do not please God. Quite the contrary, God's requirement for acceptance is the inner righteousness that comes from sincerely believing in and loving God, understanding and following His teachings, and loving others. Some of those in the Bible commended for their faith are Enoch, Noah, Jabez, Hezekiah, Job, Daniel, Simeon, Anna, Nathanael, Cornelius, Barnabas, Ananias (Acts 9:10, 22:12), and Timothy.

3. Ex. 23:33; Deut. 18:9–14; 1 Chron. 16:26; Isa. 2:8; Jer. 2:11–13, 7:28–31, 11:12, 16:20; Dan. 9:5; Mark 7:13; Acts 15; 1 Cor. 12:2; Gal. 4:8–10; Rev. 9:20—These are a few verses about counterfeits—false gods and false Christs (Matt. 24:5), false religions, legalisms (Matt. 23:23), traditions (Matt. 15:9), sanctimony or outward appearances of piety (Isa. 58:2; Matt. 6:5; Col. 2:1–23), formalism/ceremonialism (Isa. 1:13, 29:13; Matt. 15:8; Gal. 4:10), a zeal for God but not according to knowledge (Rom. 10:2), and false trusts (Ps. 52:7).
4. John 16:33—"These things I have spoken to you, that in Me you may have peace. In the world you will have tribulation; but be of good cheer, I have overcome the world."

40. Follow Me

My precious children, I love each of you with everlasting love that will sustain you through every trial and tribulation.

I have called you out of darkness and into the light of salvation by the power and glory of Jesus Christ. I have called you to be saints who are loved and honored. I have called you to reflect My love and holiness. You are my delight, My treasure. Listen carefully.

There are times are coming, My children, when you must listen and obey My voice. You must turn to the right or left to walk in My protection and provision. Your very life will depend upon it. Learn now to hear My voice and walk with Me in obedience. Not every choice and move is critical to your protection and provision, but some will be. Learn to follow Me now and you will know which way to go. Shut out other voices and come to Me in the quiet. I am waiting for you. I am waiting.

It is to those who wait upon Me—to those who seek Me with their whole heart that I shall reveal Myself. From your innermost being will flow rivers of living water. You will be refreshed, and I will strengthen your heart. My Holy Spirit will lead and guide you. Follow Me so the foundation of the church will be full of integrity and strength of heart. Follow Me, says the Lord your God.

Selected Scripture Reading

1. Deut. 7:9—"Therefore know that the LORD your God, He is God, the faithful God who keeps covenant and mercy for a thousand generations with those who love Him and keep His commandments." Deuteronomy 30:19 and Psalms 94–96 confirm that God lovingly calls all His creation to acknowledge and receive the comfort, salvation, deliverance, and protection that coming into relationship with Him brings. In these scriptures, we also learn that while our sovereign and almighty God is a refuge for those in relationship with Him, He will eventually render judgment and punishment on the proud workers of iniquity. This theme appears repeatedly in the Old and New Testaments.
2. John 3:16—"For God so loved the world that He gave His only begotten Son; that whoever believes in Him should not perish but have everlasting life." See Isa. 3:10.
3. Ps. 18:35–36—"You have also given me the shield of your salvation; your right hand has held me up, your gentleness has made me great. You enlarged my path under me, so my feet did not slip." See Ps. 37:7; Isa. 25:9; John 5:39, 7:16–17; Acts 1:4–5.
4. Ps. 37:23–24—"The steps of a good man are ordered by the LORD, and He delights in his way. Though he fall, he shall not be utterly cast down; for the LORD upholds him with His hand." See Luke 10:25–37; Gal. 6:1–2 regarding sharing one another's burdens.
5. Prov. 8:34–36—"Blessed is the man who listens to me [wisdom], watching daily at my gates ... For whoever finds me finds life, and obtains favor from the LORD; But he who sins against me [wisdom] wrongs his own soul; all those who hate me love death."

41. In Your Hearts Leave the World

My children, I would speak to you of My love. My love is powerful. My love is healing to your soul and spirit. Come to Me all you who are burdened with the cares of this world. In Me, you will find rest. In Me, you will find peace for your souls. It is by remaining in My love that you will find strength and wisdom to overcome the trials, temptations, and confusions coming upon the earth.

I am calling to My beloved bride. In your hearts, leave the world. Come to Me. Refresh yourself in My presence. Know My presence and My love. Prepare yourself, My bride, for I am returning soon to take you home. Prepare yourself. Let My love fill your hearts. You are My beloved.

Selected Scripture Reading

1. Ex. 23:4; Lev. 19:18; Deut. 5:29, 6:1–25, 31:11–20; Matt. 25:35; Prov. 25:21; Mal. 1:11; Matt. 5:43–48; Acts 13:44–52, 26:23, 28:28; Isa. 42:1–7; Rom. 12:9–21, 3:17–19; Gal. 5:6; Eph. 3:3–9; 1 Peter 4:7–10; 1 John 4:7–8; 1 Cor. 13—There are many words in Hebrew and Greek that have been translated "love." Their definitions and uses vary and may include

   - to have affection for (sexually or otherwise)
   - to delight in
   - to deliver
   - to join (figuratively)
   - to cling to
   - to have compassion upon
   - to have, obtain, or show mercy
   - to have pity
   - to be passionate
   - to love in a social or moral sense (*Strong's* no. 25, *agapao*)
   - to knock or smote (carries a sense of selfishness)
   - to be kind
   - to cherish
   - to will or wish
   - to have a love for mankind (*philanthropia*) and brotherly love (*philadelphia*).

   The scripture verses above clarify that "love" is preeminent in God's character and the preeminent character quality and behavior He expects us to honor and exemplify in our lives. God's love is not driven by lust or self-gratification; His love has the parameters of

goodness and truth. By His sovereignty, He teaches and demonstrates His love for us yet gives us free will to choose to love Him or reject Him.
2. Rom. 5:8—"But God demonstrates His own love toward us, in that while we were still sinners, Christ died for us." See John 3:16, 16:27; Eph. 2:4–10; 2 Thess. 3:5; Heb. 9:28.
3. 2 Cor. 6:17–18—"Therefore come out from among them and be separate, says the Lord. Do not touch what is unclean and I will receive you. I will be a Father to you and you shall be My sons and daughters, says the LORD Almighty." See Isa. 52:10–11; John 15:12–19; Rom. 16:17–19; 1 Cor. 5:11, 6:14–18; 2 Thess. 3:6; 2 Tim. 2:24–26, 3:1–5; 1 John 2:15–17; Rev. 18:4. Consider also Matt. 9:10–13; Mark 2:13–17—ministering to others.
4. John 15:1–17—"You are already clean because of the word which I have spoken to you. Abide in Me, and I in you. As the branch cannot bear fruit of itself, unless it abides in the vine, neither can you, unless you abide in Me … By this My Father is glorified, that you bear much fruit, so you will be My disciples. As the Father loved Me, I also have loved you; abide in My love. If you keep My commandments, you will abide in My love … These things I command you, that you love one another."

42. Put On Tender Mercies

My precious children, I am here in your midst. This is our time together. I delight in you as you enter My presence with thanksgiving and come into My courts with praise.

I am calling My people to a greater understanding and experience in repentance. I am calling you to come out and be separate from the world in order that you may live with overcoming grace and power.

There is much work to be done in My kingdom and before I return for My bride. Awake, My church. Arise, My people. Live before Me in holiness and purity. Come into the presence of your King. I have assignments and positions for you. Prepare yourselves. Hide My word in your hearts. Listen, and spend time with Me. Learn to know My voice.

My children, this greater understanding of and experience in repentance will lead you to put on tender mercies, kindness, humility, and forgiveness for one another. My love is being perfected in you. Receive My love, My bride. Receive My love.

Selected Scripture Reading

1. Ps. 100:1–5—"Make a joyful shout to the LORD, all you lands! Serve the LORD with gladness; come before His presence with singing. Know that the LORD, He is God, It is He who has made us ... We are His people and the sheep of His pasture. Enter into His gates with thanksgiving, and into His courts with praise. Be thankful to Him, and bless His name. For the LORD is good; His mercy is everlasting, and His truth endures to all generations." Additional scriptures clarify the nature, design, and purpose of worship; see 1 Chron. 16:29; 2 Chron. 5:11–14; Pss. 5:7, 31:19–24, 95:6, 96:9, 111:1, 134; Isa. 56:7; Mic. 6:8; Matt. 4:10; Luke 19:46, 24:52–53; John 4:20–26, 7:14–29. Jesus's explanation of keeping the law stressed love and doing good over religious acts and ceremonial traditions. See Eccl. 5:1–7; Isa. 2:3; Acts 2:46–3:1; Eph. 5:1–21; Heb. 10–11. For a summary perspective on worship, see Rev. 4:11–5:13.
2. 2 Chron. 7:14; Pss. 34:18, 51:17, 119:67; Isa. 30:15, 52:1; Jer. 4:12, 14; 7:5, 36:7; Hos. 3:5, 14:2; Joel 2:12–14; Matt. 3:2; Mark 1:4; Luke 24:45–53; Acts 17:29–31, 20:21; 1 Cor. 15:34; 2 Cor. 7:10; Matt. 3:8; Rom. 2:4, 12:16, 13:11–12; Eph. 5:8–17; Heb. 6; 2 Peter 3:9; James 4:1–17. Hebrew words translated "repent" (*Strong's* no. 5162, *nacham*, and no. 7725, *shub*) as well as the Greek word *metaneo* support the following understandings of what repentance means.

    - to be sorry
    - to change one's mind or purpose particularly with respect to accepting God's will
    - to regret
    - to change the inner self
    - to relent
    - to relieve
    - to think better
    - to return
    - to console oneself

3. Col. 3:1–17—Being tenderhearted and humbly recognizing our shortcomings and sins increase our compassion for others and establish a stable testimony for God.
4. Matt. 24:14—"And this gospel of the kingdom will be preached in all the world as a witness to all the nations, and then the end will come."

43. Before the Throne of God

All over this nation, I am giving prayer assignments to my intercessors. You are being called to spiritual warfare. The battle must be won in the spiritual realm by My people.

Awake, church. Arise. Open your spiritual eyes. Open your spiritual ears. I will speak to your spirit deep in your hearts and direct you to pray specific prayers. Because you will know you have heard My voice, you will pray with faith.

You must separate yourself from the world and come into My presence. You must lay aside selfish thoughts and ambitions. You must allow My Holy Spirit to wash you clean. When you come into My presence—washed in the blood of the Lamb, dressed in the pure, white robes of righteousness—your confidence, hope, and faith will give authority to your prayers.

Come up, My beloved, into the place prepared for you. Come up before the throne of God with your prayers of intercession.

Biblical Insights from the Books of Haggai and Zechariah

Haggai and Zechariah were prophets who spoke encouraging words about restoration (ca. 520–475 BC) to the civil and religious leaders and the common folk in Jerusalem when the people were very discouraged and confused about their situation and assignment.

There is much descriptive and allegorical language in these two Old Testament books that gives not only historical accounts highlighting spiritual dynamics, but also looks forward to the future restoration God has planned for Israel and all His people.

For background information, here is an abbreviated history of what the nation of Israel—both Northern/Israel and Southern/Judah kingdoms—had gone through.

1. Ca. 700s–600s BC—warnings by prophets such as Isaiah and Jeremiah to return to the Lord or face being ruled by their enemies (return to God or be ruled by sin).
2. 722 BC—The ten northern tribes that constituted the Northern Kingdom were decimated by Assyria.
3. 597, 586, 581 BC—Babylon's attacks defeated the two remaining tribes known as Judah/Southern Kingdom. The Babylonians destroyed Jerusalem including the temple and took approximately 60,000 exiles to Babylon.
4. 539 BC—King Cyrus of Persia captured Babylon.
5. Ca. 536 BC—Thanks to the Persian king Cyrus (Isa. 44:28–45:1; Ezra), the first exiles returned to Jerusalem. Cyrus had assigned them the task under governor Zerubbabel to rebuild the temple.

At the time of Haggai and Zechariah, Jerusalem and the people as a unified nation lay in ruins; they were traumatized by the past, burdened by living in a pile of rubble, and discouraged by the Samaritans and others who worked to undermine their will and ability to rebuild the temple of God. As you read these books laden with symbolism, look for the promises and principles of restoration.

44. Let Faith Well Up in Your Heart

I speak to My people. There are indeed troubling times coming upon the earth and upon this nation. Remember that I have called you to be My witnesses to reflect the love, the holiness, and the glory of Your God.

I am not a God who leaves you forsaken and hopeless. You are My beloved. You are My bride. I will walk with you through every trial. As you see the things around you crumble, let faith well up in your heart. Come to Me and hide yourself under My wings—under My authority.

I will care for you. I will provide for you. You are to be blessed and to be a blessing to all those around you. You will receive your assignment through patient prayer and worship. Be patient—walk in the grace and anointing I am giving to you. Be wise and refuse the traps and snares of the enemy of your soul.

My beloved, I am returning for you to take you home. Your reward is sure. I am, and there is none other.

Selected Scripture Reading

1. Isa. 43:10–12—"You are My witnesses, says the LORD, and My servant whom I have chosen, that you may know and believe Me. And understand that I am He. Before Me there was no God formed, nor shall there be after Me. I, even I, am the LORD, and besides Me, there is no savior. I have declared and saved, I have proclaimed, and there was no foreign god among you; therefore you are My witnesses, says the LORD, that I am God."

    Here is more information on how God identifies Himself

    - creator (Neh. 9:6; Heb. 11:3; 1 Peter 4:19)
    - counselor (Ps. 16:7; Isa. 9:6; Rev. 3:18)
    - a righteous judge and consuming fire (Ps. 50; 1 Cor. 3:11–17; Mal. 3:2; Heb. 12:25–29)
    - faithful (Deut. 7:9; Ps. 89:1; 1 Cor. 1:9; 2 Thess. 3:3; Heb. 10:23; Rev. 1:5, 19:11)
    - I am (Ex. 3:14; John 8:58; Rev. 1:18)

- gracious, patient, abounding in truth, forgiving (Ex. 34:5–7; Ps. 84:11; Acts 11:23, 13:43; 1 Cor. 3:10)
- unsearchable—far above mankind in wisdom, knowledge, and power (Ps. 147; Isa. 40:28, 55:8–9; Rom. 11:33–35)

2. John 14:26, 16:13–15; Acts 1:8; Rom. 8:26–27; Acts 10:17–19; Eph. 5:1–21; 2 Peter 1:1–11—Jesus promised to send the Holy Spirit to comfort, guide, and empower His disciples to give testimony to the existence and work of God. As we follow His teachings and Spirit, we will mature in our faith and effectiveness for Him.
3. 1 Peter 1:3–7—Our faith will be tested for the purposes of purification and strengthening.
4. Ex. 19:4; Ruth 2:12; Pss. 17:8, 36:7, 91:4; Mal. 4:2; Matt. 23:37—These verses use the metaphor "under His wings" to denote being under the protection and authority of God; the Hebrew word *kanaph* (*Strong's* no. 3671) is translated "wings, skirt, borders, corners, ends."

45. Hear the Sound of the Trumpet

My words I speak to you to direct and strengthen your hearts. Quite often, My people hear My Word and even understand it, but they do not follow through in obedience. They allow their own thoughts, they allow the cares and pleasures of this world to drown out My Word and dim the vision and call I place in their hearts.

O people of God, My children, remember the words I have spoken to you. My words are Spirit; they are life. By My words, you are delivered from death to salvation. By My words you are consecrated and dedicated to holiness and victory. By My words you are cleansed and prepared for battle.

Arise, My church. Hear the sound of the trumpet. I am calling My church to work in unity and in the power of My Spirit. No longer will you work in the power of the flesh, in the power of human wisdom.

Come up higher, says the Lord, wait on Me. Let My words direct you. Let My Spirit breathe life into you. My bride shall be beautiful. You are My bride. You are the body of Christ. I will deliver you because I delight in you and you are Mine.

Selected Scripture Reading

1. Ps. 19:7–13—"The law of the LORD is perfect, converting the soul; The testimony of the LORD is sure, making wise the simple; The statutes of the LORD are right, rejoicing the heart; The commandment of the LORD is pure, enlightening the eyes; the fear of the LORD is clean, enduring forever; The judgments of the LORD are true and righteous altogether. More to be desired are they than gold, Yea, than much fine gold; Sweeter also than honey ... Moreover by them your servant is warned, and in keeping them there is great reward. Who can understand his errors? Cleanse me from secret faults. Keep back your servant also from presumptuous sins; Let them not have dominion over me. Then I shall be blameless, and I shall be innocent of great transgression."

    The Hebrew word for "law" (*Strong's* no. 8451) is *torah*; it encompasses the meanings of direction, instruction, and law. Torah is translated into the following words throughout the Old Testament: custom, instruction, instructions, Law, law, laws, ruling, teaching, teachings.
2. Ps. 119—This psalm appears to expand on Psalm 19 as the psalmist proclaims the excellency and power of God's Word. Various similar and yet distinct words are used to describe God's teachings including law, testimonies, His ways, judgments, statutes, Word, commandments, word of truth, precepts, ordinances, and decrees. A few of the principles concerning the preeminent value of God's Word include: verse 1—we will be blessed if we live according to God's teachings; verses 3–7—as we endeavor to walk in obedience, we will have confidence in our relationship with Him; and verse 9–11—if we take His teachings to heart, we will be more aware of sin and less likely to succumb to it.
3. Neh. 8; John 6:63; Heb. 4:12–13; 1 Peter 1:22–23—More on God's Word.

46. Dig Up the Uncultivated Ground

My children, as a farmer prepares the soil to receive the seed, prepare your hearts to receive My words.

Dig up the fallow—dig up the uncultivated ground. Repent of your sins; repent of attitudes, and stubbornness. Repent of the hardness of your hearts so the rain of my Holy Spirit will penetrate your soul and spirit and renew and bring life to you.

I plead with you, My dear children, to prepare your hearts that the work of My words can take hold, grow, and bear much fruit. It is the Father's delight that you bear much fruit in your life. The beautiful and rich fruit of righteousness—the fruit of love, gentleness, kindness—the fruit of truth, peace, and joy.

I have chosen you. I have appointed you to go and bear fruit that will last forever. You will bless the nations by the fruit of My Spirit, says the Lord. Hear My words and receive life.

Selected Scripture Reading

1. Jer. 4:3–4; Hos. 10:12; Luke 8:4–15—These compare our hearts to different types of soil. We are admonished to soften and prepare our hearts so we can hear, understand, and assimilate God's truths and principles.
2. Ps. 95—This psalm calls us to worship and obedience. We are reminded that God is our Creator and to be careful to not harden our hearts against Him lest we fail to enter the peace and rest He has for us. See Heb. 3:7–15.
3. Isa. 55:10–11—"For as the rain comes down, and the snow from heaven, and do not return there, but water the earth, and make it bring forth and bud, that it may give seed to the sower and bread to the eater, so shall My word be that goes forth from My mouth; It shall not return to Me void, but it shall accomplish what I please, and it shall prosper in the thing for which I sent it."
4. Ps. 1, 92:12–15, 126:5–6; Prov. 11:18, 30; Matt. 5:18–19, 13:18–23; Luke 24:44–49; John 15:1–17; Acts 10:34–43; Rom. 5:1–5, 6:15–22; Gal. 5:18–25; Eph. 5:9; Phil. 1:9–11; Col. 1:9–12; James 3:17–18; Heb. 12:11; 2 Peter 1:2–8; Jude 20–23—When our hearts are receptive to God's Word and the work of the Holy Spirit, we are quick to recognize our sins and shortcomings. We realize we stand before a holy God who loves us and is calling us to Himself. Repentance comes naturally to the one whose heart is "broken or tilled up" before

God. His Word "rains down" righteousness on us so we might be fruitful in every area of our lives. Sometimes, we can be hard hearted and not know it. Matt. 3:8 records John the Baptist speaking to those who trusted in their religious knowledge and acts: "Therefore, bear fruits worthy of repentance." Read the above scripture references to learn more about what it means to be fruitful spiritually.

47. Living Water in a Dry and Thirsty Land

You are My children born of My Spirit, and you are to carry the characteristics and distinguishing marks of your heavenly Father. In My love you are to move and live and carry My life-giving power and strength to all those around you. Not by the power of the flesh or by the strength of men does fruitful change come. No, I say to you clearly, leave that way of doing things behind.

Come up higher, My people. Reflect the power of My goodness and love. Reflect the power of My patient heart to win the lost with the truth of My salvation. I am calling you to serve, to serve with a pure heart so My love and power will flow through you as living water in a dry and thirsty land. Receive My love. Receive My power. Cleanse yourselves. Go in the power of My love, and reflect the glory of your God. You are My children. I love you.

Selected Scripture Reading

1. Acts 17:16–34—Acts records the evangelistic endeavors of the early church and begins with the promise of the Holy Spirit's help as Jesus had told them would happen (Luke 24:46–49; Acts 1–2). On the apostle Paul's second missionary journey, he went to Athens, the premier academic and cultural center of the world at that time.

    Years prior, philosophers Socrates, Plato, and Aristotle (ca. 469–322 BC) had developed sophisticated schools and academies in Athens. Theories of thought and reasoning philosophies along with math, science, politics, and art were debated and taught. Debating was popular as there were many groups of thought. It was into this culture of philosophical, religious, and lifestyle diversity that Paul gave testimony to the existence of almighty God and the gospel message of salvation. Paul's message to the people in Athens is particularly relevant to us today.

2. Rev. 22:17—"And the Spirit and the bride say, 'Come!' And let him who hears say, 'Come!' And let him who thirsts come. Whoever desires, let him take of the water of life freely." Other scriptures speak of God's Word as living waters that yield refreshing, righteousness, and eternal life; see Ps. 46:4–5; Isa. 12:3, 44:3, 49:10, 55:1–3; Jer. 17:13; Amos 8:11; Ps. 63:1–3; Ezek. 47; John 7:37–38, 4:6–26; Eph. 5:26; Rev. 7:17, 22:1–2.

3. Matt. 5:6—"Blessed are those who hunger and thirst for righteousness, for they shall be filled." We must ask, "What are we hungry for? What are we thirsty for? What are our desires?" Psalm 42 seems to describe one who in times past "used to go with the multitude ... to the house of God" and remembers how it was—wanting now to get back to God. Verse 1 reads, "As the deer pants for the water brooks, So pants my soul for You, O God."

4. Ps. 27:1, 43:3, 97:11–12, 118:27, 119:105; Prov. 4:18–19; Isa. 2:5, 9:2, 6, 42:6, 60:1–3, 19; Matt. 4:13–17, 5:13–16; Luke 1:76–79; John 1:1–13, 8:12; 2 Cor. 4:1–6; 1 Tim. 3:16; Rev. 21:23—God is the source of spiritual light, the understanding and knowledge of what is good. As God's Messiah, God manifest in the flesh, Jesus Christ is the light of God. As the "offspring of God," we are to reflect His light (Acts 17:28–29).

48. I Shall Restore My Church

Is it not right? Is it not proper that in these last days, I restore My church? I shall restore My church. My sanctuary shall be a place where My Spirit dwells because My people shall meet there with Me. They shall know Me, and I will be their God. I will know them. I will speak clearly to them, and they will hear Me. Their worship will be pure. Their hearts will be clean. There will be no filth that blocks the power of My Spirit to work among them.

Mankind will look at this work and know in its heart, "This work is of God." It is not to be touched by man; no man shall receive the glory. No, says the Lord God. I alone shall receive the glory for what I am building here. For it shall be more than steel, mortar, and stone.

I am building a sanctuary of people who will follow Me and obey My words by the power of My Holy Spirit. They will love. They will serve. They will be what the Father has created them to be. And I shall love them and delight to do great things in their midst because they will love Me for who I am, not for what I give them—just for who I am.

O people of God, do you not see how I long for your love? How My heart aches for you to come into My presence? I love you very much, and I have so many things to share with you. I will speak to your heart—to your spirit deep within you.

Prepare your heart to listen. Prepare. Prepare. Prepare.

Selected Scripture Reading

1. Ps. 51; Jer. 36:7; Hos. 14:2; Ezek. 18:30–32; Acts 3:19; 2 Cor. 7:10; Rom. 2:4; 2 Peter 3:9; James 4—These scriptures teach that humility, repentance, and prayer are a part of restoration. These principles apply to individuals, families, and groups such as local church bodies and even nations. The well-known verse of 2 Chronicles 7:14 giving instructions and hope for national restoration was God's response to King Solomon's prayer of intercession (2 Chron. 6:19–42). God's loving discipline—quite often simply reaping the consequences of our sins—is sometimes required for us to come before Him in humility, repentance, and prayer (Deut. 31:30–32:43; Ps. 66:18, 107:17, 119:67; Isa. 30:18–26; Jer. 2:19, 12:15; Lam. 5:21; Rom. 1; 2 Cor. 13; Heb.

12:3–11). The goal of discipline and repentance is restoration and sanctification of individuals' lives, relationships, the church, and all things good (Matt. 25:31–46; John 6:27, 13:34, 17:3, 17:17; Luke 4:18–19; Acts 3:19–21; Eph. 5:25b–27; Rom. 2, 15:16; 1 Cor. 1:30; Col. 2:6–7; Gal. 6:8; Eph. 2:19–22, 4–5; Heb. 13:12, 20–21; 2 Tim. 2; 1 Peter 1:17, 2:5, 4:2; Rev. 21–22).

2. Eph. 5:25b–27—"Christ also loved the church and gave Himself for her, that He might sanctify and cleanse her with the washing of water by the word, that He might present her to Himself, a glorious church, not having spot or wrinkle … that she should be holy and without blemish." The church is composed of the hearts and spirits of those who have set themselves apart to love God and others, forsaking all filthiness of sin.

49. Washed Pure to Move Forward

Purity. Purity. Purity. My people must be washed pure to move forward. Break free, I say to you. Struggle no more. Humble yourself and come forward. Ask for prayer. Break the bondages with the past. Walk forward from here with the freedom you have been longing for. Now is the time for your heart and mind to be released.

My people shall walk in freedom. My people shall walk in liberty. You shall run and not be weary. You shall walk and not faint. Come unto Me and I shall take your hurts and pain. I am restoring My church.

Selected Scripture Reading

1. Ps. 24:3–5—"Who may ascend into the hill of the LORD? Or who may stand in His holy place? He who has clean hands and a pure heart, who has not lifted up his soul to an idol, nor sworn deceitfully. He shall receive blessing from the LORD and righteousness from the God of his salvation." See Ps. 101:3; Isa. 40:31; Matt. 5:8. The concept of purity encompasses such aspects as the quality of being pure and free from adulterating mixtures, clean without dirt or filth, and the quality of goodness or innocence without sin or evil.

Studying the scriptural context of words such as *redemption*, *salvation, deliverance, purity, sanctification,* and *holiness* will help us avoid the pitfalls of empty and outward appearances of purity. Outward appearances, works, and rituals may be devoid of the genuine purity that follows as a natural result of a relationship with our Savior, Jesus Christ, and our heavenly Father by the abiding presence of the Holy Spirit.

2. John 17:17—"Sanctify them by Your truth. Your word is truth." Acts 17:10–12 and 2 Peter 3:14–18 illustrate the importance of reading with a teachable heart—giving careful study to the scriptures. Sufficient understanding with a balanced and appropriate application of scriptural principles will result in purity, sanctification, and eternal life. See Ps. 19:8, 119:9–11; John 15:3, 20:31; Rom. 1:16; 1 Peter 1:22–25; 2 Tim. 3:16; Col. 3:16; Heb. 4:12.
3. John 8:31–32—"Then Jesus said to those Jews who believed Him, 'If you abide in My word, you are My disciples indeed. And you shall know the truth and the truth shall make you free.'" The word *abide* signifies a process dependent on reading the Bible and being prayerfully intentional to live accordingly.
4. 2 Cor. 7:1—"Therefore, having these promises beloved, let us cleanse ourselves from all filthiness of the flesh and spirit, perfecting holiness in the fear of God."
5. Gal. 5:19–26—"Now the works of the flesh are evident: which are adultery, fornication, uncleanness, lewdness, idolatry, sorcery, hatred, contentions, jealousies, outbursts of wrath, selfish ambitions, dissensions, heresies, envy, murders, drunkenness, revelries, and the like ... those who practice such things will not inherit the kingdom of God. But the fruit of the Spirit is love, joy, peace, longsuffering, kindness, goodness, faithfulness, gentleness, self-control." See Rom. 1:26–31; Eph. 5.

50. Great Joy in the Kingdom

I will strip away all the false gods, busyness, and things that have cluttered and defiled the lives and hearts of My people. They have been too busy to care about Me or My kingdom. But the Spirit of the Lord says change is coming. My people are awakening to their call. They are coming alive.

They are opening their eyes. With their ears they are hearing My words to their hearts.

Come alive, My people. There is a great harvest and a great joy in My kingdom. No longer will you serve and toil for the gods of this world and materialism. You will be free and find your freedom and great joy in the kingdom of God. My joy shall be great among you, and nothing can steal the treasures you have in My kingdom. Rejoice for your redemption is near. You will soon enter your full reward.

Selected Scripture Reading

1. Ps. 78:1–72—"Give ear, O my people, to my law [teaching] ... that the generation to come might know ... that they may set their hope in God, and not forget the works of God, but keep His commandments." Quite naturally, when we listen intently to God's words, the temporal aspects of our lives take their proper place. Stress is reduced as we see into the future with an eternal perspective.
2. Isa. 1:16–20—"Wash yourselves, make yourselves clean; put away the evil of your doings from before My eyes. Cease to do evil, learn to do good; seek justice, rebuke the oppressor; defend the fatherless; plead for the widow ... If you are willing and obedient, you shall eat of the good of the land; but if you refuse and rebel, you shall be devoured by the sword." These verses along with Isa. 58; Mal. 3; Matt. 22:1–14; Luke 6:38; John 5:24–30; Acts 20:35; 2 Cor. 9:6; James 2:14–26; 1 John 3:1–23 confirm that believing God's Word motivates us to make wise choices.
3. Ps. 16:11—"You will show me the path of life; In Your presence is fullness of joy; At Your right hand are pleasures forevermore."
4. Jer. 15:16—"Your words were found, and I ate them, And Your word was to me the joy and rejoicing of my heart; For I am called by Your name, O LORD God of Hosts." Jeremiah the prophet penned these words at a time when he felt the rejection of His fellow Israelites. Speaking the words God gave him, Jeremiah called Judah to repentance; he warned of impending national destruction if they did not change their ways.

The Southern Kingdom of Judah had watched the Northern Kingdom of Israel go into captivity in 721 BC by the Assyrians, yet the concept of the consequences of national depravity did not motivate sustained repentance and change.

Jeremiah began his prophetic ministry in approximately 626 BC, and in 587 BC, Judah was taken captive by the Babylonians. In Jeremiah 15:16, we see how even in the midst of others' rejecting God's words, those who receive His words can have great joy and peace. See Isa. 61:10; Rom. 14:17.

51. Your Heart Will See and Understand

My words will burn in your heart, and you will know it is I am who is speaking to you. My words will quicken your spirit and mind. They will teach you about Me, and I will lead you. I will guide you. What I have spoken to you in My Word will come alive and speak life into your heart.

Call upon Me and I will answer you. Seek Me and you shall find Me. All that I am and have, the Father desires to give His children—He desires to give you the very being and nature of Christ. It is for this purpose that the Father sent Jesus into the world—that the Holy Spirit could come and dwell within the hearts of mankind, lead them, guide them, and birth the love and power of God in them.

Each person, though, has the choice, has the power to accept or reject what God offers—the greatest gift to mankind—that is, Himself.

Come into that secret place with Me and I shall share the secrets of the kingdom of God with you. They are all there in My Word, but I will make them come alive in your heart, and your faith will expand because your heart will see and understand.

Selected Scripture Reading

1. Ex. 3:14—"And God said to Moses, 'I AM WHO I AM.' And He said, 'Thus you shall say to the children of Israel,' "I AM has sent me to you."'" Moses was tending sheep in the wilderness of Mount Sinai when the angel of the Lord appeared to him as flames burning in a bush without the bush being consumed. There, God assigned Moses, who had grown up in the Pharaoh's household in Egypt, to return to Egypt and negotiate the Israelites' release from slavery; God thus

began the Israelites' deliverance. From Egypt, they would go into the wilderness, where God would transform them into a people who would learn to know Him, develop a national identity and culture, and live out His commands to illustrate spiritual principles about His plan for the redemption of all mankind. It is from Ex. 3:14, "I AM WHO I AM," that we are given in Hebrew and then translated into English the names that we use for God: Jehovah, Yahweh, and Lord. The answer God gave Moses says succinctly and with profundity, drawing from the Hebrew verb for "to be," that "God is, always has been, and always will be God." See John 8:58; Acts 7; Gal. 3:19–25; Rev. 1:18.
2. Jer. 20:9—"But His word was in my heart like a burning fire shut up in my bones."
3. Luke 24:32—"And they said to one another, 'Did not our heart burn within us while He talked with us on the road, and while He opened the Scriptures to us?'"
4. John 16:13–15—"However when He, the Spirit of truth has come, He will guide you into all truth." See Ezek. 36:26–27; John 6:63–64; Rom. 8:11, 10:9–10 for more about how God's Spirit works in our hearts.

52. Will You Answer My Call to Your Heart?

Be alert, My children. Victory in prayer—receiving the full answer to your prayer—requires persistence and diligence. If you are double minded, if you are wishy-washy as you think about your concerns and requests, if you don't really care, then the fruit of your prayers will fail.

Give heed My words. Pray according to My will, and do not give up. It is the Father's good will to answer your prayers, prayers that are full of hope and faith. Love doesn't give up.

Let My love fill your heart and wash away the filth in your mind and life. Let My love give you the peace and joy you are seeking. As My love grows in you, as My love is perfected in your heart, you will see My will accomplished in your life. Then, persevering in prayer will flow naturally because of your relationship with Me.

Do you think Noah heard from Me only one time about building the ark? No—he walked in communion with Me, so his persistence in prayer and obedience was a natural result of his relationship with Me.

I am calling you up higher. I am calling you to come closer to Me. Will you come? Will you answer My call to your heart? Come, My beloved. Come, My friend.

Selected Scripture Reading

1. Matt. 11:15—At least ten times in scripture, the phrase *ears to hear* is used—Deut. 29:4; Ezek. 12:2; Matt. 13:9, 13:43; Mark 4:9, 23, 7:16; Luke 8:8, 14:35. That phrase is most often stated in the context of, "He who has ears to hear, let him hear." This is a heads-up, a call to be alert and pay attention because God has something to tell us that goes deeper than the surface level meaning of the words. In fact, from Ezek. 12:2, we may extrapolate that the attitude of our hearts may affect our ability to understand what God is saying. Luke 8:18 admonishes us to consider carefully how we listen to what God is saying. If we study and meditate on God's Word, He will increase our understanding. However, if we just read over it superficially, we will not comprehend or receive its life-giving truths and therefore have little influence on the worldly culture around us (Luke 14:34–35).
2. Ps. 143:10—"Teach me to do Your Will, for You are my God; Your Spirit is good. Lead me in the land of uprightness." See Ps. 40:8; James 1:5–8.
3. 1 John 5:14–15—"Now this is the confidence that we have in Him, that if we ask anything according to His will, He hears us. And if we know that He hears us, whatever we ask, we know that we have the petitions that we have asked of Him." What does it mean to pray according to His will? What does it mean to pray in Jesus's name? Are we talking about a verbal formula for getting what we want? Or do the scriptural references to prayer describe a surrendered child of God who hears the Good Shepherd, knows His character and nature, and understands the heart of His heavenly Father?

    Consider Christ as He prayed in the Garden of Gethsemane. He knew the cross lay before Him. Three times He agonized in prayer. Matt. 26:39 records, "O My Father if it is possible, let this cup pass from Me; nevertheless, not as I will, but as You will." See Gen. 18:16–32; John 5:19; Acts 12:5; James 5:13–18; Psalms.

53. The Perfect Gift

My children, you search for the perfect gift. Each of you has the perfect gift in you. It is love. It is grace. It is kindness. It is generosity of heart.

As My love gave and sacrificed My Son, I command you to love one another. The sacrifice of love heals. The sacrifice of love gives strength to the weak. The sacrifice of love gives hope to the hopeless.

Let go of your burdens. Let go of all your fears and receive My love. Walk in My love. Let My love be perfected in your heart so that My love will flow through you to touch all those around you.

Yes, I am returning soon. I shall be—and I am—looking for My children who are full of My love. Your love blesses Me. I receive your worship.

Biblical Insights on "Love" from 1 Corinthians 13

"The Love Chapter," "the Greatest Gift," or "the Preeminence of Love" are some of the titles given to 1 Cor. 13.

Some letters of the New Testament are addressed to multiple congregations; the letter of Galatians (Gal. 1:2) was addressed to all the churches in Galatia (north-central Asia Minor). However, the apostle Paul specified the letter known as 1 Corinthians as being written to that church alone (1 Cor. 1:2).

Corinth was a strategically positioned city that over the centuries became a commercial and maritime megacity. Estimates of its population are as high as 800,000. The Phoenicians had been among the first settlers there; they introduced the idolatrous worship of such gods as Baal and Asthoreth, which was accompanied by lewd and immoral rituals. Succeeding nations such as Greece and Rome controlled Corinth adding their own particular brands of gods and goddess mythologies and worship.

The apostle Paul established the church at Corinth around AD 50–51. This letter, 1 Corinthians, was written to the church to help them recognize and counter the spiritual pitfalls of their culture: idolatry in all its forms, immorality, corruption, and false theological beliefs and teachings. Imagine a culture in which sex was elevated and constantly idolized. The chief goddess in Corinth was Aphrodite (Venus). It is recorded that there were over 1,000 temple prostitutes who were called priestesses. Imagine the destructive influence that idolatry, immorality, corruption, and false teachings inflicted on families, relationships, social stability, and the church. In 1 Corinthians 13, Paul was defining God's pure and divine love and how essential it was for individuals and families and the functioning of the church.

Selected Scripture Reading

1. Rom. 12:9–21—"Let love be without hypocrisy. Abhor what is evil. Cling to what is good. Be kindly affectionate to one another with brotherly love, in honor giving preference to one another; not lagging in diligence, fervent in spirit, serving the Lord; rejoicing in hope, patient in tribulation, continuing steadfastly in prayer; distributing to the needs of the saints, given to hospitality. Bless those who persecute you; bless and do not curse. Rejoice with those who rejoice, and weep with those who weep. Be of the same mind toward one another. Do not set your mind on high things, but associate with the humble. Do not be wise in your own opinion. Repay no one evil for evil. Have regard for good things in the sight of all men. If it is possible, as much as it depends on you, live peaceably with all men."

54. You Shall Walk in Newness of Life and Great Joy

I am calling you up higher. I am calling you to a better way—a better way of living, a better way of loving, a better way of being.

For you are to be—you are called to be My witnesses to the power of the gospel of Jesus Christ. It is not by words only but by My words and My Spirit demonstrated in power that I shall come to deliver this people.

Look to Me and follow Me. I shall lead you away from the bondages of the past. You shall walk in newness of life and great joy. You will learn how to cast all your burdens upon Me—to trust Me, and let Me carry you to victory.

Selected Scripture Reading

1. Ps. 61:2–5—The psalmist cries out to God, "Lead me to the rock that is higher than I." In the Old and New Testaments, the metaphor of a rock describes the stabilizing strength and power of God to protect and provide salvation for those who cry out to Him. More than once, God is called "the rock of my salvation." See Deut. 32:4, 31; 1 Sam. 2:2; 2 Sam. 22:47; Ps. 18:31, 28:1, 62:1–2, 94:22, 118:22; Isa. 8:14, 17:10, 28:16; Dan. 2:34–35, 45; Matt. 21:42, 44; Mark 12:10; Luke 20:17; Acts 4:11; Rom. 9:33; 1 Cor. 10:4; 1 Peter 2:4–8.

   To further explain how God becomes our rock of salvation leading us to a higher way of living and being, Jesus told the parable of building one's house on the rock and not on sand (Matt. 7:21–29; Luke 7:46–49). God becomes the rock of our salvation when we follow His teachings.

2. Isa. 55:8–9—"For My thoughts are not your thoughts, Nor are your ways My ways, says the LORD. For as the heavens are higher than the earth, So are My ways higher than your ways, And My thoughts than your thoughts." See Isa. 1:18–20.

3. Mic. 4:1–2a—"Now it shall come to pass in the latter days That the mountain of the LORD's house Shall be established on the top of the mountains, And shall be exalted above the hills; And peoples shall flow to it. Many nations shall come and say, Come, and let us go up to the mountain of the LORD ... He will teach us His ways, And we shall walk in His paths." Compare with Matt. 3:1–2; Luke 4:16–21, 17:20–21; Eph. 5:5; Col. 1:3–6; Rev. 11:15. The word *mountain* in scripture may be used as a metaphor or simile; consider its possible meanings in Pss. 15, 30:7, 36:6, 49:11, 72; Isa. 49:11; Mark 11:22–26; Heb. 12:22-24.

4. 1 Peter 1:8–17—"Finally, all of you be of one mind, having compassion for one another ... But sanctify the Lord God in your hearts, and always be ready to give a defense to everyone who asks you a reason for the hope that is in you, with meekness and fear." These verses clearly state we are called to be a blessing to others and thereby we also are blessed. This principle applies even when we are mistreated for righteousness' sake. In fact, our response in the midst of conflict or persecution should flow from our faith and reverence for God and our

readiness to give an answer for our faith with meekness and respect. In 1 Peter 1:12, we read of the blessings we will then receive from God; receiving God's blessings results from being in relationship with Him and living according to His teachings.

55. I Give You Grace

My child—My church—you stand just before the breakthrough. You stand before the door that is about to open. Take a hold of the handle, grasp the will of the Father, and enter the destiny He has for you.

Yes, one stands against you to hinder and prevent you from fulfilling the will of the Father—from opening the doors I have placed before you. But I say to you, persevere in prayer; continue in fellowship and worship. You will drive the enemy away by your love for Me and for one another.

Rejoice. I have given you the weapons of warfare. I have given you the strength to continue to victory. Open the door; walk in the destiny I have for you to overcome the world, to overcome the deceitfulness of sin, and the hardness of heart.

I have not left you alone. My Holy Spirit is here with you to guide you to truth and understanding. Submit yourself to Me and I shall teach you how to put on the spiritual armor and use the spiritual weapons of warfare to open and walk through the doors before you.

Only have courage, My child. Strengthen and build up yourself in holy faith. Let My Holy Spirit speak through you. Pray in the Spirit, and pray with understanding. Pray the will of the Father and I will hear and answer you. The doors will open. I give you grace.

Selected Scripture Reading

1. Ps. 84:11—"For the Lord God is a sun and shield; The LORD will give grace and glory; No good thing will He withhold from those who walk uprightly."
2. John 10:7, 9—"Then Jesus said to them again, Most assuredly, I say to you, I am the door of the sheep ... I am the door. If anyone enters by Me, he will be saved, and will go in and out and find pasture." See Rev. 3:8, 20.

3. 2 Cor. 6:1–6—In speaking to the believers at Corinth, the apostle Paul pleaded with them saying he did not want them to "receive the grace of God in vain." He reminded them now is the time in history to receive God's salvation. He lists examples of times we may draw on God's grace such as in work and ministry, in seasons of tribulation, in rejoicing or in sorrow. From these verses, we learn God's grace comes in patience in tribulation, purity, knowing God and His ways, practicing kindness and sincere love, responding to the Holy Spirit (1 Cor. 2:6–16), and knowing the Bible.
4. Jude 20—"Beloved, building yourselves up on your most holy faith, praying in the Spirit, keep yourselves in the love of God, looking for the mercy of our Lord Jesus Christ."
5. Col. 4:2–6—This section of verses may be titled "Christian Graces," and Paul requests prayer that God would give him an open door to share the gospel of Christ.

56. Stand Still and See the Salvation God Has Prepared

Rest in My presence. Rest in My peace. Separate yourself from the world and commune with Me. Let us converse together. As your mind is renewed, you will hear Me more easily and clearly. Fill your heart and mind with My Word. Study the scriptures. Live My Word.

I will call and rearrange people to fulfill the jobs and assignments I have for them in My kingdom. Just as I move the stars in the heavens, I will move My people into positions to serve Me. You will see some stars being removed and new ones taking their place for I shall do a new thing.

I have been building and creating an army of mature and wise believers. When the time is right, I shall call them forth to serve in positions of leadership. They shall be empowered by My Holy Spirit to lead this nation through its dark season and to its destiny before Me. I have called them. I have prepared them for such a time as this. My saints must uphold these leaders with much prayer and even prayer in the Spirit.

As My people pray and intercede, My Holy Spirit rains down on them, cleansing and refreshing them, even washing away destructive powers and events. Oh, worship the Lord. Stand still and see the salvation God has prepared for those who love Him.

Selected Scripture Reading

1. Ps. 95:1–11—"Oh come, let us sing to the LORD! Let us shout joyfully to the Rock of our Salvation. Let us come before His presence with thanksgiving ... Today, if you will hear His voice: Do not harden your heats, as in the rebellion ... when your fathers tested Me ... They do not know My ways. So I swore in My wrath, They shall not enter My rest." Compare this with Matthew 7:15–23, in which Jesus teaches us to watch out for those who would lead us astray with wrong teachings about the kingdom of God thus yielding the fruits of rebellion, lawlessness, and separation from God.
2. Ps. 116:5–7—"Gracious is the LORD and righteous; Yes, our God is merciful ... Return to your rest, O my soul." See Ps. 119:59; Jer. 17:5–10; Heb. 4:1–13; Rom. 12:2.
3. Dan. 4:32—"The Most High rules in the kingdom of men, and gives it to whomever he chooses." See Jer. 12:17, 13:15–18; Ps. 83.
4. Matt. 25:13–29—This is the parable of the talents that gives the basic principles of good stewardship. See Luke 10:25–37, 12:35–48; 2 Cor. 5:20; Acts 20:24.
5. John 4:34–36—"Then Jesus said to them, 'My food is to do the will of Him who sent Me, and to finish His work ... And he who reaps receives wages and gathers fruit for eternal life, that both he who sows and he who reaps may rejoice together.'"
6. 1 Cor. 15:58—"Therefore, my beloved brethren, be steadfast, immovable, always abounding in the work of the Lord, knowing that your labor is not in vain in the Lord."
7. 2 Chron. 20:17—"You will not need to fight in this battle. Position yourselves, stand still and see the salvation of the LORD, who is with you." See 1 Tim. 2:1–4.

57. I Am Restoring What Has Been Lost and Stolen

There is a shifting, there is a change, there is a new sound coming. It is the sound of My Holy Spirit among you. I am coming as a mighty, rushing wind. I shall bring healing and deliverance to My people.

You will hear My voice. My sheep hear My voice. I am calling to you. Yes, change is coming. I am restoring what has been lost and stolen. Holiness, righteousness, and power will clothe My people. You shall shine; you shall radiate My love and grace.

You have a work to do. Prepare your hearts and love one another. I am coming quickly.

Selected Scripture Reading

1. Ps. 40:3—"He has put a new song in my mouth—Praise to our God; Many will see it and fear, And will trust in the LORD." This reveals the power of a godly testimony.
2. Isa. 43:19—"Behold, I will do a new thing, Now it shall spring forth; Shall you not know it? I will even make a road in the wilderness and rivers in the desert." Jeremiah 31:31–33 and Hebrews 8:7–13 confirm the new thing God is doing is the the New Covenant.
3. Isa. 60:1–3—"Arise, shine; For your light has come! And the glory of the LORD is risen upon you. For behold, the darkness shall cover the earth, And deep darkness the people; But the LORD will arise over you, And His glory will be seen upon you."
4. Lam. 5:21—"Turn us back to You, O LORD, and we will be restored."
5. Ps. 51:12–13—"Restore to me the joy of Your salvation, And uphold me by Your generous Spirit. Then I will teach transgressors Your ways, And sinners shall be converted to You." See Acts for accounts of conversion and evangelism.
6. Acts 2:1–2—"When the Day of Pentecost had fully come, they were all with one accord in one place. And suddenly there came a sound from heaven, as of a rushing mighty wind and it filled the whole house where they were sitting." See Acts 10:24–45, 19:1–6.
7. Acts 4:33—"And with great power the apostles gave witness to the resurrection of the Lord Jesus. And great grace was upon them all." Compare with Isa. 32:15, 43:10; Acts 1:4–8.
8. 1 Thess. 4:3–9—"For this is the will of God, your sanctification: that you should abstain from sexual immorality; That each of you should know how to possess his own vessel in sanctification and honor, Not in passion of lust, like the Gentiles who do not know God; That no one should take advantage of and defraud his brother in this matter,

because the Lord is the avenger of all such, as we also forewarned you and testified, For God did not call us to uncleanness, but in holiness. Therefore he who rejects this does not reject man, but God who has also given us His Holy Spirit. But concerning brotherly love you have no need that I should write to you, for you yourselves are taught by God to love one another."

58. My Disciples

My children, when I speak to you—when I say to you, "Come up higher," I am calling you to a higher standard. I am calling you to rise above the world's way of loving, the world's way of obeying and being.

You are to be what I have called you to be—that is My disciples. Some call themselves My disciples yet they are not. They give themselves to the things and ways of the world.

My sheep know My voice and follow the Good Shepherd. I will lead you. I will teach you how to live—how to overcome the deceitfulness of pride and the deceitfulness of riches esteemed by the world.

Open your heart and submit to My Word and My love. Do not fear; My grace will cover you and set you free. My truth—My Spirit—is coming to My people, and I shall set you free. Your discipleship will be affirmed for all the world to see.

Search My Word. Search the scriptures for in them, you will find life and that life will give you power to live as My disciples. I am restoring My church. She shall be magnificent. My love shall clothe you, for you are My beloved. I am preparing you to take you home to My Father.

Biblical Insights from Luke 10:25–37

An expert in the law asked Jesus, "Teacher, what must I do to inherit eternal life?" As Jesus was apt to do, he answered the man's question with a question—He asked what the law said and what his interpretation of it was. The man quoted Deuteronomy 6:5 and Leviticus 19:18, which can be summarized as "Love God and love others well." The lawyer (a student of the Mosaic law or scribe) knew what the scriptures instructed but was uncomfortable with the responsibility inherent in the commandments.

Perhaps he could have justified himself and therefore asked Jesus to define who "my neighbor or those others" were. Jesus told the parable of the Good Samaritan. The priest and Levite in the story represented those who followed the letter of the law while overlooking the heart of God. The Samaritans were a mixed Jewish group and considered to have an inferior, confused, and messed-up theology. They were despised by many.

The story took place on the road from Jerusalem to Jericho that at that time was plagued by bandits and thieves. A man was beaten, robbed, and left for dead. A priest and a Levite, known for being observers of the law, saw the man on the road but ignored him. Later, a Samaritan rescued the man. Jesus asked the scribe, "Which one of the three men was a neighbor to the injured man?"

Compare this story with 1 John 3:16–23 about the higher calling to be motivated by God's love. To further study the attributes, failures, and corrupted doctrine of dead legalisms, see Matt. 23; Mic. 6:8; Luke 11:42–44; Galatians.

59. If My People

If My people will preach and teach My words of love—My commandments—My principles of love—your nation will be healed.

Live My Word. My Word heals and gives life. Honor Me and I will bless you. Teach My love in word and deed.

Selected Scripture Reading

1. Jer. 23:22—"But if they had stood in My counsel, And had caused My people to hear My words, Then they would have turned them from their evil way And from the evil of their doings." Jeremiah 23 is a blistering oracle spoken of the shepherds and prophets in which God accused them of neglecting, scattering, and deceiving His people by false teachings, wickedness, and idolatry. Nevertheless, God said in verses 3–6 that He would gather the remnant of His flock and set shepherds over them to feed and protect them. Verses 5–6 are messianic; they speak of raising up from King David a "branch of righteousness." Jeremiah 23 looks forward in history to when Jesus

would come and speak God's unadulterated message of love, truth and salvation for all to hear.
2. Isa. 48:16–18—"Thus says, the LORD, your Redeemer, The Holy One of Israel: I am the LORD your God, Who teaches you to profit, Who leads you in the way you should go. Oh, that you had heeded My commandments! Then your peace would have been like a river, And your righteousness like the waves of the sea." The topic of Isaiah 48 may be summed up this way: "God has been talking, but we weren't listening." God directed this message to Israel, but definite applications concern everyone. God reminds us that we are obstinate and inclined to think that if anything good happens, it is because we are so clever and capable—all while being seduced by idolatry. God told us that He knows we are inclined to be stiff-necked religious but not really righteous. Therefore, He has declared prophetic words to us even detailing historical events long before they happened. Compare that concept with Revelation 19:10 and consider that the Bible is God's Word to all mankind. See also Isa.41:21-29, 42:9, 46:9-10; John 8:48–58; Acts 3:18; Rev. 22:12–16.
3. Prov. 14:34—This states simply, "Righteousness exalts a nation, but sin is a reproach to any people." Here, we learn the principles of corporate accountability, blessings, and consequences. An abundance of scriptures confirms that God deals with nations, cities, and peoples; some examples are Gen. 18:16–33; 1 Chron. 28:8; 1 Kings 9:1–9; Josh. 24:19–24; Jer. 45:4; Deut. 32; Pss. 9:5, 17, 106:40–41; Isa. 24:5, 26:2, 60:12; Jer. 12:14–17; Amos 9:8; Ezek. 14:12–23; Matt. 11:20–24, 25:31–46; Rev.
4. 2 Chron. 7:12–14—"If My people who are called by My name will humble themselves, and pray, and seek My face, and turn from their wicked ways, then I will hear from heaven, and will forgive their sin and heal their land."

60. Walking in Obedience

Rebellion is as witchcraft is, and it carries the same curse of deception. My people must come into proper relationship with their authorities to walk in liberty and blessing. I have told you that you shall know the truth and the truth shall set you free when you know and obey it.

Walking in obedience to My truth brings liberty, Walking in obedience to My truth brings wisdom, and insight. Walking in obedience to My truth brings liberty and peace. Walk in My truth and you shall be set free. Come to Me. Follow Me and you will find rest for your soul.

Know that in time, sin will lose its pleasure and you will be left to face Me. The passion of lust will fade and leave you with overwhelming emptiness. Have you not already sensed despair forming its cage around you?

This is not what you had envisioned when at the beginning you entertained evil. It all looked so good, safe, and fun. For a long time, it seemed it was that way, but then you realized you were trapped and were too afraid to look for a way out.

My child, there is only one way out. Admit your mistakes. Face Me and do not run or hide from Me. Bow your knee to Me and call Me Lord. No longer let sin be your lord. No longer be slave to lusts, greed, and evil bondages.

I have been there all along waiting for you to come to Me with your whole heart, mind, and being. Yes, I know the pain and rejection you suffered, but why didn't you bring it to Me so I could carry your burdens of guilt and shame? I will in no way reject you or belittle you when you come to Me—the returning child is received by the open arms of the Father.

Only this I say to you, repent and turn from sin and I will set you free to be your true self. Forgive all who have offended you just as I forgive you when you come to Me contrite in heart and desiring our relationship to be established in truth and purity.

Recognize and identify the enemy of your soul who lures and beats you into submission with pride, fear, and lust. Pay attention. He offers you what he cannot give—peace and salvation. He gives you only lies and deceit.

I call to you now, My child, and speak to you clearly. You must choose whom you will serve. I am your heavenly Father. I have sent My Son, My salvation, to you. Believe Him and follow Him. His name is salvation. His name is Jesus.

Selected Scripture Reading

1. See 1 Sam. 15:22–23; Ezek. 18:31–32; Hos. 3:4–5; Rom. 2:13; Matt. 7:21; Dan. 6:10; Ps. 81:11–14; Mic. 6:8; John 8:31–32; Col. 1:19–23; Heb. 4:11–12; James 1:15–16; Matt. 18:21–35; John 1:1–18.

61. Trust Me to Carry the Heavy Burdens

Again, I say to you My little ones, cast all your cares and burdens on Me. Come to Me and I will give you peace and rest. There are many burdens too heavy for you to carry. Give them to Me and trust Me to carry them for you.

Your way is ever before Me. Call on Me and I will light your path; you will not walk in darkness. Call on Me and you shall walk in My truth and love.

My truth and love will direct your heart and mind, and you will walk in My blessings. Walk, I say to you, walk in My presence and know Me.

Biblical Insights from Psalm 23:1–6

This psalm's metaphors and picturesque language speak life into our burdened hearts. We hear God say to us that when we allow Him to be our Good Shepherd, He will be the inner strength and peace we desperately seek. We may be more familiar with Jesus's identifying Himself as the Good Shepherd (John 10:11–15), but the Old Testament also speaks of God coming with a strong hand to "feed His flock like a shepherd" (Isa. 40:10–11).

In the six verses of Ps. 23, God told us many things such as,

- We will not lack anything we really need.
- He will teach us to rest and find peace in Him.
- If we follow Him, He will lead us and help us navigate through life here by teaching us to choose righteous paths.
- In the process of following His teachings, our souls—our minds, wills, and emotions—will be restored to spiritual health.
- He works in our lives for His name's sake. He has said He will bless those who seek Him, and His work in our lives brings Him glory.
- As we follow Him with a clear conscience and fully trust Him, we will have no fear of the future or of evil. He says He will be with us even when we walk through life's darkest and loneliest valleys.
- God's rod and staff may represent His correction and protection just as a shepherd would use a rod or staff to help guide the sheep and fend off predators. Our hearts are comforted because we recognize His loving correction and protection.
- God provides for us even in the midst of the trials and tribulations of this life.

Verses 5–6 give a key to overcoming difficulties—the attitude of our heart. He acknowledged God's goodness with an intensely grateful heart and with inner vision saw himself dwelling "in the house of the LORD forever."

1. Heb. 10: 36–38—These verses speak of the need for enduring faith so we may receive God's promises. They also quote the phrase from Habakkuk 2:4 and Romans 1:17—"The just shall live by faith."
2. Matt. 11:28–30—"Come to Me, all you who labor and are heavy laden, and I will give you rest. Take My yoke upon you and learn from Me, for I am gentle and lowly in heart, and you will find rest for your souls. For My yoke is easy and My burden is light."

3. Ps. 15—This answers the question, "LORD, who may abide in Your tabernacle? Who may dwell in Your holy hill?"

62. Wait upon Me

Listen, My child, for I have many things to tell you. These are difficult times for all people. The earth is going through labor pains, with many deaths and much destruction. The enemy of your souls is also destroying and deceiving many. Do not believe his lies.

Seek Me. Stay close to Me. Do not go astray. Seek not the word of truth from another source for I am the Living Water and the Bread of Life.

Let not your hearts be troubled for all that is coming over the earth. Rest in Me. Let My peace flood your mind and heart. Bask in My presence, and do not seek another source. Be cautious. Be wise. Do not run here and there trying this and that to find more of Me. Meet me in the secret place of righteous prayer and you will find Me. Meet me in the secret place of holiness in prayer and I will be there.

Those who wait upon the Lord shall renew their strength. They shall run and not be weary. They shall walk and not faint. For they shall not be ashamed who wait upon Me.

Selected Scripture Reading

1. Ps. 73:24—Scripture consistently and repeatedly refers to seeking God's counsel in all things. The first sixteen verses of Psalm 73 are a lament about the apparent prosperity and successes of the wicked with the psalmist saying how painful it was to try to understand this. However, in verses 17–28, the psalmist says that when he entered God's sanctuary to seek God's perspective and counsel, he understood the outcomes of the wicked and those who put their trust in God. What do Isaiah 11:2, John 16:13, and Ephesians 1:15–19 tell us about getting good guidance? Related to this topic is 2 Samuel 23:3–4, which records King David's last words. He warns that those in positions of leadership must rule with the counsel and respect of God.

2. Ps. 16:7—The Lord counsels us even during the night seasons by speaking to our hearts. For additional consideration on night seasons and meditation, see Josh. 1:8; Ps. 4:4, 19:14, 63:1–8, 149:5; Phil. 4:4–9.
3. Matt. 24:4–27; Mark 13:3–37; Luke 21:7–36—These passages often share a heading such as signs of the times or and end of the age and are very similar in their depictions of the difficulties on the earth shortly before the coming of the Son of Man. Commonalities include such as

    - much deception, even those presenting themselves as "christs"
    - geopolitical confusion, conflicts, wars, rumors of wars
    - ethnic and racial conflicts
    - persecution and killing of Christians
    - people getting easily offended, angry, hateful, and violent
    - people becoming apathetic, self-centered, and uncompassionate
    - lawlessness and disrespect of authority abounding
    - earthquakes
    - famines
    - pestilences
    - signs in the heavens

4. Isa. 49:23; Ps. 25:3; Matt. 24:13; Mark 13:13; Luke 21:19, 36—These remind us that those who are alert and waiting on God will not be ashamed but blessed.

63. My Love Will Bring Healing to Your Soul

I am pouring My love into your spirit, and it will flow over your mind, will, and emotions. My love will bring healing to your soul. Receive My love as it flows over and through you. Let My love wash away the hurts of the past. Let My love cleanse and purify your soul.

I am washing you with the powerful, purified water of My Word—and by My Spirit, it shall be accomplished, says the Lord God almighty. Come into My presence and receive life.

Selected Scripture Reading

1. Rom. 5:1–5—This begins by confirming that we are justified as righteous before God by believing Jesus Christ died for our sins. Because we have faith in Christ, we have access to grace, the power to stand and rejoice in the hope of God's salvation no matter what difficulties we may go through. Verses 3–4 point out that hard times actually produce perseverance and mature character qualities. How can all this work benefit in our lives? Verse 5 reads, "Now hope does not disappoint, because the love of God has been poured out in our hearts by the Holy Spirit who was given to us."

   Additional scriptures about God's love and Holy Spirit being poured into us are Luke 24:46–49 and Acts 2:1–47, 10:45. When we comprehend that our heavenly Father loves us so much that He provided Himself as a Lamb (Gen. 22:8; John 1:29), His Son, Jesus, as a sacrifice for our sins (John 3:16), we cannot but tangibly feel His love for us and want with all our hearts to be made whole by His love. In the process, we are healed spiritually and find our true identities and personalities.
2. John 3:16—"For God so loved the world that He gave His only begotten Son; that whoever believes in Him should not perish but have everlasting life." See Luke 4:17–21.
3. Jer. 31:3—God draws us to Himself with lovingkindness.
4. Ps. 119:9–11—God's life-giving words hidden in our hearts help us live pure lives. See Ps. 101; John 17:17; Eph. 5:26–27; 1 Peter 1:22–23.
5. Deut. 30:6; Mark 12:28–34—God works in our hearts to draw us to Himself so we can love Him with all our being and love others well.
6. John 4:10 (NLT)—"Jesus replied, 'If you only knew the gift God has for you and who you are speaking to, you would ask me, and I would give you living water.'"
7. 1 John 3:1–3—"Behold what manner of love the Father has bestowed on us, that we should be called children of God! … And everyone who has this hope in Him purifies himself just as He is pure." See John 15:3, 8:32.

64. There Is No Other Name

My children, I love you and share with you the mysteries of the kingdom of God. It is by one Man, the Son of God, that peace—My peace has come to the world and to your hearts. Open your hearts and hear My words to you.

The peace the world is seeking—the peace the world is crying out for—is found only in the person of Jesus Christ. There is no other name through whom peace comes. I say to you, My children, let My love, let My peace flow through you to your neighbors. Carry the presence and peace of Jesus with you everywhere you go. This is My plan—this is my purpose for you. My peace and joy in you shall reveal the kingdom of God among you.

Selected Scripture Reading

1. Prov. 25:2 (Voice)—"God's glory is shown when He conceals things; a king's glory is shown in his ability to explore the facts of the matter." When we want to learn about something or to get to know someone, we must make an effort to do so. The Bible often uses the word *seek* and admonishes us to seek God, wisdom, understanding, knowledge, discretion, and truth. See Proverbs 1–31; Matt. 6:33; 7:7–8; Heb. 11:6.
2. Deut. 29—In renewing the covenant that the Israelites have with God to be His people, Moses reviewed what God had done for them and told them if they kept the covenant, they would prosper in all they did. He warned them what would happen to them individually and as a nation if they were negligent or rebellious. In verse 29, Moses made a statement concerning the people's responsibility to obey God: "The secret things belong to the LORD our God, but those things which are revealed belong to us and to our children forever, that we may do all the words of this law."
3. Luke 8:9–10—Jesus's disciples did not readily understand the concealed meaning of the parable of the sower and asked Him its meaning. Before giving them the interpretation, Jesus said, "To you it has been given to know the mysteries of the kingdom of God, but to the rest it is given in parables, that Seeing they may not see, And hearing they may not understand." God often hides His truths in

plain sight so one must be seeking Him to find them. See Col. 1:27, 2:2–3, 4:3; Eph. 1:9, 3:3–12, 6:19; 1 Tim. 3:16; 1 Cor. 2:7, 15:50–58.
4. John 18:36—"Jesus answered, 'My kingdom is not of this world.'" See Acts 4:12.
5. Rom. 14:17–19—"For the kingdom of God is not eating and drinking but righteousness and peace and joy in the Holy Spirit. For he who serves Christ in these things is acceptable to God and approved by men. Therefore let us pursue the things which make for peace and the things by which one may edify another." See Col. 1:4–6.
6. Phil. 2:5–15—"Let this mind be in you which was also in Christ Jesus, 6. Who being in the form of God, did not consider it robbery to be equal with God, But made Himself of no reputation, taking the form of a bondservant, and coming in the likeness of men."

65. Be Faithful in Intercession

I am calling you to prayer. Pray, My people, pray. Evil forces are at work around the earth. Their goal is to start a major war and take over nations. They have many wicked plans to create fear and chaos, to control and destroy.

Yet they do not know Me. They do not know My power. Power for good, not evil. I say to you, My church, pray for your enemies. Bind the strong man. Loose My peace over your nation.

Seek Me and you will find deliverance. Your enemy will scatter, and you will wonder where they went. Only you must be faithful in intercession.

Selected Scripture Reading

1. Isa. 55:6–7—"Seek the LORD while He may be found, Call upon Him while He is near. Let the wicked forsake his way, And the unrighteous man his thoughts; Let him return to the LORD. And He will have mercy on him; And to our God, For He will abundantly pardon." See 2 Chron. 7:14; Joel 2:12–13, 15.
2. Zech. 8:16–17—Have you ever wondered what God hates? This scripture lists at least one thing most have quite likely been guilty

of multiple times—thinking evil in our hearts against someone else. For more on what God hates, see Prov. 6:16–19. Of course, from an instructional standpoint, God appoints ministers such as prophets (1 Sam. 12:23–25) to call leaders (2 Sam. 11–12; Nathan ministered to David resulting in David's repentance) and all people to return to Him (Ezek. 22; Acts 17:1–4, 19:8–20; Eph. 4:11–16). See 1 Thess. 5:12–24. We may surmise from Lamentations 2:14 that a task of the prophetic voice is to see the iniquity of the people and with God's guidance speak out to give the people an opportunity to turn away the inevitable captivity that results from doing whatever God hates (Jer. 23:22).

3. 1 Tim. 2:1–6 (NASB)—"First of all, then, I urge that entreaties and prayers, petitions and thanksgivings, be made on behalf of all men, for kings and all who are in authority, so that we may lead a tranquil and quiet life in all godliness and dignity. This is good and acceptable in the sight of God our Savior, who desires all men to be saved and to come to the knowledge of the truth. For there is one God, and one mediator also between God and men, the man Christ Jesus, who gave Himself as a ransom for all, the testimony given at the proper time." See Matt. 16:19, 18:19. An Old Testament story illustrating the power of prayer in matters of national defense is that recorded in 2 Kings 19:8–37. Sennacherib of Assyria moved to attack Judah around 701 BC. King Hezekiah, aware of the military successes of the Assyrians, went to the temple to pray to God requesting to be delivered from the hand of their approaching enemy. Verses 20–34 record God's answer, and verses 35–37 record the outcome.

4. Mark 10:42–45—Leadership motives and principles in the kingdom of God are very different from those in secular, worldly, power-centered structures. See Deut. 17: 14-20, Matt. 20:25-28; Luke 6:28.

5. Gal. 6:9–10—"And let us not grow weary while doing good, for in due season we shall reap if we do not lose heart." See Rev. 15:3–4.

66. Let Go of Past Wounds and Hurts

Some of you are holding tightly to past hurts and wounds. Your fists—your heart—is clenched shut because of the memory of the pain and the fear of being hurt again. My dear child, I love you with an everlasting love.

Remember what I have done for you—how I have extended My love and mercy to you even when you were far from Me and unlovable. I send My love, My Son, Jesus, to you to reveal to you how much I love you and to make a way for you. Does He not teach you to draw on My strength and love to love your neighbor, forgive one another, and move forward in the power of grace I give you? Receive My Holy Spirit to strengthen your heart.

Trust Me to bring healing to your broken heart. Look to Me and not another to receive affirmation and peace for your soul. Trust Me and not another to fulfill the greater joys in your heart. Let My love and grace flow through you and you will be blessed and be a blessing to others.

Trust Me to care tenderly for you. Trust Me to lead you carefully. I am here for you. Let go of your wounds and hurts. This is a new day, a new season. Rejoice in your salvation.

Selected Scripture Reading

1. Ps. 109:22–26 (NASB)—"For I am afflicted and needy, And my heart is wounded within me ... Help me, O Lord my God; Save me according to Your lovingkindness."
2. Ps. 64:1–10—"Hear my voice, O God, in my meditation; Preserve my life from fear of the enemy. Hide me from the secret plots of the wicked ... The righteous shall be glad in the LORD and trust in Him. And all the upright in heart shall glory." See 2 Chron. 5:13–14, 20:20–22; Ps. 40:16, 62:8, 119:64–68; Acts 2:47; Heb. 13:15–17.
3. Hos. 6:1—"Come, and let us return to the LORD; For He has torn, but He will heal us; He has stricken, but He will bind us up." See Ps. 41:4, 103; John 8:1–12; 1 John 1:9.
4. Mark 11:25–26—"And whenever you stand praying, if you have anything against anyone, forgive him, that your Father in heaven may also forgive you your trespasses. But if you do not forgive, neither will your Father in heaven forgive your trespasses."
5. Matt. 6:5–15—In these verses, Jesus teaches us about prayer.

    - Prayer is between God and us.
    - It is not about talking nonstop, repeating phrases or formulas.
    - God already knows what we need.

- We should acknowledge He is our sovereign Father.
- We are to ask Him for our daily sustenance; quite likely, this means spiritual as well as physical bread.
- We are to forgive others—God forgives us as we forgive others (Matt. 18:21–35).
- We are to pray for guidance.
- We are to pray for deliverance from the evil one.
- We are to praise God.

6. 2 Cor. 5:17—"Therefore, if anyone is in Christ, he is a new creation; old things have passed away; behold, all things have become new."

67. Prophecies Given Long Ago Are Soon to Be Fulfilled

Prophecies given long ago are soon to be fulfilled. You will see these things happen and know I have spoken. Have faith in My Word. My Holy Spirit is with you to lead you, to guide and to comfort you.

Set your heart on things above. Spend time with Me now and you will be prepared. I am speaking to My bride. Make your heart ready. Purify and cleanse yourselves. Let go of, put down, and walk away from sin. Walk in My love and purity and you will have no fear of the future for I shall be there with you and you will overcome with great victory.

Selected Scripture Reading

1. Deut. 4:29—"But from there you will seek the LORD your God, and you will find Him if you seek Him with all your heart and with all your soul." In Deuteronomy 4, Moses was reminding, admonishing, and teaching the Israelites many things.

   - Receive God's promises, which was dependent on their remaining faithful and obedient.
   - Remember the dire consequences of sexual and spiritual immorality and adultery.
   - Pay attention to follow God's directives for setting up a justice system that reflects His wisdom, understanding, and principles;

that would result in Israel becoming a great nation and having an exemplary society for other nations to witness the glory of God.
- Your nation's existence, your existence, depends on your following the Ten Commandments (Ex. 20:1–17; Deut. 5:6–22, 10:12–21; Matt. 22:35–40; Mark 12:28–34), which are embodied in the general command to love God and others.
- Teach your children and grandchildren about God and His ways throughout history.
- Your salvation is at stake, so individually and corporately follow God by paying attention to your lifestyle choices.
- Do not be enticed or corrupted by worshipping carved images or idols. Note that God did not appear to you in an image when giving you His commands on Horeb; rather, He spoke to you. Do not be led astray to idolize carved statues or worship the sun, moon, stars, or anything else created.
- God has chosen you and has purified and refined you in the furnace of affliction that you should be His very own people not given to worship of false gods.
- Remember what I (Moses) am saying to you; it would be disastrous if after you have entered the land, you were corrupted to do evil and suffer the consequences.
- However, if you do fall away and sin, if you call out to Him with all your heart, He will be faithful to His covenant with you and deliver you.

2. Rev. 1:1 (Voice)—"This is the revelation of Jesus the Anointed, the Liberating King: an account of visions and a heavenly journey, God granted this to Him so that He would show His followers the realities that are already breaking into the world and soon will be fulfilled." See Isa. 42:8–9.

68. Stand with Israel and You Will Be Blessed

Israel shall be spoken of as a great friend of America, and America shall be a friend of Israel.

It shall be pertaining to America, and Israel shall give warning. This is grace to you, America. Do not turn your back on Israel. Stand with Israel and you will be blessed. Curse Israel and you will be cursed.

Biblical Insights on God's Call and Purpose of Israel

In Gen. 12:1–3, we read, "Now the LORD had said to Abram: 'Get out of your country, From your family And from your father's house, To a land that I will show you. I will make you a great nation; I will bless you And make your name great; And you shall be a blessing. I will bless those who bless you, And I will curse those who curse you; And in you all the families of the earth shall be blessed.'" Was there a particular reason God chose a group of people through which to reveal Himself to all peoples? In Genesis 1–11, many good events were recorded, but a critical moral and spiritual decline had occurred in humanity (Gen. 6, 11).

In Gen. 1, we read a summary of the beginnings of creation of the heavens and the earth, the creation of plant and animal life, and the creation of humanity. Genesis 2 describes the garden where Adam lived and the creation of woman, a special companion for Adam. They had a relationship with God that was beautiful in purity and communication. God had given them free will; but He commanded them for their own good not to "eat of the tree of knowledge of good and evil for in that day they would surely die." For them to decide for themselves what was good and evil would be playing the part of God (3:5). Furthermore, their sin and rebellion resulted in increasingly destructive consequences.

In Gen. 4, we read about Cain murdering Abel; by Gen. 6, mankind has become so corrupted that God found it necessary to bring a great flood and start over again with those who were trying to follow Him (Gen. 7–10). Noah and his family weren't perfect either; just as now, each one had to choose to follow God.

Gen. 11 records what appears to be the first secular, self-willed, and prideful dynasty attempting to build a gateway to power—the Tower of Babel. One of Noah's descendants through his son, Cush, was Nimrod, "who was the first man on earth to be known as a powerful warrior" (Gen. 10:8b Voice). Nimrod built many cities in the land of Shinar including Babel. Things were in a bad way; beginning in Genesis 11, we learn about Abram's lineage; in Abram, God saw a man he could work with to change the course of history for nations and individuals (Gen. 18:19). God would make a nation of Abram's family and by and through His dealings with that nation reveal Himself and His plan for salvation for all who would respond. See Acts 7; Rom. 9–11; Gal. 3:29.

Selected Scripture Reading

1. Ps. 106:1–48; Zech. 2:8, 12:2–11; Joel 3:1–2; Hos. 3:5; Rom. 11:25—These are additional scriptures regarding Israel and the requirement God places on other nations to recognize His will and sovereignty.

69. Listen to My Holy Spirit as I Speak to Your Heart

I am directing My people in this nation to prepare for what lies ahead. First, they are to prepare their hearts and minds and set their hearts on eternal rather than earthly things.

I am also instructing that many change positions or relocate. Some I shall call home. Others are being instructed to store certain items and make physical preparations. There shall be much work for My people who are called by My name to do—to serve those around them with great compassion with the resources I have given them. Their service to others shall show My glory and love, and they shall witness to the truth of the gospel. Many will be saved because of their witness, love, and testimony during crises and difficulties.

So hear Me, My people. Listen to know My voice and not another's. Spend time with Me. Read My Word and listen to My Holy Spirit as I speak to your heart. Your heart will be refreshed and encouraged as you receive rich treasures and understanding from My Word. My words will burn in your heart, and you will receive My wisdom. My wisdom comes from above and not below. You will find rest for your souls, and you will not fear.

You are My children. You are My bride. Come to Me and receive from Me. Come and open your hearts to Me that I may fill your hearts with good things, with blessings. As I have spoken, it shall be.

Selected Scripture Reading

1. Ps. 4:8—"I will both lie down in peace, and sleep; For You alone O LORD, make me dwell in safety." See Ps. 50:15 and 91:9–10.
2. Prov. 1:20–33—Proverbs is a collection of short sayings meant to convey important truths, character qualities, and principles for living in harmony with God and mankind. Proverbs instructs those who will listen to gain knowledge of God and wisdom (Prov. 1:1–7). We are given warnings not to be influenced by evil (1:8–19).

    Beginning in verse 20, wisdom is presented figuratively as a woman calling out to everyone to "turn at her rebuke." Verse 23 promises God's Holy Spirit with wisdom and understanding will be poured out on those who repent and follow Him. To refuse the counsel of God brings destructive consequences (1:22–32), but those who follow God's counsel will dwell in safety without fear of evil (1:33). Wisdom will warn them how to avoid the consequences of evil. See Deut. 34:9; Prov. 2–4; Rom. 13:11–14; Eph. 1:17.
3. Matt. 5:16—"Let your light so shine before men, that they may see your good works and glorify your Father in heaven." See Luke 24:32.

70. My Love Will Lift You Up on Eagles' Wings

There is a new sound, a new music coming from My people. It is the sound of purity. It is the sound of holiness and it is reaching the heavens. This is a beautiful music, a powerful music and rises with the prayers of the saints.

Arise, My beloved. See and taste the good things the Lord has prepared for those who love Him. You will walk in blessings. You will know the Lord your God, and you will not fear. My love will lift you up on eagles' wings. Listen and hear the sound of My love—My love for you.

You are My children, and I watch over you with a jealous love. No one can snatch you from My hand. Only do not stray from My commands; do not stray from My protection. There is a way that seems right to man, but the end thereof is death. Stay close to Me in the secret place of My presence and you will find life for your soul and great joy. Rejoice and delight yourself in the Lord, the God of all creation.

Biblical Insights in 2 Chronicles

There is an interesting, related scripture in 2 Chronicles 20:21 that says Jehoshaphat the king "appointed those who should sing to the LORD, and who should praise the beauty of holiness, as they went out before the army and were saying: 'Praise the LORD, For His mercy endures forever.'" This comes toward the conclusion of when the Ammonites and Moabites attacked Judah around 896 BC. King Jehoshaphat, knowing of the great approaching armies, proclaimed a national fast. He stood before the people praying to God. In his prayer, he acknowledged God's power and sovereignty; he prayed as Solomon had in 2 Chronicles 7:14 when the temple was dedicated. Read 2 Chronicles 20:6–12 for critical details.

After King Jehoshaphat's prayer, the Spirit of the Lord moved upon Jahaziel to prophetically speak God's response to the people: "Thus says the LORD to you: 'Do not be afraid nor dismayed because of this great multitude, for the battle is not yours but God's ... You will not need to fight in this battle. Position yourselves, stand still and see the salvation of the LORD who is with you'" (2 Chron. 20:15–17).

The next morning, Jehoshaphat and his army went out into the wilderness of Tekoa. There, he charged his army, "Believe in the LORD your God, and you shall be established; believe in His prophets and you shall prosper" (2 Chron. 20:20). Then the king did a strange thing—he told the singers to go out in front of the army and praise the beauty of the holiness of God! Verse 22 reads, "Now when they [these singers] began to sing and to praise, the LORD set ambushes against the people of Ammon, Moab, and Mount Seir, who had come against Judah; and they were defeated!" The beauty of holiness is the state of being consecrated and set apart to God and then hearing and obeying Him with rejoicing.

71. I Have a People

And God says, I have a people in this nation who love Me completely even unto death. They are not afraid of pestilence, of harm, or persecution. Their light shall and does shine brightly and gloriously. Their testimony shall go throughout all the earth, and I shall do great exploits through them.

They shall know Me face to face. They know My voice, and faith is in their hearts. I shall call to them, and they shall do My bidding. Nothing and no one shall be able to stand against them because My Word shall come out of their mouths. My knowledge and My wisdom and My truth will be declared through them. They shall be a brilliant white and glorious light in the midst of gross darkness.

You are My children; you are that light. Do not think little of yourselves to become that brilliant light, shining and reflecting My glory. I am here with you to fill you with the light of My truth, with the light of My love. Open your hearts and receive all I have for you.

Biblical Insights in an Overview of Genesis to Revelation

From Genesis to Revelation, the scriptures tell the story of mankind—of the wise, foolish, good, and wicked alike. We learn about those who sought God and desired to walk with integrity before Him. These men and women were not perfect, but they learned from their and others' mistakes—even those whose hearts did not seek God.

We read about Adam and Eve, Cain and Abel, Noah and his family, Abraham and Lot, Jacob and Esau, Joseph and his brothers, Moses,

Joshua, Achan, Gideon, Abimelech, Ruth and Boaz, Eli and his wicked sons, Samuel, Saul and David, Solomon and Absalom, Nathan, Jeremiah, Isaiah, and all the prophets, the many wicked kings and the few good kings. In their lives—in the choices they make, we can see ourselves. In Cain, we see jealousy, self-justification, and revenge with all its destructive consequences. In Joseph, we see the naïve enthusiasm of a gifted youth tempered with affliction and thus bringing forth the wisdom and maturity necessary to fulfill his destiny. King David's story teaches us what it means to love God and desire to walk with integrity before Him—even in transparent humility—especially as he publicly repented for his sins of adultery and murder (2 Sam. 11–12; Ps. 51).

The Bible speaks of individual and corporate integrity and accountability. It teaches we must ask ourselves critical questions such as, Do we know our Creator God? Do and we acknowledge Him by the way we think and live? The recorded events of the Tower of Babel (Gen. 11), Sodom and Gomorrah (Gen. 18:16–19:29), and Achan and the defeat at Ai (Josh. 7) as well as Jesus's teaching in Matthew 11:20–24 give examples. Old and New Testament scriptures speak of nations being accountable to God: See Isa. 26:2; Jer. 11:17, 12:17, 45:4; Ps. 2:1–12, 33:12; Prov. 14:34; Ezek. 14:12–23; Obad. 1:15; Matt. 25:31–46.

Scripture states that all those in governing, teaching, and spiritual leadership positions are to speak, act, and live as good examples. Leaders are to be just and rule in the fear of God (2 Sam. 23:1–3; 1 Tim. 3:1–13; Acts 26:16).

72. Come to Me for Healing and Restoration

My grace is with you, My children, so you may become what I have created you to become.

When I let things fall apart in a life or a nation, what is in the heart of that life or nation is revealed. Do you not see that is My love calling to them to come to Me for healing and restoration? I love My people. I love My creation and I long for them to be whole and restored.

Do not rebuke the cleansing process. Call on Me to bring deliverance. Humble yourselves and seek My face. I long to bring healing and restoration to My people.

Give yourself to Me—your whole heart, mind, and soul, and you will be restored for My love shall make you whole. I am restoring My church through the power of My love and grace.

Biblical Insights on "Processing Our Mistakes"

Rarely do we comprehend the value of failures to bring enlightenment—that is, to see mistakes as stepping stones to improvement. Failures are painful and often humiliating experiences that can be paralyzing when we focus on them. How do we get beyond our mistakes and problems plaguing us? How can we process our failures to turn them into assets? How do we receive God's grace to become what He has created us to become?

Let's begin with a foundational truth in Jeremiah 17:9–10 (Voice): "The heart is most devious and incurably sick. Who can understand it? It is I, the Eternal One, who probes the innermost heart and examines the innermost thoughts. I will compensate each person justly, according to his ways and by what his actions deserve." That same concept of our hearts needing a cleaning and makeover is repeated in Mark 7:20–23: "And He said, 'What comes out of a man, that defiles a man. For from within, out of the heart of men, proceed evil thoughts, adulteries, fornications, murders, Thefts, covetousness, wickedness, deceit, lewdness, an evil eye, blasphemy, pride, foolishness. All these evil things come from within and defile a man." The fact that we struggle with character issues reveals that our hearts need renewal. We must acknowledge this truth to position ourselves to receive God's help.

Failures, troubles, and stresses come into our lives and we observe in ourselves ungodly attitudes, words, and actions. We would be wise to take immediate action.

- Call out to the Lord (Ps. 50:15, 86:5, 7; 2 Tim. 2:22).
- Have humble and repentant hearts (Ps. 34:18; Hos. 14:2; Acts 20:21; Rom. 12:16; 2 Cor. 7:10).
- Ask God for deliverance (Pss. 3:8, 6–7, 9:3–11; Isa. 61; Luke 4:16–21; 2 Kings 19:20; Mark 5:1–20; Luke 8:2; 2 Tim. 4:18).
- Practice a lifestyle of cleansing ourselves from all unrighteousness (Matt. 3:8; John 17:17; Rom. 15:16; 1 Peter 1:22–23, 4:2; Ps. 101:3; Heb. 13:20–21; James 2:18).

- Develop an attitude of gratitude (2 Chron. 20:22; Pss. 9:11, 100:4; Matt. 18:21–35; Acts 2:47; Col. 3:15; Eph. 6; 1 Tim. 5:18; Heb. 13:15; 1 Peter 2:9).

73. Receive from Me What Your Heart Seeks

Read My Word; in it, you will find the secrets of My heart and I will reveal Myself to you. You will learn that I cherish and love you. I call to you to come sit with Me and listen as I impart knowledge and wisdom to your heart. Come to Me and receive from Me that which your heart seeks.

It is the wise who set their hearts to seek and know their Creator God. Seek Me and you shall find Me. I am not far from you, but you must seek Me. Does your heart cry out for wisdom? Are you hungry and thirsty for understanding? Do you desire truth and mercy? For I am all these and more.

Some seek the knowledge of these but reject Me. They reject not only My sovereignty but My very existence. In their hearts they say, "There is no God. I can believe and do as I wish. There is no Creator who sees and hears me."

Yes, you do have the freedom to choose what you will seek and what you will follow. But will you have the wisdom to see there are consequences tied to the choices you make? Or will it be that because you have rejected Me, you will foolishly choose to believe lies—lies about who you are, lies about your purpose on earth, lies about Me, and lies about eternity? For you see, "'There is a way that seems right to a man, But its end is the way of death" (Prov. 16:25).

Look around you. What are the people choosing? Can you see life or death resulting from their choices? Do you see life or death, blessings or curses from the choices you have made and are making?

It is the foolish one who blindly and stubbornly goes his own way, not seeking My counsel. He harms himself and others. Turn away from your foolish ways and seek the Lord your God. Commit your heart and commit your ways to Me and I will direct your steps for I will lead you in the paths of wisdom and righteousness. Come to Me to find that which your heart seeks.

Selected Scripture Reading—Psalm 25

The psalmist wrote, "To You, O LORD, I lift up my soul. O my God, I trust in You; Let me not be ashamed; Let not my enemies triumph over me … Show me Your ways, O LORD; Teach me your paths. Lead me in Your truth and teach me, For You are the God of my salvation; On You I wait all the day. Remember, O LORD, Your tender mercies and Your lovingkindness, For they are from of old. Do not remember the sins of my youth nor my transgressions; According to Your mercy remember me, For Your goodness sake; O LORD. Good and upright is the LORD; Therefore He teaches sinners in the way. The humble He guides in justice, And the humble He teaches His way."

74. You Are My Child, and I Love You

I created and formed you in your mother's womb. You are created to be, in working with Me, an overcomer.

My child, to each of you I say, My love for you is great. My plans for you are good and are for blessing. Even in the midst of difficult days and seasons, know that My plan is to bless you and bring you a victorious peace.

It is you who know Me—it is you who come to Me in the secret place—you shall have the strength; you shall have the power, anointing, and presence of My Holy Spirit to overcome every challenge and difficulty.

Come to Me with your whole heart. Cast aside every sin and give Me the burdens of your heart. Abide with Me so My Holy Spirit may direct your path. You are My child, and I love you.

Biblical Insights on "Created in the Image of the Good Shepherd"

Scripture unequivocally affirms the sanctity and legitimacy of mankind. In Genesis 1:26, God said, "Let Us make man in Our image," so mankind in the form of male and female was created. In what ways do we reflect the image of God? Together, male and female are a natural, physical image or reflection of God, who the Bible says is a Spirit (John 4:24). Therefore, life and gender also are God-given attributes.

Without question, our Creator God is infinitely more complex and dimensional than we can comprehend. The Bible gives many descriptions that build understanding concerning the shared attributes of mankind and God. For example, the attribute of unity and plurality combined. God is one but has multiple dimensions or forms. As almighty God, our Creator, He is our Father (Isa. 64:8; Rom 8:15). As God manifested in the flesh, He is our Savior (Isa. 43:11; 1 Tim. 3:16). As the Spirit of God, He exists and gives us life in and by His Holy Spirit (Job 33:4; Acts 2:38).

In Matthew 28:19, the plurality and work of God is summarized in Jesus's words "Go therefore and make disciples of all the nations, baptizing them in the name of the Father and of the Son and of the Holy Spirit." The Bible teaches God is Father, Son, and Holy Spirit and is one as Deut. 6:4 affirms, "Hear, O Israel: The LORD our God, the LORD is one!" Likewise, we have a basic understanding of the plurality of man when we speak of man as having a physical body, a soul (mind, will, emotions/hearts), and a spirit (Gen. 2:7; 1 Cor. 15:35–58).

There is a reason Psalm 23 is among the most quoted scriptures. The declarations of this psalm draw for us incredible pictures of God's love, guidance, provision, and protection. These words bear witness in our hearts and spirits that the Lord God almighty is our Good Shepherd throughout life's journey and His "goodness and mercy shall follow me all the days of my life; And I will dwell in the house of the LORD Forever." See 2 Cor. 13:14.

75. I Have Plans for You, and They Are Good

Did I not tell you something big was going to happen that would blow away man's attempts to control and create? Man cannot of himself create. I am the Creator. There is none other beside Me. Mankind's pride and arrogance will always end in destruction.

The season of sowing and reaping has come. He who has sown to the wind shall reap the whirlwind. It is a fearful thing to reap the seeds of destruction. Yet it shall not be so for My people—those who know Me and are called by My name. Look up and rejoice for your redemption is very near.

I am calling My people to come closer to Me—to rise up, to stand up—and walk in the full inheritance I have given them. You shall have wisdom and understanding you have not had before. The chains of deception and confusion of the enemy will fall away, and your faith will increase.

Do not be afraid of wars, rumors of wars, pestilences, earthquakes, disasters—the signs and conditions of this age. Walk in the liberty and freedom of My Spirit. Believe Me when I say to you that I have plans for you and that they are good.

Biblical Insights from the Book of Habakkuk

The world was in depravity and turmoil when the prophet Habakkuk lived in Judah ca. 600 BC. The Egyptian and Assyrian dynasties were waning and Babylonia was rising. Judah was threatened by invasion from the North. From the time Saul was king (ca. 1093 BC) until Judah went into captivity (which happened in three phases: 607 BC, 597 BC, and 587 BC), the Israelites had gone through multiple cycles of moral and spiritual heights and depths as the people followed the examples of their leaders.

Habakkuk saw all the wickedness of his people and the victories of the aggressive and cruel Babylonians. That grieved and perplexed him. He was looking for God's justice to make things right, but that didn't seem to be happening. Habakkuk complained to God, who said He was raising up the wicked Chaldeans (Babylonians) as an instrument of correction and judgment (Hab. 1:5–11). See Ezek. 12:15; Jer. 29:10; Mic. 7:9; Heb. 12:3–11.

In verses 12–17, Habakkuk asked God why He allowed a more-wicked nation to plunder and destroy a less-wicked nation. He compared the Babylonians to fishermen who gathered up fish and plundered with a net! The prophet wondered how long God would let that happen. Habakkuk did what you and I must do in such a situation: "I will stand my watch And set myself on the rampart, And watch and see what He will say to me, And what I will answer when I am corrected." See Hab. 2:1–4; Rom. 1:17.

First God contrasted the proud and wicked Babylonians with those whose souls were upright because they lived by faith. Then God outlined the mind-set and behavior of the wicked. Habakkuk gained understanding of the plan and purposes of God. The prophet's prayer is recorded in chapter 3; you will find it powerful, poetic, and encouraging.

76. Seek Me and You Will Find Me

I have spoken repeatedly to My people to come to Me, to spend time with Me, and to learn My voice, but they have not made time for Me.

Yes, a few rest in My presence, and I delight in them, and they receive My blessings. Yet I wait on many others. The time has come that they will seek Me as never before.

Because they have not learned to know Me—to know My voice or understand My Word, they will be flooded with fear and confusion until they regain their footing on the solid rock.

I am coming soon, My people. Many things are changing quickly. Things you have trusted in and depended upon, even false gods My people have entertained, will be washed away. Seek Me and you will find Me.

How will you respond, O my heart, to the words He has spoken? Have not His words quickened my spirit and burned in my heart?

This is your opportunity to move forward and deepen your love relationship with your Creator. My heart, will you every day surrender to Him, placing your mind and will on the altar of loving obedience? Not out of self-religious piety will you please your Creator God. O my heart, hear and think upon Him, who created you—created you to be filled with His love, grace, and wisdom.

Cast away, set aside the haughty, religious, and cruel lies that cause you to despise, to hate, and to destroy yourself and others. Can you not see, my heart? There is a path that leads to life, and there is a path that leads to death. You must choose, dear heart of mine. You must choose which path you will follow.

That's right, dear one—we are on a journey. Sometimes, I call you my heart. Sometimes, I call you my spirit. Sometimes, I call you my God-conscious conscience. You are my inner being. You are like my radar and compass all in one.

How is it, O my heart, that you reside so deep within me and yet permeate and direct every aspect of this body in which I live? Oh, yes—He breathed into my body His breath—His Spirit. I became a living soul even in my mother's womb. Oh how wonderfully and fearfully I am made.

Your Word comforts me: "Though an army may encamp against me,

My heart shall not fear; Though war may rise against me, In this I will be confident. One thing I have desired of the LORD, That will I seek: That I may dwell in the house of the LORD All the days of my life … For in the time of trouble He shall hide me in His pavilion … When You said, 'Seek My face,' My heart said to You, 'Your face, LORD, will I seek'" (Ps. 27:2–8).

77. For the Beauty in My People

I hear the hoof beats. War is on the horizon. Prepare, My children, for great changes and difficulties. Many plans will be placed on hold as principalities and powers of darkness incite rebellion, riots, chaos, and anarchy. Governmental authorities will be overwhelmed and will shrink in fear and terror.

But do not be frightened, My people. Do not be afraid of those who have power over the flesh. They shall be brought to nothing on the Day of Judgment. You ask Me where I am in the midst of the darkness in the world today. I am there with those who call out to Me for help. I am with those who call out to Me for wisdom, and understanding. I am with those who seek My face and turn from their wicked ways. In humility and repentance, you will find Me.

Let not the man nor nation who comes to me in pride and self-righteousness think I shall bow to requests for personal gain and acceptance. I am waiting for My people to humble themselves and seek My face. I am waiting for My people to love and obey My words more than the pleasures of this world. I am waiting for My people to walk in the integrity of the righteousness I have given them.

Will you cleanse and purify yourselves? Will you walk in holy love toward one another? Will you obey and follow Me by My Word and by My Spirit? It is time for My bride to come out from the darkness. Separate yourselves from all unrighteousness, even subtle forms of self-righteousness and hypocrisy.

I am waiting for My bride to prepare herself, become clean, pure, and strong in My Spirit that I may anoint her with power to carry out the work of the kingdom of God in this hour. Those who love me will understand what I am saying. You will seek My face. You will wean yourselves from the deceitfulness of sin, and you will hunger and thirst for holiness and righteousness. You will desire to fulfill your calling and destiny in the kingdom of God. You will be blessed, and you will be a blessing to others.

Where am I in the midst of the darkness of this world? Is not the kingdom of God within the hearts of mankind? When I abide in you and you abide in My Word and in My Spirit, My light shines forth from your heart and dispels the darkness. Step forward, My bride, and fulfill your destiny in this hour.

Look up. Your redemption is near. Rejoice. You shall attain great reward. Remain true and faithful to Me—to My Word—and you shall overcome with magnificent and glorious testimony. I shall cleanse and purge evil from My church. Look for the beauty in My people. You shall witness My glory among My people for I will be great in their midst.

Selected Scripture Reading

1. Ps. 9:17–20, 149:4; Isa. 24, 26:9; 51; Acts 17:12–31; Rev. 15:3–4; Matt. 5:3–12.

78. I Have Called You to Be Peacemakers

I am calling My people, young and old and on all levels of life, to hear Me and obey My command; I have called you to be peacemakers and share My gospel with your neighbors and with the world to bring peace to their hearts.

My children, come close to Me and hear what I would say to you. These are indeed perilous times with much confusion and deception. That which is wicked is honored and held in high regard. That which is clean and holy is mocked and ridiculed.

But look and see what I am about to do. I shall honor My servants. You shall not walk in darkness because My light shall shine upon you and you will know the path of righteousness to walk. And you will walk in the path of righteousness and I will honor you with peace, knowledge, and understanding. You will walk in the blessings of the Lord.

It is now the world needs to see My peace reflected in your hearts, My peace reflected in your families—My peace reflected within My body of believers.

When I say I have called you to be peacemakers, know and understand; this is no easy task because both the flesh within you—your carnal nature—and evil principalities will stand against and war with you.

Search My Word. Search My scriptures diligently and humbly to find My truth and obey My commands. Do those things. Walk in the presence of My Holy Spirit, and carry My peace with you fulfilling My command to be peacemakers that you may inherit incorruptible blessings. Come close to Me, My children, and walk in My ways that I may honor and bless you.

> "Blessed are the peacemakers for they shall be called the sons of God" (Matt. 5:9).

Biblical Insights from Psalm 85:8–13

It seems contradictory that we must battle to find peace. Yet the experiences of life confirm that unless we act intentionally with strategy, skill, and diligence, things and relationships will fall into disrepair. We must invest time and effort to keep our houses and appliances in good working order. Try maintaining good relationships with others while not talking and communicating with them! Forgo genuinely connecting with friends and family in a meaningful and consistent way and see what happens to your relationships!

To maintain and improve—to grow spiritually—we have to battle distractions, laziness, discouragement, bitterness, anger, lusts, fear, demands on our time and energy, deceptions, pride, and so on.

The Bible is the story of the search and battle for peace with God, within ourselves, and with others. Will you go on that mission to search and battle for peace? The psalmist says,

> I will hear what God the LORD will speak, For He will speak peace To His people and to His saints; But let them not turn back to foolishness. Surely His salvation is near to those who fear Him, That glory may dwell in our land.

Mercy and truth have met together; Righteousness and peace have kissed. Truth shall spring out of the earth, and righteousness shall look down from heaven. Yes, the LORD will give what is good; And our land will yield its increase. Righteousness will go before Him, And shall make His footsteps our pathway. (Psalm 85:8–13)

79. Lay Up Treasures in Heaven

This is a season of harvest time for all peoples. That which you have sown, you shall reap. If you have sown the Spirit, if you have set your heart on heavenly things, then you shall reap heaven's rewards. Righteousness, peace, and joy are yours. My Spirit is pouring out gifts and anointing to those who have been and are faithful, humble, obedient servants. This is for the work of the end-times harvest. Yes, indeed, you shall go forth equipped and ready, rejoicing as you bring in a harvest of souls for the kingdom of God.

Only, be not weary in doing well, My children. These times require much strength and wisdom. If you sow to the flesh, you will lack in strength and wisdom. Come to Me. Spend time alone with Me and listen to My Holy Spirit. I will direct your thoughts. I will direct your paths and be light for your understanding.

I must speak to you clearly, My child: slow down and make time for Me. Rest your body and quiet your soul so you can hear Me speak softly to your heart. I am calling to you, My precious child, lay up treasures in heaven for where your treasure is, there also will be your heart.

Biblical Insights from the Book of Hosea

The pastoral metaphor of sowing and reaping is used in scripture to describe two kinds of sowing and reaping that are intricately related. The first use of the metaphor refers to how we live and tend the gardens of our hearts. Do we let the weeds of lies, pride, idolatry, and selfish ambition choke out wisdom, compassion, truth, and patience? We might call this the lifestyle sowing and reaping principle.

There was a time (ca. 755–715 BC) in the life of the Northern Kingdom of Israel that illustrates this first kind of sowing and reaping. We read about it in Hosea. Outwardly, Israel looked prosperous and religious. But against God's instructions, the nation had become comfortable with accepting the theological beliefs and practices of those living within and near its borders. Trade agreements and alliances for economic and political benefit were made. The people believed they were okay; but they were blind to their disobedience and its consequences.

Inwardly, the nation was succumbing to corruption, idolatry, immorality, violence, and family and social confusion. God charged them with spiritual adultery and warned of impending disastrous consequences. Through the prophet, God revealed that future defeat and exile would motivate them to return to Him. In Hosea 10:12 (Voice), God told them to soften their hearts and return to Him and live according to His principles and directives: "Plant a crop of righteousness for yourselves, harvest the fruit of unfailing love, And break up your hard soil, because it's time to seek the Eternal until He comes and waters your fields with justice."

This same principle of sowing and reaping related to lifestyle is repeated in multiple ways throughout the Old and New Testaments.[1] The scriptures teach us that it is important to understand biblical truths and principles to make judicious lifestyle choices (Matt. 6).

The sowing and reaping metaphor is also used to convey truths about the harvest of souls for salvation. What had happened that we needed saving? God gives us free will, but our choices have consequences. We have the freedom to make choices but not to change the consequences connected to them.[2]

Sin has the consequence of separating us from God (Isa. 59:1–2). Each of us must be saved or cleansed from our sins (Rom. 3:23–26). In 1 John 1:8, we read, "If we say that we have no sin, we deceive ourselves and the truth is not in us." Ecclesiastes 7:20 confirms, "For there is not a just man on earth who does good And does not sin" (Rom. 3:9–18).

Through Adam and Eve's disobedience, sin took root in the hearts of mankind. Nevertheless, God had a plan from the very beginning to

---

[1] Prov. 11:18; 22:8; Jer. 2:19; Ezek. 16:43; 22:23–31; Gal. 6:7–8; Matt. 6:33; Rom. 1:18–32; 2:1–16; 2 Cor. 9:6–15; Heb. 10:29–31.
[2] Deut. 31:14–32:43; Rom. 6:23.

- expose the existence and nature of sin through the laws and commandments He would give them[3] (Abraham's lineage[4] would carry God's message to all mankind by recording His words, even prophecies. The Israelites' history of obedience and disobedience would reflect God's truths, faithfulness, love, and mercies, and open the door for all to know God.[5]),
- reveal to mankind the inability and inadequacy of outward appearances of keeping rules,[6]
- teach mankind that its heart needed to be renewed,[7]
- provide a mediator, a propitiatory sacrifice to redeem all mankind from sin,[8]
- create a people who would by faith hunger and thirst after Him and receive His righteousness,[9]
- establish an eternal kingdom of God,[10] and
- defeat Satan and the powers of darkness.[11]

Above are seven foundational points of God's plan to offer salvation to those who choose to receive and believe Him. It is a glorious message of freedom from guilt and the power of sin. He wants us to share this message with the world and "lay up treasures in heaven."[12]

80. Let Me Be Your Refuge

My people's lives are filled with busyness and distractions. Their hearts and minds are consumed with the cares and pleasures of this world. They pursue everything but have no time for Me, so their lives feel

---

[3] Gal. 3.
[4] Gen. 12:3, Ex. 20:1–17.
[5] Deut. 7:6, 1 Peter 2:9; James 2:5.
[6] Isa. 1, Gal. 3; Heb. 10.
[7] 1 Sam. 16:7; Ps. 51:10; Ezek. 18:31; John 3:1–21; Acts 2:38; 2 Cor. 7:10.
[8] Gen. 22:8; Isa. 7:14, 9:6–7, 43:10–11; Matt. 1:21–23; John 1:29, 3:16; Acts 7:2–53.
[9] Deut. 14:2; Ps. 60:4–5; Isa. 55; Hos. 2:23; Matt. 5:6; Rom. 9:25–26, 11:28; Eph. 1:3–7; Heb. 11; 1 John 3:2.
[10] Isa. 9:7; Dan. 2:44, 7:13; Luke 17:21, 24:46–49; Acts; Col. 1:6; 2 Peter 1:11; Rev. 11:15.
[11] Col. 2:15; Eph. 6:10–18; 2 Thess. 2:8; Heb. 2:14; 1 John 3:8; Rev. 20:10.
[12] Prov. 11:30; Matt. 6:20; Mark 16:15; 2 Tim. 4:1–5; James 5:19–20; Rev. 21–22.

empty, plagued with strife, fear and confusion. Weariness and depression become their companions.

I ask you, where is your abundant life that My Son gave His life to give you? Where is your peace in the Holy Spirit? Where is your hope and confidence? Are you seeking the things in this world to give you peace and fulfillment?

Earthly pleasures cannot fulfill the needs of your heart. Earthly wisdom and direction will disappoint and fail you. Do not become angry with Me—do not blame Me when you go your own way and leave Me out of your life.

Judgment begins in the house of the Lord, for My bride shall be free of the entanglements of the world. She shall have eyes to see Me and ears to hear Me, and her heart shall be pure. She shall have great understanding and wisdom. She shall cast aside the focus and obsessions of worldliness. She shall put on the garments of praise and communion with Me. There shall be neither disappointments nor emptiness in My bride's heart. As she fulfills her destiny in Me, her joy will abound.

Awaken, My people. Pray for spiritual eyes of understanding that you may be prepared for what lies ahead. Come to Me. Let Me be your refuge and strong tower. Let Me guide you through these times that your joy shall be full.

Biblical Insights on Life

Today, it seems an unlimited amount of information and pressures come our way daily. Navigating and balancing work, family, households, and additional commitments amid the complications of expectations often leave us exhausted, frustrated, and feeling out of control. We even get stuck on images instead of life's important matters! Why does it look as if we have it all but are really "wretched, miserable, poor, blind, and naked?" (Rev. 3:14–22).

Open my eyes, O Lord, that I may see! Psalm 71:1–3 reads,

> In You, O LORD, I put my trust; Let me never be put the shame. Deliver me in Your righteousness and cause me to escape; Incline Your ear to me, and save me. Be my strong refuge, To which I resort continually; You have

given the commandment to save me, For You are my rock and my fortress.

Ps. 62:8 counsels us, "Trust in Him at all times, you people; Pour out your heart before Him; God is a refuge for us."

81. I Have Made Preparations for You

I am here with you. I stand among you. Be encouraged, My beloved child, be encouraged.

The things I have spoken to my prophets and through My Word are soon to take place. Prepare, My child, prepare your heart. Everything that can be shaken will be shaken so that which cannot be shaken shall remain. Then shall My glory be revealed in and through My church. She too must be shaken so that which is in her—that which is weighing her testimony down, causing her to be a reproach among the heathen—is removed.

Then shall My church become My bride; I shall meet you in the air, and your redemption shall be completed. Know, My beautiful bride, that I love you deeply. Those things that are coming soon over the earth shall be difficult indeed. Yet I have made preparations for you to rise above the difficulties. I have made preparations for you to fulfill the destiny to which you have been called. That is to be My witnesses to all the world and testify to the glory, power, and majesty of God.

Yes indeed, these shall be dark days, but My bride shall carry the torch of God's salvation. Holiness shall burn brightly in her bosom, and nothing the enemy throws at her shall harm her. Look up, My bride—your redemption draws nigh.

Biblical Insights from the Book of Isaiah

God desires that we receive comfort and direction by understanding the bigger picture of history, and that includes the past, present, and future as He chooses to reveal it to us.[13] An example from Isaiah helps us see

---

[13] Deut. 29:29; Dan. 2:28; John 13:19, 16:33; Acts 3:18; Matt. 24; Revelation.

how God uses forth telling and foretelling to validate His sovereignty and show His loving care for His people.

God directed Isaiah to speak to Judah concerning its backslidden condition, which was certain to bring about the consequences God had warned the Israelites about in Deuteronomy 28:15–68 hundreds of years earlier. While pronouncing sovereign judgments on Judah as well as the godless neighboring nations, Isaiah saw into the future, to when God would send salvation in the form of His Messiah—God with us—as our Redeemer and Savior.[14] In Isaiah,[15] God explained that He alone was capable of directing events on the world stage and explaining what or why certain events would happen. He alone could give the reason they happened in the past.

In 712 BC, Isaiah prophesied about a man named Cyrus who would be called by God to rebuild the foundations of Jerusalem and the temple.[16] Ezra[17] wrote about a Persian king named Cyrus. In the first year[18] of his rule over Babylon, he decreed that the Jewish exiles were to return to Jerusalem and Judah to rebuild their city and temple. At the time, Ezra lived in Babylon as an exile. He was of priestly lineage, trustworthy, faithful in studying God's Word, and teaching the people, but he wasn't among the first group to return. In 458 BC, Ezra led a second group of exiles to Judah. [19] By that time, the temple had been rebuilt. Ezra's task was to teach and lead the people into spiritual renewal.

This story from hundreds of years ago is another confirmation of God's mercy, grace, and willingness to work with imperfect human beings who lose their way on life's journey. Can we not see ourselves in this story? We come to God but get distracted by life and often without realizing it fall out of relationship with Him. We get involved in things that become sour grapes in our mouths. Life shakes us up; we are taken captive by our sins and find ourselves in Babylon.

But God knows where we are, and He meets us in Babylon. With enlightened understanding, we cry out to Him for help and learn He

---

[14] Isa. 7:14, 9:1–2, 11:2, 53:3.
[15] Isa. 41:4, 26, 42:9, 45:21, 46:9–10.
[16] Ca. 712 BC. See Isa. 44:28–45:1–7.
[17] Ezra 1:1–4.
[18] Ca. 538 BC.
[19] This second group was given authority to return by King Artaxerxes; see Ezra 7–10.

has been waiting on us: "Therefore the LORD will wait, that He may be gracious to you; And therefore He will be exalted, that He may have mercy on you, For the LORD is a God of justice; Blessed are all those who wait for Him" (Isa. 30:18).

82. Repent and Cleanse Your Hearts

Man errs not understanding Me or My words concerning prophecy.[20] Have I not told you I do nothing without revealing it first through My servants the prophets?[21] Repent and cleanse your hearts and minds that you may understand My words and not wrestle with them to your own destruction.[22]

Some words I speak to you are firmly established and describe conditions and events as they will surely happen.[23] When you see these things come to pass, you will know I have spoken and your hearts will have been prepared because of the words I have spoken.[24]

Others, many other prophetic words I have given and do give you are conditional on your obedience.[25] The pure in heart shall see Me. They shall understand their God, and not be offended by His Word. Come to Me, My children. Cleanse your hearts and minds. Seek Me with your whole heart and you shall find Me. I am that I am, and I am your heart's desire.

---

[20] Num. 12:6; Deut. 29:29; 2 Kings 17:13; 1 Chron. 16:7–36; 2 Chron. 20:20; Jer. 23:22; Ezek. 13; Dan. 5:2, 18; Hos. 6:6, 12:10; Prov. 29:18; Matt. 5:18; Rom. 12:6; 1 Cor. 12:10, 13:2, 14:1; 2 Peter 1:19–21; Eph. 5:3; 1 Tim. 4:14; Rev. 1:3, 22:10, 18–19.
[21] Amos 3:7–8; Gen. 18:17:33; Num. 9:20; Luke 12:12; John 14:26, 15:15; Acts 21:10–14; 1 Cor. 2:13; 1 John 2:27.
[22] 2 Peter 3:16; Matt. 22:29; 2 Cor. 2:17, 4:2; Heb. 5:11–14.
[23] Gen. 41:16–32; Isa. 42:8–9, 46:9–10; Dan. 2:31–45, 9:20–27; Ezek. 38; Joel 3:1–2; Zech. 12:10, 14, 16; Matt. 24; Mark 13; Luke 21; Rom. 8:29; Acts 3:18; Rev. 1–22.
[24] John 13:19, 15:26, 16:33; Isa. 42:9, 48:3–8; Acts 17:2–3, 18:28.
[25] Gen. 18:26; Deut. 28:1–6; Josh. 24:19–24; 1 Kings 9:1–9; 1 Chron. 28:8; Ps. 66:18–19; Isa. 1:19–20; Jer. 29:13; Zech. 6:15; John 15:7; Acts 2:38–39; Rom. 10:9–10; 2 Tim. 2:21:23.

Biblical Insights on Understanding God's Messages

To correctly understand biblical prophecy requires that we value our Creator in all His majesty and splendor. We ascribe to Him all knowledge, power, holiness, wisdom, truth, and glory. He alone is sovereign,. He alone has the power to give life, and has the words of life. By His words, He created the heavens, earth, and all therein even mankind.

God's words are the spirit of prophecy. His words are truth. His words speak justice and mercy. His words carry power, even the power to create. Think of the often-repeated phrase in Genesis 1: "And God said ..." Think of John 1:1–14.

> In the beginning was the Word, and the Word was with God, and the Word was God. He was in the beginning with God. All things were made through Him, and without Him nothing was made that was made. In Him was life, and the life was the light of men ... And the Word became flesh and dwelt among us, and we beheld His glory, the glory as of the only begotten of the Father, full of grace and truth.

From the beginning, God has been speaking to us in multiple ways. He has manifested Himself to us in His creation.[26] He has revealed Himself by His covenants with Abraham, Abraham's descendants, and even those Gentiles who believe.[27] The written words of God have been maintained and testify to the existence, nature, and works of the Godhead throughout history giving evidence to their power to work good in the hearts of those who hear.[28]

Ultimately, God sent His manifest presence, His Son, to seal the redemption of mankind. Thus in the ministry and testimony of Jesus Christ, God has spoken to us of His great love.[29] In John 5:39, Jesus said,

---

[26] Ps. 19:1–6. 97:6; Acts 14:15–17; Rom. 1:20.
[27] Gen. 12:2–3. 28:14; Acts 3:25–26; Gal. 3:6–9.
[28] Ex. 31:18; Deut. 6:4–12; Ps. 119; Isa. 40:8; Jer. 15:16, 36:8; Ezek. 37:7; Luke 4:16–22; John 20:31; Rom. 15:4; 1 Cor. 10:11; Eph. 6:17; 1 Peter 1:25; 2 Peter 1:21; 2 Tim. 3:16; 1 John 5:13.
[29] 1 Tim. 3:14–16.

"You search the Scriptures, for in them you think you have eternal life; and these are they which testify of Me."[30]

So what is our responsibility? What is our part in discerning and understanding what God would say to us? Do we believe just anything and everything? Do we accept just any interpretation or opinion? Surely not! Even the scriptures themselves give warnings about foolishly following teachings or people.[31] In 2 Timothy 3:16, we read, "All Scripture is given by inspiration of God, and is profitable for doctrine, for reproof, for correction, for instruction in righteousness, that the man of God may be complete, thoroughly equipped for every good work." The folks at Berea responded with wisdom when they heard the gospel preached by Paul and Silas: "They received the word with all readiness, and searched the Scriptures daily to find out whether these things were so" (Acts 17:11).

How do we evaluate what we think God might be saying to us? Does it agree with God's nature? Is it in harmony with scripture? Consider the narrative—"Repent, and Cleanse Your Hearts." Did you find it unusual to see footnotes throughout that word? Each of those footnotes indicates a scripture verse or verses that echoes the content.

Can you hear echoes of scripture in the word you are examining? Every such word should be in agreement with scriptural principles in God's Word. The Bible is our compass pointing us to the one true God. Any such word that points in a different direction than biblical true north can cause us to miss the mark.

It is difficult to recognize whether such a word or even an essay or someone's opinion is in agreement with the Bible if we have never read and studied the Bible. The more we become familiar with the genuine, the easier it is to discern between a good and a bad compass—between truth and error.

---

[30] Even the prophetic Revelation testifies of Jesus: Rev. 1:1, 19:10.
[31] Deut. 11:16, 30, 13:1–5; Ps. 43:1; Isa. 5:20–24; Prov. 12:15; Jer. 9:6, 14:16, 23:16–17, 29:8–9; Ezek. 13:1–23; Matt. 13:38, 24:11; Mark 4:18–19; 1 Cor. 3:18, 6:9–10, 15:33; 2 Cor. 3:1, 4:4, 11:3; Gal. 5:9; Eph. 5:6, 6:12; Col. 2:8; 1 Peter 5:8; 2 Peter 2–3; James 4:7; 2 Thess. 2:1–17; 1 John 2:18.

83. Awaken and Arise

Awaken and arise, My church, to the call of this hour. Grow in obedient faith, hope, and love. Your generation has lost obedient faith, hope, and love. It is your calling to live and walk in the now flow of My Holy Spirit and reveal the glory of God to this generation. Arise and awaken, My church. Learn to know My voice and obey. Meditate upon and study My Word that you may know Me. We have much work to do together in this hour before I return.

Arise, My bride, and look to Me for your redemption draws nigh. Do not look on the turbulent waves and shaking ground that is covering the earth with deep darkness. I say to you, look beyond the darkness and see My light and see the path I shall make for you. I have plans for you, and they are good. I have plans for you, and they are to be a bright and shining light to dispel the darkness.

Look up, My beloved. Look up with faith in your heart. Ask Me to reveal to you My plans for you. Watch, listen, and obey. Know My Word. Humble yourselves. Purify your hearts. Walk before Me with a clear conscience.

I have tasks and callings for each of you to reclaim the ground the enemy has stolen. Pay attention. For some of you must reclaim ground the enemy has stolen in your life. You have believed the devil's lies and have suffered. Pay attention to Me. Follow My truth, walk out My directions to you, and I will walk with you as you reclaim the ground of your inheritance in Christ.

Look up, My bride. For some of you, I have tasks and specific assignments to move you forward in your workplace and in your communities—move forward among your people to carry My light. Pay attention to Me. Listen for My Holy Spirit to direct and instruct you. Wait for Me and do not lag behind. Watch for My love to draw your heart to your assignment.

Minister in the calling where you are now. Mothers and fathers to your children. Brothers and sisters to one another. Who is your neighbor? Pay attention as My love directs you to reach out and give a cup of cold water in My name.

Arise, My bride, for in you I will be a bright light shining in the darkness. Look up, My beloved, and see the joyful victory I have prepared for you. Rejoice with comfort and joy!

Biblical Insights from Isaiah 60:1–3

Isa. 60:1–3 (Voice) gives a poetic summary.

> Arise, shine, for your light has broken through! The Eternal One's brilliance has dawned upon you. See truly; look carefully—darkness blankets the earth; people all over are cloaked in darkness. But God will rise and shine on you; The Eternal's bright glory will shine on you, a light for all to see. Nations north and south, peoples east and west will be drawn to your light, will find purpose and direction by your light, In the radiance of your rising, you will enlighten the leaders of nations.

84. I Delight in Communing with You

I am calling you to Myself, into the very presence of love. Your songs, the cries of your heart, have touched My heart.

Come to Me, My child, with clean hands and a pure heart and you will be free to hear My Holy Spirit speak to you. For it is to the humble and contrite heart that I reveal Myself. I resist the proud and arrogant heart. But to the meek and teachable—I delight to commune with you.

Seek Me and you shall find Me. Listen. Shut out other voices. Read My Word and you will learn to recognize My voice. Slow down and spend time with Me.

Many rewards and treasures in My kingdom go unopened because My people do not listen to Me. They run to and fro, exhausted and depleted of My strength and power to overcome the world and the enemy of their souls.

Awaken, My people. Awaken to who you are and what you are designed and created to be. You are designed and created to commune with your God. You are designed and created to love and worship Him. For it is in Me that you receive light. It is in Me that you receive truth, and in Me you receive strength to exist and reflect My glory. It is in Me that your joy is complete.

I long for you to come to Me—to quiet your heart and wait in My presence. Rest yourself in My presence. Soak your spirit, and heart in My Word. In My presence, life and power will fill you.

These are days—these are times and seasons you need Me. You need My Spirit within you to empower you to live as an overcomer. In these perilous times, you need the wisdom and discernment My Holy Spirit gives to you when and as you commune with Me. There is no other way to be prepared. In communion with Me, you receive the anointing, wisdom, and discernment required to avoid the deceptions and walk in My grace and protection.

All peoples shall be tested by the things coming upon the earth in these end times. My Spirit is calling to My bride, "Make yourself ready, for your Bridegroom is soon coming to take you home." Learn to know His voice now so when He calls, you will hear Him.

Selected Scripture Reading

1. Hos. 6:6 (Voice)—"For I want not animal sacrifices, but mercy. I don't want burnt offerings; I want people to know Me as God!" See Jer. 32:41; James 2:23.
2. Phil. 1:9–11—"And this I pray, that your love may abound still more and more in knowledge and all discernment ... being filled with the fruits of righteousness."

85. The Sounds of Worship

Open your heart to Me, for it is to your heart that I speak. It is to your heart that I come and give My peace.

When you open your heart completely to Me, our hearts touch and you hear the voice of the Good Shepherd, who loves you and cares for you throughout your journey on this earth. You heart—I created your heart to give and receive love. My holy love. My pure love. Let your heart be moved by My love.

Open your heart, My child, and love Me so that My love will fill your heart with great joy. I will empower you with My love. I am restoring My church. She is awaking. She is arising. The sounds of worship are reaching to the heavens.

Selected Scripture Reading

1. 1 Sam. 16:7b (Voice)—"For the Eternal One does not pay attention to what humans value. Humans only care about the external appearance, but the Eternal considers the inner character." See 1 Chron. 28:9.
2. Ps. 139:23–24 (Voice)—"Explore me, O God, and know the real me. Dig deeply and discover who I am. Put me to the test and watch how I handle the strain. Examine me to see if there is an evil bone in me, and guide me down Your path forever."
3. Ps. 117:2; Jer. 31:3; Rom. 5:8—These verses reflect the frequent and consistent themes throughout the Bible of God's mercy and unfailing love in the midst of refining trials.
4. Ezek. 36:26–27 (Voice)—"I will plant a new heart and a new spirit inside of you. I will take out your stubborn, stony heart and give you a willing, tender heart of flesh. And I will put My Spirit inside of you and inspire you to live by My statutes and follow My laws." See 1 Cor. 13; 1 Peter 1:22.
5. Ps. 31:23—Do you think this verse gives insight about how pride affects our ability to love? Compare with Ps. 10:2; Prov. 28:25; 1 John 2.
6. Eph. 2:4–7—What four character qualities does God have that motivate and empower us to experience life-changing events? Can you identify additional attributes of God from other scriptures?
7. Hab. 2:1–2 (Voice)—"I will take my place at the watchtower. I will stand at my post and watch. I will watch and see what He says to me. I need to think about how I should respond to Him When He gets back to me with His answer."
8. Heb. 3:12–13—What do these verses warn against?
9. Heb. 4:7b—"Today, if you will hear His voice, Do not harden your hearts."

86. Remain under My Wings

I am calling you. I am calling My church to holiness. It is through the holiness of My Son, Jesus Christ, that you receive salvation and deliverance.

Walk, My child, in My holiness that you receive all you have need of through My Son Jesus. Does not My Word say to you, "Be Holy for I am Holy"? Does not My Word say to you, "I desire holiness in the inward parts?" Man looks on the outward appearances but I, your Creator God look upon—I look upon your heart.

Know that in My holiness—when you walk in My holiness—you remain under My wings. My grace and protection cover you. Come to Me, My beloved and let My love be perfected in you. Let me cover you.

Selected Scripture Reading

1. Lev. 10:3—"And Moses said to Aaron, 'This is what the LORD spoke to me saying, "By those who come near Me I must be regarded as holy."'"
2. Isa. 6:3—"And one cried to another and said: 'Holy, holy, holy is the LORD of hosts; The whole earth is full of His glory!'"
3. Luke 1:68–74—"Blessed is the Lord God of Israel, For He has visited and redeemed His people And has raised up a horn of salvation for us In the house of His servant David, As He spoke by the mouth of His holy prophets, Who have been since the world began, That we should be saved from our enemies And from the hand of all who hate us, To perform the mercy promised to our fathers And to remember His holy covenant The oath which He swore to our father Abraham: To grant us that we, being delivered from the hand of our enemies Might serve Him without fear, In holiness and righteousness before Him all the days of our life."
4. Jer. 17:10 (Voice)—"It is I, the Eternal One, who probes the innermost heart and examines the innermost thoughts. I will compensate each person justly according to his ways and by which his actions deserve."
5. Ps. 51:10–13—"Create in me a clean heart, O God, And renew a steadfast spirit within me. Do not cast me away from Your presence, And do not take Your Holy Spirit from me, Restore to me the joy of Your salvation, And uphold me by Your generous Spirit. Then I will teach transgressors Your Ways, And sinners shall be converted to You."
6. 1 Peter 1:13–19—"Therefore gird up the loins of your mind, be sober, and rest your hope fully upon the grace that is to be brought to you at the revelation of Jesus Christ, as obedient children, not conforming

yourselves to the former lusts as in your ignorance; but as He who called you is holy, you also be holy in all your conduct, because it is written, 'Be holy, for I am holy.' And if you call on the Father who without partiality judges according to each one's work, conduct yourselves throughout the time of your stay here in fear; knowing that you were not redeemed with corruptible things like silver or gold, from your aimless conduct received by tradition from your fathers, but with the precious blood of Christ, as of a lamb without blemish and without spot."

7. 2 Tim. 1:8–9 (ESV)—"Therefore do not be ashamed of the testimony about our Lord, nor of me his prisoner, but share in suffering for the gospel by the power of God, who saved us and called us to a holy calling, not because of our works but because of his own purpose and grace, which he gave us in Christ Jesus before the ages began."

87. Look Ahead

Now is the time to pay attention, My child. Now is the time to wait patiently to hear My voice to you.

Come apart—come away to the quiet and secret place and be with Me. Rest in Me. I will reveal Myself as your protector and provider. You will be amazed at what I share with you.

The time is coming, and now is when you need My Word. You need My wisdom and you need My revelation to make it through what lies ahead. For many of you, up to this point, you have not really needed Me or taken your walk with Me seriously.

Look ahead. Look up. My church is awaking and preparing herself. She is recognizing the hour and searching for the white garments of purity and holiness. She is searching to know the Father's heart and she is listening for the voice of the Good Shepherd.

I am calling. I am calling you to be among the people who know their God. Come. Come. Come and be with Me.

Biblical Insights from Psalm 119:33–40 (Voice)

> O Eternal One, show me how to live according to
> Your statutes, and I will keep them always. Grant me

understanding so that I can keep Your law and keep it wholeheartedly. Guide me to walk in the way You commanded because I take joy in it. Turn my head and my heart to Your decrees and not to sinful gain. Keep my eyes from gazing upon worthless things, and give me true life according to Your plans. Verify Your word to Your servant, which will lead me to worship You. Take away the scorn that I dread because Your actions are just and good. Look and see—I long for Your guidance; restore me in Your righteousness.

88. I Am with You to Lead You

My child, do not be alarmed. Things around you in this world are about to change dramatically. There will be upheaval and chaos, but do not be alarmed.

Remember, I have already told you these things in My Word. I am with you, and I do not change. I take care of those under My protection. I take care of those under the shadow of My wings.

Only be diligent to stay with Me and not wander off. I will care for you, but you must listen and follow in obedience. Noah listened and obeyed, and he and his household were protected even in the midst of great and dangerous waters. As Noah is a testimony to My love, My grace, and My provision—even in the midst of difficult times—so also shall My bride reflect My glory even now. Seek Me, My beloved.

I am here. I am with you to lead you and protect you. You will overcome.

Selected Scripture Reading

1. Isa. 41:10—"Fear not, for I am with you; Be not dismayed, for I am your God. I will strengthen you, Yes, I will help you, I will uphold you with My righteous right hand." See Gen. 6:9–22; Heb. 11:7.
2. Deut. 31:6—"Be strong and of good courage, do not fear nor be afraid of them; for the LORD your God, He is the One who goes with you. He will not leave you nor forsake you."

3. Prov. 10:17 (NIV)—"Whoever heeds discipline shows the way to life, but whoever ignores correction leads others astray."
4. Prov. 20:1 (NLT)—"Wine produces mockers; alcohol leads to brawls. Those led astray by drink cannot be wise."
5. Rom. 13:11–14—"And do this, knowing the time, that now it is high time to awake out of sleep; for now our salvation is nearer than when we first believed. The night is far spent, the day is at hand. Therefore let us cast off the works of darkness, and let us put on the armor of light. Let us walk properly, as in the day, not in revelry and drunkenness, not in lewdness and lust, not in strife and envy. But put on the Lord Jesus Christ, and make no provision for the flesh, to fulfill its lusts."
6. Luke 21:34–36—"But take heed to yourselves, lest your hearts be weighed down with carousing, drunkenness, and cares of this life, and that Day come on you unexpectedly. For it will come as a snare on all those who dwell on the face of the whole earth. Watch, therefore, and pray always that you may be counted worthy to escape all these things that will come to pass, and to stand before the Son of Man."

7. Rev. 3:10–11—"Because you have kept My command to persevere, I also will keep you from the hour of trial which shall come upon

the whole world, to test those who dwell on the earth. Behold, I am coming quickly! Hold fast what you have, that no one may take your crown." See Zeph. 2:3.

89. I Give You This Warning and This Charge

By My Spirit, I give you this warning and this charge. There are those who are working to create civil unrest and chaos that there should be reason to order martial law and further restrict your liberty and freedoms.

But I say to you, though you walk through the valley of the shadow of death, fear no evil, for greater is He who is in you than he who is in the world. Keep My words in your heart and you shall sustain liberty, peace, and strength.

If My people who are called by My name will reflect My glory across this land, your land and people will be blessed. Only know this—there is much pollution and sin in your nation; your nation is very sick. The land is vomiting filth.

Repent for yourselves and repent for your nation. Turn from your wickedness and evil ways. The sin of this nation is a stench in My nostrils; all forms of idolatry and adultery are paraded and accepted. I teach you My principles and commands of faithfulness and love but you reject Me and walk away to follow lustful desires.

This nation must choose whom you will serve. I call to you, My people, and warn you. Cry out for mercy for your land. Humble yourselves in repentance that bears fruit of turning to Me and away from sin. Pray for your leaders and judges to have holy fear and respect for almighty God. Pray for your police force and military to walk in the anointing of God and carry My peace with them.

Yes, there are those who would destroy you, and you have an enemy who seeks to devour both soul and body. Nevertheless, My bride, know I have given you spiritual weapons of warfare.

In holiness, righteousness, and purity, look again at the spiritual weapons I have given you. Study them. Know My heart. Know My character and you will understand the spiritual weapons I have given you.

I have prepared a table before you in the presence of your enemies. I have set provisions before you to strengthen and prepare you for the battle.

Arise, My bride, and overcome evil with good. Overcome hate with love. You are My bride. Receive My anointing and blessing to go forth and reveal the glory of the kingdom of God.

Selected Scripture Reading

1. Josh. 24:15—"Choose for yourselves this day whom you will serve."

90. When My Righteous Ones Cry Out to Me

Be alert and be aware, My child; an attack of deception is being planned on your country. Those plotting this deception and distraction attack are doing so to hide their evil manipulations. Pray against these greedy attempts to control and steal economies.

I am the Lord your God, and if My people will cry out to Me as I direct you to, I will hear you and answer. I will expose and destroy wickedness when My righteous ones cry out to Me. I long for you, My people, to walk in the inheritance I have given you, not shunning the gifts and callings I have assigned you that your destiny and joy be fulfilled.

Come to Me, My beloved. Learn to know My voice and My ways that you may do My bidding.

Selected Scripture Reading

1. Isa. 14:12—"How are you fallen from heaven, O Lucifer, son of the morning! How you are cut down to the ground, you **who weakened the nations!**" (emphasis mine) See Luke 10:18; Rev. 12:7–9.
2. Isa. 24:4–6 (Voice)—"So the earth mourns ... the world languishes and droops ... The earth is polluted by those who live on it; they pay no attention to God's teaching. They violate His directives and break the everlasting covenant. Consequently, a nasty curse consumes the earth, and those who inhabit it are to blame for it."
3. 1 Sam. 12:10—"Then they cried out to the LORD, and said, 'We have sinned, because we have forsaken the LORD and served the Baals and Ashtoreths; but now deliver us from the hand of our enemies, and we will serve You.'" See 2 Chron. 7:14.

4. Isa. 61:11—"For as the earth brings forth its bud, as the garden causes the things that are sown in it to spring forth, so the Lord GOD will cause righteousness and praise to spring forth before all nations."
5. Ps. 86:5—"For You, Lord, are good, and ready to forgive, and abundant in mercy to all those who call upon You." See Acts 5:31; Eph. 1:7; 1 John 1:9.
6. Eph. 6:10–18—"Finally, my brethren, be strong in the Lord and in the power of His might. Put on the whole armor of God that you may be able to stand against the wiles of the devil. For we do not wrestle against flesh and blood, but against principalities, against powers, against the rulers of the darkness of this age, against spiritual hosts of wickedness in the heavenly places. Therefore take up the whole armor of God, that you may be able to withstand in the evil day … Stand therefore, having girded your waist with truth, having put on the breastplate of righteousness, and having shod your feet with the preparation of the gospel of peace, above all, taking the shield of faith with which you will be able to quench all the fiery darts of the wicked one. And take the helmet of salvation and the sword of the Spirit, which is the word of God; praying always with all prayer and supplication in the Spirit, being watchful to this end with all perseverance and supplication for all the saints."

91. Consecrate Your Heart and Receive from Me

My children, I have gifted you and given you talents to use for My kingdom. To each one, individually, I have called you to live the life of Christ, seeking and knowing the heart of the Father.

Love the Lord your God with all your heart and you will know Me. Know Me—connect your heart to My heart and you will see the gifts and talents I have for you. The time is now for My glory to be revealed among and through My people so the world may know I am.

My glory shall be revealed in the earth, the heavens, and My people.

Learn diligently. Learn wisely. Consecrate your heart. I desire My people to be fully prepared and equipped to manifest the callings and gifts so My presence and glory will be manifested to the lost.

Consecrate—consecrate your heart and receive from Me all you are created to be. It is time for My glory to be revealed.

Selected Scripture Reading

1. Deut. 14:2—"For you are a holy people to the LORD your God, and the LORD has chosen you to be a people for Himself, a special treasure above all the peoples who are on the face of the earth." See Gal. 3:6–14.
2. John 1:12—"But as many as received Him, to them He gave the right to become children of God, to those who believe in His name: who were born, not of blood, nor of the will of the flesh, nor of the will of man, but of God."
3. Gal. 3:26–28—"For you are all sons of God through faith in Christ Jesus. For as many of you as were baptized unto Christ have put on Christ. There is neither Jew nor Greek, there is neither slave nor free, there is neither male nor female; for you are all one in Christ Jesus."
4. Ps. 140:13—"Surely the righteous shall give thanks to Your name; The upright shall dwell in Your presence." See Matt. 25:14–30; Rom. 8:19.
5. James 1:16–25—"Do not be deceived, my beloved brethren. Every good gift and every perfect gift is from above, and comes down from the Father of lights, with whom there is no variation nor shadow of turning. Of His own will He brought us forth by the word of truth, that we might be a kind of firstfruits of His creatures. So then ... let every man be swift to hear, slow to speak, slow to wrath; for the wrath of man does not produce the righteousness of God. Therefore, lay aside all filthiness and overflow of wickedness, and receive with meekness the implanted word, which is able to save your souls. But be doers of the word and not hearers only; deceiving yourselves ... But he who looks into the perfect law of liberty and continues in it, and is not a forgetful hearer, but a doer of the work, this one will be blessed in what he does." See 1 Peter 4:7–11.

92. Will You Be Found Faithful?

The shaking is imminent. Prepare yourself and your household for you know not the moment when you can no longer make preparations. Know this. I am with you in the midst of all storms. I am with you in the midst of all difficulties. My arm is not too short to deliver you. Cry out to Me in your distress and I will hear your cry and deliver you. Make your requests known to Me and I will hear you.

Call to Me now that your land be spared great tragedy for I would have mercy upon you. I remember the covenant the forefathers of this land have with Me. But the present inhabitants must repent and renew their commitment to Me and to My chosen Israel.

Know, I am returning soon with the winnowing fork in My hand. When the Son of Man returns, will He find faith on earth? Will you be found faithful?

I am calling throughout the earth to all mankind. Alert. Alert. Warnings are going forth. Prepare your hearts and seek My face. Embrace the Lord with all your heart and you will be saved. My love is sufficient to meet your every need. I will receive you into glory.

Do not procrastinate. Do not put off seeking Me.

Selected Scripture Reading

1. Matt. 25:13—"Watch therefore, for you know neither the day nor the hour in which the Son of Man is coming." See Matt. 24:3–51; Luke 21:36.
2. Isa. 2:12–17—"For the day of the LORD of hosts shall come upon everything proud and lofty, upon everything lifted up—and it shall be brought low ... Upon every high tower, and upon every fortified wall ... The loftiness of man shall be bowed down ... The LORD alone will be exalted in that day, But the idols He shall utterly abolish."
3. Joel 3:14–17—"Multitudes, multitudes in the valley of decision! For the day of the LORD is near in the valley of decision. The sun and moon will grow dark, and the stars will diminish their brightness. The LORD also will roar from Zion, and utter His voice from Jerusalem; the heavens and earth will shake; But the LORD will be a shelter for His people, and the strength of the children of Israel." See Ps. 50:15; Acts 20:21.
4. Joel 2:12–14—"Now therefore, says the LORD, turn to Me with all your heart, with fasting, with weeping, and with mourning ... Return to the LORD your God, for He is gracious and merciful, slow to

anger and of great kindness, and He relents from doing harm." See Matt. 3:2, 8; Luke 24:47; 2 Cor. 7:10; 2 Peter 3:9.
5. Acts 10:42—"And He [Jesus] commanded us to preach to the people, and to testify that it is He who was ordained by God to be Judge of the living and the dead. To Him all the prophets witness that, through His name, whoever believes in Him will receive remission of sins." See Hos. 14:2.
6. Heb. 10:23—"Let us hold fast the confession of our hope without wavering, for He who promised is faithful." See Heb. 10:36–39; 1 Cor. 4:2.

93. Know That I Am with You

Hear Me, My child. In one hour—in a short time span—the world as you have known it will change. The things the nations have trusted will come tumbling down for I am a righteous God and I will expose and bring to ruin the false gods My people over the earth have sought out and committed adultery with.

Hear Me and seek Me now that your heart and mind will be at peace during this time of immense shaking. I am uprooting the trees that have born no fruit. Come to Me now and learn of Me. I am meek and lowly in Spirit. I am kind and compassionate toward all mankind. I desire all men be saved. Know that I am with you, and not against you.

Follow Me and I will protect you as the things around you come crashing down. Listen to My Spirit and follow Me. Your joy will be great, and you will be fruitful in My kingdom. I will greet you with "Well done, good and faithful servant. Enter your reward."

Selected Scripture Reading

1. Ps. 9:1–20—"I will praise You, O LORD, with my whole heart; I will tell of all Your marvelous works ... For You have maintained my right and my cause; You sat on the throne judging in righteousness. You have rebuked the nations, You have destroyed the wicked ... But the LORD shall endure forever ... He shall judge the world in righteousness ... The LORD also will be a refuge for the oppressed,

a refuge in times of trouble. And those who know Your name will put their trust in You; For You, LORD, have not forsaken those who seek You ... The nations have sunk down in the pit which they made ... Arise, O LORD ... Let the nations be judged in Your sight ... That the nations may know themselves to be but mere men."
2. Ps. 33:12—"Blessed is the nation whose God is the LORD, The people He has chosen as His own inheritance." See Ps. 28:9, 81.
3. 1 Cor. 10:1–22—"And do not become idolaters as were some of them. As it is written, 'The people sat down to eat and drink, and rose up to play.' Nor let us commit sexual immorality as some of them did ... Therefore, my beloved, flee from idolatry."
4. Rev. 18:17–19—Rev. 18 describes the fall of Babylon and typifies the destruction of the Antichrist, satanically driven world system. Twice in these verses the destruction is mentioned as taking place "in one hour," which means "suddenly."
5. Deut. 4:19—God says He made the sun, moon, and stars; don't worship them.
6. Eph. 5:1–7—"And walk in love, as Christ also has loved us and given Himself for us ... But fornication, and all uncleanness or covetousness, let it not even be named among you, as is fitting for saints; neither filthiness, nor foolish talking, nor coarse jesting ... but rather giving of thanks. For this you know, that no fornicator, unclean person, nor covetous man, who is an idolater has any inheritance in the kingdom of Christ and God. Let no one deceive you with empty words, for because of these things the wrath of God comes upon the sons of disobedience. Therefore, do not be partakers with them."

94. Be Wise and Gracious

Come into My presence with thanksgiving and into My courts with praise. Walk before Me in holiness and you will stand and not fall in these days of trials, tests, and tribulations.

For I will be your Good Shepherd. I will lead and protect My sheep. I will care for you and carry you. Do not fear the future, My beloved, for your future is with Me.

Trust Me and walk in obedience. Know Me, and My love will give you My power and strength to overcome. These are times of stretching and training for My people. Be wise and gracious, My beloved, that your beauty be revealed to the world. I will be glorified through you.

Come into My presence, My beloved. Come.

Selected Scripture Reading

1. 1 Chron. 16:29 (NLT)—"Give to the LORD the glory He deserves! Bring your offering and come into His presence. Worship the LORD in all His holy splendor."
2. Ps. 100:1–5—"Make a joyful shout to the LORD, all you lands! Serve the LORD with gladness; Come before His presence with singing. Know that the LORD, He is God; It is He who has made us, and not we ourselves; We are His people and the sheep of His pasture. Enter into His gates with thanksgiving, And into His courts with praise. Be thankful to Him, and bless His name. For the LORD is good; His mercy is everlasting, And His truth endures to all generations."
3. Isa. 40:10–11—"Behold, the Lord GOD shall come with a strong hand, And His arm shall rule for Him; Behold, His reward is with Him, And His work before Him. He will feed His flock like a shepherd; He will gather the lambs with His arm, And carry them in His bosom, And gently lead those who are with young."
4. Ps. 79:11—"So we, Your people and sheep of Your pasture, Will give You thanks forever; We will show forth Your praise to all generations."
5. John 10:14–16—"I am the good shepherd; and I know My sheep, and am known by My own. As the Father knows Me, even so I know the Father; and I lay down My life for the sheep. And other sheep I have which are not of this fold; them also I must bring, and they will hear My voice; and there will be one flock and one shepherd."
6. Eph. 2:11–15—"Therefore remember that you, once Gentiles in the flesh ... that at that time you were without Christ ... having no hope and without God in the world. But now in Christ Jesus you who once were far off have been brought near by the blood of Christ. For He Himself is our peace, who has made both one, and has broken down the middle wall of separation, having abolished in His flesh the enmity, that is the law of commandments contained in ordinances, so as to create in Himself one new man from the two, thus making peace."

7. Jude 24–25—"Now to Him who is able to keep you from stumbling And to present you faultless Before the presence of His glory with exceeding joy … To God our Savior Who alone is wise, Be glory and majesty, Dominion and power, Both now and forever. Amen.

95. My Gift to You

Wealth, riches, and pleasures have caused My people to be stubborn and stiff-necked. They no longer look to Me for honor, approval, and blessings but consider themselves the source of their own strength and blessings.

They have wandered far from Me while they continue to give lip service to Me. Yet they do not have reverence; they do not fear or obey My command to love the Lord their God with all their heart, strength, and mind and give Him honor in all they do.

You are My children, and as a good father disciplines His sons and daughters, so must I discipline you. No discipline is pleasant in the moment, but discipline yields the fruit of repentance and the reward of liberty from the bonds of sin.

How I desire, My people, that you would simply hear My words and repent, and turn from your wicked ways—turn from your worship of false idols and ungodly ways. Oh that you would hear and obey.

Those who do hear and obey—those who heed My call to holiness—shall be spared much grief and confusion because they shall see and understand. They shall hear and obey.

Those who see and hear shall walk and not faint. They shall run and not be weary. They shall mount up with wings as eagles. Those with understanding shall come up higher. They shall stand and not fall in the day of trouble.

Hear Me, My people. Seek Me now while times are comfortable. Come into My presence and lay aside your fleshly pursuits. Seek the kingdom of God and My righteousness so you may live in My peace and blessings. This is my gift to you. Obey and receive your reward now and in eternity.

Selected Scripture Reading

1. Ps. 90:12 (NLT)—"Teach us to realize the brevity of life, so that we may grow in wisdom." See Matt. 6:33.
2. Prov. 3:21–26 (NLT)—"My child, don't lose sight of common sense and discernment. Hang on to them, For they will refresh your soul. They are like jewels on a necklace. They keep you safe on your way, and your feet will not stumble. You can go to bed without fear; you will lie down and sleep soundly. You need not be afraid of sudden disaster or the destruction that comes upon the wicked, For the LORD is your security. He will keep your foot from being caught in a trap."
3. Deut. 8:11–14 (Voice)—"But then be very careful! Don't forget the Eternal your God and disobey the commands and decrees and rules I'm giving you today. When your stomachs are full, when you've built comfortable houses to live in, When you have large herds and flocks, when you possess plenty of silver and gold, and when you have more things than you imagined possible; Then don't become proud and puffed up and forget Him." See Rev. 3:18.

96. A Holy Nation Set Apart, Consecrated

My people, come before Me seeking My truth and My ways and you will not walk away disappointed. Seek Me faithfully and you will walk in My grace. You will walk in My strength and in the power of My Spirit. Those who worship Me in Spirit and in truth receive My joy for they walk in My freedom.

Will you not come to Me? Will you not rest in My truth and My ways? I call to you, My people. Separate yourselves from the world and the deceitfulness of sin. My heart longs for My people to walk in the fullness of the inheritance given you by My Son's sacrifice.

My beloved, you must become a holy nation set apart and consecrated unto Me. The bride shall make herself ready. She shall endure for there is great joy and anticipation in her heart.

We shall rejoice together. Lift up your hearts to Me that I may lift you up into My kingdom.

Selected Scripture Reading

1. Deut. 7:9—"Therefore know that the LORD your God, He is God, the faithful God who keeps covenant and mercy for a thousand generations with those who love Him and keep His commandments."
2. Ps. 89:1—"I will sing of the mercies of the LORD forever, With my mouth will I make known Your faithfulness to all generations."
3. Ps. 34:22—"The LORD redeems the soul of His servants, And none of those who trust in Him shall be condemned."
4. Ps. 16:11—"You will show me the path of life; In Your presence is fullness of joy; At Your right hand are pleasures forevermore." See 2 Cor. 6:16–18.
5. Matt. 6:33—"But seek first the Kingdom of God and His righteousness and all these things shall be added to you." See Ps. 31:19–24.
6. John 4:23–24—"But the hour is coming, and now is, when the true worshippers will worship the Father in spirit and truth; for the Father is seeking such to worship Him. God is Spirit, and those who worship Him must worship in spirit and truth." See Ps. 111:1.
7. John 8:31–32—"Then Jesus said to those Jews who believed in Him, 'If you abide in My word, you are My disciples indeed. And you shall know the truth, and the truth shall make you free.'"
8. James 4:10—"Humble yourselves in the sight of the Lord, and He will lift you up."
9. Ps. 25:1–3—"To You, O LORD, I lift up my soul. O My God, I trust in You; Let me not be ashamed; Let not my enemies triumph over me. Indeed no one who waits on You will be ashamed." See Ps. 119:48.
10. Mark 1:15—"The time is fulfilled, and the kingdom of God is at hand. Repent, and believe in the gospel."

97. Shall I Not Do a Great Work?

In these last days, shall I not do a great work? Shall I not restore the beauty and holiness of My people?

Shall I not call forth a mighty wave of My Spirit to sweep over the lands? Shall I not restore to My church that which the world and the enemy has stolen from her? Awaken and arise, My beloved, to your destiny, to your beauty, and calling.

The world is in great need of your testimony. Listen to My words and obey My commands and principles and your testimony to the world will be pleasing in My sight. Know this. You must seek Me with your whole heart and I will be found of you.

My Word must become precious in your heart. By My Word I created the heavens and earth. Honor My Word in your heart, in your speech, and in your life. Honor Me in Spirit and in truth and I will honor you with my presence and anointing.

Selected Scripture Reading

1. Isa. 60:1–3—"Arise, shine; For your light has come! And the glory of the LORD is risen upon you. For behold, the darkness shall cover the earth and deep darkness the people; But the LORD will arise over you and His glory will be seen upon you. The Gentiles shall come to your light, And kings to the brightness of your rising."
2. Mic. 4:1–3—"Now it shall come to pass in the latter days that the mountain of the LORD'S house Shall be established on the top of the mountains, And shall be exalted above the hills; And peoples shall flow to it. Many nations shall come and say, 'Come, and let us go up to the mountain of the LORD, To the house of the God of Jacob; He will teach us His ways, And we shall walk in His paths.'" See Pss. 80; Isa. 2:2.
3. Hos. 3:5—"Afterward the children of Israel shall return and seek the LORD their God and David their king. They shall fear the LORD and His goodness in the latter days."
4. Luke 17:20–21—"Now when He was asked by the Pharisees when the kingdom of God would come, He answer them and said, 'The kingdom of God does not come with observation; nor will they say, "See here!" or "See there!" For indeed, the kingdom of God is within you.'" See John 3:35–36.
5. Rom. 14:12–19—"So then each of us shall give account of himself to God. Therefore let us not judge one another anymore, but rather resolve this, not to put a stumbling block or a cause to fall in our

brother's way ... Therefore do not let your good be spoken of as evil; for the kingdom of God is not eating and drinking, but righteousness and peace and joy in the Holy Spirit. For he who serves Christ in these things is acceptable to God and approved by men ... let us pursue the things which make for peace and the things by which one may edify another." See Acts 3:19–21; Rev. 3:5.

98. Have Faith and Do Not Lose Hope

Dear body of Christ, I warned you of the threat of anarchy, civil chaos, and unrest in your country. I have reminded you of your spiritual weapons of warfare.

Speak to this mountain and tell it to fall into the sea for you will have the kingdom of God to be established and reign over your land. Righteousness, peace, and joy in the Holy Spirit shall prevail, shall endure. Speak this prayer aloud over your nation.

Have faith, and do not lose hope. What you loose on earth shall be loosed in heaven. What you bind on earth shall be bound in heaven. As you share My words in the power of My Holy Spirit, My anointing and power will burst forth. The gospel of salvation brings healing and restoration.

Use the spiritual weapons I have given to you and use them as I direct. Use them patiently and faithfully. And if you do not grow weary in well doing, if you remain in My Spirit in love for one another, and if you abide in Me, you will overcome in due season.

My strength will be there for you when you think you can go no further. Rest in Me. Spend time with Me in the secret place and be bountifully refreshed and rewarded.

I shall say to you and you will hear, "Come away with Me, My beloved. I am here to take you home."

Selected Scripture Reading

1. Jer. 32:33 (NLT)—"My people have turned their backs on Me and have refused to return. Even though I diligently taught them, they would not receive instruction or obey."

2. Amos 9:8 (ESV)—"Behold, the eyes of the LORD GOD are upon the sinful kingdom, and I will destroy it from the surface of the ground, except that I will not utterly destroy the house of Jacob, declares the LORD." See also Isa. 24:5; Ezek. 12:16, 14:12–23; Jer. 12:15; Amos 2:4; Pss. 9:5, 37; Isa. 34:1–2.
3. Matt. 16:19—"And I will give you the keys of the kingdom of heaven, and whatever you bind on earth will be bound in heaven, and whatever you loose on earth will be loosed in heaven."
4. Matt. 25:31–32 (NET)—"When the Son of Man comes in His glory and all the angels with Him, then He will sit on His glorious throne. All the nations will be assembled before Him, and He will separate people one from another like a shepherd separates the sheep from the goats." See Ps. 51:12–13; Acts 3:19–21; 1 John 5:4; Rev. 2:7, 5:9.
5. Isa. 26:1–4 (NIV)—"We have a strong city; God makes salvation its walls and ramparts. Open the gates that the righteous nation may enter, the nation that keeps faith. You will keep in perfect peace those whose minds are steadfast, because they trust in You. Trust in the LORD forever, for the LORD, the LORD Himself, is the Rock eternal."
6. Ps. 86:9–13—"All nations whom You have made Shall come and worship before You, O Lord ... Teach me Your way, O LORD; I will walk in Your truth."

99. Refreshed by My Spirit

You ask Me about boldness, My child. I tell you that you must first be rested and refreshed by My Spirit. My words are Spirit and life to you.

Come away with Me to the secret place that My words and Spirit empower and anoint you. Learn to know My voice. Learn to know the prompting of My Holy Spirit. Fill your heart, mind, and soul with My presence. Drink in the life and power I give to you as we meet together.

My dearly beloved and precious children, do you not know? Do you not realize that when you struggle to control, when you strive to manipulate and cause a certain path to be taken, you are pushing Me out?

When you do this, you are pushing Me out of the circumstances and hindering My purposes and plans to help you and bless you. Turn away from your fears and come to Me for healing and restoration for I desire to bless you and make you fruitful in the kingdom of God.

I give you grace, liberty, and the power of My Holy Spirit to move forward. I will reveal Myself to you as almighty God.

Hear Me carefully. Rest in Me. When you go among your people, My anointing and My Spirit will be upon you.

Biblical Insights on Spiritual Refreshing

Our bodies cannot live without food and water. Likewise, our spirits must have clean and pure spiritual refreshment. Our hearts must be refreshed to be emotionally and spiritually healthy. In scripture, this principle is described with metaphors such as "dry and thirsty," "famine," "water," "rain," and "showers of blessing." These metaphors reveal deep treasures of understanding, guidelines for obtaining spiritual refreshing. Like most Biblical truths and principles, you will not find them clumped together in one book or section of scriptures; they are sprinkled throughout the Bible and require studying to find them and comprehend their meanings.

Amos 8 is one place where the metaphors of drought and famine are used to describe spiritual destitution. Whom was Amos talking to? What was going on? When Amos gave his messages (ca. 760–750 BC), Israel and Judah had gained control of trade and shipping routes and were enjoying prosperity, political power, and military accomplishments. Wealth, power, and prestige were taken as a sign of God's blessing, but hidden below the images of success, God saw greed, violence, injustice, self-righteous religious hypocrisy, idolatry, and rebellion against His teachings.

What form would God's judgment against the people's backsliding initially take? Amos 8:11 answers that question: "'Behold the days are coming,' says the LORD God, 'That I will send a famine on the land, Not a famine of bread, Nor a thirst for water, But of hearing the words of the LORD.'" There is lots of "food" for thought in that verse.

Amos 8:11 compares hearing God's words to receiving physical bread and water; God was saying His words were critical to our spiritual existence. Listen to Moses as he sang about God's words: "Let my teaching fall on you like raindrops; let what I say collect like the dew,

Like rain sprinkling the grass, like showers on the green plants. I will proclaim the name of the Eternal" (Deut. 32:2–3 Voice).

Psalm 72 proclaims the name of the Eternal and tells of God's Son who would "come down like rain upon the grass before mowing, Like showers that water the earth" (Ps. 72:6). Hosea 6:1–3 is a call to repentance and the pursuit of knowledge of the Lord; it uses the metaphor of rain signifying refreshing: "He will come to us like the rain, Like the latter and former rain to the earth."

"Sow for yourselves righteousness; Reap in mercy; Break up your fallow ground, For it is time to seek the LORD, Till He comes and rains righteousness on you." This verse in Hosea 10:12 is part of a call to repentance with a promise of spiritual refreshing for obedience. Acts 3:19–21 says it quite succinctly and clearly.

> Repent therefore and be converted, that your sins may be blotted out, so that times of refreshing may come from the presence of the Lord, And that He may send Jesus Christ, who was preached to you before, Whom heaven must receive until the times of restoration of all things, which God has spoken by the mouth of all His holy prophets since the world began.

100. Lift Up the Name and Love of Jesus

My people, must commit to Me and remain committed to Me to overcome the challenges that lay before you. You must hear My voice, obey, pray, and do as I direct.

The enemy is deceitful, and you will not know how to fight this battle in the flesh. Likewise, you must stand together in the unity of My Spirit and in My love to negate his attacks. I have given you every weapon and every provision to assure victory.

I am with you in the battle. Lift up the name and love of Jesus Christ and demons must flee. My Son bought the victory for you to live. Rejoice. Commit to serve Me and you will persevere and receive the reward.

The day has come for the revealing of the saints of God. They are the little people who heretofore have not been known by others. But I know them because they have been faithful, gracious, and loving. They have honored Me by their obedience and faithfulness to My truth, and I will honor them with My anointing.

The world will know that I am because they are a reflection of My glory. Now is the time for My church, My bride, to be revealed.

Selected Scripture Reading

1. 2 Chron. 20:12 (NLT)—"O our God, won't you stop them? We are powerless against this mighty army that is about to attack us. We do not know what to do, but we are looking to You for help."
2. Ps. 31:19 (Voice)—"Your overflowing goodness You have kept for those who live in awe of You, And You share Your goodness with those who make You their sanctuary."
3. Prov. 16:7 (NIV)—"When the LORD takes pleasure in anyone's way, He causes their enemies to make peace with them."
4. Prov. 29:25 (Voice)—"If you fear other people, you are walking into a dangerous trap; but if you trust in the Eternal, you will be safe."
5. Isa. 26:3 (Voice)—"You will keep the peace, a perfect peace, for all who trust in You, for those who dedicate their hearts and minds to You."
6. 2 Cor. 3:5 (NCV)—"We are not saying that we can do this work ourselves. It is God who makes us able to do all that we do."
7. Luke 9:62—"But Jesus said to him, 'No one having put his hand to the plow, and looking back is fit for the kingdom of God.'"
8. John 8:27–29—"They did not understand that He spoke to them of the Father. Then Jesus said to them, 'When you lift up the Son of Man, then you will know that I am He, and that I do nothing of Myself; but as My Father taught Me, I speak these things. And He who sent Me is with Me. The Father has not left Me alone, for I always do those things that please Him.'"
9. Mal. 3:16–18—"Then those who feared the LORD spoke to one another, And the LORD listened and heard them … 'They shall be Mine,' says the LORD of hosts."

101. See What I Am Doing among You

My Spirit is here with you to lead and guide you through these turbulent times. I have told you of the wind. I have told you of the great storms over the seas and over the seas of mankind. I have spoken to you of the shaking of all that can be shaken so that those things that cannot be shaken shall remain.

Now again, I speak to you of the restoration of My bride, spotless, glorious, most beautiful, and gracious. Hear Me carefully, each one of you. My children must know My voice. You must obey Me individually—and also come together in obedience corporately.

Throughout the generations, I have given to My sheep, shepherds, tried and proven in the furnace of affliction.. They have given themselves and all they have to Me. In these days of restoration, I shall put My Spirit and My anointing on them to lead My sheep into good pastures and places of shelter.

Understand what I am doing among you and be not deceived by the spirit of this age. I am restoring My church. See. See what I am doing among you. Follow Me and the windows of heaven will be opened unto you.

Selected Scripture Reading

1. John 16:13—"However, when He, the Spirit of truth has come, He will guide you into all truth for He will not speak on His own authority, but whatever He hears He will speak; and He will tell you things to come." See Zech. 4:6; Ezek. 36:27; Joel 2:28.
2. John 14:26—"But the Helper, the Holy Spirit, whom the Father will send in My name, He will teach you all things, and bring to your remembrance all things that I said to you."
3. Rom. 8:14—"For as many as are led by the Spirit of God, these are sons of God."
4. John 17:17–26—"I do not pray for these alone, but also for those who will believe in Me through their word; that they all may be one, as You, Father, are in Me, and I in You; that they also may be one in Us, that the world may believe that You sent Me ... I in them, and You in Me; that they may be made perfect in one." See also Eph. 4:23–24.

5. Jer. 3:12–15—"'Return, backsliding Israel,' says the LORD ... 'only acknowledge your iniquity ... you have not obeyed My voice ... Return ... And I will give you shepherds according to My heart, who will feed you with knowledge and understanding.'"
6. Acts 20:17–38—"serving God with all humility, with many tears and trials ... how I kept back nothing that was helpful, but proclaimed it to you." See Eph. 4:1–32.

102. I Make Clean What Is Mine

Even now I am at work to pull up and destroy whatever among you is unclean and defiles My creation. I am a holy God. I purify and make clean what is Mine and dedicated to Me. I shall be a refiner's fire and a fuller's soap to cleanse and make ready My people so they shall walk in blessing and anointing.

I am raising up a mighty army among the youth of this nation—among the youth and children of this nation and around the world. They will have undivided loyalty and passion for Me because My Spirit will be strong upon and strong in them. I am making them a banner and a sign in the house of the Lord. They will see and understand what generations before them have not seen nor understood.

To all peoples and nations of the earth, I say, walk circumspectly and soberly before your God that you may see and understand what I am doing in the earth and among My people in this hour before My return. From the least to the greatest, from all nations, from the youngest to the oldest, I will have a people who know their God—a people who understand My ways and My heart.

You are called to be a people set apart unto your God, holy and undefiled, that you may reflect My glory and goodness. How I delight in My people. We shall rejoice and celebrate the great victory together. That day is coming when your fulfilled redemption will be complete. Be steadfast. Remain faithful and you will overcome.

Selected Scripture Reading

1. Isa. 1:21–26—"How the faithful city has become a harlot! It was full of justice; Righteousness lodged in it, But now murderers. Your silver has become dross, Your wine mixed with water. Your princes are rebellious, And companions of thieves; Everyone loves bribes, And follows after rewards. They do not defend the fatherless, Nor does the cause of the widow come before them. Therefore, the Lord says, The LORD of hosts, the Mighty One of Israel, 'Ah, I will rid Myself of My adversaries, And take vengeance on My enemies. I will turn My hand against you. And thoroughly purge away your dross, And take away all of your alloy [mixture]. I will restore your judges as at the first, And your counselors as at the beginning. Afterward you shall be called the city of righteousness, the faithful city.'"
2. Zech. 13:9—"I will bring the one-third through the fire, Will refine them as silver is refined, And test them as gold is tested. They will call on My name, And I will answer them. I will say, 'This is My people'; And each one will way, 'The LORD is my God.'"
3. Mal. 3:1–5 (NIV)—"'I will send My messenger, who will prepare the way before Me. Then suddenly the Lord you are seeking will come to His temple; the messenger of the covenant, whom you desire, will come,' says the LORD Almighty. 'But who can endure the day of His coming? Who can stand when He appears? For He will be like a refiner's fire or a launderer's soap. He will sit as a refiner and purifier of silver.'"
4. 1 Cor. 3:11–17 (Voice)—"There is, in fact, only one foundation, and no one can lay any foundation other than Jesus the Anointed. As others build on the foundation (whether with gold, silver, gemstones, wood, hay, or straw), the quality of each person's work will be revealed in time as it is tested by fire. If a man's work stands the test of fire, he will be rewarded. If a man's work is consumed by the fire, his reward will be lost but he will be spared, rescued from the fire. Don't you understand that together you form a temple to the living God and His Spirit lives among you? If someone comes along to corrupt, vandalize, and destroy the temple of God, you can be sure that God will see to it that he meets destruction because the temple of God is sacred. You, together, are His temple." See also Deut. 14:2; Titus 2:14; 1 Peter 2:9.

103. Shine and Be My Light

I am the Lord your God, and I am here in your midst. I am here in your midst to awaken in you the gifts I have given you. I am here to lead and guide you in the way of holiness and abundant life.

The thief comes to rob, steal, and destroy your hope and your blessings in this life and in life eternal. But I have made a way for you to overcome all evil.

My gifts to you, My people, are salvation, healing, and restoration. You are My children, and I delight in you. Receive the gifts I give you and encourage one another. I have given you gifts to share and bless My people over the whole earth.

While there is indeed much evil and darkness at this time, I am awakening and restoring My church to the gifts and light I have given you. Shine, My people. Shine and be My light reflected in you. Let My love be in you so My glory may be reflected throughout the whole earth.

Selected Scripture Reading

1. Deut. 23:14—"For the LORD your God walks in the midst of your camp, to deliver you and give your enemies over to you; therefore your camp shall be holy, that He may see no unclean thing among you, and turn away from you." See Jer. 14:7–9; 2 Chron. 7:14.
2. Ps. 46:1–11—"God is our refuge and strength, a very present help in trouble. Therefore we will not fear, Even though the earth be removed, And though the mountains be carried into the midst of the sea ... There is a river who streams shall make glad the city of God, The holy place of the tabernacle of the Most High. God is in the midst of her, she shall not be moved; God shall help her, just at the break of dawn ... Come, behold the works of the LORD ... Be still and know that I am God; I will be exalted among the nations, I will be exalted in the earth! The LORD of hosts is with us; The God of Jacob is our refuge." See Ps. 27:1; Eph. 5:8–21.
3. Ps. 119:10–11—These verses explain the keys to recognizing God's gifts and maintaining His active presence in our lives. See Zeph. 3:17.
4. John 10:10—"The thief does not come except to steal, and to kill, and to destroy. I have come that they may have life, and that they

may have it more abundantly." In John 10, Jesus used the metaphor of His being the door of the sheepfold, the gate by which we enter the kingdom of God. He said that all those who taught any other doctrine were thieves and robbers. See John 6:63; Acts 4:12.
5. Luke 4:18–19—In these verses, Jesus explained His mission and purpose. See Isa. 49:8–9, 60:3, 61:1–11; Matt. 11:5–6, 12:18–21.
6. 2 Cor. 4:6–7—"For it is the God who commanded light to shine out of darkness, who has shone is our hearts to give the light of the knowledge of the glory of God in the face of Jesus Christ. But we have this treasure in earthen vessels, that the excellence of the power may be of God and not of us." See 1 Peter 4:7–11.

104. Choose Wisely

The time has come for you to choose whom you will serve.

Many of My children have had divided loyalty to Me. They have loved Me but have also loved the world and followed the ways of the world. They have been lovers of pleasure more than lovers of God.

This shall cease. Either you will turn from Me or you will turn to Me, for the trials and tribulations that are coming over the earth will try people's hearts and reveal hidden things both good and bad.

I say to you, turn now to Me with your whole heart so that you may stand, and not fall, in the day of trouble. I will be a rock and fortress to you if you will seek Me with your whole heart and turn away from all wickedness.

You cannot bite and devour one another and walk in My blessing and protection. Repent. Give forgiveness as I have forgiven you. Remember what My Son has done for you, and lay down your lives for one another. This is My commandment to you: love one another with a godly love all the more so as you see the day of trouble approaching.

There is little time left, My children, for you to choose whom you will serve with your whole heart; the day approaches that shall reveal whom you have chosen. Choose wisely. Choose now.

Selected Scripture Reading

1. Deut. 30:11–20—"For this commandment ... is not too mysterious for you ... But the word is very near you, in your mouth and in your heart, that you may do it. See, I have set before you today life and good, death and evil, in that I command you today to love the LORD your God, to walk in His ways, and to keep His commandments."
2. Ps. 139:23–24—"Search me, O God, and know my heart; Try me, and know my anxieties; And see if there is any wicked way in me, And lead me in the way everlasting."
3. Ps. 90:12—"So teach us to number our days, That we may gain a heart of wisdom."
4. Matt. 6:9–15—"Our Father in heaven, Hallowed be Your name. Your kingdom come, Your will be done on earth as it is in heaven. Give us this day our daily bread And forgive us our debts, As we forgive our debtors. And do not lead us into temptation, But deliver us from the evil one. For Yours is the kingdom and the power and the glory forever. Amen. For if you forgive men their trespasses, your heavenly Father will also forgive you. But if you do not forgive men, their trespasses, neither will your Father forgive your trespasses." See Matt. 7:5; Rom. 12:10–21; Gal. 5:13–26.
5. 1 Peter 1:6–7—These verses give perspective and purposes concerning difficulties and trials. See Ps. 59:16–17. In light of these verses, how might you pray when going through a hard time?

105. Hunger and Thirst

Walk with Me in purity and you will walk with Me in power. Hunger and thirst after righteousness and you will be filled with My presence.

I am calling to you. I am calling to you. Leave the ways of the world. Leave the ways of the flesh. Seek Me with your whole heart, soul, and mind. I will be found of you..

Do not be discouraged or fearful by the shaking, the confusion, and sin around you. This is a time of sifting. This is a time of calling to awaken the souls of mankind.

Walk with Me in purity and you will walk with Me in power. And you will overcome and receive the rewards of righteousness.

Selected Scripture Reading

1. Ps. 27:4–5—"One thing I have desired of the LORD. That will I seek: That I may dwell in the house of the LORD All the days of my life; to behold the beauty of the LORD, And to inquire in His temple. For in the time of trouble He shall hide me in His pavilion; In the secret place of His tabernacle He shall hide me; He shall set me high upon a rock." What do you think the phrase "high upon a rock" might be describing?
2. Isa. 26—This chapter is a song of salvation and describes the peace that follows living in relationship with God. People and nations whose minds are faithful to God shall experience well-being in all its aspects. See Ps. 24:3–5; Matt. 5:8.
3. Joel 3:14–16—"Multitudes, multitudes in the valley of decision! For the day of the LORD is near in the valley of decision. The sun and moon will grow dark, And the stars will diminish their brightness ... The heavens and earth will shake: But the LORD will be a shelter for His people and the strength of the children of Israel."
4. Prov. 20:26—"A wise king sifts out the wicked, And brings the threshing wheel over them." Prov. 21:15 and Rom. 13 give insight to the meaning of this verse.
5. 2 Cor. 7:1—"Therefore, having these promises, beloved, let us cleans ourselves from all filthiness of the flesh and spirit, perfecting holiness in the fear of God."
6. Gal. 5:16–24—"Now the works of the flesh are evident, which are: adultery, fornication, uncleanness, lewdness, idolatry, sorcery, hatred, contentions, jealousies, outbursts of wrath, selfish ambitions, dissentions, heresies, envy, murders, drunkenness, revelries, and the like ... those who are Christ's have crucified the flesh with its passions and desires." See Pss. 101:3, 17:15; 1 Tim. 5:22.
7. Luke 22:31–32—We all make mistakes and have failures, but this verse gives us hope, perspective, and direction.
8. Luke 6:47–48—"Whoever comes to Me, and hears My sayings, and does them, I will show you whom he is like: He is like a man building

a house, who dug deep and laid the foundation on the rock. And when the flood arose, the stream beat vehemently against that house, and could not shake it, for it was founded on the rock."

106. My Love Gives Wisdom and Grace

Hold on tightly to your most holy faith and do not lose heart, My beloved. Persevere and you shall overcome and win the race, be received into glory, and attain the overcomer's crown. Remember who you are. Remember your calling. Remember who I am. I have made the way for you to overcome every obstacle.

Have faith in Me. Do not doubt My Word. Do not doubt My love for you. Fill your heart and mind with My Word and you shall be strengthened such that no weapon the enemy fashions against you shall bring you to ruin.

My words are life and power. They will fill you with My love that gives wisdom and grace to endure and overcome. Hold on tightly to your faith, My bride. I am coming soon to receive you to Myself.

Selected Scripture Reading

1. Deut. 4:9; 6:1–25—These are admonitions to hold onto faith in God by making an effort to remember what we have seen and heard and pass it on to our children and future generations. See Deut. 8; Rom. 15:4. There appears to be a simple progression: believing or having faith in God and what He says leads to the fruit of obedience to Him that together constitute righteousness before Him. Genesis 15:6, Romans 4:3, and Galatians 3:6 say that Abraham believed God and the Lord counted him righteous.
2. Joel 2:27–32—Writing around 835–805 BC, the prophet Joel spoke of times far in the future when God's Spirit would do a work in the hearts and lives of people that would be evidence of God's existence and fulfill the promise of restoring relationship with His creation.

    On the day of Pentecost in Acts 2, Peter quoted from Joel and connected the events of that day to what God had promised. Joel 2:30–32, which Peter also quoted, seems to indicate that at the end

of that season or age of repentance and salvation, signs in heaven and earth would warn of impending judgment. Peter's sermon is a call to repent and come into God's plan of salvation while there is time.
3. Isa. 1:10–20, 54:17; Eccl. 7:20; Pss. 4:5, 14:1–3, 51:16–17; Hos. 6:6; Mal. 3:3; Matt. 9:13, Matt. 23; 1 Cor. 1:26–31; Romans; Phil. 1:9–11, 3:8–9; 1 John 3:8–12—Many scriptures like these teach what righteousness is and isn't. See Isa. 53:5; 1 Peter 2:24.
4. Eph. 1:3–4—"Blessed be the God and Father of our Lord Jesus Christ, who has blessed us with every spiritual blessing in the heavenly places in Christ Just as He chose us in Him before the foundation of the world, that we should be holy and without blame before Him in love … In Him you also trusted, after you heard the word of truth, the gospel of your salvation, in whom also, having believed, you were sealed with the Holy Spirit of promise, who is the guarantee of our inheritance until the redemption of the purchased possession to the praise of His glory."

107. Rejoice, My Beloved

This is a season—this is harvest time for My church, for My people. Rejoice, My beloved, for you who have been faithful and obedient shall reap great rewards. In the natural and spiritual, you will see the efforts and prayers you have given will bear fruit.

Be not weary in well doing and do not lose heart, for soon, for very soon, you shall see the reward. There is much work to be done in My kingdom. As you move forward in grace and love, I will empower you. I will anoint you for the work I have called you to do.

Listen with your heart tuned to My heart and you will hear and have understanding. Hear My words to your heart and walk in My ways and you will know it is My Spirit who is leading and teaching you.

To My children who love Me and seek My face, I speak clearly that you may know the path to take. Do not be weary in seeking Me. Do not be weary in obeying and following My ways because at the proper time and in due season, you will reap great rewards.

All people are tested and challenged. To whom will you listen? Whom will you serve? Consider and understand the words I speak to you. Turn your heart to Me and receive My life-giving words to you. Rejoice and see what I see. This is a season of harvest.

Selected Scripture Reading

1. Josh. 1:9—"Have I not commanded you? Be strong and of good courage; do not be afraid nor be dismayed, for the LORD your God is with you wherever you go."
2. Pss. 1, 89:32, 126:3–6; Prov. 11:18, 22:29; Jer. 2:19; Ezek. 16:43, 22:23–31; Matt. 9:37, 4:29; Luke 8:4–15, 10:2; John 4:34–37; Hos. 10:12; Rom. 2:6–11; Gal. 5:17, 6:8–9; Heb. 10:35—The scriptures teach that the principles of sowing and reaping apply to natural as well as spiritual investments and actions.
3. Acts 1:7–8 (Voice)—"The Father, on His own authority, has determined the ages and epochs of history, but you have not been given this knowledge. Here's the knowledge you need: you will receive power when the Holy Spirit comes on you. And you will be My witnesses, first here in Jerusalem, then beyond to Judea and Samaria, and finally to the farthest places on earth."
4. Gal. 6:6–10—"Let him who is taught the word share in all good things with him who teaches. Do not be deceived. God is not mocked; for whatever a man sows, that he will also reap. For he who sows to his flesh will of the flesh reap corruption, but he who sows to the Spirit will of the Spirit reap everlasting life. And let us not grow weary while doing good, for in due season we shall reap if we do not lose heart. Therefore, as we have opportunity, let us do good to all, especially to those who are of the household of faith."

108. I Will Speak to Your Heart

My people, hear and listen to My voice. I am calling to you for the times are perilous—the times of the end are here. But do not be fearful or confused.

Remember how I have always cared for My people. Noah listened and obeyed. Daniel listened and obeyed. Joseph listened and obeyed. I speak clearly to you. Listen and obey. Know My Word and I will speak to your heart. Know My voice. Know Me and you will walk together in unity and peace.

Understand this. You cannot seek your own way, your own will, your own plan and enter into My rest or provisions. In My kingdom, it is to him who gives up his life for the kingdom who receives all in My kingdom.

I am calling to you, My people. Listen to the wind. Listen to My Spirit and obey.

Selected Scripture Reading

1. Prov. 8:1–36—"Does not wisdom cry out, And understanding lift her voice? ... Receive my instruction, and not silver, And knowledge rather than choice gold; For wisdom is better than rubies ... I, wisdom, dwell with prudence, And find out knowledge and discretion. The fear of the LORD is to hate evil; Pride and arrogance and the evil way And the perverse mouth I hate. Counsel is mine, and sound wisdom; I am understanding, I have strength ... I love those who love me, And those who seek me diligently will find me. Riches and honor are with me, Enduring riches and righteousness ... I traverse the way of righteousness, In the midst of the paths of justice, That I may cause those who love me to inherit wealth, That I may fill their treasuries. The LORD possessed me at the beginning of His way, Before His works of old. I have been established from everlasting. From the beginning, before there was ever an earth ... Then I was beside Him as a master craftsman; And I was daily His delight, Rejoicing always before Him. Rejoicing in His inhabited world, And my delight was with the sons of men. Now therefore, listen to me, my children, For blessed are those who keep my ways. Hear instruction and be wise, And do not disdain it. Blessed is the man who listens to me, Watching daily at my gates, Waiting at the posts of my doors. For whoever finds me finds life, And obtains favor from the LORD; But he who sins against me wrongs his own soul; All those who hate me love death." This is a metaphor of wisdom speaking to our hearts teaching us that wisdom is found in God. God is the source of wisdom.

2. Habakkuk 2:1 (ONMB)—"I shall stand my watch and set myself on the tower and will watch to see what He will say to me and what I will answer when I am reproved."
3. Mark 8:34–38—Jesus explains what "taking up your cross daily and following Him" means to our focus, priorities, and behavior.

109. The Time Is Short

I speak clearly to My people about those things that are to take place shortly, but they do not take heed or prepare their hearts or households. Have I not warned you to have oil in your lamps lest you have no light in the coming days of darkness?

The heavens and the earth shall be shaken and men's hearts shall fail them for fear, but My people who know Me, who know My voice, shall have no fear. Their lights shall burn brightly, and they shall be a testimony to their God. Great exploits shall they do as they hear My voice and do My bidding.

Come before Me each day now and learn to know My voice then you will have oil for your lamps in the days of darkness. My people, will you not heed the calling and warnings of your Good Shepherd? The time is short. There is little time left to prepare. There is little time left to get your house in order. I give you warnings so you may prepare.

Do not be deceived into thinking everything will continue in a comfortable way as it has for so long. Your nation was blessed because she honored the covenant of her founding—a covenant with almighty God. But America has defiled herself, embraced many false gods, and behaved like a harlot with perversity and wickedness in her heart. She has called down curses upon herself.

Return to Me now, My people who are lost in this nation. Awaken. See that the time for repentance is short. Shake yourselves free from the bondages of sin and carnality. Come to Me before it is too late for redemption. Call out to Me for deliverance for the devil is about to attack you in great fury. Repent now or in the confusion of the battle you will destroy one another and what is good that remains among you.

Listen well, My little ones, for I am leading you into liberty and out of bondage that you may have oil in your lamps and that your light will shine brightly and glorify God.

Selected Scripture Reading

1. Isa. 59:1–2—"Behold the LORD's hand is not shortened, That it cannot save; Nor His ear heavy, That it cannot hear. But your iniquities have separated you from your God." See Isa. 58–62.
2. Luke 21:25–28—"And there will be signs in the sun, in the moon, and in the stars; and on the earth distress of nations… Then they will see the Son of Man coming in a cloud with power and great glory. Now when these things begin to happen, look up and lift up your heads because your redemption draws near." See Matt. 24:29; Isa. 13:13, 24:18b–20; Joel 3:14–17; Hag. 2:6–7; Rev. 6:12–13.
3. Acts 17:29–31—"Therefore, since we are the offspring of God, we ought not to think that the Divine Nature is like gold or silver or stone, something shaped by art and man's devising. Truly, these times of ignorance God overlooked, but now commands all men everywhere to repent." See Ps. 16:8–9; Luke 6:47–49.

110. No Longer Tossed About

Come to Me all you who are weary and burdened with the cares of this world and I will give you rest for your souls.

Seek Me. Seek My kingdom, and My righteousness—and your eyes will see, your ears will hear, and your heart will understand. Then you shall no longer be tossed about as the waves upon the sea. You shall know how to reject the busyness and distractions that eat away at the time you would spend resting in My presence.

Rest in Me and you will find peace and strength for your souls. Indeed, there may be confusion, distress, and fear all about you—fighting and turmoil. But hear this. My people who know Me—My people who have put My words into their hearts—My people who live My words—shall not be moved by any of these difficulties or attacks of the enemy.

You shall rise as with wings of eagles for you shall have My peace in your hearts. I will guide you.

Come. Come away with Me to the secret place of obedience so I may restore your soul, take your burdens, and give you rest. I give you My peace.

Selected Scripture Reading

1. Ps. 16:5–9—"O LORD, You are the portion of my inheritance and my cup. You maintain my lot ... I will bless the LORD who has given me counsel; My heart also instructs me in the night seasons, I have set the LORD always before me; Because He is at my right hand I shall not be moved. Therefore my heart is glad, and my glory rejoices; My flesh also will rest in hope." See Ps. 85:8–9.
2. Matt. 11:28–30—"Come to Me, all you who labor and are heavy laden, and I will give you rest. Take My yoke upon you and learn from Me, for I am gentle and lowly in heart, and you will find rest for your souls. For My Yoke is easy and My burden is light." See Ps. 23; Matt. 3:8; Luke 1:67–79; Heb. 4:1–6.
3. Eph. 4:11–32—"And He Himself gave some to be apostles, some prophets, some evangelists and some pastors and teachers, for the equipping of the saints for the work of ministry, for the edifying of the body of Christ, till we all come to the unity of the faith and of the knowledge of the Son of God ... that we should no longer be children tossed to and fro carried about with every wind of doctrine, by the trickery of men, in the cunning craftiness of deceitful plotting, but, speaking the truth in love, may grow up in all things into Him who is the head—Christ ... that you put off, concerning your former conduct, the old man which grows corrupt according to the deceitful lusts, and be renewed in the spirit of your mind." See Col. 2:8.

111. Righteousness Shall Take Root in the Earth

There is a crisis in the houses of leadership. The leaders are perplexed and do not know what to do. Their plans and strategies fail them, and their hearts fill with fear. I am the Lord God almighty and the kings of the earth answer to Me. I set in place and I tear down.

Hear Me, peoples of the nations. I am a righteous judge and I do not share My glory. I lift up and I tear down. You who think highly of yourself shall be brought low for I shall show you who is God. I shall show you who is Lord.

Will you shake your fist at Me? Will you plan the destruction of My people? Know the evil you have planned shall befall you instead! For My people cry out to Me. I hear their righteous cries for help and deliverance. I shall be their swift avenger. I shall uphold them through these trials. I shall be the Lord of the hosts of the armies of heaven to them. The will of the God of heaven shall come to earth.

My people shall pray in the Spirit and in understanding—and righteousness shall take root in the earth. Call out to Me, My people, and know that I hear your prayers. Have faith in Me and your heart will be strengthened and established to do My work in this hour.

Do not listen to the boasting and lies of the enemy and thereby fall into confusion. Rather, stay focused on My Word to you that I place in your heart. Purity. Holiness. Righteousness. Serving others. Seek first the kingdom of God and His righteousness and all things will be in their proper place before you.

I am seeking your heart. Love the Lord your God with your whole heart, soul, and mind and you will walk in My blessing and in My provision. You shall see the salvation and deliverance I have prepared for you.

Selected Scripture Reading

1. Isa. 34:1—"Come here and listen, O nations of the earth. Let the world and everything in it hear My words. 2. For the LORD is enraged against the nations. His fury is against all their armies." See Ps. 9:17–20; Jer. 32:33, 12:17; Amos 9:8; Hos. 4:1–4; Zeph. 3:8b; Ps. 102:15; Isa. 29:14; Matt. 25:31–32; 1 Cor. 3:19–20.
2. Isa. 24:5–6 (NLT)—"The earth suffers for the sins of its people, for they have twisted the instructions of God, violated His laws and broken His everlasting covenant. Therefore, a curse consumes the earth and its people." See Ezek. 22, 14:12–23; Hab. 2:7–8; Rom. 1; 1 Peter 4:3; Gal. 5:19–20; 1 Tim. 1:10; Mal. 2:17; 2 Tim. 3; Ps. 66:18.
3. Hos. 6:1–3 (NLT)—"Come, let us return to the LORD! He has torn us in pieces; now He will heal us. He has injured us; now He will bandage our wounds. In just a short time, He will restore us so we can live in His presence. Oh, that we might know the LORD! Let us press on to know Him! Then He will respond to us as surely as the arrival of dawn or the coming of rains in early spring." See 2 Chron. 7:14; Isa. 26:2; Jer. 12:15.

4. Ps. 33:12—"Blessed is the nation whose God is the LORD, The people He has chosen as His own inheritance." See Ex. 19:6; Ps. 72; 1 Peter 2:5–9; Rom. 10:13; Rev. 15:3–4.

112. Do Not Harden Your Hearts

When My children do not listen—when they do not make time to hear My words to them—I become quiet for a season. I wait for them to return to Me. I wait until they have ears to hear. There is a drought of the Word of the Lord in the land.

Do not harden your hearts in the days of testing. Rather, consider your ways and return to Me that I may lead and guide you and you may walk in My ways.

Selected Scripture Reading

1. Ps. 81:11–13—"But My people would not heed My voice, And Israel would have none of Me. So I gave them over to their own stubborn heart, to walk in their own counsels. Oh, that My people would listen to Me." See Deut. 8:3; Amos 8:11–12; Hos. 14:1; 2 Eph. 5:5; Thess. 2:11. After reading these scriptures, consider the connection between a stubborn heart forming false beliefs/teachings and what is necessary for returning to a good relationship with God.
2. Isa. 59:2—"But your iniquities have separated you and your God and your sins have hid His face from you, that He will not hear." See Ps. 78:34; Isa. 2:3; Hos. 14:9.
3. Rom. 1:18–2:6—"For the wrath of God is revealed from heaven against all ungodliness and unrighteousness of men, who suppress the truth in unrighteousness … Therefore God also gave them up to uncleanness, in the lusts of their hearts, to dishonor their bodies among themselves … Or do you despise the riches of His goodness, forbearance, and longsuffering, not knowing that the goodness of God leads you to repentance?"
4. Isa. 30:18 (Voice)—"Meanwhile, the Eternal One yearns to give you grace and boundless compassion; that's why He waits. For the Eternal

is a God of justice. Those inclined toward Him, waiting for His help, will find happiness."

5. Hebrews 2 is an admonition to not neglect one's salvation; Hebrews 3 builds on that theme by defining faithfulness and alerting us to what would cause us to lose out for not following through. Chapter 4 has more on this topic.
6. 2 Cor. 7:10—This verse speaks of two kinds of sorrow with very different effects.
7. Acts 20:20–21—These verses describe at least one aspect of how the apostle Paul lived faithful to the gospel of Christ.
8. Matt. 4:4—"But He answered and said, 'It is written Man shall not live by bread alone, but by every word that proceeds from the mouth of God.'" How might you write a paraphrase of this verse and capture its meaning?
9. Heb. 4:11–12—"Let us therefore be diligent to enter that rest, lest anyone fall according to the same example of disobedience. For the word of God is living and powerful, and sharper than any two-edged sword, piercing even to the division of soul and spirit ... and is a discerner of the thoughts and intents of the heart. And there is no creature hidden from His sight, but all things are naked and open to the eyes of Him to whom we must give account."
10. Isa. 30:15—"In returning and rest you shall be saved; in quietness and confidence shall be your strength." When we receive God's truths into our minds and hearts, it brings peace and rest to our inner being. See Luke 2:14.
11. Isa. 55:6–7—"Seek the LORD while He may be found, Call upon Him while He is near. Let the wicked forsake his way and the unrighteous man his thoughts; Let him return to the LORD, And He will have mercy on him; And to our God, For He will abundantly pardon."

113. That Only I Can Give You

I pronounce judgment on the false gods of the nations. For the peoples have looked to—they have worshipped false gods—and do not look to

Me, their Creator. My heart longs for My people over the face of the whole earth to come to Me that I may heal their wounds and bless them, but they refuse and follow gods that are no gods, the works of their own hands, and even demons.

Turn to Me, says the Lord your God. Turn from your sins and see the righteousness and freedom only I can give you. Do you not see you need a Savior? Look on My Son, Jesus, who died for your sins—who paid the price for your sins. He is the only way to salvation and eternal life. There is no other way.

Forsake all other attempts to make yourselves self-righteous and powerful. The end thereof is destruction. Come to Me with your whole heart, soul, strength, and mind so you may be delivered from the ways of death and that you may enter into the way of life.

Selected Scripture Reading

1. Isa. 2:8, 17—"Their land is also full of idols; They worship the work of their own hands. That which their own fingers have made … The loftiness of man shall be bowed down, And the haughtiness of men shall be brought low; The LORD alone will be exalted in that day, But the idols He shall utterly abolish." An idol is something we worship besides our Creator. The Bible gives some examples: images and statues (Isa. 41:29; Hab. 2:18); sun, moon, and stars (Deut. 4:19; Acts 7:42–43); sacred pillars or stones (Lev. 26:1); and greed (Eph. 5:5). What other things might become idols?
2. Gen. 35:2; Ex. 20:4; Deut. 11:16; 2 Kings 17:7–23; Jer. 16:20—From the time of the fall (Gen. 3–6:4), people have been drawn to idol worship, sexual immorality, violence, and occult practices. The scriptures list many false gods including these.

    - Ishtar (Ashtoreth, Astarte, Ashtartu)—goddess of love/sex and war/violence of Babylonian origin (Judg. 2:13, 10:6; 1 Sam. 7:3, 31:10; 1 Kings 11:33; 2 Kings 23:13). As is common, the worship of this deity changed over time and from culture to culture. The warlike attributes were prominent in Assyria. In Canaan, the goddess evolved to include worship of the moon.

- Baal, Baalim (pl.)—(Num. 22:41; Judg. 2:11–13, 8:33; 2 Kings 17:16). Of Semitic origin from ancient Phoenicia (area along the Eastern Mediterranean coastline northwest of the Sea of Galilee that included parts of present-day Syria, Israel, Lebanon, and southwest Turkey). They practiced public worship of many gods called Baal. This geographical area during the time of Jesus was labeled Tyre after one of the main city states of Phoenicia. The worship of Baal in Jeremiah 19:5 was identified with the worship of the false god Molech and included human and even child sacrifice. Jeremiah 7:9–15 will motivate us to identify and get rid of the false gods in our hearts.
- Molech (Moloch, Molech, Milcom, Malcam)—derived from Hebrew words meaning "the reigning one." God specifically forbad the worship of this heathen god of the Ammonites (Ex. 20:13; Lev. 18:21, 20:1–5). Nevertheless, 1 Kings 11:4–13 records how worship of Molech gained a controlling foothold among God's people. It was a case of tolerance and accommodation with disastrous consequences. See Ezek. 23:37–39; Acts 7:43. Consider how we might be doing the same thing today. What are the guidelines for maintaining a balance between tolerance and accommodation for others and obedience to God's directives? See Rom. 14.
- Chemosh—god of the Moabites (2 Kings 23:13). Child sacrifice was also a part of worship to Chemosh (2 Kings 3:4–27).

According to Rev. 9:11, one may infer that as was in the Garden of Eden, there is a malevolent, satanic influence at work to motivate mankind into self-destructive behaviors including rebellion against God. Revelation describes end-times events and the spiritual condition of those who have continued to resist the grace of God (Rev. 9:20).

3. Isa. 43:11—"I, even I, am the LORD, And besides Me there is no savior." See Isa. 12:2, 25:9, 59:16–20; Zeph. 3:17; Rom. 11:25–36.
4. Isa. 45:22—God calls all people from all nations to come to Him for salvation.
5. Jer. 2—Although in this chapter God is speaking specifically concerning the nation of Israel, the principles of staying in good

relationship with Him apply to individuals as well. What do you think verse 11 is saying about idolatry and misguided pursuit of prosperity? Why was it counterproductive for Israel to make alliances for protection and support with their pagan neighbors? (vv. 14–17, 36–37) Read this chapter and make a list of principles of staying in good relationship with God.
6. Jer. 16:19–21—"LORD, You are my strength and fortress, my refuge in the day of trouble! Nations from around the world will come to You and say, 'Our ancestors were foolish, for they worshiped worthless idols. Can people make their own god? The gods they make are not real gods at all!' 'So now I will show them My power and might,' says the LORD. 'At last they will know that I am the LORD.'"
7. 1 Tim. 4:10—"For to this end we both labor and suffer reproach, because we trust in the living God, who is the Savior of all men, especially of those who believe."
8. John 4:10—It is necessary to believe in Jesus to receive salvation.

114. You Are Precious

You are My treasure. You are My prized possession, the precious fruit of the earth.

My Son died to give you life. His resurrection foretells your resurrection into newness of life. Know that I love you and care for you perfectly. I have made every provision for you to walk out this moment in history in My blessing and in the glory I have prepared for you.

You will not understand everything that will happen, nevertheless, have faith in Me—have faith in My words to you—and you will overcome and receive the crown of life and righteousness. Rejoice, My beloved, for your name is written in the Lamb's Book of Life. You are precious. You are My treasure.

Selected Scripture Reading

1. Ex. 19:5–6—"'Now therefore, if you will indeed obey My voice and keep My covenant, then you shall be a special treasure to Me above all people; for all the earth is Mine. And you shall be to Me a kingdom of

priests and a holy nation.' These are the words which you shall speak to the children of Israel." See 2 Cor. 4:6–7, which further defines the "treasure."

2. Ps. 2:7–8—"I will declare the decree: The LORD has said to Me, 'You are My Son, Today I have begotten You, Ask of Me, and I will give You the nations for Your inheritance, And the ends of the earth for Your possession.'" This verse describes God the Father addressing His purposes for God the Son to provide salvation for all mankind.

3. Ps. 16—Written by David, this psalm is a suitable prayer for us. David cries out to the Lord to sustain and preserve him, and we follow David as he instructs his soul on how to think and respond to God effectively. See Acts 2:25–36 for corresponding New Testament scriptures indicating prophecies about the Messiah's divine nature and resurrection.

4. Acts 10:34–43 (Voice)—"Then Peter opened his mouth and said: 'In truth I perceive that God shows no partiality. But in every nation whoever fears Him and works righteousness is accepted by Him. The word which God sent to the children of Israel, preaching peace through Jesus Christ—He is Lord of all—That word you know, which was proclaimed throughout all Judea, and began from Galilee after the baptism which John preached: How God anointed Jesus of Nazareth with the Holy Spirit and with power, who went about doing good and healing all who were oppressed by the devil, for God was with Him. And we are witnesses of all things which He did ... whom they killed by hanging on a tree. Him God raised up on the third day ... And He commanded us to preach to the people and to testify that it is He who was ordained by God to be Judge of the living and the dead. To Him all the prophets witness that, through His name, whoever believes in Him will receive remission of sins.'"

5. John 6:40 (Voice)—"So if you want to know the will of the Father, know this: everyone who sees the Son and believes in Him will live eternally; and on the last day, I am the One who will resurrect him." See Dan. 12:2; Acts 24:15–16; Rom. 6:1–23; 1 Thess. 4:13–18.

6. James 5:7—"Therefore be patient, brethren, until the coming of the Lord. See how the farmer waits for the precious fruit of the earth, waiting patiently for it." See 2 Peter 3:3–9

115. You Will Know Which Path to Take

I am going to take My people back to a more simple way of living, for their lives are so harried and cluttered that it is difficult for them to think and evaluate what is happening around them.

Because I love you, I shall bring you to a place of rest. You shall work but not in confusion. You shall understand My ways and purposes. You shall be at peace because you will understand.

Leave the world and its ways. Walk away from the lusts and strivings of sinful ways. Walk away from the battles and quarrels thereof. Come. Come sit with Me and drink in the water of life. Let My love and peace fill your heart and you will know which path to take.

There is a journey ahead. Stay close to Me. We will walk together. I will lead you through and around the dangerous places, and no harm will come to you. You will be strengthened and increased. Put on the armor of God and take up the sword of the Spirit. Prepare for the journey we will walk together. I will be your strength. Come, sit with me and drink in the water of life.

Selected Scripture Reading

1. Ps. 39:6 (Voice)—"In truth, each of us journeys through life like a shadow. We busy ourselves accomplishing nothing, piling up assets we can never keep; We can't even know who will end up with those things." Psalms 127, 128, and Matthew 6 offer more on this topic. Ecclesiastes develops this theme in detail from the perspective of one who has struggled with making sense of life. The author echoes many of the philosophies and pursuits one might have in life apart from a belief in a Creator God. Hedonism (2:1–11) and materialism (5:8–14) are specifically mentioned. Chapter 12 gives the concluding advice that concurs with Hos. 6:6; Mic. 6:8; Mark 12:33; Rom. 13:10; James 1:27.
2. Luke 21:34–36—"But take heed to yourselves, lest your hearts be weighed down with carousing, drunkenness, and cares of this life, and that Day come on you unexpectedly." See 1 Thess. 5; Luke 8:11–15.
3. Luke 10:38–42—Mary and Martha were sisters who lived two thousand years ago. When Jesus went to their village of Bethany, Martha worked very hard to prepare food and make all the

arrangements for accommodating the guests. Her sister, Mary, wasn't helping with the work; she was just listening to Jesus's every word. Out of an anxious heart, Martha complained about Mary to Jesus. In verses 41–42, Jesus said, "Oh Martha, Martha, you are so anxious and concerned about a million details, but really only one thing matters. Mary has chosen that one thing, and I won't take it away from her." What does this story tell you about perspective, insight, and priorities? In John 11:21–27, we learn that Martha had significant spiritual knowledge and faith as well as being very hospitable. What was it that Mary chose and Jesus wasn't going to deny her?

4. Phil. 4:4–6—This gives keys to dealing with anxieties and overcoming the temptation to worry.
5. Isa. 58—God teaches obedience and accepting correction brings blessings.

116. Come and Work with Me

Where is the sound of My Word in the spotlights? I want My Word to go forth in the spotlights. I will raise up My voice to speak in the spotlights of the media—in all places—in arts, politics and government, business, sports, law, medicine, and education so the Word of the Lord will go forth.

The people will hear and know I am. They must know I am, and they must fear and respect the Lord—no longer walking in rebellion and hardness of heart. Change is coming. This time, I will be in the change. The winds will blow, and My breath will give life to those who turn to Me.

I am seeking souls for this is the time of a great harvest. Come work with Me and we shall rejoice together bringing in a rich and bountiful harvest. Then I shall say to you, "Well done, good and faithful servant. Enter into your rest. Enter into your reward. You shall be with Me at the marriage supper of the Lamb."

Selected Scripture Reading

1. Isa. 53:1–6—"Who has believed our report? And to whom has the arm of the LORD been revealed? For He shall grow up before Him

as a tender plant ... He is despised and rejected by men, A Man of sorrows and acquainted with grief ... Surely He has borne our griefs and carried our sorrows; Yet we esteemed Him stricken, Smitten by God, and afflicted. But He was wounded for our transgressions, He was bruised for our iniquities ... All we like sheep have gone astray; We have turned every one, to his own way; And the LORD has lain on Him the iniquity of us all."

2. Isa. 57:13—"When you cry out, Let your collection of idols deliver you, But the wind will carry them all away, A breath will take them. But he who puts his trust in Me shall possess the land, And shall inherit My holy mountain." See John 3:8.

3. Acts 5:30–32—"The God of our fathers raised up Jesus ... Him God has exalted to His right hand to be Prince and Savior, to give repentance to Israel and forgiveness of sins. And we are His witnesses to these things, and so also is the Holy Spirit whom God has given to those who obey Him." See Ezek. 37:5–9.

4. Ps. 43:10–12—"You are My witnesses, says the LORD, And My servant whom I have chosen That you may know and believe Me, And understand that I am He. Before Me there was no God formed, Nor shall there be after Me. I, even I, am the LORD, And besides Me there is no savior." See Matt. 10:18–20; Luke 21:13; Acts 1:8.

5. Ps. 60:4–5—"You have given a banner to those who fear You, That it may be displayed because of the truth. That Your beloved may be delivered." See Acts 22:15.

6. Luke 10:2—"The harvest truly is great, but the laborers are few; therefore pray the Lord of the harvest to send out laborers into His harvest." See Ps. 126:6; John 4:35–38.

7. Mt 25:14–30—"His lord said to him, Well done, good and faithful servant."

8. Rev. 19:9—"Blessed are those who are called to the marriage supper of the Lamb."

117. This Is a Good Time

Hear Me, My child. The enemy is seeking whom he may devour. My people must be diligent as spirits of both fear and anger have been sent to attack and create chaos. Do not be moved by them, My children. Do not be moved by them.

Rather, be prepared and wear the spiritual armor you have been given—the shield of faith and the sword of the Spirit—to defeat the enemy. Walk in love and obedience and you shall be victorious. Be alert and vigilant. Persevere.

The battle will not be easy as the enemy will change strategies, but stay with Me. Listen carefully and follow My directives; you shall move mountains with intercessory prayer as you are led by My Holy Spirit and speak the words I give you to speak.

This is a good time and good season as it is a time for My people to turn to Me and be empowered by My truth and empowered by My Spirit. Give your whole heart to Me. Love Me with your whole heart, soul, strength, and mind so you may connect with Me and receive. In this season, the righteousness of My righteous ones shall be revealed because My glory will be upon you.

Selected Scripture Reading

1. Prov. 11:3—"The integrity of the upright will guide them, But the perversity of the unfaithful will destroy them." See Ps. 20; 1 John 5:14–21.
2. Isa. 14:12–17—"How you are fallen from heaven, O Lucifer, son of the morning! How you are cut down to the ground, You who weakened the nations! For you have said in your heart: I will ascend into heaven, I will exalt my throne above the stars of God."
3. Deut. 18:9–15 (ONMB)—"When you have come into the land which the LORD your God gives you, you will not learn to do after the abominations of those nations. There will not be found among you anyone who makes his son or his daughter pass through the fire [killing/sacrificing children], who uses divination, is a soothsayer, an enchanter, a sorcerer. a charmer, a consulter with familiar spirits, a wizard, or a necromancer. For all who do these things are an abomination to the LORD, and it is because of these abominations that the LORD your God drives them out before you. You will be innocent with the LORD your God. For these nations which you will dispossess hearkened to soothsayers and diviners, but as for you, the LORD your God has

not allowed you to do so. The LORD your God will raise up for you a prophet (Y'shua) like me from among you, of your brothers. You will listen to Him." See Matt. 17:3; Mark 1:1, 9:7; Luke 24:27; John 5:16, 7:40; Acts 3:22, 7:1–53, esp. v. 37; Acts 19:18–20; Galatians 5. Are there contemporary occult influences in today's cultures?
4. 1 Chron. 21:1—"Now Satan stood up against Israel, and moved David to number Israel."
5. 1 Peter 5:8—"Be sober, be vigilant; because your adversary the devil walks about like a roaring lion seeking whom he may devour." See Luke 4:1–13; 1 Tim. 6:9; James 1:14–15.
6. 1 John 3:3–8—"And everyone who has this hope in Him purifies himself... For this purpose the Son of God was manifested, that He might destroy the works of the devil." See Ps. 55:16–18; Luke 18:1–8; Eph. 6:1–18; 1 Thess. 5:12–23; Rev. 20:10.

118. Must Birth It by Prayer

I have many things to tell My people, to direct your prayers and prepare for what lies ahead. An attack against America is being planned. Pray that the identity of those behind the attack be revealed and made known.

For this is not a simple attack by an outside enemy. Authority has been granted to execute this attack. My people must pray calling upon My authority to foil the plans of the wicked and bring them to naught. Ask Me to destroy the plans of the wicked and divide their camp. I will hear and answer the cry of My people. I will come to your rescue.

There is much spiritual dullness among My people, and they are entangled in the affairs, pleasures, and confusion of the world. Awaken, My people! Come out of the world that you may see and understand. Come out of your lethargy. Come out of your apathy lest you believe lies and are destroyed.

There are natural and spiritual battles. You must wake up and intercede because the time is short. I will send a great revival, but you must birth it by prayer. It is through prayer that the ground of hearts and minds are watered to prepare them to hear and receive the message of repentance and salvation. Do not underestimate the power of revival and the blessings and protection it brings when peoples' hearts turn to Me.

Pray for unity to come quickly among My people that regardless of denominations and affiliations they have a genuine love and respect for one another. My faith works through love, and you must let My love flow through you to others. My love flowing through you will cast out fear and doubt.

There is something new that will be introduced with much ado. I say to you, do not trust in this. Seek first the kingdom of God and the righteousness that comes from Me. All other pathways end in destruction and deceit. I am a righteous and jealous God for I am truth and love.

I am seeking the hearts of My people to turn to Me that I may deliver, heal, and restore. Open your hearts to Me that I may bring life and restoration.

Selected Scripture Reading

1. Ps. 5:1–12—"Give ear to my words, O LORD … Give heed to the voice of my cry … You shall destroy those who speak falsehood; The LORD abhors the bloodthirsty and deceitful man. But as for me, I will come into Your house in the multitude of Your mercy … For You, O LORD, will bless the righteous; With favor You will surround him as with a shield." See Prov. 29:2; Isa. 56; 2 Tim. 2:2–4; 1 Peter 2:13.
2. Ps. 55:17—"Evening and morning and at noon I will pray, and cry aloud, And He shall hear my voice." See Pss. 3:8, 5:1–10, 80:1–20; Prov. 21:31; Zech. 14.
3. Lam. 5:21 (Voice)—"We are so sorry and have suffered for it. Eternal One, take us back again, That we may be restored to You and You to us, just as it used to be."
4. Rom. 13:11–14—"It is high time to awake out of sleep." See 2 Chron. 7:14; Matt. 25:13.

119. Decide Whom You Will Serve

Do I not test the reins of a man's heart? Do I not give opportunity for you to choose between good and evil? Choose the good and walk away from the evil that you may live.

My Spirit will not always strive with mankind. There is a time for repentance. Call on Me while I may be found and turn away from your wickedness. Come into My light so you may see. Wash yourself with the water of My Word and be clean. Give everything you have to Me so you may walk in My provision.

The time is short. There is little time left to decide whom you will serve. Evil is lurking at the door. Come under My protection and you will find safety. Eternal life will be your reward. Call upon Me in the day of trouble and I will hear and answer you. I am not weak that I cannot save you.

I am the Lord of the hosts, the Lord of the armies of heaven, and I shall deliver My people—those who know Me, those who love Me, those who follow Me. Come, turn away from sin and wickedness. Follow Me. I am calling you to safety. I am calling you to Myself. Come to Me.

Selected Scripture Reading

1. Ex. 32—The Israelites left Egypt in approximately 1491 BC. Later that year, they arrived at Mount Sinai, and God called Moses to the mountain to receive the two tablets of stone with the Ten Commandments— foundational directives for personal and social governance.

    Because Moses was gone from the people for forty days, the people began to be insecure; they wanted the familiar idols of Egypt for comfort. They asked Moses's brother, Aaron, to make an image for them to rally around and worship. Both Moses and God were very angry with the people. Moses gave them a ultimatum to decide whom they would follow (vs. 26). This moment of decision was critical to the survival of the fledgling nation called to be God's people. God had intended them to be an example to all nations showing them how to hear and obey Him. The command to choose also foreshadowed the decision every individual must make. See Deut. 30:15–19; 1 Kings 9:1–9; Prov. 3:31, 1:29; John 11:27; 1Thess. 5:21.
2. Jer. 17:9–10—"The heart is deceitful above all things, And desperately wicked; Who can know it? I, the LORD, search the heart, I test the mind, Even to give every man according to his ways, According to the fruit of his doings." See Rev. 2:18–29.
3. Ps. 26:1–12 (NLT)—"Put me on trial, LORD, and cross-examine me. Test my motives and affections. For I am constantly aware of

Your unfailing love, and I have lived according to Your truth ... I hate the gatherings of those who do evil, and I refuse to join in with the wicked ... I have taken a stand, and I will publicly praise the LORD." See Josh. 24:15.
4. Ps. 50:15—"Call upon Me in the day of trouble; I will deliver you, and you shall glorify Me." See Pss. 20:1, 59:16, 77:2, 86:7, 102:2.
5. Nah. 1:7—"The LORD is good, A stronghold in the day of trouble; And He knows those who trust in Him."

120. Put On White Garments

It is time to prepare yourselves, My people. It is time to cleanse yourselves and put on white garments of purity. For I desire to do a good work in your midst. I desire to release My glory and power so the kingdom of God will be manifested in this place.

Come away with Me to the quiet of the secret place so I may speak to your heart and you may hear My words. Sit quietly and consider My words—My scriptures written to cleanse and sanctify you in preparation for your calling and work in My kingdom.

I have many gifts, callings, and anointings for My people, but the work of purification and sanctification must take place first.

Come to Me with your whole heart. Leave the world and its way of thinking and doing. Enter My presence and you will find your heart's desire. You will find great treasure. You will find faith, hope, and love. My pure love heals, cleanses, and sanctifies My beloved, and you are My beloved. Come to Me.

Selected Scripture Reading

1. Isa. 1:18—"Come now, and let us reason together, says the LORD, Though your sins are like scarlet, They shall be as white as snow; Though they are red like crimson, They shall be as wool." Compare with Rom. 10:12; 1 Tim. 2:4.
2. Isa. 61:10—"I will greatly rejoice in the LORD, My soul shall be joyful in My God; For He has clothed me with the garments of salvation, He has covered me with the robe of righteousness, As a

bridegroom decks himself with ornaments, And as a bride adorns herself with her jewels." Describe how salvation clothes your spirit.
3. Ps. 91:1–2—"He who dwells in the secret place of the Most High shall abide under the shadow of the Almighty. I will say of the LORD, 'He is my refuge and my fortress; My God, in Him I will trust.'"
4. Ps. 131:2—"Surely I have calmed and quieted my soul, like a weaned child with his mother; like a weaned child is my soul within me." See 1 Thess. 4:11.
5. Ps. 143:10—"Teach me to do Your will, For You are my God; Your Spirit is good. Lead me in the land of uprightness." How would you define the land of uprightness?
6. 1 Peter 1:22—"Since you have purified your souls in obeying the truth through the Spirit in sincere love of the brethren, love one another fervently with a pure heart."
7. Matt. 24:45–46—"Who then is a faithful and wise servant, whom his master made ruler over his household, to give them food in due season? Blessed is that servant whom his master, when he comes, will find so doing." See 1 Cor. 15:58. Do you think the phrase "to give them food in due season" is a meaningful part of this statement? What does it mean? Who is the wise and faithful servant whom the master has made a ruler?
8. Rom. 13:14—"But put on the Lord Jesus Christ, and make no provision for the flesh, to fulfill its lusts." See Gal. 5:16–25; Titus 2:12; 1 John 2:15. What would an example be of making a provision to fulfill the lusts of the flesh?
9. Rev. 19:8—"And to her it was granted to be arrayed in fine linen, clean and bright, for the fine linen is the righteous acts of the saints." See 1 Cor. 13; 2 Peter 2:2–11.

121. Grace to Overcome All Things

Why do I call My people to purity? Why do I tell you to cleanse yourselves and prepare for My return? Why do I tell you to clothe yourselves in righteousness and purity?

Is it not because I love you with a pure love that calls you to fulfill the destiny I have designed and created for you? You are My chosen vessels to carry forth the message of the gospel to all mankind—to those you are with every day.

The pure in heart shall see Me and know My ways. They rest under the shadow of My wings, and I am their covering. They carry no burdens for they know I carry them. They have no fear because they trust Me to work all things to accomplish good for them.

I am calling you to purity that I may protect and empower you with grace to overcome all things. Rise up, My beloved. In purity and righteousness you will put the enemy to flight. In purity and righteousness you will find great delight and joy as your destiny is fulfilled. I have created you with purpose.

Selected Scripture Reading

1. Ps. 85:8–9—"I will hear what God the LORD will speak, for He will speak peace to His people and to His saints; but let them not turn back to folly. Surely His salvation is near to those who fear Him, that glory may dwell in our land."
2. Heb. 12–14—"Pursue peace with all people and holiness, without which no one will see the LORD: looking carefully lest anyone fall short of the grace of God ; lest any root of bitterness springing up cause trouble, and by this many become defiled."
3. Ps. 24:3—"Who may ascend into the hill of the LORD? Or who may stand in His holy place? He who has clean hands and a pure heart, Who has not lifted up his soul to an idol, Nor sworn deceitfully." See 1 Thess. 4:1–12; Titus 2:1–15.
4. Matt. 5:8—"Blessed are the pure in heart, for they shall see God." See 1 Tim. 1:5.
5. 2 Cor. 7:1—"Therefore, having these promises, beloved, let us cleanse ourselves from all filthiness of the flesh and spirit, perfecting holiness in the fear of God."
6. 1 John 4:18—"There is no fear in love; but perfect love casts out fear, because fear involves torment. But he who fears has not been made perfect in love." See Matt. 18:21–35.
7. Ps. 29:11—"The LORD will give strength to His people; The LORD will bless His people with peace." See Isa. 40:31; Rom. 8:28.

8. Isa. 30:18—"Therefore the LORD will wait, that He may be gracious to you; and therefore He will be exalted, that He may have mercy on you. For the LORD is a God of justice; Blessed are all those who wait for Him."

   Isa. 30 speaks of God's children. When we are in rebellion to Him, trusting in other things and other people, He waits for us to return to Him; the fruit of our sins will discipline us.
9. 2 Cor. 9:8—This passage explains the purpose of grace.
10. Ps. 36:7—When we comprehend God's kindness to us, we are motivated to trust Him.

122. Restoration for My People

I shall reveal to you My plan of restoration for My people. I am coming to send a sweeping revival of restoration of families. That which the enemy has stolen from My people shall be returned for I have ordained you to be victorious over the enemies of your soul.

I will pour out My love among My people, and the hearts of the fathers will be turned toward their children and their families. The headship of authority will be returned because My love will flow through them and they will embrace with compassion and wisdom their loved ones. They will sacrifice themselves because they love with My love.

No longer will My people bite and devour one another for I will be strong in their midst.

Mothers will rise and take their place in the ministry of their homes and among their families and among My people. Their eyes will be opened, and they will see and comprehend the miracles they will do in My name.

I am restoring My church. I am restoring families. Ground that has been lost to the enemy will be retaken. Call out to Me to heal your land. Call out to Me to heal your families. For I would do this work among you and it shall be a testimony to the power and glory of God.

I am a redeeming God and I delight to restore the beauty and glory of what I have created. Call unto Me to bring restoration.

Selected Scripture Reading

1. Mal. 4:5–6—"Behold, I will send you Elijah the prophet Before the coming of the great and dreadful day of the LORD. And he will turn The hearts of the fathers to the children, And the hearts of the children to their fathers, Lest I come and strike the earth with a curse." Read Matthew 17:11–13 and explain who Jesus said came in the spirit of Elijah as a forerunner to initiate a season of restoration. See Luke 1:17, 57–80.
2. Pss. 27:10, 68:5—These verses are a must-read for those whose earthly parents for whatever reason haven't been there for them.
3. Matt. 5:9 (Voice)—Blessed are the peacemakers—they will be called children of God."
4. John 11:51–52—"Now this he did not say on his own authority; but being high priest that year he prophesied that Jesus would die for the nation, and not for that nation only but also that He would gather together in one the children of God who were scattered abroad." See Isa. 49:6; John 17:15–26; Acts 10:45; 1 Peter 3:1–12. How would you answer the question, "Who are "God's children"?
5. Ps. 22:27–28—"All the ends of the world Shall remember and turn to the LORD, And all the families of the nations Shall worship before You. For the kingdom is the LORD's, And He rules over the nations." See Ps. 112; Matt. 12:47–50.
6. Ps. 103:13; Prov. 1:8, 3:12; Eph. 5, 6:1–4—Compassion with godly wisdom is the key to effective parenting and leadership. Nevertheless, children and those under authority are accountable for listening and responding with good judgment according to their mental and physical abilities.
7. Prov. 31:1–31—"Who can find a virtuous woman? ... Strength and honor are her clothing ... She opens her mouth with wisdom, and on her tongue is the law of kindness."

123. I Will Teach You

I have spoken to you that I shall restore My church. I shall restore that which has been lost, and I shall empower you with My Spirit to walk in

My ways. I shall turn the hearts of the fathers to their children and I shall work in your hearts to give you wisdom and compassion for one other.

In this hour of darkness, I shall give you My light and love. I will teach you how love overcomes evil. I will instruct your hearts in the principles of kingdom authority, which work by and through divine love and respect. The enemy shall have no power over you.

I will release you from the bondages and chains that have hindered you. Come to Me and spend time with Me that I may instruct your heart. From Me, you will receive life, and the love of the Father will comfort you.

Selected Scripture Reading

1. Ps. 143:10—"Teach me to do Your will, For You are my God; Your Spirit is good. Lead me in the land of uprightness." See Ps. 94.
2. Pss. 26:2, 32:8, 3; Jer. 17:10; Joel 2:25, 29; Ezek. 26:37—If we acknowledge and accept almighty God as our teacher in life, He will lead and guide us in the way of health and blessings. This principle applies to individuals, families, communities, and nations.
3. John 14:26—"But the Helper, the Holy Spirit whom the Father will send in My name, He will teach you all things, and bring to your remembrance all things that I said to you."
4. John 16:13—"However, when He, the Spirit of truth has come, He will guide you into all truth for He will not speak on His own authority but whatever He hears He will speak; and He will tell you things to come." See Acts 1:8, 10:9–48, 13:2; Rom. 8:14.
5. Isa. 11:2; Acts 26:18; 2 Cor. 4:6—These verses state the main teaching mission and message.
6. Rom. 12:1–12—"Brothers and sisters, in light of all I have shared with you about God's mercies, I urge you to offer your bodies as a living and holy sacrifice to God, a sacred offering that brings Him pleasure; this is your reasonable, essential worship. Do not allow this world to mold you in its own image. Instead, be transformed from the inside out by renewing your mind. As a result, you will be able to discern what God wills and whatever God finds good, pleasing, and complete." Read the rest of this passage and ask God if any of your thinking, words, or actions offend Him. Listen with your heart to what His Holy Spirit says to you and respond as He directs you.

7. Nehemiah 9—This is an account of the Israelites who had returned to Jerusalem after seventy years of captivity in Babylon. They corporately read God's Word, confessed their sins, and recounted God's faithfulness to not only discipline them but to lead and guide them throughout their nation's history. In this story, we can see ourselves. We can see our own nations. Read this chapter and the closing verse 38 to learn what the people and leaders did as a part of restoring their relationship with God.

124. My Peace in Turbulent Storms

I speak to the hearts of My children. I am here in your midst to bring you My peace in the turbulent storms raging all around you.

Look not on the hatred, anger, and confusion, where deceptions abound. Look instead to Me. Keep your focus on My goodness and keep your confidence in My words to you. Study My scriptures with hunger and a humble heart and you will receive strength to endure and overcome. For my peace and hope will flood your hearts as you meet with Me; I will bathe you in My love and peace.

Cease striving. Wait upon Me and receive My plan for reconciliation and victory over confusion and darkness. Know this. I am in your midst and will do a good work among you. Only yield yourself to Me and not to carnal lusts or manipulations.

Walk with Me into liberty and your reward will be My peace in your heart. I am here to work among you. Give Me your heart so I may impart My peace into your life.

Selected Scripture Reading

1. Ps. 85:8 (Voice)—"I will hear what the True God—the Eternal—will say, for He will speak peace over His people, peace over those who faithfully follow Him [but do not let them abuse His gift and return to foolish ways]. Without a doubt, His salvation is near to those who revere Him so that He will be with us again and all His glory will fill this land." God's call is to everyone. His sustained blessings are for those who respond in loving obedience. See Ps. 49;

Mal. 2:2; Gen. 18:26; Isa. 1:19–20; 1 Kings 9:1–9; Josh. 24:19–24; 1 Chron. 28:8.

2. Nahum—Nahum was likely written between 663 BC and 612 BC. This prophetic judgment against the cruel Assyrian empire describes the fall of the city of Nineveh (on the east bank of the Tigris River in today's Iraq). Nahum says God is very patient and loving with mankind but will eventually bring the wicked—including the violent, aggressive, and cruel Assyrians—to justice.

    Nahum contains vital principles concerning God's nature (Nah. 1:2–3) and how He works in the geopolitical affairs of mankind. One of those exemplified principles is that if a nation stays faithful to His teachings, its people will be protected from their enemies. See Pss. 5:11, 33:12, 41:11; Prov. 13:34; Zeph. 2:3. However, if they fall away from a relationship with God, their enemies will harass, terrorize, and overpower them. See Ezek. 39:23–24; Deut. 28:33, 36, 49–52, 67–68; Ps. 106:40–41; Jer. 11:17; 12:17.

    The Southern Kingdom of Judah had seen the Northern Kingdom of Israel become idolatrous and wicked with the consequences of being conquered by the Assyrians in 722 BC. Nevertheless, Judah did not remain faithful to God's instructions regarding their lifestyle choices; in 586 BC, the Babylonians conquered them.

    Nahum 1:7–8, Jeremiah 12:15, and Psalms 37:34, 107 explain the principle of patiently crying out to God during hard times. An additional noteworthy principle is that God may allow a wicked nation to exist for a season and even use it to afflict a rebellious and backslidden people. Nevertheless, He will bring justice in the end. See Ezek. 14:12–23; Nah. 1; Hab. 1:12b; Isa. 51; Jer. 25:12; Matt. 25:31–32; 1 Cor. 2:6; Rev. 20:11–15, 21:22–25.

3. Isa. 26:3—"You will keep him in perfect peace, Whose mind is stayed on You, Because he trusts in You." How does Matthew 5:43–48 apply to receiving God's grace and peace? See John 5:39; Col. 3:15; Phil. 4:1–20; Gal. 5:22–26.

4. James 3:13–17 (Voice)—"Who in your community is understanding and wise? Let his example, which is marked by wisdom and gentleness, blaze a trail for others. If your heart is one that bleeds dark streams of jealousy and selfishness, do not be so proud that you ignore your depraved state. The wisdom of this world should never be mistaken

for heavenly wisdom; it originates below in the earthly realms, with the demons. Any place where you find jealousy and selfish ambition, you will discover chaos and evil thriving under its rule. Heavenly wisdom centers on purity, peace, gentleness, deference, mercy, and other good fruits untainted by hypocrisy." See Prov. 3:30, 17:14, 20:3, 25:8, 26:17, 21; 2 Tim. 2:14, 24.

5. Phil. 2:3-4—These verses define humility. See Prov. 10:12, 13:10. What is the opposite of humility?
6. 2 Tim. 2:24-26—Read this verse and give examples of how one might be "taken captive by the devil to do his will." Is being argumentative acceptable behavior for Christians?

125. According to Kingdom Principles

Make yourselves ready. Prepare your hearts. Set your life in order according to kingdom principles for I am a just judge and will reward you according to the light you have received.

Humble your hearts and hear My Holy Spirit direct and teach you how to follow Me and walk in obedience. I will gather you as a mother hen gathers her chicks. I will protect you and I will see that you have all you need to overcome and gain spiritual strength.

Learn to know My voice now. Know Me now and you will hear My voice in the day of intense battle. Learn obedience now and obedience will come quickly and easily in difficult times.

The Holy Spirit says to you, prepare. Prepare yourselves and make ready for the Lord's return. Prepare.

Selected Scripture Reading

1. Dan. 12:3—"Those who are wise shall shine like the brightness of the firmament, And those who turn many to righteousness Like the stars forever and ever."
2. Matt. 13:40–43—Jesus described what will happen at the end of this age to those who practice lawlessness.
3. Matt. 24:36–44—"Be ready all the time, because you are not going to know when Jesus is going to return." The warning expressed in these verses reveals that the time of Jesus's return will have similarities to the days of Noah; it will come as a surprise to the wicked.
4. 1 Thess. 4:3–12—It is God plan for us to be consecrated and set apart to Him—our hearts and behavior are to be consistent with the gospel and kingdom principles. This is called sanctification. Our sanctification begins with salvation then moves forward each day as we submit our carnal thinking, behavior, and passions to the lordship of Christ. The goal is to become more like Him. Sanctification is a lifelong process by which we aspire to God's higher moral and ethical code. We give honor to God, ourselves, and others by living graciously in moral purity.
5. 2 Tim. 2:15 (Voice)—"Do everything you can to present yourself to God as a man who is fully genuine, a worker unashamed of your mission, a guide capable of leading others along the correct path defined by the word of truth." See Ps. 119:10–11; John 5:39; Rom. 15:4; Acts 17:11; James 1–5; 1 Tim. 4:13; Titus 2, 3.
6. Titus 2:8—"This is a faithful saying, and these things I want you to affirm constantly, that those who have believed in God should be careful to maintain good works. These things are good and profitable to men."

7. Eph. 5:25–27—"Christ also loved the church and gave Himself for her, that He might sanctify and cleanse her with the washing of water by the Word, that He might present her to Himself a glorious church, not having spot or wrinkle or any such thing, but that she should be holy and without blemish." See Rev. 19:6. The concept here is that by reading and studying the scriptures, our minds will be recalibrated to recognize and live by kingdom truths and principles. Apart from learning God's truths and acting upon them, there is no sanctification.

126. Build Your House upon the Rock

My child, I say to you, come to Me and build your house upon the rock of My words—My truth and My gospel. Build your life upon the Rock and you will not fear the coming storms because your house shall have a strong foundation and you will stand.

I have given you My Word to use skillfully to defeat the enemy of your soul. Does not the good swordsman know how to use his sword correctly and effectively? So also you must know My Word, come before Me in humility, seek Me with your whole heart, and walk uprightly before Me. Then you will understand Me and know My ways. Then you will walk in My grace to comprehend and live My Word.

In the coming trials, some will be offended because of difficulties. Others will be offended because of the holiness and righteousness of the gospel. You do have an enemy. Satan is a thief who will lie, steal, kill, and destroy. Hear what I say to you. Be of good heart and know My Word. By My Spirit and by My truth you shall be free. Overcome, My little ones. Overcome. I have made provision for you to overcome.

Those who hear and obey My words shall stand and not be moved. Come to Me and learn how to build your life—your house—upon the Rock.

Selected Scripture Reading

1. Ps. 40:1–2—"I waited patiently for the LORD; and He inclined to me, And heard my cry. He also brought me up out of a horrible pit,

out of the miry clay, And set my feet upon a rock, And established my steps." See Deut. 8:3; Ps. 37:23–24; John 6:63.
2. Ps. 78:35—"Then they remembered that God was their rock, And the Most High God their Redeemer." See 2 Sam. 23:2; Isa. 44:6–8, 28:16; 1 Cor. 10:1–4; 1 Peter 2:6–8.
3. John 8:21–27—"Not everyone who says to me, 'Lord, Lord,' shall enter the kingdom of heaven, but he who does the will of My Father in heaven. Many will say to Me in that day, 'Lord, Lord, have we not prophesied in Your name, cast out demons in Your name and done many wonders in Your name?' And then I will declare to them, 'I never knew you; depart from Me, you who practice lawlessness!' Therefore, whoever hears these sayings of Mine, and does them, I will liken him to a wise man who built his house on the rock; and the rain descended, the floods came, and the winds blew and beat on that house; and it did not fall, for it was founded on the rock. But everyone who hears these sayings of Mine, and does not do them, will be like a foolish man who built his house on the sand; and the rain descended, the floods came, and the winds blew and beat on that house; and it fell. And great was its fall." See John 5:39; James 1:21–25.
4. Matt. 11:6—"And blessed is he who is not offended because of Me." See John 3:19.
5. 2 Peter 3:9—"The Lord is not slack concerning His promise, as some count slackness, but is longsuffering toward us, not willing that any should perish but that all should come to repentance." See John 1:12, 3:14–15, 5:24; Rom. 1:16.

127. Love and Honor One Another

Hear Me, My children. The enemy of your souls desires to sift you, to bring you into harm and destruction. But I say to you, pay attention to Me. Focus on My words to you and walk in the confidence that obedience brings. This is the confidence that the enemy cannot duplicate nor stand against.

These are indeed perilous times, yet hear Me. I desire to protect My children—to provide shelter for you in the midst of the storm. You and your generation will go through the sifting process. Direct your hearts to make wise choices. Follow Me; walk in My love and grace.

I command you to love and honor one another for this is critical to walking in My protection and anointing. Only a little while longer and I shall receive you into the heavenly kingdom.

Be faithful, My little ones. Be faithful. Hold on tightly to your faith. We shall soon celebrate joyously together. The reward of faithfulness is great.

Biblical Insights on the "Enemy of Your Soul"

Throughout the Bible—Genesis to Revelation—there are consistent bits of information about an evil force, influence, or being that works against God and against His creation. Who or what is this influence or being? Where did it come from? What does it do? And what is its end? How can we recognize evil's presence and agenda? How can we position and defend ourselves against destructive influences and forces?

The Bible often uses names and their meanings to give depth of understanding. The personal name for God's and mankind's arch enemy is Satan (adversary, opposer; 1 Chron. 21:1; Job 1–2; Luke 22:31). Other names are devil (slanderer, false accuser; Job 1:9; Rev. 12:10), serpent (Gen. 3; Rev. 12:9), dragon (Rev. 12:9), tempter (1 Thess. 3:5), evil or wicked one (Matt. 13:19), Beelzebub (chief of evil spirits, devil; Matt. 12:24; Luke 11:15), prince, ruler, or tyrant of this world (John 12:31), god of this age (2 Cor. 4:4), Belial (worthless person; 2 Cor. 6:15; 10), prince of the power of the air (Eph. 2:2), Lucifer (day star, morning star (Isa. 14:12–17; 2 Cor. 11:14), accuser of the brethren (Rev. 12:10), roaring lion (1 Peter 5:8), Abaddon (destroyer; Rev. 9:11), angel of the bottomless pit or messenger of the abyss (Rev. 9:11), murderer (John 8:44), and Leviathan (monster of chaos and terror; Lev. 27:1).

From Isaiah 14:12–17, Ezekiel 28:11–19, Luke 10:18, John 8:44, and Revelation 12:3–4, we learn how wickedness creeps into God's creation through such avenues as pride, greed, lusts, and thirst for glory. Many other supporting scriptures as well as our life experiences confirm the existence and destructive work of evil and wickedness.

One example of evil's creeping influence is the story of Uzziah (also called Azariah), Judah's eleventh king (2 Kings 14:21) who initially did what was right in God's eyes as his father Amaziah had done (2 Chron. 26:1–23 Voice). Verse 5 reads, "While Zechariah the seer was alive, Uzziah followed the True God, listening to Zechariah's messages from God as Joash had listened to Jehoiada's counsel, and the True God blessed the king in battles, in building, and in wealth as long as he was obedient." Who are we listening to?

So Uzziah started out well, but in verse 16, we see wickedness crept into his heart while he was enjoying the blessings of God. "But when Uzziah had built his army and he no longer thought he needed God's help in battles, he became prideful and corrupt." Uzziah overstepped the boundaries of good and godly behavior. He entered the temple to burn incense to God, a job that belonged to the priests. Uzziah saw himself above God's designated structure of authority. We too must examine our hearts so pride, lustful desires and even false assumptions do not lure us into willful disobedience and disaster such as happened to Uzziah. (Read vv. 16–21 to get the details and consider the implications.)

God placed checks and balances in the Jewish governmental and social infrastructure. Prophets and priests (those anointed by God and true to His Word) were to speak to the hearts and lives of individuals and to the nation (2 Kings 17:13–23; Isa. 52:7–8; Acts 4:7–33; Eph. 4:1–32; Rev. 10:7). We see those elements in 2 Chron. 26 in the ministries of Zechariah, the seer prophet (v. 5), and Azariah, the priest (v. 17). This division of power and ministry gives people the opportunity to submit themselves one to another for accountability and thus work together to understand and follow God's principles. As you read the story about Uzziah in 2 Chronicles 26, review the names and descriptions of Satan because they are clues as to how evil influences will attempt to bring corruption and destruction into your life.

Selected Scripture Reading

1. Zech. 3:1—"Then he showed me Joshua the high priest standing before the Angel of the LORD, and Satan standing at his right hand to oppose him."
2. Luke 22:31—"And the Lord said, 'Simon, Simon! Indeed, Satan has asked for you, that he may sift you as wheat. But I have prayed for you that your faith should not fail; and when you have returned to

Me, strengthen your brethren.'" See Gen. 3:14; Job 1:6; Matt. 4:1–17; Luke 9:42; John 8:44, 13:2; Acts 4:12; 2 Cor. 11:3, 14; 1 Thess. 3:5; 1 Peter 5:8; 2 Peter 2:1–20; Rev. 9:11, 20:2, 7.
3. Ps. 25:15 (KJV)—"My eyes are ever toward the LORD, For He shall pluck my feet out of the net." See Ps. 145:15; Eph. 1:15–23.
4. Ps. 141:8–9 (Voice)—"My gaze is fixed upon You, Eternal One, my Lord; in You I find safety and protection. Do not abandon me and leave me defenseless. Protect me from the jaws of the trap my enemies have set for me and from the snares of those who work evil."
5. Ps. 101:1–8—"I will sing of mercy and justice; To You, O LORD, I will sing praises. I will behave wisely in a perfect way. Oh, when will You come to me? I will walk within my house with a perfect heart. I will set nothing wicked before my eyes; I hate the work of those who fall away; It shall not cling to me. A perverse heart shall depart from me; I will not know wickedness."
6. Zeph. 2:3 (KJV)—"Seek the LORD, all you meek of the earth, Who have upheld His justice. Seek righteousness, seek humility. It may be that you will be hidden in the day of the LORD's anger." See Gen. 7:1; Ps. 91; Luke 21:36; Rev. 3:10.
7. 1 Peter 1:3–9—"Blessed be the God and Father of our Lord Jesus Christ, who according to His abundant mercy has begotten us again to a living hope through the resurrection of Jesus Christ from the dead, To an inheritance incorruptible and undefiled and that does not fade away, reserved in heaven for you. Who are kept by the power of God through faith for salvation ready to be revealed in the last time. In this you greatly rejoice, though now for a little while, if need be, you have been grieved by various trials. That the genuineness of your faith, being much more precious that gold that perishes, though it is tested by fire, may be found to praise, honor, and glory at the revelation of Jesus Christ ... Receiving the end of your faith—the salvation of your souls."

128. Give No Place to Evil

I have come to deliver My people. I have come to rescue My children. Seek Me with your whole heart. Hold nothing back from Me. Come to

Me with your whole heart—with your whole soul, and with your whole mind. Worship Me with all your being. Give no place to the enemy. Give no place to evil. Give no place to anger. Give no place to impurity. Give no place to uncleanness.

You look ahead and you look around you and you see darkness and difficulties. You ask Me, "How can I get through this? How can I have the strength or knowledge to do what I should do?" I say to you, My child, look to Me and focus your heart upon Me for I will be your light. I will be your strength. I will show you the path to take and I will give you the strength to walk. Now listen carefully. My Spirit is within you. Cleanse yourselves and purify yourselves with the pure water of my Word. Let My Word within your heart, soul, and mind permeate your thinking and being so My Spirit and My love will increase in you.

It is the power of My Spirit within you that will give you the light, the strength, and knowledge you need to walk down the path. I say to you, draw from the power of My Holy Spirit within you to have the wisdom and strength you need. Remember I said to you, out of your innermost being will flow living waters. I am your living water. Draw living waters from My Spirit I have placed within you and I will rain My holy presence upon you and rescue you from all your enemies. I will rescue you from the hardness of your heart. I will deliver you.

Selected Scripture Reading

1. Matt. 24:7–13—These verses confirm that geopolitical turmoil, natural disasters, deceptions, extreme lawlessness, violence, and hatred may cause us to become hard hearted. Yet a promise is given to those who endure in loving God and others.
2. Ps. 9:1–20—"I will praise You, O LORD, with my whole heart; I will tell of all your marvelous works… The LORD also will be a refuge for the oppressed, A refuge in times of trouble. And those who know Your name will put their trust in You; For You, LORD, have not forsaken those who seek You." See Prov. 21:31.
3. Eph. 4:25–32—"Therefore putting away lying, Let each one of you speak truth with his neighbor,' for we are members of one another. Be angry, and do not sin: do not let the sun go down on your wrath, nor give place to the devil. Let him who stole steal no longer, but rather

let him labor, working with his hands what is good, that he may have something to give him who has need. Let no corrupt word proceed out of your mouth, but what is good for necessary edification, that it may impart grace to the hearers. And do not grieve the Holy Spirit of God, by whom you were sealed for the Day of Redemption. Let all bitterness, wrath, anger, clamor, and evil speaking be put away from you, with all malice. And be kind to one another, tenderhearted, forgiving one another, even as God in Christ forgave you." See Hos. 10:12.

129. You Are My Living Church

The enemy wants you to panic and act in fear to your own destruction. But I say to you, quiet your hearts and put your trust in Me. Come to Me and rest in Me. Call out to Me and stand fast in My love.

Do not fear and do not waver. Stand fast. Stand upright in all your ways. Stand upright in your hearts. Stand upright in your thoughts. Stand upright and you will see the salvation of the Lord. The righteous—those who know Me—those who know My voice and obey Me in the midst of the storm, in the midst of confusion—they will bring peace and light. They will give stability and strength. They will build up and not tear down.

Prepare yourselves now, My children. Prepare your hearts. You are My living church. You are a shelter in this world. You are a place of strength, hope, and love because of My presence in you. Be in Me, and I will be in you and the light of the Lord shall be upon you.

Selected Scripture Reading

1. Isa. 40:10—"Fear not, for I am with you; Be not dismayed, for I am your God. I will strengthen you, Yes, I will help you, I will uphold you with My righteous right hand."
2. Deut. 31:6—"Be strong and of good courage, do not fear nor be afraid of them; for the LORD your God, He is the One who goes with you. He will not leave you nor forsake you." See Num. 14:9; Deut. 3:22; Prov. 1:33; Ps. 118:6, 56; Matt. 10:26–28.

3. Rom. 8:15—"For you did not receive the spirit of bondage again to fear, but you received the Spirit of adoption by whom we cry out, 'Abba, Father.'" See Luke 12:32.
4. 2 Tim. 1:7—For God has not given us a spirit of fear, but of power and of love and of a sound mind. See Matt. 18:21–35; Col. 3; 1 Cor. 14:33.
5. Phil. 1:27—"Only let your conduct be worthy of the gospel of Christ ... that you stand fast in one spirit, with one mind striving together for the faith of the gospel."
6. 1 Cor. 15:58—"Therefore, my beloved brethren, be steadfast, immovable, always abounding in the work of the Lord, knowing that your labor is not in vain in the Lord."
7. 1 Peter 2:1–5—"Therefore, laying aside all malice, all deceit, hypocrisy, envy, and all evil speaking, as newborn babes desire the pure milk of the word, that you may grow thereby ... coming to Him as to a living stone, rejected indeed by men, but chosen by God and precious, you also, as living stones, are being built up a spiritual house, a holy priesthood, to offer up spiritual sacrifices acceptable to God through Jesus Christ." See Hos. 6:6; Matt. 9:13; Eph. 2:20–22; Col. 1; Phil. 2:17–18.
8. 1 Cor. 3:16—"Do you not know that you are the temple of God and that the Spirit of God dwells in you?" See Ezek. 36:27; John 14:17; Rom. 8:9; 1 Cor. 6:19; 2 Tim. 1:14.
9. Matt. 5:16—"Let your light so shine before men, that they may see your good works and glorify your Father in heaven." See John 15:8; 1 Peter 2:11–12.
10. Phil. 2:14–15—"Do all things without complaining and disputing, that you may become blameless and harmless, children of God, without fault in the midst of a crooked and perverse generation, among whom you shine as lights in the world."

130. Come Closer to My Heart

When I allow you to be sifted—when I allow you to be tested—I am calling you to come up higher. I am calling you to come closer to Me. I am calling you to walk in a more excellent way. My dearly beloved children.

Do you not know? Do you not realize when you struggle to control—when you strive to manipulate and cause a certain path to be taken, you are pushing me out?

When you do this, you are pushing me out of the circumstances and hindering My purposes and plans to help and to bless you. Turn away from your fears and come to Me for healing and restoration, for I desire to bless you and make you fruitful in the kingdom of God.

Yes, I must remove those things from you that hinder My Spirit in you. For I will have a pure bride, one who knows Me in righteousness, one whom I can trust to receive and operate in My glory and the gifts I shall impart to her.

Do not fear nor be afraid of the sifting for I am separating from you that which hinders and defiles. Do not be offended by My discipline or walk away from My correction. Do not judge your brother or sister.

Others look at outward appearances, but I look upon your heart. I desire your heart to be one with Me. I am calling to you. Come closer to Me. Come closer to My heart. Know Me. I am your God, and I desire your heart.

Selected Scripture Reading

1. Gen. 7:1—"Then the LORD said to Noah, 'Come into the ark, you and all your household, because I have seen that you are righteous before Me in this generation.'" Apparently, the wickedness of mankind as described in Genesis 6:1–7 had increased to the point that without intervention, goodness was threatened with extinction. The meaning of verses 1–7 has been greatly debated. Views range from just the normal downward spiral of fallen humanity to the interpretation of the phrase "sons of God" (*B'nai Elohim*) to be referring to a group of fallen angels. Verse 4 indicates that the offspring (Hebrew, *Nephilim*) of this super powerful wickedness and the "daughters of men" resulted in large, powerful, and wicked beings that were a terror and extremely wicked influence on the rest of mankind.

    Verses 8 and 9 reveal that God looked at Noah's heart and found a man of integrity. See Num. 13:33; Deut. 1:28, 3:11, 9:1–2; Josh. 11:22; 1 Sam. 17:4–7; Job 1:6; Ps. 121:7–8; Prov. 20:26; Isa. 14:12; Amos 9:8–12; Matt. 24:37; Luke 17:26; Heb. 11:7; 2 Peter 2:4–9;

Jude 6, 7. The main point here is to be wise and avoid evil in all its forms.
2. Luke 22:31–32 (Voice)—"Simon, Simon, how Satan has pursued you, that he might make you part of his harvest. But I have prayed for you. I have prayed that your faith will hold firm and that you will recover from your failure and become a source of strength for your brothers here." Another example of how Jesus prays for us is in John 17:6–26.
3. 1 Peter 5:8–9—These verses depict how evil seeks to destroy us and how we should respond.
4. Ps. 139:23–24—"Search me, O God, and know my heart; Try me, and know my anxieties; And see if there is any wicked way in me, And lead me in the way everlasting."

131. Created to Be Clothed in My Light

I love you, My child. You were made and created in My image. I have created each one of you unique and special. Each one of you has your own combination of qualities in your personality. You are created with unique similarities and unique differences. You are beautiful to Me and are the crown of My creation.

In this season, I am restoring the beauty of My creation, which has been defiled, perverted, and destroyed by the enemy. My people themselves have gone astray and lost the glorious light that was their covering for I created you to be clothed in My light and in My presence.

Return to Me. Step into My light. Submit every part of you—who you are—to Me and I shall restore you. I shall heal your personality. I shall restore you to be the person I created you to be—full of joy, wisdom, and peace, delightfully unique—a lively stone well fitted and positioned in My household and among your brothers and sisters.

You are created to love and support one another. You are designed to edify and build up—to nurture and protect—one another with all wisdom and grace.

I have created you unique and similar. I have created you with many differences, qualities, and talents. Can you all run fast? Can you all make fine-stitched works? Know this. I have created you, each of you unique and different, yet I have created you to be one in Me. I have created you to come together in unity in Me.

To do this, you must submit to Me. You must submit your personality to Me that I may strengthen those qualities that are of Me and take away those that are not of Me. For I will restore the beauty of My creation so that My Son, Jesus Christ, be perfected in your hearts and reflect the glory of God. You are created to be clothed in My light.

Come to Me that I may restore you.

Selected Scripture Reading

1. Gen. 1:26–27—God created humanity in His image, that is, reflecting His qualities and characteristics. Scripture indicates that the ordered uniqueness and differences of male and female were meant to reveal to us more about who we are meant to be as a reflection of our Creator.
2. Ps. 30:11 (Voice)—"You did it: You turned my deepest pains into joyful dancing; You stripped off my dark clothing and covered me with joyful light." See Ps. 16:11; Matt. 15:1–20; James 1:5.
3. John 8:12—"Then Jesus spoke to them again, saying, 'I am the light of the world. He who follows Me shall not walk in darkness, but have the light of life!'"
4. Matt. 5:14–16—"And you, beloved, are the light of the world." See 2 Cor. 4:1–7; Gal. 3:26–27; Ps. 101:3.

132. Take My Yoke

I am the Lord God almighty and I am the healer of your souls. I am your Creator God and I am the one who restores. My dear and precious children, come close to Me and learn of Me. Follow Me and you will find the life you are seeking for I will lead you into My peace and joy.

My people suffer destruction for lack of knowledge. Come to Me and learn of Me. Take My yoke and learn My ways for My yoke is easy and My burden is light. Lay down the burdens of this world and take instead the gospel of salvation—My words of truth, mercy, and justice—for then you shall walk in My freedom.

Do not suffer—do not be destroyed—for lack of knowledge. Lay aside worldliness and come unto Me. Seek Me. Search My Word with all your heart and I will be found by you. I will come to you and I will teach you the path of life.

I will lead you and I will instruct you in the path of righteousness. Know this. These are perilous times, and many suffer because they seek after carnal knowledge, refusing and rebelling against My truth and wisdom. In this season of trials—in this season of hearts being tested—I have made provisions for you to overcome. I have provisions by My Holy Spirit for you to hear My Word, and understand more clearly what I say to you so you are not led astray by carnal thinking and the influences of rebellion. Consider carefully and examine your heart that you walk before Me in pure love and devotion for I have many things to teach you that will protect you during these difficult times.

You are My child, and I have made provision for you to receive My peace and joy. Come to Me that I may breathe My life into you. Come to Me and learn of Me that I may restore you and lift your heavy burdens. Come.

Selected Scripture Reading

1. Ps. 100:3 (Voice)—"Know this: the Eternal One Himself is the True God. He is the One who made us; we have not made ourselves; we are His people, like sheep grazing in His fields."
2. Mal. 2:10 (Voice)—"Do we not all share one father? Has not one God created us all? Why do we all act deceitfully with our brothers and sisters and soil the covenant between God and our ancestors?"
3. Ps. 143:10—"Teach me to do Your will, For You are my God; Your Spirit is good. Lead me in the land of uprightness." See John 14:26, 16:7–8, 13, 17:17.
4. Isa. 45:22; Acts 2:38—Notice the universal call to salvation even to those far away.
5. Ps. 82:5, 92:6; Isa. 1:3, 59:8; Jer. 5:4; Amos 3:10; Mic. 4:12; Hos. 4:6; Matt. 22:29; Luke 12:56; Acts 13:27, 28:27; Rom. 10:3; Eph. 4:17–32; Heb. 5:11; 1 Peter 1:14—These scriptures are about spiritual ignorance and its consequences.
6. Isa. 30:15; Eph. 5:17—These scriptures instruct us to return to God with knowledgeable intention.

7. Matt. 11:28–30—"Come to Me, all you who labor and are heavy laden, and I will give you rest. Take My yoke upon you and learn from Me, for I am gentle and lowly in heart and you will find rest for your souls. For My yoke is easy and My burden is light."

133. Written in My Word

I am calling My people to come up higher and commune with Me. Open your heart that I may come in and dine with you. I have many things to share with you, to teach you, to remind you of what is written in My Word.

My heart desires to comfort you and give you clarity so you are not drawn into fear and confusion. These are times that try—these are times that test people's hearts. Hold on tightly to your faith and come closer to Me. I will be your strength and shield.

You shall be tried. You shall be tested. My bride shall be purified and come forth brilliantly white, spotless, and pure. Her motives and actions shall be under the power of My Holy Spirit. She shall speak My truth. She shall do My works. She shall arise, and the gates of hell shall not stand against her.

Look up, My beloved, for your full redemption draws near. Give heed to My words. Look unto Me. Do not focus on the stormy seas around you. Fill your heart with My Word and enter My presence; we shall rejoice together.

Selected Scripture Reading

1. Isa. 55:1–3—How has it been working for mankind to come up with its own answers for joy, peace, and safety in our world? In these scriptures, God teaches us that He has put in our hearts a hunger and thirst for understanding the meaning of life and where we fit into the bigger picture. He invites us to come to Him for real answers.
2. Ps. 23 (Voice)—"The Eternal is my shepherd, He cares for me always. He provides me rest in rich, green fields besides streams of refreshing water. He soothes my fears; He makes me whole again, steering me off worn, hard paths to roads where truth and righteousness echo His

name. Even in the unending shadows of death's darkness, I am not overcome by fear. Because You are with me in those dark moments, near with Your protection and guidance, I am comforted. You spread out a table before me, provisions in the midst of attack from my enemies; You care for all my needs, anointing my head with soothing fragrant oil, filling my cup again and again with Your grace. Certainly Your faithful protection and loving provision will pursue me where I go, always, everywhere. I will always be with the Eternal, in Your house forever."

3. Jer. 3:19 (Voice)—"I thought to Myself how much I wanted to welcome you home as children and bless you with a good land and a future to be envied by all the world. I hoped for the day when you would call Me, 'My Father,' and no longer pull away from Me and My ways." God is pouring out His heart to them about how much He wanted to bless them but couldn't because they had not been faithful to His teachings. He pleads with them to repent, to change their hearts and ways. In Jeremiah 3:15, He tells them that if they repent and change their lifestyles to follow Him, He will give them godly shepherds who will feed them with knowledge and understanding. See Luke 13:34; 1 Cor. 10.

4. Rev. 2:7—In this verse, God reminds us what to expect if we heed His words.

134. America, Repent

Those who have embraced death and destruction shall reap death and destruction. They have forsaken Me and have instead run after false gods. They have idolized fame, power, wealth, and possessions. They have lusted and murdered.

They call evil good and good evil. Because they have turned their backs on Me, I cannot stand in the way of the path they have chosen.

I am calling to you, America, to repent before it is too late and you suffer destruction. Turn away from your wickedness and sins or in your pride and arrogance you will reap death and destruction. The wicked continue in blind stubbornness and rebellion, suffering the consequences. Open your eyes and ears so you can hear Me pleading with you.

Humble yourselves and change your ways so your nation may continue to exist.

Biblical Insights on What God Expects from Nations

God has a lot to say about nations in the Bible. There are approximately 559 uses of the word *nation* and 434 uses of the word *nations*. Genesis 10 is often subtitled the Table of Nations and records the descendants of Noah and his sons, Shem, Ham, and Japeth, after the flood. Some Bibles have maps of where these groups of peoples settled throughout what is now Turkey, Syria, Lebanon, parts of Russia, Iran, Iraq, Jordan, Israel, Saudi Arabia, and Egypt, the areas bordered by the Black, Aegean, Caspian, Mediterranean, and Red Seas and the Persian Gulf.

Using several translations to study Genesis 10:5, one may possibly get a glimpse of the beginning of what is known as the Gentile nations. Through Noah's son Japeth and Japeth's descendant, Javan, came a group of people who were seafaring and settled coastal lands. Some Bible maps even have the word *Greeks* written below Javan's name. Many translations state that these maritime peoples settled in coastal areas and over time developed their own language dialects and cultures thus becoming different nations.

Of particular significance is Genesis 12, which describes God's choosing a man He knew would have the leadership skills and consistent dedication to create a nation of his descendants. Abraham's descendants were not sinless, but as a nation, they were able to develop a God awareness and live before all mankind in a way that validated and witnessed God's existence, goodness, and holiness.

Studying the heritage of different groups of people and their languages can be quite intriguing and even give insight into languages, similarities, animosities, and alliances. It is also important to keep in mind that cultures and nations are made up of individuals. Psalm 53 speaks of the folly of the godless in a nation and their subsequent demise with the last verse declaring hope for restoration for the nation. Verses 1–3 state clearly that the problem of sin and even doubting the existence of God are universal problems.

Throughout the Bible, God revealed principles specifically applicable to nations and their leaders. These principles are tied to their character qualities and behaviors. Scripture uses such adjectives as *godly, righteous, wise, foolish, violent, rebellious, idolatrous,* and *wicked* to describe individuals. It also speaks of nations using the same words and phrases.

Below are a few principles and statements concerning nations.

1. God is sovereign. He rules over the nations and instructs them to follow Him, but like individuals, they choose obedience or rebellion. See Deut. 30:15, 19, 8; Josh. 24:15; Pss. 47:8, 103:9; Prov. 1:29; Jer. 32:33; Ezek. 39:6, 23–24; Dan. 2:44, 4:32; Zech. 7:8–11; Matt. 10:30; John 17:3; Eph. 4:6; Phil. 2:11; 1 Tim. 6:15; Rev. 11:17; 22:11–12.
2. Sins put our relationship with God in jeopardy. See Deut. 23:14; 1 Kings 8:22–9:9; Pss. 66:18, 64:7; Isa. 1:1–26, 3:9, 59:1–2, 43:24b; Ezek. 14:13–14; Hos. 5:4; Rom. 11:22; Heb. 3:7–14. Who determines what is sinful? Who determines what is good and what is evil? What do you think the Tree of the Knowledge of Good and Evil in Genesis 2:9 represents for mankind? Is this a heart issue, a behavior issue, or both? See Gen. 4:7; Pss. 66:18, 64:7; Isa. 59:1–2; Jer. 10:23, 17:10; Heb. 3:13.
3. Godliness brings blessings while willful disobedience brings difficulties. See Gen. 4:10–11; Deut. 32; Ps. 33:12; Prov. 14:34; Isa. 26:2. 30:1–26, 44:1–11; Jer. 17:1–14, 18:8, 45:4; Zech. 2:11, 7:11–14; Matt. 25:31–46; Gal. 5; Eph. 4:17–5:7; Col. 1:9–23; 1 Peter 2:11.
4. Prosperity can cause pride, which can cause individuals to forget God. See Deut. 8:11–20; Ezek. 16:49; Rev. 3:17.
5. God announces some events long before they happen as a confirmation of who He is. See Isa. 42:8–9, 44:6–8, 46:9–10; Dan. 2:28; Acts 3:18, 15:6–18; Rom. 11:7–36.
6. Leaders who live and work without integrity create many problems for themselves and those they lead, but leaders who follow God's principles in personal and public matters impart blessings. When godly leaders make mistakes, they acknowledge responsibility. See Deut. 34:9; Lev. 25:43; 1 Sam. 23:1–5; 2 Sam. 23:3; 2 Kings 19; 1 Chron. 21; 2 Chron. 6:12–7:14, 19:6; Neh.; Ps. 2:10–11; Prov. 20:28, 29:4, 14; Mic. 3:1–12; 1 Tim. 3:1–13.
7. The citizens of a nation are accountable to God and their leaders. How average citizens live affects their leaders and nations. The

people must use discernment and wisdom while prayerfully supporting their leaders. See 2 Chron. 36:14; Neh. 9:16–17; 1 Tim. 2:1–4.
8. God has appointed spiritual leaders as ministers to speak into the lives of those in authority and all people to encourage them to obey Him. The people must use discernment and wisdom. See Neh. 8–10; Jer. 29:1–14; Mic. 3:8; Matt. 23:1–36; 1 Thess. 5:16–22; 1 Tim. 6; Titus 1:10–16.
9. God calls all nations to repent of their sins. See Ezekiel 22 for sins that lead to judgment of a nation. Isaiah 54 describes the pattern of sin, correction, repentance, and redemption of a nation. Verse 14 states that a nation is established in righteousness and it is righteousness that will protect it from oppression and terrorism. See 2 Chron. 7:12–14; Ps. 81.

Selected Scripture Reading

1. 2 Chron. 15:1–2—"Now the Spirit of God came upon Azariah the son of Oded. And he went out to meet Asa, and said to him: 'Hear me, Asa, and all Judah and Benjamin. The LORD is with you while you are with Him. If you seek Him, He will be found by you; but if you forsake Him, He will forsake you.'"
2. Isa. 26:1–13 (Voice)—"By the grace of God, our city is strong; its structures and defenses He made secure. Now open the gates to welcome the righteous, so that those who keep faith may enter in. You will keep the peace, a perfect peace, for all who trust in You, for those who dedicate their hearts and minds to You. So trust in the Eternal One forever, for He is like a great Rock—strong, stable, trustworthy, and lasting. He humbles the high and mighty. Even the indomitable city falls before His strength, reducing it to dust. The feet of the poor, the weak, the infirm and forgotten will trample the dust of the formerly great. The path of those who do right is straight and smooth. O God You who are upright. You make the way of the righteous level. When we act in justice and righteousness—following Your laws—we wait for You. We are eager to hear Your holy name and remember Your ways. At night I long for You with all that is in Me. When morning comes, I seek You with all my heart. For when Your justice is

done on earth, then everyone in the world will learn righteousness. If grace is extended to those who do wrong, the perpetrators never learn what is right. Even when surrounded by upright people, they gravitate to evil and never even notice the awesome beauty of the Eternal. O Eternal One, even when Your hand is raised against them, they do not see it. When they finally do see how passionately You act on the people's behalf, they will be ashamed. Ah, let the fire that consumes Your enemies consume them. Eternal One, You are preparing peace for us; in fact everything we have accomplished has come from You. Others have tried to rule over us, but You, Eternal One, are our God. At the end of the day, when all is done, we acknowledge only You." See Mic. 6:6–8.

135. That I May Impart to You

I shall place My Spirit of wisdom and understanding on chosen servants of Mine. They will be called to speak before kings, presidents, and rulers in authority. I will place them in strategic positions to give counsel and witness for My name's sake.

Shall I not reveal the sons of God by My Spirit of wisdom and understanding that rests on them? Humble yourselves, My children, and learn of Me for I have many things to teach you and prepare you for the times and seasons to come.

Come to Me that I may impart to you My grace and wisdom for service in My kingdom. The time is short. Prepare yourself.

Selected Scripture Reading

1. Prov. 4:6–8—Proverbs' purpose is stated in Proverbs 1:2–3: "to know wisdom and instruction, To perceive the words of understanding, To receive the instruction of wisdom." Proverbs 4:6–8 speaks of the personal choices required to learn wisdom and its benefits. Give examples from scripture and your life experiences of how biblical wisdom may influence attitudes and behaviors.
2. Job 28:28—"And to man He said, 'behold, the fear of the Lord, that is wisdom, And to depart from evil is understanding.'" Compare this

verse with Ephesians 5:15–21. Why do these verses tie fearing and respecting God to departing from evil?

3. Matt. 10:16–20—"Behold, I send you out as sheep in the midst of wolves. Therefore be wise as serpents and harmless as doves. But beware of men, for they will deliver you up to councils and scourge you in their synagogues. You will be brought before governors and kings for My sake, as a testimony to them and to the Gentiles. But when they deliver you up, do not worry about how or what you should speak. For it will be given to you in that hour what you should speak; For it is not you who speak, but the Spirit of your Father who speaks in you." This message is repeated in Luke 12:11–12. See Acts 6:8–7:60 for an example.

4. 2 Tim. 3:12–4:5—"Yes, and all who desire to live godly in Christ Jesus will suffer persecution. But evil men and impostors will grow worse and worse, deceiving and being deceived. But you must continue in the things which you have learned and been assured of, knowing from whom you have learned them, And that from childhood you have known the Holy Scriptures, which are able to make you wise for salvation through faith which is in Christ Jesus. All Scripture is given by inspiration of God, and is profitable for doctrine, for reproof,

for correction, for instruction in righteousness, That the man of God may be complete thoroughly equipped for every good work."

136. Lifted Up in Purity and Righteousness

I am doing a new thing in your midst, and you will see My glory revealed among you.

The hard times, the difficult trials you have had and are going through have been seasons of refining and polishing for I am about to do a new work in the earth today.

The world is looking for answers, truth, comfort, and rest. The world is looking for deliverance.

I am calling forth My people to come clean and reflect My glory that the name of Jesus be lifted up in purity and righteousness for the world to see. It is through My people that My glory will be revealed to the world. Prepare yourselves, My people. Prepare your hearts and lives to reflect the purity, love and brilliance of My presence to the world.

Selected Scripture Reading

1. Ex. 15—When the Israelites were facing extermination by their enemies, they followed their leader Moses, who walked in obedience to God's instructions. Their enemies were defeated, and Moses and the people sang this song in Exodus 15. Read it carefully for insights on who God is. How do you think Leviticus 11:45, Luke 1:74–75, and 1 Peter 1:16 relate to Exodus 15? Are there spiritual parallels to a Christian's walk today?
2. Ps. 99—This is a song of praise to God acknowledging His holiness. In it are examples and principles of how He interacts with people.
3. 2 Cor. 7:1 (Voice)—"Because we have these promises, dearly loved ones, out of respect for God we should scour the filth from our flesh and spirit and move toward perfect beauty and holiness." See 2 Cor. 6 for clarification on the promises and admonitions.
4. 1 Peter 1:22–23—"Since you have purified your souls in obeying the truth through the Spirit in sincere love of the brethren, love one another fervently with a pure heart, Having been born again, not of

corruptible seed but incorruptible, through the word of God which lives and abides forever." Describe how we are born again by the words God has spoken.
5. 1 Peter 2:9—"But you are a chosen generation, a royal priesthood, a holy nation, His own special people, that you may proclaim the praises of Him who called you out of darkness into His marvelous light." Compare with Rom. 8:12–19.
6. Rev. 15:4—"Who shall not fear You, O Lord, and glorify Your name? For You alone are holy, For all nations shall come and worship before You, For Your judgments have been manifested." This verse is written within the descriptions of the end-time judgments upon nations.

137. A Higher Way

I have a destiny and a purpose for each of you. I have given you gifts and talents, and you are to grow and mature in the development and exercise of these tools I have placed in your hands. There is a bigger cause, a bigger plan than what you can presently see or are ready to comprehend at this time.

It is by faith that you will enter the promises and destiny that is yours in My kingdom. Many come close but do not enter the full potential of their destiny in My kingdom because their hearts are not fully surrendered to Me.

You must lie down all your earthly desires and pick up the cross of total surrender to Me. Will you serve Me first and not yourself? Will you give yourself to My plan for your life? Will you be a tool in the hand of the Lord for righteousness?

I am calling you to a higher way of love, service, and obedience so I may equip and prepare you for the destiny that is yours in Me. You must surrender and give to Me your future. You must come alone to Me.

Selected Scripture Reading

1. Ps. 139:1–24—"O LORD, You have searched me and known me. You know my sitting down and my rising up; You understand my

thought afar off. You comprehend my path and my lying down, And are acquainted with all my ways. For there is not a word on my tongue, But behold, O LORD, You know it altogether. You have hedged me behind and before, And laid Your hand upon me. Such knowledge is too wonderful for me; It is high, I cannot attain it ... For You formed my inward parts; You covered me in my mother's womb. I will praise You, for I am fearfully and wonderfully made; Marvelous are Your works, And that my soul knows very well ... How precious also are Your thoughts to me, O God! How great is the sum of them! ... Search me, O God, and know my heart; Try me, and know my anxieties; And see if there is any wicked way in me, And lead me in the way everlasting." See Phil. 3:1–11.

2. Ex. 31:1–6—"Then the LORD spoke to Moses, saying: See, I have called by name Bezalel the son of Uri, the son of Hur, of the tribe of Judah. And I have filled him with the Spirit of God, in wisdom, in understanding, in knowledge, and in all manner of workmanship, To design artistic works, to work in gold, silver, in bronze." What are the gifts God has entrusted you with?

3. Matt. 25—Jesus taught principles of moral character as reflected in the ability to make wise use of time and investments. He told the parable of the wise and foolish virgins and the parable of the talents. Do you think He is speaking of life on earth and eternal life as well? Verses 31–46 speak of the Son of Man judging the nations in the future. How would you summarize the basis on which nations are judged?

138. Faith Works by Love

My Spirit is calling My people to arise and stand in the gap, interceding—calling forth—for mercy, healing, and protection for their families, friends, and neighbors. I shall do the work of restoration if My church shall prevail in prayer.

I say to you, do the works I have set before you. You will know what these works are when you surrender your heart to Me completely and come humbly into My presence daily. Seek Me with your whole heart and you will find that My presence will be with you. My Spirit will commune with you and teach you My ways. You will walk in the blessings of My presence.

Come before Me in the night seasons when I call to you for I would speak to you and direct you how to intercede—how to pray for your nation and your families. My Spirit will direct your words to be in harmony with My will to accomplish the works of righteousness and blessing that I would do.

Remember, faith works by love. Let My love and My truth embrace your whole being that you may walk with Me and walk with one another in unity. Arise, My church and stand in the gap.

Selected Scripture Reading

1. Ezek. 22:29–31—"The people of the land have used oppressions, committed robbery, and mistreated the poor and needy; and they wrongfully oppress the stranger. So I sought for a man among them who would make a wall, and stand in the gap before Me on behalf of the land, that I should not destroy it."
2. Ps. 106:23—"Therefore He said that He would destroy them, Had not Moses His chosen one stood before Him in the breach, To turn away His wrath, lest He destroy them." One way Moses interceded for his people was by writing a song inspired by God. See Deut. 31:19–22, 32:1–47. What are the main principles this song teaches? How does it encourage a group of people—a nation—to believe in God's love and justice?
3. Jer. 10:23–24—"O LORD, I know the way of man is not in himself; It is not in man who walks to direct his own steps. O LORD, correct me, but with justice; Not in your anger, lest You bring me to nothing." See Ps. 20.
4. 2 Chron. 7:14—"If My people who are called by My name will humble themselves, and pray and seek My face, and turn from their wicked ways, then I will hear from heaven, and will forgive their sin and heal their land." See Ps. 81.
5. Ps. 55:16–17—"As for me, I will call upon God, And the LORD shall save me. Evening and morning, and at noon I will pray, and cry aloud, And He shall hear my voice." See Matt. 7:7, 26:41; Luke 18:1, 21:36; Eph. 6:18; Phil. 4:6; Col. 4:2; 1 Thess. 5:17, 5:16–22; 1 Tim. 2:8; James 5:13.

139. Come, My Beloved, and Follow Me

My people—My children, why do you go your own way? Why do you walk in rebellion to My commands and principles then wonder why your hearts and souls do not prosper? You live in a dry and thirsty land. You live plagued by mildew and pestilence. You are encircled and harassed by the enemies of your soul.

Stop walking in darkness. No longer follow the spiritually blind who lead you into the paths of confusion and destruction. It is time to turn around. It is time to walk in the light. It is time to embrace My truth. It is time to honor correction.

Come out, My children. Come out from the ways of the rebellious. Come out from darkness and into the light and glory of God. Follow Me and your heart and soul will be refreshed with living water. Follow Me and you will walk in the light of My truth, My wisdom, and My love.

Follow Me and you will find peace and hope. I will shut the mouths of the lions and I will make even your enemies to be at peace with you for you will overcome evil with good. You will know Me. You will obey My commands and My will for your life, and it will be good.

Grasp the vision I have for you—a holy nation and a royal priesthood—that you shall shine forth the glory and presence of God. Come, My beloved, and follow Me.

Selected Scripture Reading

1. Isa. 48:17–18 (Voice)—"The Eternal One, who rescued you, the Holy One of Israel declares, 'I am the Eternal One your God. I have given you My instruction for living well and right, leading you in how you should be and do. If only you had listened to My instruction, then you would have been flooded with peace; Your righteousness would have risen and crested like waves on the sea.'" Chapter 48 specifically addresses the nation of Israel yet reveals multiple principles and truths for all peoples and nations. See Ps. 106; Jer. 5; Rom. 1:18–3:26.
2. Isa. 30:1–26—"'Woe to the rebellious children,' says the LORD, 'Who take counsel, but not of Me, And who devise plans, but not of My Spirit, That they may add sin to sin … Therefore the LORD will wait, that He may be gracious to you; And therefore He will be

exalted, that He may have mercy on you. For the LORD is a God of justice; Blessed are all those who wait for Him.'" See Acts 20:21; Jude 1:1–25.
3. Ps. 81:11–14—"But My people would not heed My voice, And Israel would have none of Me. So I gave them over to their own stubborn heart, To walk in their own counsels. Oh, that My people would listen to Me ... I would soon subdue their enemies, And turn My hand against their adversaries." See Rom. 8:6, 14:17.
4. Heb. 3:8—"Today, if you will hear His voice, Do not harden your hearts as in the rebellion, In the day of trial in the wilderness." See Ps. 95:8; Hos. 14:2.

140. You Shall Come Forth

Some things are going to happen soon that My people will not understand. They will think I am not hearing and answering their prayers. Stand strong. Stand steadfast.

These things—these trials will test your faith and prove your faithfulness. I will never leave you. I will never forsake you. I am with you in the midst of the tribulations. You shall come forth as gold tried in the fire, worthy vessels for the Master's use.

Take time to rest and refresh yourself now for you will need all your physical strength. Stay close to Me and I will give you spiritual food to nourish and sustain you. Great opportunities lie ahead. Prepare yourself. Prepare your heart.

Yes, some things that happen will look bad. But those very things will open doors, even the doors of people's hearts that My gospel can touch them. Have faith. Trust in Me to work through all things and accomplish good among My people. I am restoring what has been lost. Come before Me and receive comfort and understanding of My grace and love for you.

Selected Scripture Reading

1. Isa. 55:6–11—"Seek the LORD while He may be found, Call upon Him while He is near. Let the wicked forsake his way, And the unrighteous man his thoughts; Let him return to the LORD, And

He will have mercy on him; And to our God, For He will abundantly pardon. 'For My thoughts are not your thoughts, Nor are your ways My ways,' says the LORD. For as the heavens are higher than the earth, So are My ways higher than your ways, And My thoughts than your thoughts. For as the rain comes down, and the snow from heaven, And do not return there, But water the earth, And make it bring forth and bud, That it may give seed to the sower and bread to the eater, So shall My word be that goes forth from My mouth, It shall not return to Me void, But it shall accomplish what I please, And it shall prosper in the thing for which I sent it."

God sees the bigger picture. How can we broaden our perspective and understanding? What should our attitude be when we face difficulties and hardships? See examples of prayers in Pss.; Rom. 11:33–36.

2. 2 Cor. 4:16–18—"Therefore we do not lose heart. Even though our outward man is perishing, yet the inward man is being renewed day by day. For our light affliction, which is but for a moment, is working for us a far more exceeding and eternal weight of glory, While we do not look at the things which are seen, but at the things which are not seen. For the things which are seen are temporary, but the things which are not seen are eternal." See Isa. 40:28–31.

141. I Will Welcome You Home

My people—even My church in the United States—have often played the part of a harlot. She is betrothed to Me to be My pure and chaste—My holy bride, but she has given herself over to the lusts of a wayward heart. She has sought out other lovers.

I am calling out to you. Return to Me and walk away from worldly pursuits that have brought you only confusion and deception. You have been in bed with your enemy, who is suffocating the life out of you. Awaken, My bride. Open your eyes before it is too late. Arise from your drunken stupor and depart from your false lovers who abuse you and leave you stricken and wounded.

I say to you clearly and plainly. Do not look to the world for truth and comfort because the ways of the world cause blindness. The ways of the world poison and defile. The ways of the world lead to death. Come to Me. Give your whole heart to Me. Live faithfully, obeying My words to you. Walk in My love. Walk in the liberty I give you and I will heal you of your backsliding.

The hour is late and the time is short. Now is the time of salvation. Now is the season of restoration. Make yourselves ready and you will be prepared for My Spirit will lead and guide you into all truth as you humbly and obediently follow Me.

Selected Scripture Reading

1. Ezek. 16:15—How might you write a definition of spiritual harlotry based on this verse?
2. Jer. 2:19—"'Your own wickedness will correct you, And your backsliding will rebuke you. Know therefore and see that it is an evil and bitter thing That you have forsaken the LORD your God, And the fear of Me is not in you,' Says the Lord GOD of hosts."
3. Mark 4:13–20—"And He said to them, 'Do you not understand this parable? ... The sower sows the word. And these are the ones by the wayside where the word is sown. When they hear, Satan comes immediately and takes away the word that was sown in their hearts. These likewise are the ones sown on stony ground who, when they hear the word, immediately receive it with gladness; And they have no root in themselves, and so endure only for a time. Afterward, when tribulation or persecution arises for the word's sake, immediately they stumble. Now these are the ones sown among the thorns; they are the ones who hear the word, And the cares of this world, the deceitfulness of riches, and the desires for other things entering in choke the word, and it becomes unfruitful. But these are the ones sown on good ground, those who hear the word, accept it, and bear fruit: some thirtyfold, some sixty, and some a hundred."
    Give examples of each metaphor.
4. Ps. 51:12–13—"Restore to me the joy of Your salvation, And uphold me by Your generous Spirit. Then I will teach transgressors Your ways, And sinners will be converted to You." See Isa. 57:15; Heb. 11:31; James 2:23–26. How does our hearts' condition affect our faith in God?

142. Will You Walk with Me?

I am separating the light from the darkness. I am calling out My people to come closer to Me and turn away from the deceitfulness of sin.

Will you walk with Me? Will you leave the ways of the world? In your hearts, will you learn to hate the ways of the spirit of Jezebel? Will you embrace My truth and will you reject the seducing beliefs of Balaam and the Nicolaitans?

Now is the time of separation. Now is the season of choosing whom you will serve for I will have a people who are pure and holy. I will have a people who walk in the freedom of righteousness.

You will know Me and you will know My voice. You will be fearless for you will know that I am with you and you will know that you are about the work of the kingdom of God.

Come to Me now and spend time in My presence. Learn to know My voice and walk in My ways. Come out of the darkness and into My light and you will see My glory as you walk in obedience.

Biblical Insights on the Metaphorical Meanings of Jezebel, Balaam, and the Nicolaitans

Jezebel, a princess from Phoenicia, lived ca. 874–853 BC. Apparently, Phoenicians were descendants of the Bronze Age Canaanites and settled along the coast of present-day Lebanon, in the center of trade routes and commercial activity. They became premier ship builders and sea merchants, exporting purple dyes, oil, wine, grains, glass, and the renowned cedar wood from the forests of Lebanon. They established colonies along the Mediterranean, even Carthage. Tyre and Sidon were two of their main cities.

Jezebel's father, Ethbaal (1 Kings 16:31), was king of Sidon (Zidonians), and like many Phoenicians before him, he had economic ties with Israel that dated back at least to David's and Solomon's times. Ethbaal and Israel's King Omri solidified their relationship and alliance by the marriage of Jezebel to Omri's son, Ahab (1 Kings 16:25–26, 30–33).

What was Jezebel's spiritual heritage? What influence did she bring with her into her new homeland of Israel? Phoenicia was a collection of city states, and each city had its local god or gods and places of worship; the gods were often adaptations of gods and goddesses from Syria and Canaan. The names of the gods had many variants from culture to culture; they included Ishtar, Ashtoreth, Asherah, Assir, Astarte, Ashtartu, Moloch, Malcam, Molech, and Chemosh.

The pagan worship associated with these gods often involved immoral fertility rites (Num. 25:1–2; Deut. 23:17; 1 Kings 14:22–24), gruesome orgies, and child sacrifice (Jer. 19:5). In some sources, you will read that Baal is not the name of one god but is rather the supposed lord over a certain geographical area. Other sources will define Baal as the principal male god of the Phoenicians and note that it is often used in the plural form (Judg. 2:11; 1 Kings 18:18; Hos. 2:17).

Omri and his son, Ahab, had been following the perverted worship practices of backslidden King Jeroboam, who ruled after King Solomon, by establishing locations for worship, building idols, changing feast times, appointing priests, and acting as a priest himself. Therefore, when Ahab married Jezebel, the spiritual condition of the nation plummeted further into unprecedented idolatry, confusion, corruption, and violence.

Because of what Jezebel did and what she is known for, even *Webster's Dictionary* defines *Jezebel* as "any woman regarded as shameless, impudent, morally unrestrained, and wicked, etc." Read more about Jezebel in 1 Kings 16:31, 18:4, 19:1, 21:5, 23; 2 Kings 9:10, 30, 36. She promoted idolatry, incited corruption, plotted murder of the innocent, and used the court system for her own gain. She was ruthless, controlling and manipulative—very politically involved. She killed the genuine prophets and believers of God. In summary Jezebel led the people away from the one true God to embrace false gods and wickedness.

Who was Balaam, and what did he believe? Read the details in Num. 22–25, 31:8, 16; Deut. 23:4; Josh. 33:22, 24:9; Neh. 13:2; Mic. 6:5; 2 Peter 2:15–16; Jude 11; and Rev. 2:14. It appears that Balaam was a well-known and accepted pagan prophet/seer from Pethor (possibly on the Euphrates River) who used divination to get information (Josh. 13:22). Because the Israelites had been successful in fighting Sihon and Og, the fearful Moabite and Midianite kings called in Balaam to curse the Israelites. God did not allow Balaam to curse the Israelites, but Balaam advised the kings on how to cause the Israelites to fall out of favor with their God and no longer be under His protection and blessing (Num. 31:16). Balaam suggested they use the Moabite women to seduce the Israelite men and get them involved in Baal worship.

What did Baalam teach? Because of his desire for personal gain, Balaam taught promotion of sin and acceptance of all religious beliefs and practices; he used sex as bait for unsuspecting victims. He redefined "sin" to fit current cultural standards, and in the process, the people alienated themselves from God.

The Bible doesn't have a great deal to say about the Nicolaitans, but in Revelation 2:6, 2:14–16, we see that the church at Ephesus and our Lord Jesus despised the teaching, deeds, and practices of the Nicolaitans. You can read these passages in several translations for more insight. The Voice translation for Revelation 2:6 reads, "But you do have this to your credit: you despise the deeds of the Nicolaitans and how they concede to evil. I also hate what they do."

It appears the Nicolaitan problem is conceding to evil. Concession may take several different forms. Saying we don't have to be concerned about sin is likely a perversion of the grace of God. Yes, salvation is by faith alone, but faith is completed by our good works and our desire to please God in all things.

How does this apply to me today? I simply might not recognize or consider that the things I do are sin in God's view. I might be so contaminated by the world, so affected by my culture, fashion, and politically correct rhetoric about abortion or same-sex marriage, evolutionary theories, etc., that although I may not consciously hold to a Nicolaitan belief, in reality, I live a compromised life.

How can I protect myself against such a deception? Perhaps a key is a soft and teachable heart that seeks God and realizes it is about fruit—not legalisms. We are free to be righteous and live righteously. If we are sensitive to God's Holy Spirit, He will lead and guide us in all things, step by step, little by little.

This word is never about pointing an accusing finger at another or looking for characteristics of Balaam, Jezebel, or the Nicolaitans in others; it is to alert us to be careful of these things in our own lives.

Selected Scripture Reading

1. Isa. 9:2–7—"The people who walked in darkness Have seen a great light; Those who dwelt in the land of the shadow of death, Upon them a light has shined ... For unto us a Child is born, Unto us a Son

is given; And the government will be upon His shoulder. And His name will be called Wonderful, Counselor, Mighty God, Everlasting Father, Prince of Peace. Of the increase of His government and peace There will be no end, Upon the throne of David and over His kingdom, To order and establish it with judgment and justice From that time forward, even forever." The New Testament reference to this scripture foretelling of the Messiah, the Christ, is Matthew 4:14–17.
2. Rom. 13:12—"The night is far spent, the day is at hand. Therefore let us cast off the works of darkness, and let us put on the armor of light. Let us walk properly, as in the day, not in revelry and drunkenness, not in lewdness and lust, not in strife and envy. But put on the Lord Jesus Christ, and make no provision for the flesh, to fulfill its lusts." See Gal. 5:16–25; Eph. 5:8–14. How do we "cast off the works of darkness?" Give examples.
3. Ps. 16:11—"You will show me the path of life; In Your presence is fullness of joy; At Your right hand are pleasures forevermore." See Ps. 139:23–24.

143. I Am Calling My People to Walk in Holiness

I am the Lord your God, and I am in your midst. I am coming among you in a great visitation of My Spirit. I am bringing restoration to My people.

I am bringing restoration to your hearts. I am bring restoration to your minds. I am bringing restoration to your families. I shall bring cleansing and deliverance to My people. No longer will you be mocked and shamed because of your failures and entrapments.

For I am calling My people to walk in My holiness. I am calling you to walk in My light—that the darkness in your heart—the darkness in your mind—and the darkness around you shall flee. Come out, My children, from the Spirit of Babylon. Come out from the Spirit of wickedness and sin. For My Spirit shall not always strive with the spirit of man. Choose you this day whom you will serve.

Will you bow to the gods of mammon and sensuality? Will you sacrifice your life to emptiness and the traps of sin? No, My little ones. Hear your God! And walk in the liberty and freedom of purity that you have in Me. Keep yourselves pure, and do not become entangled in unrighteousness.

Do not stare at the world for the world is being consumed by a spirit of madness. Many have embraced pride and arrogance. They have rejected Me and race forward into darkness and debauchery.[32] Come out from among them!

I am calling you to be bright and glorious lights in the kingdom of God. Do not be afraid of the darkness for light dispels the darkness. Fill your mind and fill your heart with My love, humility, and truth. You will not be ashamed. You will not be disappointed. For you will stand tall and you will straight in the midst of a perverse and crooked generation.

I have called you to come forth, My beloved, and overcome all things because of the power of My Spirit that dwells within you. Rejoice, My child; you can do all things in Christ who is your strength. Rejoice. You will overcome.

Let My light surround you. Let My light fill you and let My glory shine through you. For I will reveal Myself to all peoples over the earth. You shall be restored and you shall be My witnesses throughout the earth.

Selected Scripture Reading

1. Deut. 23:24—"For the LORD your God walks in the midst of your camp, to deliver you and give your enemies over to you; therefore your camp shall be holy that He may see no unclean thing among you, and turn away from you."
2. Ps. 119:9–11—"How can a young man cleanse his way? By taking heed according to Your word. With my whole heart I have sought You; Oh, let me not wander from Your commandments! Your word I have hidden in my heart, That I might not sin against You."
3. Ps. 119:65–68—"You have dealt well with Your servant, O LORD, according to Your word, Teach me good judgment and knowledge, For I believe Your commandments. Before I was afflicted I went astray, But now I keep Your word. You are good, and do good; Teach me Your statutes." See verses 73–80.

---

[32] Debauchery: 1. Extreme indulgence of one's appetites, especially for sensual pleasure; gross intemperance; lustfulness, gluttony. 2. Seduction from duty or allegiance; a leading astray morally.

4. Matt. 18:20—"For where two or three are gathered together in My name, I am there in the midst of them." See 1 Cor. 14:26.
5. Heb. 2:9–13—"But we see Jesus, who was made a little lower than the angels, for the suffering of death crowned with glory and honor, that He, by the grace of God, might taste death for everyone. For it was fitting for Him, for whom are all things and by whom are all things, in bringing many sons to glory, to make the captain of their salvation perfect through sufferings. For both He who sanctifies and those who are being sanctified are all of one, for which reason He is not ashamed to call them brethren, Saying: 'I will declare Your name to My brethren; In the midst of the assembly I will sing praise to You.' And again: 'I will put my trust in Him.' And again: 'Here am I and the children whom God has given Me.'"
6. Phil. 2:14–15—"Do all things without complaining and disputing, That you may become blameless and harmless, children of God without fault in the midst of a crooked and perverse generation, among whom you shine as lights in the world, 16. Holding fast the word of life." See 1 Peter 4:7–11.
7. Matt. 5:16—"Let your light so shine before men, that they may see your good works and glorify your Father in heaven." See John 15:8.

144. Then Shall Your Light Shine

Will you build your life on a foundation of righteousness and holiness that I may impart to you the tools and ministries and resources to build My kingdom?

Many seek their own glory, but I am seeking the humble in spirit so I may reveal to them the kingdom of heaven. Many seek the wealth of this world, but I am seeking those who hunger and thirst for righteousness.

I am looking for those who hearts want to know Me. Will you seek Me with your whole heart? Will you let My Spirit teach you what is holy, pleasing, and acceptable in My sight? This is the hour I am restoring the beauty of holiness and purity to My people for you shall shine forth My truth and My glory among the nations.

Be faithful in the little things, My children, and you will see Me do greater things in your midst. Love one another. Seek to serve your God and seek to serve one another out of a pure heart. Love justice for I am a God of justice.

In all these things, seek to know Me and My holiness and you will find Me. Then, shall your light shine forth, for I will have My glory revealed to the nations through My people.

Selected Scripture Reading

1. Prov. 10:25—"When the whirlwind passes by, the wicked is no more, But the righteous has an everlasting foundation."
2. Ps. 11—Don't we all want to get away from our troubles? This psalm was written by David, who for years struggled with a man who hunted him down to kill him, enemy armies, and a murderous rebellion in his family. This psalm helps us set our hearts and understanding on eternal values and principles. See Ps. 14:2; 2 Chron. 6:19.
3. Isa. 51:4—"Listen to Me, My people; And give ear to Me, O My nation: For the law will proceed from Me, And I will make My justice rest As a light of the peoples." See Isa. 61:8.
4. Ps. 25:9—"The humble He guides in justice. And the humble He teaches His way."
5. Ps. 37:6—"He shall bring forth your righteousness as the light, And your justice as the noonday." See Isa. 53.
6. Matt. 12:18—"Behold! My Servant whom I have chosen, My beloved in whom My soul is well pleased! I will put My Spirit upon Him, And he will declare justice to the Gentiles." This is a quote from Isa. 42:1-4.
7. 1 Tim. 6:9–19—"But those who desire to be rich fall into temptation and a snare, and into many foolish and harmful lusts which drown men in destruction and perdition … But you, O man of God, flee these things and pursue righteousness, godliness, faith, love, patience, gentleness. Fight the good fight of faith, lay hold on eternal life … Let them do good, that they be rich in good works, ready to give, willing to share, Storing up for themselves a good foundation for the time to come, that they may lay hold on eternal life."
8. Ps. 96:9—"Oh, worship the LORD in the beauty of holiness! Tremble before Him, all the earth." See 2 Chron. 20:21; Ps. 29:2.

145. Come Out of Your Complacency

My people who are in this nation, wake up! Come out of your complacency. Know that the comfort you have worshipped will no longer be there. Every idol is going to fail.

Soften your hearts and pay attention to My Holy Spirit for I will lead and direct My people in a good path. You will have eyes that see, ears that hear, and hearts that understand. You will know which way to go. You will know which way to turn for I will be your guide. I will be your protection. I will provide for you.

Prepare your hearts and minds because the hour of darkness is upon you. Come to Me. Take the light I give you—a bright light to shine in the darkness—My light of truth, honor, and justice. Only the light of My truth will stand against the darkness of this hour.

To a great degree, My people have lost My light. They do not know My Word, the Scriptures. They twist My words to their own destruction. Awaken your hearts and come humbly before Me that I may teach you—for My Holy Spirit desires to instruct you and to bring you into understanding and maturity that you may walk in My grace and abundant blessings.

Yes, I say to you clearly. Follow Me and you will walk in My light. Follow Me and you will walk in My blessings even in the midst of chaos and darkness. Your light will shine and go forth; great will be that light. Great will be your blessings. Great will be your reward.

Persevere, My beloved. Persevere. Remain faithful until I return.

Selected Scripture Reading

1. Ps. 57:7–11 (Voice)—"My heart is ready, O God; my heart is ready, And I will sing! Yes, I will sing praise! Wake up, my glory! Wake up, harp and lyre; I will stir the sleepy dawn with praise! I will offer You my thanks, O Lord, before the nations of the world; I will sing of Your greatness no matter where I am."
2. Rev. 2:14–15, 20—These verses were written to believers who lived in a culture saturated with satanic lies and practices. They point out the severe dangers of becoming complacent and comfortable with godless festivities, rituals, and sexually driven lifestyles.

3. Rev. 3:2–3 (Voice)—"Wake up from your death-sleep, and strengthen what remains of the life you have been given that is in danger of death. I have judged your deeds as far from complete in the sight of My God. Therefore, remember what you have received and heard; it's time to keep these instructions and turn back from your ways (repent). If you do not wake up from this sleep, I will come in judgment. I will creep up on you like a thief—you will have no way of knowing when I will come." When we are spiritually asleep we are oblivious to impending spiritual dangers.
4. Ps. 32:5–8—"I acknowledge my sin to You, And my iniquity I have not hidden. I said, 'I will confess my transgressions to the LORD,' And You forgave the iniquity of my sin. For this cause everyone who is godly shall pray to You In a time when You may be found … You are my hiding place; You shall preserve me from trouble; You shall surround me with songs of deliverance."

146. Grow in Grace

My people, have entertained great evil, and now, great evil is attacking your families, your schools, your government, and your faith. I the Lord am your God. My heart pleads with you. Return to Me, America, and perhaps you may be spared some of the great destruction the enemy has planned for you.

Soften your hearts. Hear My words to you. The hour is late. There is little time left for you to repent and turn from your idolatries, violence and whoredoms.[33] These things are a stench in my nostrils, and I cannot spare you. My patience with you will not go on forever as you pollute and defile the land.

For the sake of My people, My judgments—the fruit of unrighteousness—have been delayed to give you time to turn your hearts to Me. I desire to burst forth with My glory and healing redemption in this nation. Work with Me to accomplish this task and to bring many souls into the kingdom.

---

[33] Whoredoms—in the Bible, the desertion of the worship of God for the worship of idols.

I have good plans for you, America. Return to Me, grow in grace to overcome the gross darkness, and reflect My light in this difficult season.

Selected Scripture Reading

1. Isa. 26:2–3—"Open the gates, That the righteous nation which keeps the truth may enter in. You will keep him in perfect peace, Whose mind is stayed on You, Because he trusts in You." See Ps. 33:12, 130.
2. Jer. 17:3–10—"Cursed is the man who trusts in man And makes flesh his strength, Whose heart departs from the LORD ... I the LORD, search the heart, I test the mind, Even to give every man according to his ways, According to the fruit of his doings." See Jer. 17:3–4; Amos 9:8; Hos. 4:1–3; Matt. 25:31–32; Rom. 11:22; Ps. 9.
3. Jer. 2:7—"I brought you into a bountiful country, To eat its fruit and its goodness. But when you entered, you defiled My land And made My heritage an abomination."
4. Jer. 3:23—It is futile to trust and hope in anything other than almighty God.
5. Ps. 106:44–45—"Nevertheless He regarded their affliction, When He heard their cry; And for their sake He remembered His covenant, And relented according to the multitude of His mercies." See 2 Chron. 7:14.
6. 2 Peter 3:9 (Voice)—"Now the Lord is not slow about enacting His promise—slow is how some people want to characterize it—no, He is not slow but patient and merciful to you, not wanting anyone to be destroyed, but wanting everyone to turn away from following his own path and to turn toward God's."

147. Call unto Me with a Heart of Repentance

I have a covenant with you, America. You are to be a light to the nations. I have set you, I have established you as an example of a nation whose God is the Lord. You have been blessed because of your covenant with Me.

As long as your heart was to follow Me, I have carried you, protected you, and been your guardian. But you have turned your back on Me. Your blessings have been turned into curses, and you shall receive severe discipline. Why do you choose to become an example of what I will do to a nation who forsakes Me and runs toward wickedness?

Call unto Me to save you. Call unto Me with a heart of repentance. Turn from your lusts and violence. Return to Me and walk in My grace to obey My commands and principles that you may receive mercy and blessing. I desire to bless you and fulfill your destiny to be a light among the nations.

Selected Scripture Reading

1. Deut. 8:5–18—"You should know in your heart that as a man chastens his son, so the LORD your God chastens you. Therefore you shall keep the commands of the LORD your God, to walk in His ways and to fear Him. For the LORD your God is bringing you into a good land, a land of brooks of water, of fountains and springs … a land in which you will eat bread without scarcity, in which you will lack nothing … When you have eaten and are full, then you shall bless the LORD your God for the good land which He has given you. Beware that you do not forget the LORD your God by not keeping His commandments … when your heart is lifted up, and you forget the LORD … Then you say in your heart, 'My power and the might of my hand have gained me this wealth' … remember the LORD your God, for it is He who gives you power to get wealth that He may confirm His covenant which He swore to your fathers." See Ezek. 34:23–31; John 10:11; Rom. 9; Heb. 13:20; 1 Peter 2:25.
2. Isa. 55:1–7—"Ho! Everyone who thirsts, Come to the waters; And you who have no money, Come, buy and eat … Incline your ear, and come to Me. Hear, and your soul shall live; And I will make an everlasting covenant with you—The sure mercies of David … Surely you shall call a nation you do not know, And nations who do not know you shall run to you, Because of the LORD your God, And the Holy One of Israel; For He has glorified you. Seek the LORD while He may be found, Call upon Him while He is near. Let the wicked forsake his way, And the unrighteous man his thoughts; Let him return to the LORD, And He will have mercy on him; And to our God, For He will abundantly pardon." See Deut. 11:26–28; Ezek. 14:13, 22; Zech. 7–8. God calls all nations to come to Him.

3. Prov. 14:34—"Righteousness exalts a nation, But sin is a reproach to any people."
4. Ps. 72:11—"Yes, all kings shall fall down before Him; All nations shall serve Him." See Ps. 48:14; Ezek. 34:23–31; Isa. 46:3–4; Mal. 3:6–7; Rev. 15:3–4.

148. Know the Foundations of Your Faith

My children, the hour is late and the battle—the spiritual battle is intense. The battle is for the souls of mankind. Listen carefully. Be alert as My Holy Spirit directs you. The enemy is using fear and deceptions to bring confusion and herd many into enslavement.

For those whose minds and hearts are renewed in Christ, it will not be so. You will not be moved by fear and deception—for you know Me and have faith in almighty God.

Now I say to you, consider and think carefully. Know the foundations of your faith so you can stand firm in this time—in this season of shaking and testing. Know the foundations of your faith.

Study My Word and show yourself to be a disciple who understands My commandments, knows My principles, and honors My character. Do this by taking on the mind, nature, and power of Christ.

Search My words for within them you will find life. You will find power to overcome all attacks of the enemies of your soul. I am giving you a warning, My beloved. In this hour, the enemy is fiercely attacking your thinking to destroy your mind and soul.

Know My Word and walk together in My love and you cannot—you cannot—be defeated. Stay balanced in faith and works. You will receive My grace to win this race. You have been chosen for such a time as this. Your reward is great in the kingdom of heaven. Rejoice, My beloved. Your redemption draws near.

Selected Scripture Reading

1. Ps. 119:145–149 (Voice)—"I called to You wholeheartedly: 'Answer me, O Eternal One!' I will respect, I will follow Your statutes. I cried out to You: 'Rescue me, and I will live according to Your decrees.' I

wake before the dawn and call for help; I hope in Your words. My eyes do not shut before each watch of the night so that I can fix my mind on Your word. Listen to my voice, in keeping with Your unfailing love. Preserve my life, O Eternal One, according to Your just rulings."

2. Ps. 97:10—What does God tell you to hate for your own good? See James 1:21, 2:22.
3. Ps. 111:2—What does "study the works of God" mean?
4. 2 Tim. 2—In these verses, the apostle Paul admonished Timothy to present himself to God as one who correctly understood God's teachings and lived by them. Make a list of Paul's advice—what to do and not do. See Prov. 11:30, 14:25; John 5:39; 1 Tim. 1:4–10; Titus 2:12; Acts 28:23.
5. Matt. 10:7, 27; Mark 16:15; Luke 9:2, 60; Acts 5:20; 2 Tim. 4:1–5—What are we commanded to do with what we understand and believe about God?

149. Be a Source of Strength

I delight in you, the work of My creation. Know that I have good plans for you—to bless you and not to harm you. My desire is for you to walk in wholeness before Me, nothing lacking. As I told you, this is a season of restoration for you, My people.

The world is in chaos and travail, but I would have you, My people, to be a source of strength, stability, and light in the darkness. Into the darkness, I command you—I give you the grace of God to bring My peace and calming love.

The enemy of your souls is fomenting chaos, violence, and destruction. Take your stand. Be on guard. I commission you to go forth with the gospel of salvation and bring peace to overcome the chaos of the enemy.

Follow Me. Be patient and wise. I will direct you in intercessory prayer by My Spirit. Some things will be allowed to be destroyed because they are not profitable to godliness. Your work shall be to further the kingdom of God on earth. I will use you to bring peace, light, and order into the chaos. I will use My people to bring restoration by the power of My Spirit.

I love My creation, and I delight in you. Follow Me to fulfill your destiny. Follow Me to wholeness and restoration. I am your Father, and I love you.

Selected Scripture Reading

1. Jer. 29:11–14—"For I know the thoughts that I think toward you, says the LORD, thoughts of peace and not of evil, to give you a future and a hope. Then you will call upon Me and go and pray to Me, and I will listen to you. And you will seek Me and find Me, when you search for Me with all your heart." This was written as part of a prophetic letter around 599 BC by the prophet Jeremiah from Jerusalem to the Israelites who had been taken as captives to Babylon in 597 BC. This promise is spoken to a people who had been uprooted from their homeland and taken hundreds of miles away because of their multiple decades, even generations, of sins against God and each other.

    Verses 12 and 13 teach us that repentance of individuals and the nation as a whole set in motion the steps toward divine deliverance and redemption. Jeremiah told the exiles that it would not be a quick trip back to Jerusalem as a few false prophets claimed it would be.

    Nearly seventy years later, Daniel, who had been taken as an exile to Babylon in 605 BC, read Jeremiah's letter and knew that according to verse 10, the time of the exile was coming to a close. Daniel's response was to pray and seek God. See Dan. 9. What principles in this story are applicable to our lives today?
2. John 3:16—"For God so loved the world that He gave His only begotten Son, that whoever believes in Him should not perish but have everlasting life." See John 10:7–11.
3. Rom. 10:8–10—"The word is near you, in your mouth and in your heart (that is, the word of faith which we preach): That if you confess with your mouth the Lord Jesus and believe in your heart that God has raised Him from the dead, you will be saved. For with the heart one believes unto righteousness, and with the mouth confession is made unto salvation." Paraphrase these verses for greater understanding.
4. 1 Tim. 4:1–2—"Now the Spirit expressly says that in the latter times some will depart from the faith, giving heed to deceiving spirits and doctrines of demons, speaking lies in hypocrisy, having their own conscience seared with a hot iron." Matthew 16:5–12 is a metaphor

warning us to beware of false teachings such as those that promote pride and self-righteousness.
5. Mark 13:5–27—"And Jesus, answering them, began to say, 'Take heed that no one deceives you ... But when you hear of wars and rumors of wars, do not be troubled; for such things must happen ... For nation will rise against nation ... earthquakes ... famines ... troubles. These are the beginnings of sorrows ... And the gospel must first be preached to all the nations.'" See Isa. 12:1–6; 1 Peter 3:8–16. How might we be deceived or misled by bad news?
6. James 1:2–5—"My brethren, count it all joy when you fall into various trials, knowing that the testing of your faith produces patience. But let patience have its perfect work, that you may be perfect and complete, lacking nothing." What does it mean to "count it as joy"?

150. I Will Open Your Eyes to Hope

Do not be discouraged nor alarmed, My children, for these things must take place—will take place in the end times. There is much turmoil as both the spiritual and natural realms are in the midst of battle—good against evil. The earth is in travail.

Stay close to Me, My little ones, and you will find comfort and rest from the turmoil for I will open your eyes to hope. Call on Me so I may send My warring angels—My protecting angels—to work in your behalf.

I say to you, place no hindrances to their work before them. Remove all sin and wickedness from your lives and hearts so My good work in your lives be not hindered—that My angels be not hindered in their assignments.

For My glory shall be revealed among My bride. She shall be pure and spotless, tried in the fire, and found altogether lovely and pleasing. She understands the times, knows and is alert to put on the full armor of God doing spiritual battle and doing the good works of the kingdom of God.

Know the plans I have for you are good—to bless you and bring you peace, and joy, and every good thing. I will not leave you nor forsake you. Do not be misled by what you see or hear happening around you. Have faith in Me. Put your trust in Me. Hold fast to what is good.

Many difficult things will take place in these times. You must hold onto tightly to My Word so My grace may flow into your heart and mind. You will stand up and and take your place in this time of history.

You will rise above the turmoil. You will be victorious for you are seated in heavenly places with Christ. Your position and authority come through Jesus Christ. Let His love rule in your hearts so just as Christ endured and overcame, you also may persevere and overcome.

Be strong and overcome. Join the heavenly multitudes—the heavenly assembly—who rejoice and jubilantly proclaim, "The Lord is God and there is none beside Him. He is our God and we shall praise Him."

Selected Scripture Reading

1. Ps. 50:15—"Call upon Me in the day of trouble; I will deliver you, and you shall glorify Me." See Matt. 24:3–44; Mark 13:4–37; 2 Tim. 3:1–5; Titus 1:16.
2. 1 Peter 1:3–7—"Blessed be the God and Father of our Lord Jesus Christ, who according to His abundant mercy has begotten us again to a living hope through the resurrection of Jesus Christ from the dead, To an inheritance incorruptible and undefiled and that does not fade away, reserved in heaven for you, Who are kept by the power of God."
3. Heb. 12:1–2—"Therefore we also, since we are surrounded by so great a cloud of witnesses, let us lay aside every weight, and the sin which so easily ensnares us, and let us run with endurance the race that is set before us, Looking unto Jesus."

151. Ask Me for Eye Salve

The battle you are in is a battle for the souls of mankind. The battle is for the affections of your heart. Will you give your heart to Me, or will you be deceived and lured into placing your trust and love in the hands of an evil taskmaster who has neither mercy nor love?

Awaken, My bride, and do not listen to the lies of the enemy who will ensnare you in foolishness and trap you in wickedness and sin such that you separate yourself from Me and separate yourself from My provision and protection.

Ask Me for eye salve that your eyes may be healed and that you may discern between good and evil. Ask Me to give you eyes to see, ears to hear, and hearts to understand. Then see, hear, and understand. Flee from the enemies of your soul. Flee from wickedness. Turn from sin that I may be your shield and defender. Give no place to the enemy so I may be your protector.

For I will defend, I will protect My own. I protect them in the fiery furnace. I protect them in the flood. I protect them in the storms. I bring them safely through tribulations. I bring you home to Me. I receive you into fullness of joy.

Selected Scripture Reading

1. Rev. 3:18–19—"I counsel you to buy from Me gold refined in the fire, that you may be rich; and white garments, that you may be clothed, that the shame of your nakedness may not be revealed; and anoint your eyes with eye salve, that you may see. As many as I love, I rebuke and chasten. Therefore, be zealous and repent." How do these verses apply to your life? What true riches does God have for you? What is the meaning of the white garments?
2. Ps. 139—The psalmist affirms God's perfect knowledge of mankind; He understands everything about us. Verses 23 and 24 are a prayer: "Search me, O God, and know my heart; Try me, and know my anxieties; And see if there is any wicked way in me, And lead me in the way everlasting." What is the benefit of this prayer? Compare it with Psalm 19:12–14. What do you think presumptuous sins might be?
3. Isa. 59:1–2—"Behold, the LORD's hand is not shortened, That it cannot save; Nor His ear heavy, That it cannot hear. But your iniquities have separated you from your God; And your sins have hidden His face from you, So that He will not hear."
4. Heb. 3:12–14 (Voice)—"Brothers and sisters, pay close attention so you won't develop an evil and unbelieving heart that causes you to abandon the living God. Encourage each other every day… so none of you let the deceitfulness of sin harden your hearts." See Prov. 4:23.
5. 2 Cor. 6:1–2—"We then, as workers together with Him also plead with you not to receive the grace of God in vain. For He says: 'In an

acceptable time I have heard you, And in the day of salvation I have helped you.' Behold, now is the accepted time; behold now is the day of salvation." See Luke 24:31–45; Heb. 10:19–39; James 5:16.

152. I Will Lead You Safely and Triumphantly

To My Beloved I say, count it all joy when you suffer for My name's sake. There are two kingdoms in this world: the kingdom of light and the kingdom of darkness. The kingdom of darkness hates the kingdom of light—that is, My truth of the gospel of salvation.

You are mine. You are born of My Spirit and born of My love. You carry the gospel of salvation within you. You carry My truth and My light. That is why the darkness hates you.

Rejoice, My beloved, for just as natural light dispels natural darkness, so does My truth and light reflected in you dispel spiritual darkness. As you face trials, as you face temptations, as you face tribulations, yield yourself to Me so My light and truth are perfected in you. You will shine all the more brightly as My grace and glory cover you.

My power in you will increase, and you will see greater things in My kingdom. You will see and understand, and your joy will abound.

Keep your eyes and hearts focused on Me and I will lead you safely and triumphantly through what lies ahead.

Look beyond the difficulty and see the joy.

Selected Scripture Reading

1. Ps. 27:1 (Voice)—"The Eternal is my light amidst my darkness and my rescue in times of trouble. So whom shall I fear?" See Matt. 10:27–31.
2. John 3:16–21 (Voice)—These verses explain the gospel of salvation: "For God expressed His love for the world in this way: He gave His only Son so that whoever believes in Him will not face everlasting destruction, but will have everlasting life. Here's the point. God didn't send His Son into the world to judge it; instead, He is here to rescue a world headed toward certain destruction. No one who believes in Him has to fear condemnation, yet condemnation is already the reality for everyone who refuses to believe because they reject the name of the only Son of God. Why does God allow for judgment and condemnation? Because the Light, sent from God, pierced through the world's darkness to expose ill motives, hatred, gossip, greed, violence, and the like. Still some people preferred the darkness over the light because their actions were dark. Some of mankind hated the light. They scampered hurriedly back into the darkness where vices thrive and wickedness flourishes. Those who abandon deceit and embrace what is true, they will enter into the light where it will be clear that their deeds come from God." See Luke 24; John 3:5, 14:6; Acts 1–2; Rom. 8:12–25, 11:22; Col. 1:9–15, 22–23; Phil. 2:12; Heb. 9:27–28; 1 Peter 5:6–11; 2 Peter 1:2–11; 3:9.
3. Eph. 5—Throughout the New Testament, we are taught that when we first believe the gospel of salvation, we begin walking in God's light. Nevertheless, we choose to live in accordance with God's teachings or not. See Prov. 6:23.
4. Ps. 43:3—"Oh, send out Your light and Your truth! Let them lead me; Let them bring me to Your holy hill And to Your tabernacle." See Rev. 22.

153. Come into Alignment

My beloved, I must warn you. Great deceptions have been planned against My people—against mankind—that they should embrace a lie and reject the truth.

Now is the time like never before that you must be steadfast in your faith and fully devoted and committed to Me. Seek Me. Know Me. Follow Me. In My truth, in My righteousness, in My holiness shall you possess your souls unto salvation.

You are in a spiritual battle and the confusion, chaos, and shakings reflect this spiritual battle. Do not be deceived. Cleanse your hearts and mend your ways. Come into alignment with My commands and principles so you suffer not because of sin and disobedience.

It is My will during this season to counter the attacks of the enemy with My truth revealed in glory through My people. My people will hear Me. My people will believe Me and they will speak My words in humble obedience. They will not seek to serve themselves for their love will be purified.

Receive My Holy Spirit. Receive My love and let it be perfected in you so you may overcome the darkness. Remain in Me—in My love, in My truth, in My holiness, and righteousness—and you will not be deceived. You will be victorious and full of joy.

Selected Scripture Reading

1. Deut. 11:16—"Take heed to yourselves, lest your heart be deceived, and you turn aside and serve other gods and worship them." See 2 Thess. 2.
2. Prov. 14:12—"Before every person lies a road that seems to be right, but the end of that road is death and destruction." For additional information on deception, see Prov. 27:6; Isa. 5:20–24, 66:4–5; Jer. 29:8b–9, 24:11; Mark 4:18–19; Luke 21:8; 1 Cor. 4:4, 6:9–10, 15:33; 2 Cor. 11:3, 14; Gal. 6:6–8; Eph. 6:10–18; James 1:16; 1 Peter 5:8; 2 Peter 2–3; James 4:7; 1 John 2:18; Rev. 12:9.
3. Ps. 38—This is a Psalm to read for perspective and comfort when we sorrowfully recognize our personal responsibility for how badly things have gone. The psalmist was chastened by the Lord and

plagued by his enemies natural and spiritual, yet he remembered God is his Lord and Savior. See Ps. 43:1; 1 Cor. 10:13; 2 Tim. 4:18; Heb. 13:6; 2 Peter 2:9.
4. 1 Cor. 10:6–14—Verse 6 begins by saying the Old Testament stories teach us spiritual lessons applicable to every generation. The apostle Paul then speaks of the Israelites' spiritual battle with idolatry recorded in Exodus 32. He points out that we can fall into similar confusion with its consequences. Read Stephen's sermon on this event in Acts 7.
5. Ps. 119:86–88—"Indeed all Your commands are trustworthy, but my enemies have harassed me with their lies; help me ... According to your unfailing love, spare my life so that I can live according to the decrees of Your mouth."
6. Rom. 8:18–23—"For I consider that the sufferings of this present time are not worthy to be compared with the glory which shall be revealed in us."

154. Trust Me to Do a Good Work

I see the trial, I see the difficulty, I see the heartache you are going through. Cling to Me. Come before Me and surrender all you are to Me that I may comfort you.

In the midst of this battle, I say to you, trust Me to do a good work in your heart and a good work in your life. Trust Me. Believe in Me and My love for you. Obey Me, and My glory will come over you as you come into My presence.

My glory will cover you and bring deliverance for you. You shall overcome because My glory shall be revealed in and through you. You are precious to Me.

Selected Scripture Reading

1. Ps. 86:15—"But You, O LORD, are a God full of compassion, and gracious, Longsuffering and abundant in mercy and truth."
2. 2 Chron. 16:9a—"For the eyes of the LORD run to and fro throughout the whole earth, to show Himself strong on behalf of those whose heart is loyal to Him."

3. Ps. 33:13–15 (Voice)—"The Eternal peers down from heaven and watches all of humanity; He observes every soul from His divine residence. He has formed every human heart, breathing life into every human spirit; He knows the deeds of each person, inside and out." See Gen. 16:13.
4. Ps. 62—Have you ever been hurt or disappointed by others? Do the injustices endured by the oppressed weigh heavily on your spirit? Don't miss the perspective and wisdom in this psalm, a plan of action that will unleash God's power and intervention.
5. Heb. 3:19–4:16—To trust someone requires believing in him or her. Speaking of the example of those Israelites who did not enter the Promised Land (Num. 14:29), the apostle Paul said, "And we can see that they couldn't enter because they did not believe." Hebrews 4 explains God's promise to us of salvation requires that we trust and believe what He says to us. In verse 11, we are warned, "So let us move forward to enter this rest, so that none of us fall into the kind of faithless disobedience that prevented them from entering." The closing verses of this chapter remind us that Jesus is both our great High Priest and our example, one who is intimately aware of our inadequacies. Therefore, we are told to come boldly to him and ask Him for grace, mercy, and strength to overcome.
6. 2 Peter 1:2–8—"Grace and peace be multiplied to you in the knowledge of God and of Jesus our Lord, As His divine power has given to us all things that pertain to life and godliness, through the knowledge of Him who called us by glory and virtue, By which have been given to us exceedingly great and precious promises, that through these you may be partakers of the divine nature, having escaped the corruption that is in the world through lust. But also for this very reason, giving all diligence, add to your faith virtue, to virtue knowledge, to knowledge self-control, to self-control perseverance, to perseverance godliness, to godliness brotherly kindness, to brotherly kindness love. For if these things are yours and abound, you will be neither barren nor unfruitful in the knowledge of our Lord Jesus Christ."

155. Clothe Yourselves in My Humility

Will My people attempt to justify themselves in their own eyes? Will you stand before Me and say, "I am right in my own eyes. I do not need to come before You in humility. I do not need to repent and come before You in the righteousness of Jesus Christ." Will you say these things to Me in your heart?

Do you not know you shall be judged by the very words you speak? Do you not know that I, the Lord God, know the thoughts and intents of your heart? Do you not know that you are in danger of hell fire when you attack and accuse your brother? I will not hold him guiltless who hates his brother.

My Son, Jesus Christ, came to earth to reveal to you the righteousness of God. The righteousness I have to give to you is birthed in humility and love. The righteousness of Christ is revealed in the sacrifice of His entire life and death. He gave His life that you may receive the righteousness of God.

Have I not commanded you to love your brother? Have I not taught you by example how to lay down your life for one another—turning from and putting away all filthiness of lust and greed?

In this hour, your enemy—the devil—is inciting all mankind into hatred and arrogant rebellion. Do not—do not fall into this trap of self-righteousness and pride. Instead, clothe yourselves in My humility, loving one another with pure love and you will receive My grace to walk in overcoming power.

For My light and glory will cover you, and great will be your reward. Come to Me and walk with Me, My beloved. Love one another and walk in My love and in My righteousness.

Selected Scripture Reading

1. Isa. 57:15—"For thus says the High and Lofty One Who inhabits eternity, whose name is Holy: I dwell in the high and holy place, With him who has a contrite and humble spirit, To revive the spirit of the humble, And to revive the heart of the contrite ones."
2. Rom. 3:20–24 (NIV)—"Therefore no one will be declared righteous in God's sight by the works of the law; rather, through the law we become

conscious of our sin. But now apart from the law the righteousness of God has been made known, to which the Law and the Prophets testify. This righteousness is given through faith in Jesus Christ to all who believe. There is no difference between Jew and Gentile, for all have sinned and fall short of the glory of God, and all are justified freely by his grace through the redemption that came by Christ Jesus."
3. Ps. 39:7–8—"And now, LORD, what do I wait for? My hope is in You. Deliver me from all my transgressions." See Rom. 10:8–13.

156. Soften Your Hearts

I call out to you, My children. I am speaking to your heart. My Holy Spirit is here to comfort, instruct, and direct you in the way of life and truth.

I call out to you, but you must listen and obey. My dear children, soften your hearts and make time for Me. Quiet your souls and know that I am God. You have struggled with so many doubts and confusion. You have asked why your faith wavers and is often weak.

My child, have I not loved you with all My heart giving My very best to you in My Word becoming flesh and being sacrificed for you that you might live? My Word gives life as you hear what I am saying to you and as you let it take root, and grow, and mature in your heart.

You must guard your heart with all diligence so My Word can do its perfecting work in your life that your destiny in Me will be fulfilled. My Word growing in your heart and maturing in grace, purity, and love will push out the fears and doubts that trouble and hinder you.

Look not on your fears and doubts but to Me, My child. I am the author and finisher of your faith. I love you with all My heart. I give you everything in Christ. Come to Me with all your heart and you will know I am God.

Selected Scripture Reading

1. Isa. 45:22—"Look to Me, and be saved, All you ends of the earth! For I am God, and there is no other." No one—not any people group—is excluded in the call to be saved.

2. Matt. 22:9—"Therefore go into the highways, and as many as you find, invite to the wedding." Compare this verse with Proverbs 11:30 and Matthew 4:17–20. What should be a priority in your life?
3. John 7:37–38—"On the last day, that great day of the feast, Jesus stood and cried out, saying, 'If anyone thirsts, let him come to Me and drink. He who believes in Me, as the Scripture has said, out of his heart will flow rivers of living water.'" What does living water refer to?
4. Rom. 10:12–13—"For there is no distinction between Jew and Greek, for the same Lord over all is rich to all who call upon Him. For whoever calls on the name of the LORD shall be saved." See 1 Tim. 2:4. How do these verses apply to the concept of ethnic and organized religious groups?
5. 2 Chron. 34:27—"Because your heart was tender, and you humbled yourself before God when you heard His words against this place and against its inhabitants, and you humbled yourself before Me, and you tore your clothes and wept before Me, I also have heard you, says the LORD." See 2 Chron. 30:18b–19; Rom. 5.
6. John 6:35–40—"And Jesus said to them, 'I am the bread of life. He who comes to Me shall never hunger, and he who believes in Me shall never thirst. But I said to you that you have seen Me and yet do not believe. All that the Father gives Me will come to Me, and the one who comes to Me I will by no means cast out. For I have come down from heaven not to do My own will, but the will of Him who sent Me. This is the will of the Father who sent Me, that of all He has given Me I should lose nothing, but should raise it up at the last day. And this is the will of Him who sent me, that everyone who sees the Son and believes in Him may have everlasting life and I will raise him up at the last day.'"

157. The Windows of Heaven's Blessings

My children, I am calling to you. I am seeking those, who will give to Me their whole hearts, souls, and minds. I am seeking those who will love Me with all their being and follow Me in obedience such that the windows of heaven's blessings will be opened to them.

I am seeking those who will spearhead a revival all over this land. Will you be of those people? Will you follow Me in the grace I have for you to overcome every obstacle and every hardship?

If My children will hear—if My children will listen to My heart—they will understand I am calling them to rise up and bless the nations. For I have given to you the message of the kingdom of God. I have given to you the words of the gospel of salvation that has power to bring peace to the hearts of mankind. You have the sword of truth under the banner of My love.

Follow the counsel of My Holy Spirit and I will direct your words and steps to grow in My grace to receive a greater anointing and to be a greater testimony to all peoples. So great will be your joy when you learn to lay aside selfish ways and ambitions. As you walk with Me in blessing others, you will find the meaning and fulfillment you have been seeking.

I am your God. You are created to be a blessing. Worship and serve your God. Love Me and one another. You are created to be a blessing. For I have a plan and a destiny for you to reflect My glory so My presence will be revealed and known on this earth before My Son returns.

Selected Scripture Reading

1. 1 Chron. 28:9b (Voice)—"The Eternal searches all hearts for their desires and understands the intentions of every thought. If you search for Him as He searches you, then He will let you find Him. But if you abandon Him, then He will reject you forever."
2. Mal. 3:10 (Voice)—"To rectify this situation [national backsliding] you must bring the entire tithe into the storage house in the temple so that there may be food for Me and for the Levites in My house. Feel free to test Me now in this. See whether or not I, the Eternal, Commander of heavenly armies, will open the windows of heaven to you and pour a blessing down upon you until all your needs are satisfied." See 2 Chron. 31:10; Matt. 6:25–34. How is tithing meant to be a means of blessing God and others? Does our attitude about giving money, time, and effort matter?
3. Ps. 84:11—"For the LORD God is a sun and shield; The LORD will give grace and glory; No good thing will He withhold From those who walk uprightly." See Ps. 62:7.

4. Ps. 85:9–13—"Surely His salvation is near to those who fear Him, That glory may dwell in our land. Mercy and truth have met together, Righteousness and peace have kissed. Truth shall spring out of the earth, And righteousness shall look down from heaven. Yes, the LORD will give what is good; And our land will yield its increase. Righteousness will go before Him, And shall make His footsteps our pathway."
5. Prov. 11:30—"The fruit of the righteous is a tree of life, And he who wins souls is wise." See Dan. 12:3; Matt. 4:19; James 5:19–20; Jude 20–23.
6. John 4:34–38—"Jesus said to them, 'My food is to do the will of Him who sent Me, and to finish His work. Do you not say, "There are still four months and then comes the harvest"? Behold, I say to you, lift up your eyes and look at the fields, for they are already white for harvest! And he who reaps receives wages and gathers fruit for eternal life, that both he who sows and he who reaps may rejoice together.'"

158. All the Nations Will Know

Because of the praises and obedience of My people, I will answer the cry of your hearts. I will deliver you from the snare of the enemy. I will call you forth to arise and stand before Me. My glory shall cover you, and all the nations will know "I AM WHO I AM," the Lord God almighty.

I say to you, My precious children—My creation—prepare, for the cold winds of adversity are blowing over your nation and over the earth. These are bitter winds. These are fierce winds and have no equals in past history.

Listen to My Holy Spirit for He will direct and guide you through this season when men's hearts are hardened and driven by cold winds. My Spirit will open your eyes and show you the path to walk in My sunshine. You will have supernatural warmth and comfort.

Do not be afraid of the cold winds. Come together in purity and unity and My Spirit will be with you and you will be covered with My warmth and grace. You will stand as a warm fire and a bright light among a wicked and perverse generation. I will turn around what the enemy has meant to harm and destroy. I will put a stop to it and I will bring a blessing to My people.

These are not easy or comfortable times. Hardships and deceptions—gross darkness—cover the earth. Stand firm, My people. Know that the light of the gospel of salvation through Jesus Christ shall burst forth over all nations. The burning love and passion I have for My people and My creation shall be revealed, and I will comfort My people.

Look unto Me. Look for Me because I am coming to deliver and bless My people. Look up. I am in your midst. I AM WHO I AM and I am with you.

Selected Scripture Reading

1. Exodus 3 records God giving Moses the assignment to bring the Israelites out of Egypt. Moses knew the people would ask the name of who it was that sent him. He asked God how he should answer them. In God's response, "I AM WHO I AM" He reveals His preeminence and eternal existence. That answer also puts into perspective Moses' feelings of inadequacy. Moses now knows, it is God's power not his own that will bring about the deliverance of the Israelites from the bondage of slavery. How does our understanding of who God is help us to have faith?
2. 2 Chron. 5–7—In the Old Testament, worship of God was meant to be a heartfelt appreciation and obedience to almighty God and very much a community experience with worship taking place in the tabernacle or temple. Early on in King Solomon's reign, he built a most magnificent house of worship. At the dedication, the people wholeheartedly embraced God and came together with praise and singing. Read 2 Chronicles 5:13 to find out how God responded, and read chapters 6–7 about how to maintain a relationship with God and how He reveals Himself. Compare the principles in these chapters to New Testament teachings in 1 Cor. 3:16–17, 6:19–20; Eph. 2:20–22; Heb. 3:6; 1 Peter 2:5.
3. 2 Chron. 20:22 (Voice)—"As they sang and praised, the Eternal was ready to cause great confusion in battle for the men from Ammon, Moab, and Mount Seir (in Edom) who had come to attack Judah.

They were utterly defeated, turning on one another." See Deut. 28:1; 1 Cor. 16:13–14.
4. Ps. 34:4–6—Scripture teaches us that we must "cry out to the Lord" for help.
5. Neh. 6:16—"And it happened, when all our enemies heard of it, and all the nations around us saw these things, that they were very disheartened in their own eyes; for they perceived that this work was done by our God."
6. Ps. 22:27—"All the ends of the world Shall remember and turn to the LORD, And all the families of the nations Shall worship before You." See Ps. 96:3.
7. Isa. 2:2—"Now it shall come to pass in the latter days That the mountain of the LORD's house Shall be established on the top of the mountains, And shall be exalted above the hills; And all nations shall flow to it."
8. Acts 4:19–20—"But Peter and John answered and said to them, 'Whether it is right in the sight of God to listen to you more than to God, you judge. For we cannot but speak the things which we have seen and heard.'" See vv. 23–31.
9. Heb. 10:23–25—"Let us hold fast the confession of our hope without wavering, for He who promised is faithful. And let us consider one another in order to stir up love and good works, Not forsaking the assembling of ourselves together."
10. 1 Cor. 15:58—This verse admonishes us to intentionally persevere in our walk with God keeping in mind His eternal values and rewards.
11. Rev. 19:5—"Then a voice came from the throne, saying, 'Praise our God, all you His servants, and those who fear Him, both small and great.'"

159. With Meekness and Humility

Cry aloud and weep, My precious ones, for My beloved is not yet ready for her Bridegroom to appear. Her garments are soiled. Iniquity is in her heart. Cry out for her that her eyes be opened and she can see to make herself ready for My return. It is the pure in heart who see God.

    I speak to you clearly. Purify yourselves. Turn from all lusts and iniquity. With meekness and humility, receive My words—My teaching—to instruct you how to think and live. Receive Me into your heart and you will be made clean.

My people, I have spoken to you about the dangers and perils of this time—of these days. You must be alert and give thought to your ways because your enemy plans your destruction. I say to you, be wise and discerning so you do not fall into the traps of temptations.

Cleanse your hearts and minds—and walk away from lust and pride. There is a spirit of seduction at work to separate you from Me. That which is of My Spirit will draw you closer to Me. That which is of My Spirit will bring peace and the beauty of holiness to your heart. You will walk in My love and you will love others with grace and wisdom.

Be alert, My children, and do not be seduced by lies and deceptions. There is only one way to salvation. There is only one name that washes away sin. Stay close to Me, and do not be deceived. My Holy Spirit will lead and direct you if you ask and if you walk with Me.

Daily you must seek Me. Daily you must present yourselves before Me. Direct your heart to know Me that we may have communion together.

Selected Scripture Reading

1. Jer. 3:21–23—"A voice was heard on the desolate heights, Weeping and supplications of the children of Israel. For they have perverted their way. They have forgotten the LORD their God. Return, you backsliding children, And I will heal your backslidings. Indeed we do come to You, For You are the LORD our God. Truly, in vain is salvation hoped for from the hills, And from the multitude of mountains; Truly, in the LORD our God Is the salvation of Israel." See 1 Cor. 10:1–33 for an explanation of how Israel's experiences carry instructions for the church and believers today.
2. Mic. 6:8—Read this verse to find out a one-sentence summary of what God requires from you.
3. Matt. 5:8—What can you do to increase your "seeing" God and understanding Him and His ways?
4. 1 Peter 1:22–2:3—"Since you have purified your souls in obeying the truth through the Spirit in sincere love of the brethren, love one another fervently with a pure heart, Having been born again, not of

corruptible seed but incorruptible through the word of God which lives and abides forever ... Therefore, laying aside all malice, all deceit, hypocrisy, envy, and all evil speaking, As newborn babes, desire the pure milk of the word, that you may grow thereby, If indeed you have tasted that the Lord is gracious."
5. Phil. 1:27–2:4—"Only let your conduct be worthy of the gospel of Christ ... that you stand fast in one spirit, with one mind striving together for the faith of the gospel ... Let nothing be done through selfish ambition or conceit, but in lowliness of mind let each esteem others better than himself." See Rom. 12:1–21.
6. Rom. 12:17–18 (Voice)—"Do not retaliate with evil, regardless of the evil brought against you. Try to do what is good and right and honorable as agreed upon by all people. If it is within your power, make peace with all people."
7. Mal. 2:6—What character qualities and "fruit" should we look for in the lives of ministers, priests, preachers, and teachers of the Bible? See Hos. 6:6; Ps. 46:10; Luke 10:39.
8. Rev. 7:9–10—"After these things I looked, and behold, a great multitude which no one could number, standing before the throne and before the Lamb, clothed with white robes, with palm branches in their hands, And crying out with a loud voice, saying, 'Salvation belongs to our God who sits on the throne, and to the Lamb!'"

160. Let Go of the Sins of Previous Generations

Hear, My child, what I would say to you. Open your ears and soften your hearts that you may come under My wings of protection.

Do not slip and fall over the same obstacles and into the same pits as your parents, grandparents, and ancestors before you. For it is the little foxes that spoil the vine and steal and destroy the grapes. It is the little foxes that attack your fruitfulness in the kingdom of God.

Hear Me carefully, My children. You are in a very dangerous time in history. It is essential you remain in My Word, seeking Me daily, and laying everything on the altar. Lay everything on the altar and you will receive what I have for you. Your spirit will be quickened, and you will discern between good and evil. You will recognize the dangers of the little foxes.

I have made every provision for you to walk in My grace and overcoming victory. Let go of the sins of previous generations and come into the brighter light so you can bear much fruit in the kingdom of God.

I am your heavenly Father, and I love you, My child. I love you. Come under My wings and be prepared for your destiny.

Selected Scripture Reading

1. Song of Solomon 2:15 (AMP)—"Catch the foxes for us, The little foxes that spoil and ruin the vineyards [of love], While our vineyards are in blossom." What are the metaphorical little foxes that create problems in relationships between people? What little foxes hinder the ministries of the church?
2. Eccl. 10:1—"Dead flies putrefy the perfumer's ointment, And cause it to give off a foul odor; So does a little folly to one respected for wisdom and honor." See Matt. 16:6; 1 Cor. 5:6; Gal. 5:9. In these metaphors, dead flies and leaven describe how a little of something bad can neutralize or destroy something good. Give examples of such dead flies and leaven.
3. Ps. 78:4b–8—"... telling to the generation to come the praises of the LORD ... That they may set their hope in God, and not forget the works of God, But keep His commandments; And may not be like their fathers, a stubborn and rebellious generation, a generation that did not set its heart aright, and whose spirit was not faithful to God." See Jer. 11:10. How do you think one generation successfully conveys to the next the knowledge of and respect for almighty God? What in a culture hinders the older generation's ability to transmit values and knowledge to the next?
4. Col. 1:9–13—"Be filled with the knowledge of His will in all wisdom and spiritual understanding; that you may walk worthy of the Lord, fully pleasing Him, being fruitful in every good work and increasing in the knowledge of God; strengthened with all might, according to His glorious power, for all patience and longsuffering with joy; giving thanks to the Father who has qualified us to be partakers of the inheritance of the saints in the light. He has delivered us from the power of darkness and conveyed us into the kingdom of the Son of His love."

161. The Holy Spirit Will Witness to the Truth

My Holy Spirit is given to My children to guide, comfort, and direct you. If you will fill your heart and mind with My Word, He—the Holy Spirit—will witness to the truth and bring to your mind My words that you may be instructed and trained in righteousness. Thereby, you will grow in grace and maturity, increasing in strength and fruitfulness.

The carnal mind is at enmity with the working of God. The carnal mind cannot see the purposes of God or comprehend how the Spirit of God works because it is with the heart that man receives the gifts of God and understands spiritual truth. The pure in heart shall see God.

This is an hour in history where there is much darkness, confusion, fear, and deception. Build up yourselves in your most Holy faith. Honor My Spirit's work in your heart and mind and among My people so He may comfort you and be a shield of protection against all the attacks of the enemy.

Pray with understanding and pray in the Spirit as He directs you. In so doing, He will help you stay focused and pray according to the will of your heavenly Father, even with humility and obedience. Guard your heart diligently. Place My Spirit as guardian over your heart because all the issues of life flow through the heart. Allow My Holy Spirit to teach and guide your heart.

This is the meaning of "Love the Lord God with all your heart, soul, strength, and mind." Follow Me, My little ones, for My yoke is easy and My burden is light and you will find rest for your souls. I have come that you might have life and life more abundantly. Rejoice! Rejoice!

Selected Scripture Reading

1. Zech. 4:6—The prophet Zechariah spoke into the life of the nation of Israel beginning around 520 BC. The first Jewish exiles had returned from Babylon to Jerusalem by permission from Cyrus in 536 BC and had begun rebuilding the altar and temple. Because of opposition and apathy, work became neglected. Zechariah 4:6 says that God told Zerubbabel (the first man in charge of leading the exiles in the work of restoration): "Your strength and prowess will not be enough to finish My temple, but My Spirit will be." Zechariah and his contemporary,

Haggai, spoke God's words to the people to repent and finish the work He had called them to do.

As is often the case in scripture, there appears to be double applications to the prophet's words that clearly point to the future coming of the Messiah (Zech. 3). In the New Testament Gospels, Zechariah is often quoted. Ezekiel and Zechariah are the most-often quoted prophets in Revelation. See Neh. 9:5–38; Ps. 51:11.
2. Joel 2:28–29—"And it shall come to pass afterward. That I will pour out My Spirit on all flesh; Your sons and your daughters shall prophesy. Your old men shall dream dreams, Your young men shall see visions. And also on My menservants and on My maidservants I will pour out My Spirit in those days." See Acts 2:1–47.
3. Luke 11:13—Ask your heavenly Father to give to you His Holy Spirit.
4. John 14:26 (Voice)—"The Father is sending a great Helper, the Holy Spirit, in My name to teach you everything and to remind you of all that I have said to you."
5. Rom. 8:13–14 (Voice)—"For if your life is just about satisfying the impulses of your sinful nature, then prepare to die. But if you have invited the Spirit to destroy these selfish desires, you will experience life. If the Spirit of God is leading you, then take comfort in knowing you are His children." See John 14:15–24, 15:26, 16:7–15.
6. 1 John 4:16—"And we have known and believed the love that God has for us. God is love and he who abides in love, abides in God, and God in him."

162. No Compromise or Confusion Shall Blind Your Eyes

Be cautious, My bride. There is one coming—there is one who shall put himself forward as a rescuer. An image and aura shall be created to make him appear to be anointed to bring peace, solve problems, and bring peoples and groups together into harmony and order.

He will work to gain wealth and control of wealth. Those around him are cunning, wicked, and cruel for they will be driven by the demonic hordes of hell. Satan knows his time is short; he works swiftly to consolidate his power and forces. You will see this consolidation of power, but do not be afraid, and do not be deceived. Do not be intimidated.

For I stand with you. I stand beside you and I am within you. Let My words be released in your heart. Hear My Holy Spirit in you for I will comfort you. I will direct you. You will have no doubts about Me. You will know Me and you will know who you are in Me. By the strength of My Spirit in you, you will be bold and fearless.

My bride shall rise up in beauty and truth. My glory shall cover you. No compromise or confusion shall blind your eyes because your heart is given wholly, completely, and in purity to Me. I will say of you, "This is My bride. She is altogether lovely and pure. Her heart belongs to Me alone. She is willing to sacrifice all and come with Me. She is mine and I will receive her into eternal glory. She will be with Me forever."

Selected Scripture Reading

1. Isa. 14:12–13—"How you are fallen from heaven, O Lucifer, son of the morning! How you are cut down to the ground, You who weakened the nations! For you have said in your heart: 'I will ascend into heaven, I will exalt my throne above the stars of God.'" See Ps. 2; 1 Chron. 21:1; Dan. 11:36; 2 Thess. 2:4; Dan. 7–12; Luke 10:18; Rev. 13:1–8.
2. 2 Cor. 11:14–15—"And no wonder! For Satan himself transforms himself into an angel of light. Therefore it is no great thing if his ministers also transform themselves into ministers of righteousness, whose end will be according to their works."
3. 1 Thess. 5:1–11—"For you yourselves know perfectly that the day of the LORD comes as a thief in the night … But you brethren are not in darkness." See Prov. 14:33.
4. Isa. 27:1—"In that day the LORD with His severe sword, great and strong, Will punish Leviathan the fleeing serpent, Leviathan that twisted serpent; And He will slay the reptile that is in the sea." See 2 Thess. 2:1–17.
5. 1 John 4:17 (NLT)—"And as we live in God, our love grows more perfect. So we will not be afraid on the day of judgment, but we can face him with confidence because we live like Jesus here in this world." See Heb. 4:16; Acts 9:29.
6. 1 Peter 1:13–19 (Voice)—"So get yourselves ready, prepare your minds to act, control yourselves, and look forward in hope …" Verses

13-19 give clear instructions about how those who believe in God are to live.

163. Your Bridegroom Comes

Now is the time, My beloved. Now is the time to come out and separate yourselves from all ungodliness and rebellion. I am warning you for you are at a crossroads in history. You must choose to walk with Me and to follow Me closely or the deceptions of darkness will lead you astray into much harm and destruction.

These are the dangerous times the prophets and My Word warn about: people doing what is right in their own eyes and calling evil good and calling good evil.

I say to you, have no part of the spirit of Babylon that exalts itself against God. Come out from her. Wash and cleanse yourselves from haughty arrogance that leads to deception.

The hour is late. Be prepared, My beloved. Your bridegroom comes. He is coming for those whose hearts are looking for Him. He is coming for those who shall rejoice to see Him.

Selected Scripture Reading

1. Gen. 7:1—"Then the LORD said to Noah, 'Come into the ark, you and all your household, because I have seen that you are righteous before Me in this generation.'" Can you draw any present-day parallels?
2. Isa. 45:22—"Look to Me, and be saved, All you ends of the earth!"
3. Deut. 30:15–20—"See, I have set before you today life and good, death and evil. In that I command you today to love the LORD your God, to walk in His ways … that you may live and multiply; and the LORD your God will bless you in the land which you go to possess. But if your heart turns away." Continue reading this passage to find out what happens if they do follow God's teachings. See Prov. 1:20–33.
4. Prov. 12:15—"The way of a fool is right in his own eyes, But he who heeds counsel is wise." See Ps. 36; Matt. 24:4–25:13.

5. 1 John 1:11—"But he who hates his brother is in darkness and walks in darkness, and does not know where he is going, because the darkness has blinded his eyes."
6. Isa. 5:20–24—"Woe to those who call evil good, and good evil, Who put darkness for light, and light for darkness… Woe to those who are wise in their own eyes … Therefore, as the fire devours the stubble … So their root will be as rottenness … Because they have rejected the law of the LORD of hosts And despised the word of the Holy One of Israel."
7. Jer. 51:6–10—"Flee from the midst of Babylon, And every one save his life! Do not be cut off in her iniquity, For this is the time of the LORD's vengeance. He shall recompense her. Babylon was a golden cup in the LORD's hand, That made all the earth drunk. The nations drank her wine; Therefore the nations are deranged." What do you think Babylon represents?
8. 2 Cor. 10:3–5 (Voice)—"For though we walk in the world, we do not fight according to this world's rules of warfare. The weapons of the war we're fighting are not of this world but are powered by God and effective at tearing down the strongholds erected against His truth. We are demolishing arguments and ideas, every high-and-mighty philosophy that pits itself against the knowledge of the one true God."

164. You Will Understand My Words because You Know Me

My words speak life to you. Receive My words into your heart and live. Know that I love you and know that what I have for you is good. Know that I withhold nothing from you that is good. Trust Me and know that if I withhold something or someone from you, it is for your benefit.

You have the power to choose what you receive and what you reject. However, if your heart is seeking Me, My Spirit will be empowered—will be strong in you—and you will hear with your heart and know in your spirit how to discern between good and evil.

Let no one take from you what I have given to you. My gifts and callings to you are sure and irrevocable, yet may be forfeited, refused, or given up by you. Do not allow man or spirit to steal your peace and blessings in My kingdom. Remember the battle is not yours. It is Mine says the Lord of the hosts of the armies of heaven.

You put on the armor of God. You put on righteousness through faith in the Name and atoning work of Jesus Christ. You carry with you in your heart My Word of truth—know the scriptures. Stand firm in My grace and in the power of My Holy Spirit and you will see what I will do.

For I am a holy, righteous, and merciful God who will deliver and save My people. Your salvation is not found in a formula—not in a ritual, nor works of good deeds. Do not trust in these. Do not put your faith in them for they cannot provide redemption.

I speak to you clearly. Your salvation is in relationship with Me. Open your heart completely. Bow you knee—that is, bow your heart—give Me your heart so I may give you a new heart, renewed by My Holy Spirit. It is then you will see and understand the majesty and glory of the power of the kingdom of God—the power to change the hearts of mankind— power to destroy the evil works of Satan and set man free to walk in My truth and love.

Come to Me and continue with Me. Follow Me daily, yielding to My teachings and My Holy Spirit. . Guard your heart from pride and deceptions. Do not become ensnared by evil or you will become its slave and forfeit your blessings.

Stand firm, My child. You are worthy to be in relationship with Me for I have called all mankind to be saved from sin. Have confidence in My love for you. Did I not send My Son, Jesus, to make atonement for your sins and teach you how to live in relationship with God and your fellow man?

Love Me with your whole being and your whole life. Love one another with My love by My Spirit and you will remain in Me and I in you. You will know which path to take. You will understand My words because you know Me.

Selected Scripture Reading

1. Deut. 8:3—"So He humbled you, allowed you to hunger, and fed you with manna which you did not know nor did your fathers know, that He might make you know that man shall not live by bread alone;

but man lives by every word that proceeds from the mouth of the LORD." See Deut. 4:29; Ps. 119:130; Matt. 4:4; Luke 24:15–53.
2. Jer. 10:23 (AMP)—"O LORD, I know that the path of [life of] a man is not in himself; It is not within [the limited ability of] man [even one at his best] to choose and direct his steps [in life]."
3. Prov. 3:5–8—"Trust in the LORD with all your heart, And lean not on your own understanding; In all your ways acknowledge Him, And He shall direct your paths. Do not be wise in your own eyes; Fear the LORD and depart from evil. It will be health to your flesh, And strength to your bones."
4. Jer. 23:29 (Voice)—"Does not My word burn like fire? Does it not shatter rock like a strong hammer?" See Luke 24:32; Rom. 1:16.
5. Heb. 4:12—This verse explains how God's Word is a living diagnostic tool.
6. Ps. 84:11—"For the LORD God is a sun and shield; The LORD will give grace and glory; No good thing will He withhold From those who walk uprightly." See Ps. 34:10.
7. Luke 11:9–10—"So I say to you, ask, and it will be given to you; seek, and you will find; knock, and it will be opened to you. For everyone who asks receives, and he who seeks finds, and to him who knocks it will be opened." See Jer. 33:3; Prov. 8:17.
8. 1 Cor. 2:12 (AMP)—"Now we have received, not the spirit of the world, but the [Holy] Spirit who is from God, so that we may know and understand the [wonderful] things freely given to us by God."
9. John 17:1–3—These verses explain what eternal life embodies.

165. The Secret Place of Intimacy and Communion

Seek Me and you will find Me. Search for Me with your whole heart and you will know Me for I reveal Myself to those who come before Me in humility and hunger to learn of Me.

I delight to reveal Myself to those whose hearts are pure. I delight to reveal Myself to those who hunger and thirst for righteousness for you stay on the straight and narrow path to find spiritual treasures. You do not look to the right or left or lust after worldliness and self-gratification.

Come away with Me, My beloved one, to the secret place of intimacy and communion. My Spirit shall lead and guide you; your heart will be strong and unwavering even in the midst of all the shaking and confusion coming upon the world. For this is a perilous time—a time when people's hearts are being tested and what is in their hearts is being revealed.

My people who know Me and desire to walk with Me in obedience to My truth will by My Holy Spirit evaluate and test those things in their own hearts and be able to discern good from evil. My people who know Me will repent of the evil and they will embrace the goodness of God—the goodness of God which leads them to repentance. Thereby you will receive the grace of God to walk in overcoming power regardless of the chaos, confusion, and difficulties surrounding you.

You shall shine as bright lights in a season of gross darkness. Be not deceived. Hold fast to My words in purity and humble obedience. Seek Me and you will find Me.

Selected Scripture Reading

1. Deut. 30:6—"And the LORD your God will circumcise your heart and the heart of your descendants, to love the LORD your God with all your heart and with all your soul, that you may live." See Rom. 2:28–29.
2. Jer. 29:13—"And you will seek Me and find Me, when you search for Me with all your heart."
3. Matt. 5:3–10—"Blessed are the poor in spirit, for theirs is the kingdom of heaven. Blessed are those who mourn, for they shall be comforted. Blessed are the meek, for they shall inherit the earth. Blessed are those who hunger and thirst for righteousness for they shall be filled. Blessed are the merciful, for they shall obtain mercy. 8. Blessed are the pure in heart for they shall see God. Blessed are the peacemakers for they shall be called the sons of God. Blessed are those who are persecuted for righteousness sake, for theirs is the kingdom of heaven."

166. Come, All You Saints

There is a great dragon is rising in the east. He is gaining strength and power. He is an enemy of the one true God. He is wise, cunning, and deceitful. He will slay many because of his cunning and craftiness. For they will say, "He is not capable. He cannot do what he says."

Hear Me and know this. He is cunning and deceitful, and there is one who will assist this dragon, for he too is wicked and seeks to do others harm. He says to himself, I will let this dragon do a work for me and no one will know I have enabled him to do it. Then I will take the prey for I am the strong one. I will take what I want.

The wicked of the earth are plotting and scheming. They are devising plans to conquer nations and wealth and power. They will kill and destroy for they have no fear of God or respect for mankind. In their greed and lust for power, they have given possession of their souls to the devil, and he empowers them to do great wickedness and harm. For a season, it will look like the dragons are conquering and no one can stop them.

But there is One coming who with the brilliance of His glory shall completely destroy all the enemies of God. His Name is true, and His coming is sure. At a time when the people of the earth do not expect or wait for Him, He will split the skies and appear as the righteous judge of earth.

Fear not, you who love the Lord and wait patiently for Him, for He has come to avenge the blood of His faithful saints. He has come to reward the righteous, condemn the wicked, and take vengeance on those whose hearts are intent on doing evil.

Come, all you saints of the most high God. Do not fear those things coming upon the earth. Do not fear him who is able to destroy the body. Rather, fear Him who has the power to destroy both body and soul in hell.

Stand before your God in purity and righteousness. Apply the blood of the Lamb to the doorpost of your heart and walk in sanctification before Him. You are marked for salvation. Fear not what man may do. You belong to God, and He will keep you.

Arise, My people. Arise, My lovely bride. Adorn yourself with the beauty of holiness, and let My glory shine through you. Let My words and My Spirit within you grow and become mighty to the tearing down of spiritual strongholds and wickedness in high places. Arise and take your positions, My people. Take your positions in this spiritual battle at the end of times. Take your place. Now is the time.

Selected Scripture Reading

1. Rev. 19:11–16—"Now I saw heaven opened and behold a white horse, and He who sat upon Him was called Faithful and True, and in righteousness, He judges and makes war ... He was clothed with a robe dipped in blood, and His name is called the Word of God ... KING OF KINGS AND LORD OF LORDS." See Ps. 149; Dan. 7:13–14; 1 John 2:18–22, 4:1–6; 2 John 7; 2 Thess. 2:1–12; Revelation.
2. Psalm 2 indicates a hostile power would bring an attack against God's people. This attack would be crushed by almighty God. See Ezekiel, Zechariah, and Daniel. Consider how the verses in Acts 4:23–31 might apply.

167. Come Out from among the Spirit of Babylon

My people are being tossed about and confused by the winds blowing over the earth. They stumble and fall because they do not know My Word. They have not hidden My Word in their hearts. They are tempted to embrace many lies and deceptions.

I speak to you clearly, My people, whom I have chosen as My inheritance. Come out from among the spirit of Babylon. You cannot follow the ways of Baal and God and walk in blessing. You must choose this day whom you will serve.

This day I call to you. Come out from the deceitfulness of sin. Cleanse yourselves in the pure water of My Word. Search My Word diligently and you will find life. You will know the truth, and the truth will set you free. Do not be deceived by the many beguiling words in the winds blowing over the earth.

Hear and pay attention to Me, My children. I desire to give you living water that you may be refreshed and that you may live. Hear Me, My children. I am the true Bread of Life. Only I can satisfy your hunger.

It is My Spirit—the Holy Spirit of God—who breathes life into you. Drink of Me, eat of Me, and breathe of Me. Live in Me. Abide in Me and you will come alive. For you will see, you will hear, and you will know your God. You will say those things you hear Me say and you will do those things you see Me do; you will be Me to those around you. You will testify of My love, My grace, and the salvation of My Son, Jesus Christ. The world awaits the revealing of the sons of God.

Drink of Me, eat of My Word, and breathe of My Spirit so you can walk in the power of My salvation and speak in My Name. My children have eyes to see, ears to hear, and hearts to understand because they are with Me. They are with Me and they are in Me and I am in them. Hear Me, My children. Turn from the world and abide in Me.

Seek first the kingdom of God and His righteousness and My Holy Spirit will lead, direct, and comfort you. You will grow and learn to discern good from evil. Be faithful and diligent in your search to know Me.

Selected Scripture Reading

1. Jer. 51:6—"Flee from the midst of Babylon, and every one save his life! Do not be cut off in her iniquity for this is the time of the LORD's vengeance; He shall recompense her." If "Babylon" is being used as a metaphor, what might it represent?
2. 2 Cor. 6:17–7:1—"'Therefore, come out from among them and be separate,' says the Lord. 'Do not touch what is unclean, and I will receive you. I will be a Father to you and you shall be My sons and daughters,' says the LORD Almighty. Therefore, having these promises beloved, let us cleanse ourselves from all filthiness of the flesh and spirit, perfecting holiness in the fear of God."
3. Ps. 51—This prayer of repentance applies to everyone.
4. Ps. 119:11—"I have hidden Your Word in my heart that I might not sin against You."
5. Prov. 1:7—"The fear of the LORD is the beginning of knowledge, But fools despise wisdom and instruction."
6. Pss. 105, 106—These psalms give insight on how God works in our affairs and uses circumstances to draw us to Himself.
7. Rom. 1:16–17—"For I am not ashamed of the gospel of Christ, for it is the power of God to salvation ... Jew ... Greek ... just shall live by faith."
8. Rom. 1:18–32—God's wrath on unrighteousness is outlined, and sin and works of rebellion are listed.

9. Isa. 13; Jer. 51; Rev. 18; 2 Cor. 6:14–7:1; Gal. 5:16–25; Titus 3:3–5— These scriptures reflect God's call to His people to come away from sin
10. Matt. 6:33 (NLT)—"Seek the Kingdom of God above all else, and live righteously, and He will give you everything you need." See John 14:15–15:17.

168. I Am Calling to My People

I am calling to My people. Come out of the busyness. Come out of the distractions that are separating you from Me. My heart longs to draw you closer, to speak to your heart, and to lead you in the paths of righteousness and freedom.

The time is short. The enemy of your souls is planning many deceptions to lead mankind astray. But for those who have separated themselves from the spirit of Babylon, for those who have stood against the spirit of Jezebel, it shall not be so. They humble themselves daily and seek Me with their whole heart. They follow Me to learn of Me, and I reveal Myself to them.

I will empower My servants who know Me. I will empower My servants who are My friends as they hear Me and know My heart.

Selected Scripture Reading

1. Ps. 39:6–7 (Voice)—"In truth, each of us journeys through life like a shadow. We busy ourselves accomplishing nothing, piling up assets we can never keep; We can't even know who will end up with those things. In light of all this, Lord, what am I really waiting for? You are my hope." Ask God to give you His perspective on what is important in life.
2. Jer. 32:36–44 (God is speaking)—"And I will make an everlasting covenant with them, that I will not turn away from doing them good, but I will put My fear in their hearts so that they will not depart from Me. Yes, I will rejoice over them to do them good, and I will assuredly plant them in this land, with all My heart and with all My soul."

3. Luke 10:38–42—"A certain woman named Martha welcomed Him into her house. And she had a sister called Mary who also sat at Jesus' feet and heard His word. But Martha was distracted with much serving, and she approached Him and said, 'Lord, do You not care that my sister has left me to serve alone? Therefore, tell her to help me.' And Jesus answered and said to her, 'Martha, Martha, you are worried and troubled about many things. But one thing is needed, and Mary has chosen that good part, which will not be taken away from her.'"

We can be distracted by unimportant things and neglect the more important. John 11:24, 27 notes a positive report on Martha.

4. Phil. 4:4–7—"Rejoice in the Lord always ... Be anxious for nothing, but in everything by prayer and supplication, with thanksgiving, let your requests be made known to God; And the peace of God, which surpasses all understanding, will guard your hearts and minds through Christ Jesus."

5. 1 Peter 5:6–11—"Therefore humble yourselves under the mighty hand of God, that He may exalt you in due time, Casting all your care upon Him, for He cares for you. Be sober, be vigilant; because your adversary the devil walks about like a roaring lion seeking whom he may devour." See Rev. 2:20.

6. Ps. 40:1–17—"I waited patiently for the LORD, and He inclined to me, And heard my cry ... He has put a new song in my mouth ... Sacrifice and offering You did not desire; My ears You have opened. Burnt offering and sin offering You did not require. Then I said, 'Behold, I come; In the scroll of the book it is written of me. I delight to do Your will, O my God, and Your law is within my heart.'"

We often think of the Old Testament rituals of sacrifice as defining worship at that time. This passage challenges that simplistic belief and points to the Messianic fulfillment of the promises of God.

169. A Living Sanctuary

My beloved children—you who know Me, you who hear My voice and eagerly await My return—you are most precious to Me, and I am building you into a living sanctuary. Walk before Me in purity and holiness. Be faithful in all your ways for My Spirit desires to dwell in power in My sanctuary.

I have many things to say to you, but you must cleanse and purify your hearts. Walk under the shadow of My wings that I might bless and protect you. These are perilous times, and you will be tempted in many ways, tempted to lose the simplicity of your faith and trust in Me.

In this season of restoration and purification of My church, I am speaking and revealing many things to you. For you who turn your hearts to Me–for you who seek Me with your whole heart–you shall see and understand. The scriptures shall come to life for you as you spend time in My Word and in My presence.

My church, this is the key. I desire intimacy with you. I desire purity of love, and communion with you. I speak clearly to you. The key to restoration is intimacy with Me. Come into My presence and learn of Me for I am meek and humble and you will find rest for your soul. Come into My presence and you shall be refreshed and restored. Do not miss this provision for My church in the end times. Come into My heart.

I say to you, My beloved, do not doubt. In your heart, remember our love for one another, for all in the household of faith. Let My love be in you and flow through you.

I dwell in My sanctuary.

Selected Scripture Reading

1. 1 Chron. 16:27 (Voice)—"Honor and majesty precede Him; strength and beauty infuse His holy sanctuary." See Ps. 127:1.
2. 2 Chron. 2:6—King Solomon said that God inhabits the universe and that no earthly building could contain him. He clarified that the temple he would build was simply a place for the people to go to acknowledge and meet with God. See Pss. 26:8, 40:6–10; Heb. 10:1–39.
3. Acts 7:48–50—"However, the Most High does not dwell in temples made with hands, as the prophet says, 'Heaven is My throne, And earth is My footstool. What house will you build for Me? Says the LORD, Or what is the place of My rest? Has My hand not made all these things.'" See Isa. 66:1–2; Ps. 102:25.

4. Amos. 9:11–12—"'On that day I will raise up the tabernacle of David, which has fallen down, And repair its damages; I will raise up its ruins, And rebuild it as in the days of old; That they may possess the remnant of Edom, And all the Gentiles who are called by My name.' Says the LORD who does this thing." See Luke 3:23–31; John 2:19, Heb. 3:4–6; Acts 15:14–18.
5. 1 Cor. 3:16—"Do you not know that you are the temple of God and that the Spirit of God dwells in you?" See Ps. 51:10–13; 1 Peter 2:4–10.
6. Titus 3:3–8—"For we ourselves were also once foolish, disobedient, deceived, serving various lusts and pleasures, living in malice and envy, hateful and hating one another. But when the kindness and the love of God our Savior toward man appeared, Not by works of righteousness which we have done, but according to His mercy He saved us, through the washing of the regeneration and renewing of the Holy Spirit, Whom He poured out on us abundantly through Jesus Christ our Savior, That having been justified by His grace we should become heirs according to the hope of eternal life, This is a faithful saying, and these things I want you to affirm constantly, that those who have believed in God should be careful to maintain good works. These things are good and profitable to men." See Eph. 2:19–22; 2 Cor. 11:3; Pss. 36:7, 17:8.

170. That You May Walk above the Confusion

Will My people hunger and thirst after righteousness? Will you come before Me desiring to love Me with your whole heart?

I have given My all for you. Will you give Me all of you? Know, My precious one, that I love you with My whole heart and that the plans I have for you are good, plans to bless you and bring you closer to Me. Seek Me. Turn from every evil and sin that will separate you from Me. Set your heart and place your affections on spiritual things so you may walk above the confusion of this world.

Know that I have come to bring you life abundantly, but you must follow Me and obey My commands. In obedience to My words, you shall walk in truth and the truth will set you free from the power of sin and death.

Arise, My beloved, and come up higher. Seek Me with all your heart for I am your joy. I am your peace. I am your righteousness.

Selected Scripture Reading

1. 2 Chron. 15:12–15—"Then they entered into a covenant to seek the LORD God of their fathers with all their heart and with all their soul ... And all Judah rejoiced at the oath, for they had sworn with all their heart and sought Him with all their soul, and He was found by them, and the LORD gave them rest all around." See Ps. 37:34; Prov. 4:23.
2. Matt. 5:6—"Blessed are those who hunger and thirst for righteousness, For they shall be filled."
3. Isa. 26:9 (Voice)—"At night I long for You with all that is in Me. When morning comes, I seek You with all my heart. For when Your justice is done on earth, then everyone in the world will learn righteousness."
4. Ps. 26:2–3 (Voice)—"Put me on trial and examine me, O Eternal One! Search me through and through—from my deepest longings to every thought that crosses my mind. Your unfailing love is always before me; I have journeyed down Your path of truth."
5. Col. 3:2–3 (Voice)—"Stay focused on what's above, not on earthly things, Because your old life is dead and gone."
6. James 3:16 (Voice)—"Any place where you find jealousy and selfish ambition, you will discover chaos and evil thriving under its rule." See Deut. 28:20.
7. 1 John 2:15–17—"Do not love the world or the things in the world. If anyone loves the world, the love of the Father is not in him. For all that is in the world—the lust of the flesh, the lust of the eyes, and the pride of life—is not of the Father but is of the world. And the world is passing away, and the lust of it; but he who does the will of God abides forever."
8. John 10:10—"The thief does not come except to steal, and to kill, and to destroy. I have come that they may have life, and that they may

have it more abundantly. Who or what might be the thief?" Read all of chapter 10 for more information and insight.
9. John 8:31–32—"Then Jesus said to those Jews who believed Him, 'If you abide in My word, you are my disciples indeed. And you shall know the truth, and the truth shall make you free.'"

171. It Is with Your Heart

Have I not called you out of this world to Myself? Have I not set you apart unto righteousness that you may live and have your existence in My kingdom and not of this world?

Listen to My Word and learn to know Me. I am calling My people to rest in Me. To rest in Me, you must know Me with your heart. For it is with your heart that you receive My words and know My love for you. It is with your heart that you believe and salvation is manifested in your life.

I am calling My people to rest in Me. Sanctify your hearts unto Me and you will find peace and rest for your souls. Do not give yourself to the evil taskmaster of this world. Do not give yourself to sin and unrighteousness for you will become entangled–you will become entrapped by it.

Instead, know the truth and flee from sin. Come to Me, and I will give you the peace and rest your heart is seeking. Do not set your heart on the things of this world; set your heart on Me and you will know My rest.

Selected Scripture Reading

1. Isa. 45:22–23—"Look to Me, and be saved, All you ends of the earth! For I am God, and there is no other. I have sworn by Myself; The word has gone out of My mouth in righteousness, And shall not return, That to Me every knee shall bow, Every tongue shall take an oath." See Luke 4:17–21; 1 Tim. 2:4.
2. Rom. 14:10–12—Do you struggle with being critical and judgmental of others, leaving them with a feeling of condemnation and leaving you puffed up, feeling self-righteous? Prayerfully read these verses and do a topical study of related scriptures to bring greater understanding and peace into your relationships with others.

3. Ps. 86:3–5—"Be merciful to me, O Lord, For I cry to You all day long. Rejoice the soul of your servant, For to You, O Lord, I lift up my soul. For You, Lord, are good, and ready to forgive, And abundant in mercy to all those who call upon You." See Ps. 29:11.
4. Heb. 4:1–12—"Therefore, since a promise remains of entering His rest, let us fear lest any of you seem to have come short of it. For indeed the gospel was preached to us as well as to them; but the word which they heard did not profit them, not being mixed with faith in those who heard it. For we who have believed do enter that rest."
5. Phil. 4:6–8—"Be anxious for nothing but in everything by prayer and supplication, with thanksgiving, let your requests be made known to God And the peace of God, which surpasses all understanding, will guard your hearts and minds through Christ Jesus. Finally, brethren, whatever things are true, whatever things are noble, whatever things are just, whatever this are pure, whatever things are lovely, whatever things are of good report, if there is any virtue and if there is anything praiseworthy—meditate on these things."

172. Will You Stand for Truth?

Will you stand for truth, or will you compromise? Will your lusts lead to blindness? Will your lusts lead to making excuses for your sins instead of repentance? If you cling to your rebellion, if you do not turn from your sins, you will gather wrath and judgment upon yourself and your people.

I say to you, My people, buy eye salve from Me and heal your blindness. Turn from your sinful behavior. Crucify the flesh and its lustful desires. You cannot continue to have a pretense of godliness and purity yet be resistant to My grace. My grace is moving upon your heart. You must choose whom you will serve.

Trust Me to do a good work in your heart. Trust Me to do a good work in your life; I am calling My people to come out from the world. Come out and separate yourselves in purity and holiness. I am calling you to come up higher and walk with Me in heavenly places. I have a work for you. I have a destiny for you. Come up higher and walk in the presence of your God.

Selected Scripture Reading

1. Gen. 19:1–14—Lot chose to live in the wicked city of Sodom and he and his family lived a compromised life. Because of his uncle Abraham's prayers, two angels warned Lot of Sodom's impending destruction. Lot tried to warn the men who were pledged to marry his daughters, but they ignored him thinking he was joking. Why did they miss the warning?
2. Ps. 19:8–14—"The statutes of the LORD are right, rejoicing the heart; The commandment of the LORD is pure, enlightening the eyes; The fear of the LORD is clean, enduring forever; The judgments of the LORD are true and righteous altogether. More to be desired are they than gold, Yea, than much fine gold; Sweeter also than honey and the honeycomb. Moreover by them Your servant is warned, And in keeping them there is great reward. Who can understand his errors? Cleanse me from my secret faults. Keep back Your servant also from presumptuous sins; Let them not have dominion over me. Then shall I be blameless, And I shall be innocent of great transgression. Let the words of my mouth and the meditation of my heart Be acceptable in Your sight, O LORD, my strength and my Redeemer." See Acts 4:1–37; Rev. 3:14–22.
3. Prov. 26:23–26 (Voice)—"Like a shiny glaze coating a rough clay pot, so are burning lips that conceal an evil heart ... And though he covers his hatred with cleverness, his wicked ways will be publicly exposed." What do you think the metaphor "burning lips" describes?
4. 1 Thess. 4:1–5 (Voice)—"Remember what we have taught you: live a life that is pleasing to God as you are already doing ... For you know the instructions we gave you, instructions that came through the Lord Jesus. Now this is God's will for you: set yourselves apart and live holy lives; avoid polluting yourselves with sexual defilement. Learn how to take charge over your own body, maintaining purity and honor." See Jude 20–25.

173. Into These Times of Shaking and Storms

My people cannot hear My voice. They do not know the voice of their Shepherd. Their lives are full of busyness and the voices of this world.

Will you not come to Me and find rest for your soul? Will you not come to Me and find the peace you are seeking? Oh, My little ones. Seek Me now, and learn to know Me now. Learn to recognize My voice.

As the world is shaken, as foundations crumble, fear and confusion will increase. I am calling you to come forth during this season as bright and shining stars of the glory of God. I am calling you to bring peace and stability into these times of shaking and storms. I am calling you to bring My words and My presence before the people.

By My Word and by My Spirit, I speak to you. Hear and understand. Know what I am saying to you and you will be strengthened. You will see beyond the confusion. You will see beyond the chaos and destruction. You will see through the deceptions.

Hear and know My Word. Live by My Spirit and you will stand. You will live victoriously as you walk in My love My truth, and My wisdom. Know My Word and put it into your heart so My Spirit may give you discernment. These are perilous times, and you must have discernment to see through the strategies of the enemy.

To fulfill your destiny, you must surrender completely to Me. You must walk away from the world's ways and voices. Seek Me and know My Word. Rest in My presence and I will fill your heart with Myself. Come to Me, My little ones. Come to Me.

I am restoring My people; I am restoring your vision and understanding. Be wise, My little ones, and you will see. By My Word and by My Spirit, says the Lord your God, you will see.

Selected Scripture Reading

1. Gen. 22:18—We are a blessing to ourselves and others when we obey God.
2. Deut. 4:25–31—"When you beget children and grandchildren and have grown old in the land, and act corruptly and make a carved image in the form of anything, and do evil in the sight of the LORD your God to provoke Him to anger … And the LORD will scatter you among the peoples … But from there you will seek the LORD your God, and you will find Him if you seek Him with all your heart and with all your soul. When you are in distress and all these things come upon you in the latter days, when you turn to the LORD your

God and obey His voice. (For the LORD your God is a merciful God); He will not forsake you nor destroy you, nor forget the covenant of your fathers which He swore to them."

Outline the sequence of events and consequences described in these verses. Is there a pattern that might also describe what people experience today?

3. Hab. 2:1–4—"I will stand my watch And set myself on the rampart, And watch to see what He will say to me. And what I will answer when I am corrected. Then the LORD answered me and said: "Write down the vision! And make it plain on tablets, That he may run who reads it. For the vision is yet for an appointed time; But at the end it will speak, and it will not lie. Though it tarries, wait for it; Because it will surely come. It will not tarry. Behold the proud, His soul is not upright in him; But the just shall live by faith." See Rom. 1:16–20; John 10; Acts 7. What did the prophet mean when he said he was watching to see what he would answer when he was corrected?

4. Luke 14:15–24—"Blessed is he who shall eat bread in the kingdom of God! Then He said to him, 'A certain man gave a great supper and invited many, And sent his servant at supper time to say to those who were invited, "Come, for all things are now ready." But they all with one accord began to make excuses. The first said to him, "I have bought a piece of ground, and I must go and see it. I ask you to have me excused."'"

What temptations or challenges do you encounter when planning to read the Bible or go to church?

174. Look to Me and See

Look and see what I am doing among My people. Restoration. Purification. My Spirit is working among you, and I am leading and guiding you into restoration, into holiness, purity, and righteousness. For I will reveal Myself—I will reveal My glory—to all people of the earth through My beloved children.

Think it not strange, My children, that you are going through trials and tests; for I am creating–I am fashioning you into worthy vessels, vessels worthy to carry My gospel and My presence to this generation.

Be patient, My child. Restoration is a process that takes time. You must have faith and vision to see into the future.

Yield yourself to Me. Follow Me in obedience. Choose the good and reject the evil and you will be restored. Old strongholds and ungodly ways of thinking and doing must be identified, forsaken, and torn down.

I am restoring My bride to be altogether lovely adorned with the beauty of grace, love, and truth. She is majestic, filled with the glory and power of Christ–fully committed and devoted to Me. Have faith to see the restoration of My church. Be patient and full of My love and grace as I work among you and in your midst to do this work of restoration. I am among you to do a good work. Look and see what I am doing in your hearts. Look to Me and see.

Selected Scripture Reading

1. Ps. 123:1–2—"Unto You I lift up my eyes, O You who dwell in the heavens. Behold, as the eyes of servants look to the hand of their masters, As the eyes of a maid to the hand of her mistress, So our eyes look to the LORD our God, Until He has mercy on us."
2. Isa. 45:22–25—"Look to Me, and be saved, All you ends of the earth! For I have sworn by Myself; The word has gone out of My mouth in righteousness, And shall not return, That to Me every knee shall bow, Every tongue shall take an oath. He shall say, 'Surely in the LORD I have righteousness and strength. To Him men shall come, And all shall be ashamed Who are incensed against Him. In the LORD all the descendants of Israel Shall be justified and give glory.'" See Isa. 55–56; Rom. 11.
3. Lam. 5:21—"Turn us back to You, O LORD, and we will be restored."
4. Zech. 12:10–12—"And I will pour on the house of David and on the inhabitants of Jerusalem the Spirit of grace and supplication; then they will look on Me, whom they pierced. Yes, they will mourn for Him as one mourns for his only son, and grieve for Him as one grieves for a firstborn." See Isa. 11:11; Matt. 23:37–39; Luke 21:24.
5. Mal. 4:5–6—"Behold, I will send you Elijah the prophet Before the coming of the great and dreadful day of the LORD. And he will turn the hearts of the fathers to the children, And the hearts of the children to their fathers, Lest I come and strike the earth with a curse." See

Matt. 17:10–13. Notice the call of God to look on others, especially children, with compassion.

6. Heb. 12:1–13:9—"Therefore we also since we are surrounded by so great a cloud of witnesses, let us lay aside every weight, and the sin which so easily ensnares us, and let us run with endurance the race that is set before us, Looking unto Jesus, the author and finisher of our faith, who for the joy that was set before Him endured the cross, despising the shame, and has sat down at the right hand of the throne of God ... Let brotherly love continue ... Do not be carried about with various and strange doctrines. For it is good that the heart be established by grace, not with foods which have not profited those who have been occupied with them." See 1 Peter 1–4.

In all these verses is the call to endure hardships and discipline while maintaining an attitude of appreciation and love. We are admonished not to be carried away by strange doctrines or beliefs. Why do you think we are prone to be carried away by false doctrines? How can we prepare our hearts and minds to recognize and refuse strange doctrines?

175. Welcome My Correction

Who are My children? Who are truly Mine? Have I not told you that by their fruits you shall know them? Have I not told you that My sheep know My voice? They know the voice of the Good Shepherd and the voice of another they shall not follow.

Listen carefully, My children, and do not be deceived by those who have a form and talk of godliness but walk in disobedience to My Word and reject My counsel. They will lead you astray as they themselves are led astray by their lustful desires. Turn away from such and do not reap the rewards of their foolish rebellions.

You must carefully consider and judge between good and evil, between the profitable and the unprofitable, and between what is righteous and what is unrighteous so you may choose the good and walk in it. Is it not I, the Lord, who tests the reins of your heart? Is it not I, the Lord, who sets choices before you?

If you seek Me with your whole heart, you will find Me. My children have soft hearts for Me, and they hunger and thirst for My words of instruction and counsel to them. Hear Me. Those who are Mine welcome My correction in their lives. They do not reject My discipline for I do discipline My children that they may grow in wisdom and godly love.

These are perilous times, and the love of many turns cold–cold toward their fellow man and cold toward God. This is the harvest season and both good and evil are ripening–maturing like fruit in the fields.

I am calling to you, My children, to fill your hearts with My love. Embrace with eagerness My Word, and welcome My instruction, correction, and discipline. You shall know the truth and you shall be set free to walk in Me.

Selected Scripture Reading

1. Ps. 33:18–22—"Behold, the eye of the LORD is on those who fear Him, On those who hope in His mercy, 19. To deliver their soul from death, And to keep them alive in famine. Our soul waits for the LORD; He is our help and our shield. For our heart shall rejoice in Him, Because we have trusted in His holy name. Let Your mercy, O LORD, be upon us, Just as we hope in You." See Ps. 94:12–13.
2. Rom. 8:14 (Voice)—"If the Spirit of God is leading you, then take comfort in knowing you are His children." See Deut. 7:6; 1 Peter 2:9.
3. Matt. 7:15–20—"Beware of false prophets who come to you in sheep's clothing but inwardly they are ravenous wolves. You will know them by their fruits. Do men gather grapes from thornbushes or figs from thistles? Even so, every good tree bears good fruit, but a bad tree bears bad fruit." See 1 John 3:10.
4. Heb. 12:11—"Now no chastening seems to be joyful for the present, but painful; nevertheless afterward it yields the peaceable fruit of righteousness to those who have been trained by it."

176. Wisdom, Insight, and Diligence Are Required

In My end-times harvest, the wheat and the tares will grow together until the time of the very end. The good will mature and bear worthy and good fruit. Wickedness will mature, and great evil will abound.

Conflict, chaos, and upheaval will open the eyes of many who have walked in comfortable complacency. They will have hearts to see and understand. Many will move from complacency into My kingdom. Jew and Gentile alike will come together into one new man.

For I am calling My people out of the world. I am calling you to Myself. Oh, hear Me, come to Me, and learn of Me. Take My burden upon you—the knowledge and understanding of righteousness and the kingdom of God. Then, you shall know the way to walk, and you will find rest for your soul.

You shall be gathered together with Me, and great will be your joy. Great wisdom, insight, and diligence are required during this harvest time.

Selected Scripture Reading

1. Dan. 12:1–4—"At that time Michael shall stand up, The great prince who stands watch over the sons of your people, And there shall be a time of trouble, Such as never was since there was a nation, Even to that time. And at that time your people shall be delivered, Everyone who is found written in the book. And many of those who sleep in the dust of the earth shall awake, Some to everlasting life, Some to shame and everlasting contempt. Those who are wise shall shine Like the brightness of the firmament, And those who turn many to righteousness Like the stars forever and ever. But you, Daniel, shut up the words, and seal the book until the time of the end; many shall run to and fro, and knowledge shall increase." See Matt. 13, 24.
2. John 10:11–18—"I am the good shepherd. The good shepherd gives His life for the sheep ... And other sheep I have which are not of this fold; them also I must bring, and they will hear My voice; and there will be one flock and one shepherd."
3. Eph. 2:11–22—"Therefore remember that you, once Gentiles in the flesh ... That at that time you were without Christ, being aliens from the commonwealth of Israel and strangers from the covenants of promise, having no hope and without God in the world. But now in Christ Jesus... For He Himself is our peace, who has made both one, and has broken down the middle wall of separation ... so as to create in Himself one new man from the two, thus making peace, And that

He might reconcile them both to God in one body through the cross." See 2 Cor. 6:1–2; Gal. 3:8; Matt. 11:28–30.

177. Embrace Instruction in Righteousness

Listen carefully and understand. My people are pregnant with sin. They work diligently to cover their lusts and misdeeds. Do you not know I see and I hear you when you justify yourselves calling good evil and evil good?

Return to Me now lest your shame and destruction overtake you. Do not persist in your stubbornness and evil ways. Turn from lusts and greed that you may be free from the bondages of sin.

Sin conceived matures and brings spiritual blindness, destruction of what is good, and death. Turn from sin that you may live.

Embrace truth. Embrace instruction in righteousness. Humble yourselves before Me and I will lift you up. Call to Me and I will answer you.

Selected Scripture Reading

1. Ps. 33:18–19—These verses state that fearing God brings significant blessings. Consider this verse along with Deut. 10:12; Josh. 24:14; Matt. 10:28; Rom. 11:22; Phil. 2:12; 1 Peter 1:17; 2 Peter 2:17; Rev. 14:7 for a more complete and balanced understanding of fearing God.
2. Isa. 5:20—"Woe to those who call evil good, and good evil, who put darkness for light, and light for darkness; who put bitter for sweet, and sweet for bitter. Woe to those who are wise in their own eyes, and prudent in their own sight."

    The ultimate question for individuals and mankind is, "Who decides what is right and what is wrong?" This question was exemplified in Genesis 3 with the story of the beguiling serpent. God's concluding judgments are described in Revelation—judgments on evil and rewards for good (Rev. 22:12–17). How should these truths impact a culture? Judicial, educational, and governmental structures?
3. Isa. 32:17—"The work of righteousness will be peace, And the effect of righteousness, quietness and assurance forever. My people will

dwell in a peaceful habitation, In secure dwellings, and in quiet resting places." See Ps. 101.

4. 2 Tim. 2:15—"Be diligent to present yourself approved to God, a worker who does not need to be ashamed, rightly dividing the word of truth." See Deut. 6:5–7, 11:19, 17:14–20; 2 Chron. 17:9; Ps. 119; Isa. 2:3, 34:16; John 5:39; Acts 10:33–48, 17:11; Rom. 15:4; Eph. 4:11; Col. 4:16; James 3:1; 2 Tim. 2:25.

   Given Jesus's statement in Matthew 7:15–29 that not everyone who calls Him Lord will enter the kingdom of heaven, do you think it is possible to be a Christian and have no desire to study and live by His teachings?

5. James 1:14—"But each one is tempted when he is drawn away by his own desires and enticed, then, when desire has conceived, it gives birth to sin; and sin, when it is full grown, brings forth death." See James 4:10.

6. Rom. 1:18–32—"For the wrath of God is revealed from heaven against all ungodliness and unrighteousness of men, who suppress the truth in unrighteousness ... although they knew God, they did not glorify Him as God, nor were they thankful, but became futile in their thoughts and their foolish hearts were darkened ... Therefore God also gave them up to uncleanness in the lusts of their hearts to dishonor their bodies ... For this reason, God gave them up to vile passions ... even as they did not like to retain God in their knowledge, God gave them over to a debased mind, to do those things which are not fitting; being filled with all unrighteousness, sexual immorality, wickedness, full of envy, murder, strife, deceit, evil-mindedness; they are whisperers, backbiters, haters of God, violent, proud, boasters, inventors of evil things, disobedient to parents, undiscerning, untrustworthy, unloving, unforgiving, unmerciful ... [they] also approve of those who practice them."

178. I Am the Good Shepherd

I am the Good Shepherd. I keep watch over My flock. I always know where you are even when you stray from Me and leave My protection.

By My Spirit, I speak to your heart and call you to return to Me. Stay on the straight and narrow path that leads to righteousness and faith in

Me. If you choose to listen with an obedient heart and learn to know Me, you will develop a discerning heart and know to choose good and turn away from evil.

These are perilous times, and deceptions abound. There are traps and pitfalls that will ensnare many who fall into them. Do not be sheep who are led astray. Stay close to Me, your Good Shepherd. I will lead you and provide for you. I will be your protector. Do not listen to enticing voices that tickle your ears and incite your lusts to lead you astray.

Remember who I am, and follow the voice of your Shepherd that I may lead you safely home.

Selected Scripture Reading

1. Ps. 23:1–6—"The LORD is my shepherd; I shall not want. He makes me to lie down in green pastures … He restores my soul. He leads me in the paths of righteousness for His name's sake … I will fear no evil; for You are with me. Your rod and staff, they comfort me. You prepare a table before me in the presence of my enemies … Surely goodness and mercy shall follow me." See Ps. 79:13; Ezek. 34:11–12.
2. Isa. 40:10–11—"Behold, the Lord GOD shall come with a strong hand, and His arm shall rule for Him, Behold, His reward is with Him, and His work before Him. He will feed His flock like a shepherd; He will gather the lambs with His arm and carry them to His bosom, and gently lead those who are with young." See Isa. 53:1–12; 1 Peter 2:21–25; John 12:38.
3. John 10:1–11 (Jesus speaking)—"But he who enters by the door is the shepherd of the sheep … and the sheep hear his voice; and he calls his own sheep by name and leads them out. And when he brings out his own sheep, he goes before them, and the sheep follow him, for they know his voice … I am the door of the sheep … If anyone enters by Me, he will be saved … I am the good shepherd. The good shepherd gives His life for the sheep."
4. 1 Peter 2:25—"For you were like sheep going astray but have now returned to the Shepherd and Overseer of your souls." See Matt. 18:10–14.
5. 1 Peter 5:4—"When the Chief Shepherd appears, you will receive the crown of glory that does not fade away."

6. Rev. 7:17—"The Lamb who is in the midst of the throne will shepherd them and lead them to living fountains of waters. And God will wipe away every tear from their eyes."

179. Understanding and Wisdom Will Be Your Companions

My children, do not be alarmed or afraid as you see dangers and troubles approaching. Do not give in to worry or fretting. Remember how I have always walked with My children through the valleys, storms, and battles. I will hear and answer your cries for help.

Strengthen your heart in Me. Know My Word, and let My words to you go deep into your heart and take root so your faith may grow and flourish. Then you shall be steadfast and unwavering in your faith regardless of what is going on around you.

Separate your heart from worldliness, and set your affections on things above. Then understanding and wisdom will be your companions. Put My Word in your heart, and My truth shall set you free for My words shall teach you.

My words shall divide between what is of the soul—of the flesh—and what is of My Spirit and gives life. Welcome the conviction of the Holy Spirit as He bears witness to the truth.

I will lead and guide you. I will protect you. Follow Me.

Selected Scripture Reading

1. Ps. 37:1–40—"Do not fret because of evildoers, nor be envious of the workers of iniquity ... Commit your way to the LORD, Trust also in Him, And He shall bring it to pass. He shall bring forth your righteousness as the light And your justice as the noonday. Rest in the LORD and wait patiently for Him ... The LORD knows the days of the upright, And their inheritance shall be forever. They shall not be ashamed in the evil time, And in the days of famine they shall be satisfied ... The steps of a good man are ordered by the LORD, And He delights in his way. Though he fall, he shall not be utterly cast down, For the LORD upholds him with His hand ... Depart from evil, and do good, And dwell forevermore. For the LORD

loves justice, And does not forsake His saints. They are preserved forever ... Wait on the LORD, And keep His way, And He shall exalt you to inherit the land, When the wicked are cut off, you shall see it ... But the salvation of the righteous is from the LORD; He is their strength in the time of trouble." See Ps. 51:6; Prov. 3:13; 1 Peter 3:12.
2. Ezek. 36:27–28—"I will put My Spirit within you and cause you to walk in My statutes, and you will keep My judgments and do them. Then you shall dwell in the land that I gave to your fathers, you shall be My people, and I will be your God." See John 8:31–36, 14:2–21; John 17:17, Rom. 15:16, Col. 3.
3. Heb. 4:12—"For the word of God is living and powerful, and sharper than any two-edged sword, piercing even to the division of soul and spirit..."

180. I Desire to Comfort and Protect My People

My people seek people who tickle their ears and entertain them. They follow smooth words and do not follow My truth because they do not hunger and thirst for My righteousness. They do not follow Me because they have lost their first love.

I am calling and gathering My children close to Me, close to My heart. Seek Me and you shall find Me. Learn to know My voice and you will hear My Spirit speak to your heart, "This is the way. Walk in it."

I desire to gather you as a mother hen gathers her chicks. I desire to comfort and protect My people. I desire to prepare you for what lies ahead.

Do not seek to be tickled and entertained. Rather, seek to know the will and purposes of God that you may walk in My blessings and protection.

The hour is late. You must choose whom you will serve. Come to Me. Follow Me.

Selected Scripture Reading

1. 2 Tim. 4:3–4—"For the time will come when they will not endure sound doctrine, but according to their own desires, because they have itching ears, they will heap up for themselves teachers; and they will turn their ears away from the truth, and be turned aside to fables."

2. Jer. 2—This passage describes God's words to Israel about remembering the love they had for Him at the beginning. God describes how they lost their first love and fell into spiritual adultery and idolatry. Does this happen to Christians today? How can we position and guard ourselves against falling away from a vibrant, personal relationship with God?
3. Rev. 2:1–7—This was written to the church at Ephesus; it complimented them for their work, patience, and rejection of evil and yet admonished them to return to intimate communion and relationship with the Lord.
4. Matt. 23:37—"O Jerusalem, Jerusalem, the one who kills the prophets and stones those who are sent to her! How often I wanted to gather your children together, as a hen gathers her chicks under her wings, but you were not willing." Have you ever rejected the one thing you really were seeking and hoping for? What causes this? How can we avoid that mistake?
5. Ps. 91:4—"He shall cover you with His feathers, and under His wings you shall take refuge; His truth shall be your shield and buckler." Psalm 91 discloses the protection one has when "dwelling in the secret place of the Most High." How would you define the "secret place of the Most High?"
6. 2 Chron. 24:20b—"Thus says God, 'Why do you transgress the commandments of the LORD, so that you cannot prosper? Because you have forsaken the LORD, He also has forsaken you.'" See Deut. 30:19–20. Can you think of historical accounts in the Bible illustrating this truth?
7. Rev. 2:7—"He who has an ear, let him hear what the Spirit says to the churches. To him who overcomes, I will give to eat from the tree of life, which is in the midst of the Paradise of God."

181. Walk with Me and You Will Walk in My Glory

My Holy Spirit is here to lead and guide you in the way of life and completeness in Me. You are My creation, and it is My will that you be strong in spirit and understanding, walking in My truth and light.

Consider carefully what My Word teaches you, and take to heart

My commands and precepts so you may live and overcome trials and difficulties. The enemy of your souls would have you be fearful, angry, greedy, controlled by lusts, and full of arrogance and pride. The enemy of your souls entices you to hatred against your brothers and sisters, against your fellow man. Be alert—do not enter these snares and traps.

Look to Me. Study My Word and follow Me. I am holy. I am righteous. I am pure love. Let My love flow through you to your brothers and sisters, to your fellow man. In patience and wisdom, encourage one another. Lift one another up in godliness and righteousness.

Have I not given you this commandment to love one another as I have loved you? For My glory to be revealed in the earth before all peoples, it is necessary that you love, honor, and esteem one another as I have taught you to do. Is not My Spirit in each of My children? Honor Me by honoring one another. Let your speech be seasoned with grace, and come to Me for refreshment and rest.

I am restoring the glory of My people. I am restoring what the enemy has stolen from My people. In knowing Me, in following My precepts and commands to grow in purity and love, you will find My glory surrounding you. Walk with Me and you will walk in My glory.

Selected Scripture Reading

1. Isa. 60:1–2—"Arise, shine; For your light has come! And the glory of the LORD is risen upon you. For behold the darkness shall cover the earth and deep darkness the people; But the LORD will arise over you, and His glory will be seen upon you." See 1 Cor. 3:16.
2. Ps. 8—This passage highlights the glory of the Lord.
3. 2 Tim. 2:15—Why is this a necessity?
4. Eph. 5—This teaches us that as we walk in God's love, we will be sanctified and cleansed by the water of the word and clothed in the glory of God (vv. 26–27).
5. 1 Peter 5:8–10—"Be sober, be vigilant; because your adversary the devil walks about like a roaring lion, seeking whom he may devour. Resist him, steadfast in the faith, knowing that the same sufferings are experienced by your brotherhood in the world. But may the God of all grace who called us to His eternal glory by Christ Jesus, after you have suffered a while, perfect, establish, strengthen, and settle you."

6. Jude exhorts us to "contend earnestly for the faith." This book instructs us about recognizing false teachers and false doctrines then closes with an admonition of maintaining our life with God. See Col. 4:6.

182. Know the Plans I Have for You Are Good

Know the plans I have for you are good; they are plans to give you a hope—a knowing of My blessing and goodness in your life. Follow Me carefully with all diligence.

I have many things to teach you by My Holy Spirit. I delight to bring understanding and freedom to My children. I delight to inspire you—to put My plans into your heart. As you surrender your whole being to me, I will enable you to see creative solutions to your challenges and situations. My Holy Spirit will give you ideas and plans. I will direct your paths.

Surrender and walk in faithfulness to receive what I have for you. Look to Me so your joy will be great and your destiny will be fulfilled.

Some of My children give up and do not believe I love them or have compassion in My heart for them. Consider, My precious ones, how much I have given to give you deliverance and eternal life. My mercies are new every morning for you. Do not refuse the grace I give you to open your heart and receive encouragement and life from Me. The way may not always be easy, yet have faith in Me to bring you safely and joyously to your destination.

Be strong. Be brave. Be courageous. Reach out with your heart to Me. Know the plans I have for you are good.

Selected Scripture Reading

1. Ps. 33:11 (Voice)—"The Eternal's purposes will last to the end of time; the thoughts of His heart will awaken and stir all generations." See John 16:12–14; 2 Cor. 5:17–21.
2. Jer. 29:11—Read this to find out how God thinks about you and what He desires for you. See 2 Cor. 1:3–4, 2:9–16.
3. Ps. 32:1–11—"Blessed is he whose transgression is forgiven, Whose sin is covered. Blessed is the man to whom the LORD does not impute iniquity, And in whose spirit there is no deceit … I acknowledged my

sin to You, And my iniquity I have not hidden. I said, 'I will confess my transgressions to the LORD,' And You forgave the iniquity of my sin. For this cause everyone who is godly shall pray to You In a time when You may be found … You are my hiding place; You shall preserve me from trouble; You shall surround me with songs of deliverance. I will instruct you and teach you in the way you should go; I will guide you with My eye. Do not be like the horse or like the mule, Which have no understanding, Which must be harnessed with bit and bridle, Else they will not come near you. Many sorrows shall be to the wicked; But he who trusts in the LORD, mercy shall surround him. Be glad in the LORD and rejoice, you righteous; And shout for joy, all you upright in heart!" See Ps. 37:4; Prov. 3; 1 John 3:21–23.

183. The Time Appointed for Salvation

I am your Creator and God. I have appointed and set forth times and seasons. There is a time to sow seed. There is a season for watering and tending to growth, and there is a harvest time.

The earth has seasons and mankind also has seasons and times. Now is the accepted time of salvation. Now is the time to cleanse yourselves in the blood of the Lamb, Jesus Christ, for there is no other name by which you may be saved. He is the only door to salvation and eternal life.

Seasons and times come and go. Man does not know when his season—his time shall end. It is the wise man, however, who considers carefully and understands the seasons and times he is in. He knows the time to work. He knows the time to learn and create. He understands the time to build up and the time to tear down.

Now is the accepted time, the time appointed for salvation. Seek Me while I may be found. For the one who has finished and completed his work in its appointed time there is satisfaction and joy.

Selected Scripture Reading

1. Gen. 1:14–18—"Then God said, 'Let there be lights in the firmament of the heavens to divide the day from the night; and let them be for signs and seasons, and for days and years.'" See Gen. 8:22.

2. 1 Cor. 3:6–11—Planting, watering, and harvesting are symbolic of spiritual birth and maturity.
3. Gal. 6:7–10—The principles of sowing and reaping apply to spiritual and emotional growth.
4. Ps. 32; Matt; Mark; Luke; John; Acts—These teach us that now is the time for salvation, for learning to know our Creator in a close and loving relationship.
5. Acts 4:12—"Nor is there salvation in any other for there is no other name under heaven given among men by which we must be saved." See John 10:7–9.
6. Eccl. 9:12—"For man also does not know his time."
7. 1 Chron. 12:32—The sons of Issachar were wise and understood the times.
8. Ps. 119:104—"Through Your precepts I get understanding; Therefore, I hate every false way."
9. Luke 12:54–56; Matt. 16:1–4—Jesus rebuked those who claimed to be discerning yet were not. In Luke 19:41–44, Jesus said that Jerusalem did not understand the time of its visitation—recognizing the Messiah and the new covenant as the prophets foretold.
10. Isa. 55:6–7—"Seek the LORD while He may be found, Call upon Him while He is near. Let the wicked forsake his way and the unrighteous man his thoughts; Let him return to the LORD and He will have mercy on him; and to our God, For He will abundantly pardon."
11. Jer. 5:23–25—Defiance and rebellion cause one to miss the appointed season thus causing good to be withheld or lost.
12. Matt. 25—This chapter discusses aspects of being prepared and wise stewardship.

184. I Have a Calling and a Purpose for Each of My Children

I have a calling and a purpose for each of My children. You have a unique destiny fitted to your God-given personality, talents, and gifts—fitted to your place to serve in My kingdom.

Submit yourself, submit your plans, submit your thoughts, submit your heart—your whole being—to Me that you may see and walk in the blessings I have for you. You will be blessed and you will be a blessing to others.

Know this. I will direct your steps. The steps of a righteous man are ordered by the Lord. I will direct you. I will speak to your heart. Give your heart to listen and obey. Give your heart to seek Me. Give your heart to know My ways.

You choose. You have a choice. Will you obey? Will you listen? Will you turn away from the lustful, selfish temptations that rob you of your destiny in Me? Will you follow Me with your whole heart? Will you choose to serve the Lord, your God? Will you choose to walk in the abundance of spiritual understanding and gifts I have set before you?

Surrender to Me and follow Me and your joy will be complete as you walk in My ways, as you walk in the destiny that is yours in My kingdom. Come with Me.

Selected Scripture Reading

1. Ex. 31:2–5—"See, I have called by name Bezalel the son of Uri ... And I have filled him with the Spirit of God, in wisdom, in understanding, in knowledge, and in all manner of workmanship, To design artistic works, to work in gold, in silver, in bronze, In cutting jewels for setting, in carving wood, and to work in all manner of workmanship."
2. Prov. 3:3–4—"Let not mercy and truth forsake you; Bind them around your neck, Write them on the tablet of your heart, And so find favor and high esteem In the sight of God and man."
3. Eph. 2:10—"For we are His workmanship, created in Christ Jesus for good works, which God prepared beforehand that we should walk in them." See Matt. 5:13–16.
4. Matt. 25:14–30—Jesus told the parable of the talents, which teaches the importance of good development, investment, and management of the talents and gifts God has given.
5. 1 Cor. 12–14—Just as Ex. 31:2–5 describes how God gifted Bezalel to work in artistic creations, 1 Cor. 12–14 describes the essence of spiritual understanding and gifts that God by His Holy Spirit imparts to believers to promote their spiritual and emotional maturity as well as to make them blessings to all people. While gifts are diverse, they

all are for the purpose of godly encouragement for God's children with love being the critical element. See Col. 3:17; Rom. 12.
6. Eph. 4:7–13—"But to each of us grace was given ... And He Himself gave some to be apostles, some prophets, some evangelists, and some pastors and teachers, For the equipping of the saints for the work of the ministry, for the edifying of the body of Christ, Till we all come to the unity of the faith and of the knowledge of the Son of God." See John 14:12.

185. Remain in Communion with Me

It is with your heart you hear My voice to you. It is with your heart that you believe My words to you and faith is born in you that leads to salvation and righteousness.

Hear and obey. Remain in communion with Me so you will bear the fruits of righteousness. For it is by remaining in Me that your redemption and destiny are fulfilled. I have commanded and appointed you to bear fruit. Blessed are you when you remain in communion with Me. Blessed are you when you meditate day and night on My words to you, walking in obedience and love.

The fruit of My Spirit shall be your reward. Your heart shall be filled with My love, joy, peace, patience, and purity in thoughts and deeds. You shall hear and understand My command to you to go forth and share the message of the gospel of Christ with all the nations, with your neighbors. You shall bear fruit.

It is not an easy task to bear fruit in the kingdom of God. You must walk in obedience and love for God and His precepts. You must deny the lusts of the flesh so you may attain the fruits of the Spirit of God.

Those who hear My words speaking to their hearts and leave the bondages of sin shall walk forward in freedom. You shall find life and true riches.

Selected Scripture Reading

1. Jer. 17:10—"I the LORD, search the heart, I test the mind, Even to give every man according to his ways, According to the fruit of his doings."

2. Rom. 10:8–10—"The word is near you, in your mouth and in your heart. That if you confess with your mouth the Lord Jesus and believe in your heart that God has raised Him from the dead, you will be saved. For with the heart one believes unto righteousness, and with the mouth confession is made unto salvation."
3. Prov. 18:15—"The heart of the prudent acquires knowledge, and the ear of the wise seeks knowledge." See Prov. 4 about the security that wisdom provides.
4. Matt. 13:3–23—Jesus told the parable of the sower, which illustrates hearing the teachings of God and our responsibility to live out those teachings and thus bear fruit.
5. Matt. 28:18–20—"And Jesus came and spoke to them, saying, 'All authority has been given to Me in heaven and on earth. Go therefore and make disciples of all the nations, baptizing them in the name of the Father and of the Son and of the Holy Spirit, teaching them to observe all things that I have commanded you.'"
6. Gal. 5:22–25—"But the fruit of the Spirit is love, joy, peace, longsuffering, kindness, goodness, faithfulness, gentleness, self-control … And those who are Christ's have crucified the flesh with its passions and desires." See John 15.

186. Be Merciful and Gracious to One Another

I am the Good Shepherd, and I care for My sheep. I have compassion for My lambs. I work tenderly with My flock. I lead and guide you to safe pastures. I look to your future for I desire to bring you safely home, to your eternal home.

You must choose to follow Me. You must choose to watch Me. You must choose to listen to Me. You must choose to become one with Me. You must love one another as I have loved you.

No, you are not yet perfect. Your brothers and sisters are not yet perfect. But as I have compassion for you, have compassion for one another Know this. I am the judge of My people. Each one shall all stand before Me and give an account of their words and actions. They stand or fall before Me, not you.

Be merciful and gracious to one another, yet you must judge behavior. You must say, "The Lord condemns sin. We must cleanse ourselves. Our Lord commands us to be pure and holy."

Not in arrogance but in humility, build up, edify, and encourage one another to lay up for yourselves spiritual treasures in heaven where moth and rust cannot destroy them. In grace and humility, reach out and snatch your brothers and sisters from the dangers of hellfire.

I am the Good Shepherd. Learn from Me. Care tenderly for one another. I am gathering you together in unity. You will become My lovely and glorious church without spot or wrinkle, altogether lovely. I shall lift you up into the heavenlies.

Selected Scripture Reading

1. Isa. 40:11—"He will feed His flock like a shepherd; He will gather the lambs with His arm and carry them in His bosom, and gently lead those who are with young." See John 2:11.
2. Ps. 23:1–6 (NCV)—"The LORD is my shepherd; I have everything I need. He lets me rest in green pastures. He leads me to calm water. He gives me new strength. He leads me on paths that are right for the good of his name. Even if I walk through a very dark valley, I will not be afraid, because you are with me. Your rod and your shepherd's staff comfort me. You prepare a meal for me in front of my enemies ... Surely your love and goodness will be with me all my life, and I will live in the house of the LORD forever."
3. Matt. 22:37–39—"Jesus said to him, 'You shall love the LORD your God with all your heart, with all your soul and with all your mind. This is the first and great commandment. And the second is like it: You shall love your neighbor as yourself.'" See Matt. 12:36–37.
4. Matt. 5:7—Do you want others to treat you kindly with mercy? Do you want God to treat you with kindness and mercy? Consider the many aspects of this verse. See John 13:34.
5. Rom. 14:19—"Therefore let us pursue the things which make for peace and the things by which we may edify another." See 1 Peter 4:8; 1 John 4:7–8; Rom. 12:10–13; Gal. 5.

187. For My Shepherds

My heart is heavy, says the Lord, for My shepherds. Many, many of My shepherds are weak and confused and even follow after strange unions.

Some who claim My name have never known Me. Some have known Me but have turned aside and no longer seek Me.

You who are in positions of leadership—you to whom My sheep look for protection and guidance—awaken and hear My voice calling to you.

I call you out from your slumber and apathy. I call you out from your fear of man and your pride. I call you out from the compromises with wickedness, idolatry, and uncleanness. I call you out from the deceptions of the spirit of Babylon.

Set no other gods before your face. I am the Lord your God, and I am calling to you. Give me your whole heart and follow Me. Know My voice and know My love for you. Believe My words as My Spirit bears witness to the truth.

How can you lead My sheep into safe and bountiful pastures when you yourself do not know My heart and follow My ways? How can you be the example My sheep need when you do not follow My example?

I am doing a work of restoration in My people for I will have a glorious church, a pure and beautiful bride. Come aside. Hear My voice speaking to your heart for I desire to give you seasons of refreshing and renewal. For you, I say, give Me your burdens and come with Me.

Selected Scripture Reading

1. Isa. 52:7—"How beautiful upon the mountains are the feet of him who brings good news, who proclaims peace, who brings glad tidings of good things, who proclaims salvation, who says to Zion, 'Your God reigns!'" See Rom. 10–11.
2. Jer. 32:37–41—God reveals His heart to restore His people after their backsliding. He says in verse 41, "Yes, I will rejoice over them to do them good, and I will assuredly plant them in this land, with all My heart and with all My soul."
3. 2 Chron. 12:14 (spoken of King Rehoboam)—"And he did evil, because he did not prepare his heart to seek the LORD." See Jer. 23:1–2; Ezek. 22:23–30.
4. Jer. 50:6–7 (Voice)—"My people have become like lost sheep, and their shepherds have led them astray. They wandered so far from My protection—on the mountaintops and hills they lost their way,

worshiping false gods, forgetting where I was and where they could find rest. And whoever found My lost sheep devoured them. Their enemies said to themselves, 'Why worry? We are not the guilty ones here. They are the ones who sinned against their God.'"

5. John 21:16–17—In this conversation, Jesus asked Peter three times, stressing the importance of the question, "Do you love Me?" Peter confirmed how much He loved the Lord. Jesus said, "Look after My sheep." Compare with Ezek. 44:23; Acts 20:18–35.

188. All the Issues of Life

Among My shepherds, some have not given My children the pure and complete teaching of My Word. My people have sought out substitutes and have embraced lies that separate them from Me.

I say to you, purify your hearts. Repent and come before Me in humility that you may seek Me with you whole heart. Search for Me; do not seek after strange flesh.

Honor My Word with obedience and your faith and wisdom will grow. Remember, all the issues of life are centered in your heart. Keep your heart pure by My Word and you will find genuine intimacy with your God.

Selected Scripture Reading

1. Ezek. 34:7–11—"As I live, says the LORD GOD, surely because My flock became a prey ... nor did My shepherds search for My flock ... Indeed I Myself will search for My sheep and seek them out."
2. Isa. 40:10–11—"Behold, the Lord GOD shall come with a strong hand, And His arm shall rule for Him ... He will feed His flock like a shepherd; He will gather the lambs with His arm." See John 10:11; Heb. 13:20–21.
3. 2 Tim. 3:1–5—"But know this, that in the last days perilous times will come: for men will be lovers of themselves, lovers of money, boasters, proud, blasphemers, disobedient to parents, unthankful, unholy, unloving, unforgiving, slanderers, without self-control, brutal, despisers of good, traitors, headstrong, haughty, lovers of

pleasure rather than lovers of God, having a form of godliness but denying its power. And from such people turn away!"
4. Titus 1:16—"They profess to know God, but in works they deny Him, being abominable, disobedient, and disqualified for every good work."
5. Jude 1–25—While affirming God's power to sanctify and keep the saints, Jude gives a clear, sharp warning concerning false teachers who pervert the grace of God, cause confusion and division, and even promote sexual immorality and all manner of carnality. See Rom. 1–2.
6. James 4:8—"Draw near to God and He will draw near to you. Cleanse your hands, you sinners; and purify your hearts, you double minded." See Prov. 4:23; Matt. 12:34b–35.
7. Heb. 9:14—"How much more shall the blood of Christ, who through the eternal Spirit offered Himself without spot to God, cleanse your conscience from dead works to serve the living God?" See Ps. 145.
8. Rev. 7:17—"The Lamb who is in the midst of the throne will shepherd them and lead them to living fountains of waters. And God will wipe away every tear from their eyes."

189. My Kingdom Is Not of This World

I am doing a new thing in the earth today among My people. I am going to and fro over the earth. My eyes are searching for hearts who are hungry for Me, searching for hearts who are desperate for truth and righteousness. Blessed are the pure in heart, for they shall see Me.

Set your heart to know things above. Ask Me for wisdom to understand spiritual matters. Open your heart to walk in My love, grace, and forgiveness. For My kingdom is not of this world. My kingdom is not about lands, territories, natural power, and wealth. My kingdom is not about crushing the hearts and spirits of mankind.

By My Word of truth—the gospel of salvation—is My kingdom established. My Word says to you: repent and turn from sin. Walk in the way of good standing with your God.

The kingdom of God is not about meat and drink—not about what you possess and consume. My kingdom is in your hearts. Following My words will bring you righteousness, peace, and joy by the power of My Holy Spirit.

Follow Me with your whole heart, and let—allow—My will to be done in your heart that My kingdom be established on the earth.

Selected Scripture Reading

1. Isa. 43:19—"Watch closely: I am preparing something new; it's happening now, even as I speak, and you're about to see it. I am preparing a way through the desert; Waters will flow where there had been none." Compare with Prov. 21:3; Isa. 48. What do you think God's priorities and goals are in his dealings with mankind? Name one or two methods He uses.
2. Isa. 11:1–2—"There shall come forth a Rod from the stem of Jesse, and a Branch shall grow out of his roots. The Spirit of the LORD shall rest upon Him, The Spirit of wisdom and understanding, The Spirit of counsel and might, the Spirit of knowledge and of the fear [reverence] of the LORD." Compare with John 1:1–34; Rom. 1:4. Who is being described?
3. Isa. 42:1—"Behold! My Servant whom I uphold, My Elect One in whom My soul delights! I have put My Spirit upon Him; He will bring forth justice to the Gentiles."
4. John 16:13–14—"However, when He, the Spirit of truth has come, He will guide you into all truth for He will not speak on His own authority, but whatever He hears, He will speak, and He will tell you things to come. He will glorify Me, for He will take of what is Mine, and declare it to you." Who is the Spirit of Truth?
5. Rom. 14:17–19—"The kingdom of God is not eating and drinking, but righteousness and peace and joy in the Holy Spirit for he who serves Christ in these things is acceptable to God and approved by men. Therefore let us pursue the things which make for peace and the things by which one may edify another." How would you describe the kingdom of God?
6. John 18:36—"Jesus answered, 'My kingdom is not of this world.'" See Luke 17:20b–21.

190. Guard Your Heart and Your Thoughts

My children, hear Me and give heed to My instructions. Pay attention and seek the truth. Be diligent and focused in your pursuit of righteousness.

For the upright in heart—those who walk by My Spirit according to My teaching and example—will be blessed with the rewards of righteousness in this life and in the life to come. Hear Me and do not underestimate this truth: you must evaluate and bring every thought into captivity. As a man thinks in his heart, so he becomes.

A good man will bring treasure out of his heart—love, mercy, grace, wisdom, truth, honesty—seeking to serve and bless his neighbors. A man who is led astray by wicked and lustful thoughts, puffed up by pride and greed, will bring forth fruit from his heart: deceit, and destruction with sorrow.

Therefore, if you desire to walk uprightly in my grace and blessings, guard your heart and your thoughts. Ask Me for wisdom and discernment. Choose this day whom you will serve.

Selected Scripture Reading

1. Ps. 5:8—"Lead me, O LORD, in Your righteousness because of my enemies; Make Your way straight before my face."
2. Ps. 25:4–5—"Show me Your ways, O LORD; Teach me Your paths. Lead me in Your truth and teach me, For You are the God of my salvation; On You I wait all the day."
3. Ps. 143:10—"Teach me to do Your will, For You are my God; Your Spirit is good. Lead me in the land of uprightness."
4. Ps. 119:101–105—"I have restrained my feet from every evil way, That I may keep Your word. I have not departed from Your judgments, For You Yourself have taught me, How sweet are Your words to my taste, Sweeter than honey to my mouth! Through Your precepts I get understanding; Therefore I hate every false way. Your word is a lamp to my feet And a light to my path."
5. Ezra—Ezra was an example of a faithful priest and scribe who was knowledgeable and careful to obey the words and principles of God (7:11). Under Ezra's leadership, the Babylonian king, Artaxerxes (Ezra 7–10) authorized him to lead a second colony of exiled Jews back

to Jerusalem (ca. 457 BC). The story of Ezra is one of the struggle to restore relationship with God by seeking Him, hearing instructions from Him, and doing what it took to be obedient to His words. Once, Ezra was faced with transporting the valuable temple possessions through a dangerous territory. Ezra 8:21 records what he did as he faced potential disaster: "Then I proclaimed a fast there at the river of Ahava that we might humble ourselves before God to seek from Him the right way."

191. As You Wait Patiently

I delight in you when you wait upon Me. As you wait patiently upon Me, your faithfulness is revealed and I delight in you.

My beloved child, will you not spend time with Me that I may speak to your heart? My Holy Spirit is calling you. Come away with Me and learn to know My heart so your heart will be strengthened. Take My words into your heart for My words are living and will give life and strength to you.

The words of the world—the many voices of the world—will distract and mislead you. The enemy desires to steal your life and destroy your hope. Wait, I say, wait upon the Lord your God that you may see the grace I have for you to overcome—the grace I have for you to be victorious over the enemy of your souls.

Wait upon Me and hear My words to your heart; your strength will be renewed. You shall run and not grow weary, for My Spirit will lead you. I will direct your heart and your steps. Your hope and confidence will be established.

There is much work to do in My kingdom, and you must be strong. Wait upon Me. Hear My words to your heart and receive Me.

Selected Scripture Reading

1. Ps. 27:14—"Wait on the LORD; Be of good courage, And He shall strengthen your heart; Wait, I say on the LORD!"
2. Ps. 62:5—"My soul, wait silently for God alone, For my expectation is from Him."

3. Ps. 18:19—"He also brought me out into a broad place; He delivered me because He delighted in me."
4. Prov. 11:20; Ps. 31:19–20—These passages tell us that God delights in the ways of the blameless and will hide them in the secret place of His presence to protect them.
5. 1 Sam. 15:22—"Has the LORD as great delight in burnt offerings and sacrifices, as in obeying the voice of the LORD? Behold, to obey is better than sacrifice."
6. Prov. 20:22; Rom. 12:9–21—These passages admonish us to wait and think carefully about how we respond when we are offended by or irritated with others. This is in harmony with both Old and New Testament teachings on loving our neighbor as ourselves. See Lev. 19:18; Luke 10:25–37.
7. Heb. 3—This chapter begins with reminding us of the faithfulness of both Moses and Jesus to God's directives and assignments. Then in verses 7–19, we read about the example of those wandering in the wilderness who listened to the voices of sin and rebellion. God did not allow them to enter the rest He had intended for them.

192. Only Remain Faithful

Hear Me, My child, as I speak to your heart. I speak to your heart because it is with your heart you believe and receive salvation. It is with your heart that you learn to know My voice and My heart. It is with your heart that you receive every gift I speak to you.

He who is faithful in the little things will find his heart enlarged to receive more from Me. My Father and I will come to the faithful and rest upon them.

Your love and faithfulness will draw us to you, and we will dwell with you to comfort and strengthen you. As My Father and I are one, so shall you be one with us. Only remain faithful.

Remain faithful, My beloved. Remain faithful.

Selected Scripture Reading

1. 2 Chron. 31:18—"And to all who were written in the genealogy—their little ones and their wives, their sons and daughters, the whole company of them—for in their faithfulness they sanctified themselves in holiness." See Jer. 32:38–41; Mark 12:30–31.
2. Ps. 37:3—"Trust in the LORD, and do good; Dwell in the land, and feed on His faithfulness." See Ps. 119:9–11; Heb. 10:23.
3. Gal. 5:6 (NLT)—"For when we place our faith in Christ Jesus, there is no benefit in being circumcised or being uncircumcised. What is important is faith expressing itself in love." This point is further confirmed in Rom. 1:17, 4.
4. Gal. 5:22—"But the fruit of the Spirit is love, joy, peace, longsuffering, kindness, goodness, faithfulness, gentleness, self-control. Against such there is no law."
5. Luke 16:1–12—This is Jesus's parable about the unjust steward/dishonest manager. The dishonest man was commended not for being dishonest but rather for planning for what he was going to do after he got fired from his job. Jesus was teaching that if dishonest people are wise and shrewd enough to plan for the future, so ought the people of God be wise enough to plan ahead and lay up treasures in heaven.
6. John 17:6–26—This is Jesus's prayer for all believers throughout the ages that we be in spiritual unity, a unity energized by the power of God's love and His truth. This divine, supernatural unity would testify to the world God sent Jesus to the world to bring deliverance, healing, and salvation.
7. Matt. 25:14–This is the parable of the talents, which illustrates the principles and rewards of faithful stewardship in the kingdom of God. We are taught to use talents, resources, and opportunities wisely or we will suffer loss; this principle applies in the natural as well as in the spiritual. See Ps. 119:32.

193. You Are Created in My Image

Consider this carefully, My child, and know that I am your Creator. I am God, and there is none beside Me. I designed and formed mankind in My image, giving you a body, soul, and spirit.

I created you for the joy of communion and fellowship. Know that I am your God, and I desire communion and fellowship with you. Know that I am your God. I desire you to walk in communion and fellowship with one another to fulfill your designed purposes and destiny.

Be wise and alert. Do not let sin and the enemy of your souls steal your joy and steal your understanding of your identity and gifts. For you are created in My image to do good works which are the fruit of communion and fellowship with Me.

In communion and fellowship with Me, My love will flow into you. My love will empower you to love one another more perfectly, increasing My glory among you.

Walk in My love so your joy and destiny in Me will be fulfilled. I am your God, and you are My child.

Selected Scripture Reading

1. Gen. 1:26–27, 5:1, 9:6; James 3:9–10—These passages speak of mankind being created in the image of God.
2. Ps. 100:1–5—"Make a joyful shout to the LORD, all you lands! Serve the LORD with gladness; Come before His presence with singing. Know that the LORD, He is God; It is He who has made us, and not we ourselves; We are His people and the sheep of His pasture. Enter into His gates with thanksgiving, And into His courts with praise. Be thankful to Him, and bless His name. For the LORD is good." See Ps. 16:10.
3. Mal. 2:10—"Have we not all one Father? Has not one God created us?"
4. John 15—Jesus taught the importance of maintaining a vibrant relationship with our heavenly Father and living in accordance with His teachings. "These things I have spoken to you, that My joy remain in you, and that your joy may be full (v. 11).
5. Acts 17:22–34—The apostle Paul spoke at the Areopagus in Athens and referred to an altar he saw there dedicated to the unknown

god. Paul revealed to them that the true God created the world and everything in it. He taught that God commanded all people to repent because there was an appointed Day of Judgment, "for in Him we live and move and have our being (v. 28).

6. 1 John 1:7—"But if we walk in the light as He is in the light, we have fellowship with one another, and the blood of Jesus Christ His Son cleanses us from all sin." See Isa. 2:5.
7. Ps. 43:3–4—"Oh, send out Your light and Your truth! Let them bring me to Your holy hill! And to Your tabernacle ... And on the harp I will praise You, O God, my God."

194. Take on My Nature and You Will See Clearly

Take courage, My little one, and know I am with you. I am with you to lead and guide you through these times. Give Me your heart and I will be your salvation. Seek Me first above everything in this world and you will find Me. You will find your heart's desire.

I come to those who seek Me with all their heart. I walk with you through the hills and through the valleys. Keep your eyes on Me and you will see and understand. There are many obstacles, perils, dangers—challenges to overcome. Look to Me. I will direct you. Listen carefully.

It is as you become like Me—it is as you take off the old carnal, fleshly nature and put on the nature of Christ—that you are empowered to overcome. Keep your eyes and your heart focused on Me so your mind will be renewed.

In humility, study My Word and love one another with My love. Take on My nature and you will see clearly how to walk in these times, for I will be with you and strong in you. Walk with Me and I shall walk with you.

Selected Scripture Reading

1. Deut. 31:6—"Be strong and of good courage, do not fear nor be afraid of them; for the LORD your God, He is the One who goes with you. He will not leave you nor forsake you." Deuteronomy 31:6–8 records the words of Moses to Joshua and the people. These are comforting words as the people knew they faced formidable challenges. In the

previous chapter, Moses had warned the people that their protection and blessing depended on their continuing to love God with all their heart and follow Him.
2. Ps. 31:24—"Be of good courage, And He shall strengthen your heart, All you who hope in the LORD." Acts 28:15 is an example of how we can encourage others.
3. Prov. 14:6; Isa. 6:9–10—These passages explain the result of seeking wisdom while rejecting God.
4. Rom. 8:14 (Voice)—"If the Spirit of God is leading you, then take comfort in knowing you are His children."
5. Col. 2:1–3:11—Paul establishes the preeminence of Christ over all things making it clear that holiness was only because of the sacrifice of Jesus's blood. In Colossians 2:1–3:11, Paul identified the perils and challenges that were facing the believers at Colossae—the teachings of man that ascribe power and energy to legalisms, rituals, or asceticism and in effect cheat believers by deceiving them. Paul was addressing the tolerance and infiltration of a combination of pagan occult and Jewish legalism influences. Again speaking boldly, in chapters 3 and 4, Paul gave clear commands on living pure lives, walking in God's love, and letting the Word of Christ dwell richly in our hearts.

195. The Simplicity of the Gospel

I am calling you to return to the simplicity of the gospel I have given you. Remember what the heralding angels spoke at the birth of Messiah: "Peace on earth; good will toward mankind."

The words of life My Son brings to you reveal true peace for your soul—salvation from sin and eternal life. My words teach you the way of peace for your soul and how to live in My peace with one another. My truth brings you freedom to love, freedom to live with goodwill toward one another.

Look again at the simplicity of the gospel. I have called you to love. Love Me with your whole heart, and love one another. My love reveals My truth and peace. Walk in My love as Christ did and reveal the power and glory of God to redeem and save.

Love Me and know Me, My beloved. Know Me.

Selected Scripture Reading

1. Ps. 85:8–9—"I will hear what God the LORD will speak, For He will speak peace to His people and to His saints; But let them not turn back to folly. Surely His salvation is near to those who fear Him, That glory may dwell in our land."
2. Isa. 57:19—"'I create the fruit of the lips: Peace, peace to him who is far off and to him who is near,' says the LORD, 'And I will heal him.'" See Acts 2:38–39.
3. Luke 2:13–14—"And suddenly there was with the angel a multitude of the heavenly host praising God and saying, 'Glory to God in the highest, And on earth peace, goodwill toward men!'" See Eph. 2:4–9. God, who is rich in mercy, sent Jesus to give us peace by providing salvation from our sins that is activated by our believing in God's plan for redemption.
4. Heb. 11:6—"But without faith it is impossible to please Him, for he who comes to God must believe that He is, and that He is a rewarder of those who diligently seek Him."

5. 2 Cor. 11:3—"But I fear, lest somehow as the serpent deceived Eve by his craftiness, so your minds may be corrupted from the

simplicity [NU adds "and purity"] that is in Christ. Combined with 1 Corinthians 1:12 and Ephesians 6:24, we understand the importance of sincerity.
6. Rom. 14–15—Paul sorts through the fruit (in-house squabbling) of trying to be right about issues that were really a matter of opinion. He gave two examples of such issues: what food you should eat or not eat, and which days should be holidays. Paul reminds us in 14:10–19 that we shall all "stand before the judgment seat of Christ" and that the kingdom of God was really about "righteousness, peace, and joy in the Holy Spirit."

196. I Will Be All Things to You

Hear Me, My beloved and learn to know My voice. Know My voice and learn to know Me.

You listen and watch many voices in the world and fill your mind and heart with the knowledge and ways of the world. Yes, you live in the world, but you are not to be of this world.

You are of My Spirit, and I call you to live in and by My Spirit so you may have victory over the darkness of sin and deception in the world. Come out and be separated from sin and darkness. Do not have fellowship with darkness, and do not walk in lustful thinking.

Choose Me. Seek Me with your whole heart and you will find the love, peace, and joy your heart desires. I will be all things to you. I will lead and guide you. We will have communion together. You will know Me, and I shall know you.

Come. Come to Me, My beloved.

Selected Scripture Reading

1. Ps. 29:1–11—"The voice of the LORD is over the waters … The voice of the LORD is powerful; The voice of the LORD is full of majesty. The voice of the LORD breaks the cedars … The voice of the LORD divides the flames of fire. The voice of the LORD shakes the wilderness … The LORD sat enthroned at the Flood, And the LORD sits as King forever. The LORD will give strength to His

      people; The LORD will bless His people with peace." See Ex. 19:19; 1 Kings 19:9–18; Matt. 17:5; Acts 10.
2. According to Bible Gateway, the NKJV has the phrase "God speaks" 15 times, "God spoke" 134 times, "God said" 618 times, and "God says" 375 times.
3. Ps. 8:1–36—In poetic form, wisdom is personified as a woman raising her voice to all mankind: "O people! I have a message for all humanity." We learn that wisdom speaks only truth and promotes justice. Perceptive people understand the value of wisdom and the correction it may require. Wisdom respects the eternal and so despises all forms of evil conduct and talk.

      Honorable leaders decree what is right by following wisdom. Verse 17 says one must choose to hear the voice of wisdom: "I love those who love me; those who search hard for me will find me." Then Lady Wisdom identified herself in verse 22: "The Eternal created me; it happened when His work was beginning, one of His first acts long ago. Before time He established me, before the earth saw its first sunrise." Surprisingly, Lady Wisdom said she was "elated by the world He was making and all its fine creatures; I was especially pleased with humanity." So God created wisdom, and wisdom was delighted with mankind! Don't miss the admonitions, however, that Lady Wisdom has for all humanity in verses 32–36.
4. Eph. 1:15–23—This is the apostle Paul's prayer for us to receive the spirit of wisdom.

197. Listen with Your Heart and Hear Me Calling

Can you not see I am a God who gives time for My people to repent, time for you to see, and understand? Time for you to turn your hearts to seek Me?

      I give you time to desire Me. I give you time to find Me. Listen with your heart and hear Me calling you. Soften your heart and believe in Me. Receive My words and receive life.

      Redeem the time given to you and receive Me. Now is the time.

      Do not become distracted and thus miss what I desire to do in your heart and in your life. Consider carefully the choices you make and the pathway those choices place before you. Now is the appointed time for you to come into My presence.

Selected Scripture Reading

1. Num. 14:11–20; Ezek. 20:15–17—Both illustrate that God was very angry with His people for rejecting His teachings, ignoring His will for them, disregarding the Sabbaths as times set apart to rest and consider their relationship with Him, and being led astray into various forms of idolatry. The idolatrous practices included child sacrifice, idol worship connected with sexual immorality, worship of demons in the form of false gods, and violence/war. He is nevertheless very patient, and he waits for people to repent and turn their hearts to Him.
2. 2 Peter 3:1–9—Peter said he wanted to stir up their pure minds. The word *pure* (Greek *eilikrines*, Strong's no. 1506) literally means "tested by sunlight." Peter told them to remember the words spoken by the holy prophets before and what the apostles taught. He acknowledges that there are scoffers who make fun of and demean what God has said. Peter noted that these mockers and scoffers walk according to their own lusts saying, "Where is the promise of His coming? For since the fathers fell asleep, all things continue as they were from the beginning of creation." Peter appears to refer to the error that the scoffers made when Noah was building the ark and compares that to present scoffers who do not believe there will be a future judgment. The Lord is not slack concerning His promise as some count slackness, but is longsuffering toward us, not willing that any should perish but that all should come to repentance (v. 9). See Mark 1:14–15; Gal. 4:4–5; Eph. 1:10.
3. Matt. 24:14—"And this gospel of the kingdom will be preached in all the world as a witness to all the nations, and then the end will come."
4. John 14:2–3—"In My Father's house are many mansions; if it were not so, I would have told you. I go to prepare a place for you." See John 12:26; Acts 1:11.

198. Surrender to Me and Receive from Me

I would have you understand this, My child. There are many gifts and talents I have for each of you to grow and develop in your lives. These talents and gifts are to help you in your daily lives as you go about living and reaching out to love and serve one another.

To be equipped and to receive what you need to live and work in My kingdom, you must receive from Me. The gifts and empowering of My Spirit come only from Me. No amount of carnal effort and striving will give you the wisdom, grace, and spiritual power you need to overcome.

To have what you need, you must come to Me, spend time with Me, and listen to My Word and listen to what My Holy Spirit is saying to your heart. Surrender to Me and receive of Me. For I will come to you. I will meet with you. I will empower you to receive spiritual strength to overcome.

Hear and understand My words to you. Receive from Me that which I have for you. This is how you will overcome with great joy.

Selected Scripture Reading

1. Ps. 71:17—"O God, You have taught me from my youth; And to this day I declare Your wondrous works." See Eph. 4–5 about walking in unity, love and spiritual gifts.
2. Ps. 68:19—"Blessed be the Lord, Who daily loads us with benefits, The God of our Salvation." Multiple scriptures in the Old and New Testaments confirm that God Himself through His Son has provided the gift of salvation for His people. See Isa. 9:6–7, 7:14, 43:11; Mic. 5:2–5; Luke 2:11.
3. Deut. 32:3–4—"Let my teaching drop as the rain, My speech distill as the dew, As raindrops on the tender herb, And as showers on the grass. For I proclaim the name of the LORD: Ascribe greatness to our God. He is the Rock, His work is perfect; For all His ways are justice, A God of truth and without injustice; Righteous and upright is He."
4. Ex. 31:1–11; 1 Kings 7:13–14; Ps. 40:3; 2 Chron. 5:13—These indicate that natural talents are also God given; this too is evidence of our being created in God's image.

5. Matt. 25:14–30—Jesus tells the parable of the talents, which illustrates the principles of the use and stewardship of resources, money, time, and effort. Note the first word in verse 14—*For*. This denotes an admonition to be alert and make the most of natural and spiritual opportunities that God gives us using His principles and in His timing.
6. Mal. 3:8–12; 2 Chron. 31:10 balanced against Matt. 23:23; Luke 18:9–14—These point out the blessings for individuals and nations alike of giving to God with sincerity and humility. The scriptures also teach giving according to ability (2 Cor. 8:12; Acts 11:29) and giving sacrificially (1 Kings 17:8–16; Luke 21:4; Acts 4:34; 2 Cor. 8:1–15). Generosity and giving are attributes of our heavenly Father he desires we demonstrate (Lev. 25:35; Deut. 15:7; Prov. 19:17; Matt. 6:1; Gal. 2:10).

199. I Will Feed You with Manna from Heaven and Water from the Rock

I speak to you very clearly, My children. The god of this world is working to lull and blind mankind into great deceptions. You must be alert and on guard to identify by the Holy Spirit and by the truth of My Word that which is true and that which is designed to deceive and destroy that which is true and good, even your salvation. Be alert and be on your guard.

The Deceiver is at work to take from you your will and strength to resist that which is wrong. Hear Me carefully. To overcome in this hour, you must separate yourself from the world. You must come out from the spirit of Babylon. Shut your ears—shut your heart—to the lusts and greed that entice and motivate you to accept deceptions.

I call to you, My beloved, come with Me. Stand under My wings. Eat at My table. I have prepared a feast of truth and understanding for you. Yes, even in the midst of your enemies.

Come with Me and you shall see. Come with Me and you shall hear. Come with Me and you shall understand, and be satisfied. For I will feed you with manna from heaven and water from the Rock. You will find the genuine. You will find Me.

My love for you is great. I have made a way for you to come to Me.

Selected Scripture Reading

1. Ps. 15:1–5—"LORD, who may abide in Your tabernacle? Who may dwell in Your holy hill? He who walks uprightly and works righteousness, and speaks the truth in his heart; He who does not backbite with his tongue, nor does evil to his neighbor, nor does he take up a reproach against his friend; In whose eyes a vile person is despised, but he honors those who fear the LORD ... He who does these things shall never be moved."
2. Ps. 119:115–117—"Depart from me, you evildoers, for I will keep the commandments of my God! Uphold me according to Your word, that I may live; and do not let me be ashamed of my hope. Hold me up, and I shall be safe. And I shall observe Your statutes continually." See Jer. 51:6–9; Rev. 18:1–5.
3. 2 Cor. 11:13–15—"And no wonder! For Satan himself transforms himself into an angel of light. Therefore it is no great thing if his ministers also transform themselves into ministers of righteousness." See Jer. 23:25–32; 2 Peter 2–3.
4. Col. 2:8—"Beware lest anyone cheat you through philosophy and empty deceit, according to the tradition of men, according to the basic principles of the world, and not according to Christ." See Acts 17:11.
5. Jer. 29:13—"And you will seek Me and find Me, when you search for Me with all your heart." See Luke 11:9–13; John 6:31–35, 7:37–38; Rev. 22:1–2.

200. Come, Return to the Lord Your God

At the end of the age, I am speaking to the nations and people all over the world. I am speaking through nature. I am speaking through the wind and the waves. I am speaking on the earth and in the heavens.

Watch and hear Me. I am calling My people. I am your God. Follow Me, and not another. For I will lead you to safety. I will not deceive you. I will not tickle your ears to lead you astray.

Repent and cleanse your hearts, and you will see Me and know what I say is true. You will live and not die. I am speaking to all My creation.

Hear what I say to you. The Spirit and the bride say, "Come, return to the Lord your God and He will save you. He will deliver you."

Selected Scripture Reading

1. Ps. 19:1–4 (Voice)—"The celestial realms announce God's glory; the skies testify of His hands' great work. Each day pours out more of their sayings; each night, more to hear and more to learn. Inaudible words are their manner of speech, and silence, their means to convey. Yet from here to the ends of the earth, their voices have gone out; the whole world can hear what they say." See Acts 2; Rom. 1.
2. Ps. 29:3–11—This psalm has six verses that specifically mention the voice of God upon and through nature. There may be symbolism in some of the descriptions. For example, verse 5 says, "The voice of the LORD breaks the cedars, Yes, the LORD splinters the cedars of Lebanon." Compare the phrase about God's voice breaking the cedars to Isaiah 2:11–18.
3. Isa. 2—We read about the future house of God in the latter days when the knowledge of God will be the preeminent power on earth. People from all nations will say, "Come and let us go up to the mountain of the LORD, To the house of the God of Jacob; He will teach us His ways, And we shall walk in His paths." Isaiah 2:4 has the well-known phrase about this season in history: "He shall judge between the nations, And rebuke many people; They shall beat their swords into plowshares And their spears into pruning hooks; Nation shall not lift up sword against nation, Neither shall they learn war anymore." Do you think this relates to Hosea 3:5?
4. Isa. 2:5–22—This gives a rather somber description of the day of the Lord, the time when God will rebuke many for their occult practices, pride, worship of materialism, and idolatries. Verses 12–13 mention the cedars of Lebanon: "For the day of the LORD of hosts Shall come upon everything proud and lofty, Upon everything lifted up—And it shall be brought low—Upon all the cedars of Lebanon that are high and lifted up." Verse 11 seems to indicate that the phrase "cedars of Lebanon" is symbolic of more than just the trees themselves. What do you think this metaphor means?

201. Move Forward with Me

I have created you to move forward. I have created you to come up higher.

The difficulties and sorrows of mankind are many. When your heart is burdened, cry out to Me. As you give yourself to Me, all you have and all you are, I will comfort you and redeem the situation. Watch in faithful patience and see what I will do for you.

I am the Lord your God. You are my creation. Never doubt My love for you. Know I have a plan for you—to overcome in all things. Rejoice in Me and be courageous. You shall overcome. Move forward with Me.

Selected Scripture Reading

1. Prov. 24:16 (Voice)—"For a good man may fall seven times and get back up again, but the wicked will stumble around and fall into misfortune." This principle is confirmed and expanded in Ps. 37:23–24; Rom. 8:26–28.
2. Isa. 55:6–9—"Seek the Lord while He may be found, Call upon Him while He is near. Let the wicked forsake his way, And the unrighteous man his thoughts, Let him return to the LORD, And He will have mercy on him … 'For My thoughts are not your thoughts, Nor are your ways My ways,' says the LORD. For as the heavens are higher than the earth, So are My ways higher than your ways, And My thoughts than your thoughts."
3. Rom. 15:4—"For whatever things were written before were written for our learning, that we through the patience and comfort of the Scriptures might have hope."
4. Micah—There is much to learn from the book of Micah because there are many parallels in it to our present time. Micah succinctly states what God requires of us (6:8). Like many prophetic words, there were current and as well future applications. Micah 5:2 is a prophecy about where the Christ would be born. See John 7:40–42.

    Apostasy, greed, social injustice, corruption by leaders, and idolatry bring division and attacks by enemies as was described in prophetic warnings of Micah 1–3, and 6:9–16. The people had long since lost their pure devotion, obedience to right living, and worship of Jehovah God especially through the influence of Solomon's foreign wives (1 Kings 11). Altars and places of worship were built for false gods such as Ashtoreth (Ishtar, Astarte, a goddess of sexual immorality and perversions, prostitution and violence/war); Molech (Milcom, Moloch), child sacrifice practiced in worship of Molech; and Chemosh, which like the worship of Molech practiced child sacrifice.

In Micah are clear declarations of impending judgment by foreign invaders; there are also repeated messages of God restoring a remnant of His people (Mic. 2:12–13, 7:7–20). God is calling His people to move forward through repentance and come up higher through obedience to His teachings (Mic. 4; 2 Peter 1:2–8).

202. The Key to Restoration

In this season of restoration and purification of My church, I am speaking and revealing many things to you. For you who turn your hearts to me—for you who seek Me with your whole heart—you shall see and understand.

The scriptures shall come to life for you as you spend time in My Word and in My presence. My church, this is the key: I desire intimacy with you. I desire purity of love, and communion with you. I speak clearly to you. The key to restoration is intimacy with Me.

Come into My presence and learn of Me for I am meek and humble—and you will find rest for your souls. Come into My presence and be refreshed and restored. Do not miss this provision for My church in the end times. Come into My heart.

Selected Scripture Reading

1. Jer. 32:38–41—"They shall be My people, and I will be their God; then I will give them one heart and one way, that they may fear Me forever, for the good of them and their children after them. And I will make an everlasting covenant with them, that I will not turn away from doing them good; but I will put My fear in their hearts so that they will not depart from Me. Yes, I will rejoice over them to do them good, and I will assuredly plant them in this land, with all My heart and with all My soul."

2. Eph. 5:25b–27—"Christ also loved the church and gave Himself for her, that He might sanctify and cleanse her with the washing of water by the word, that He might present her to Himself a glorious church, not having spot or wrinkle or any such thing, but that she should be holy and without blemish." See Phil. 1:6; 1 Thess. 4, 5.
3. 1 John 1:3b—"Truly our fellowship is with the Father and with His Son Jesus Christ."
4. John 15:5—"I am the vine, you are the branches. He who abides in Me, and I in him, bears much fruit; for without Me you can do nothing."
5. John 16:13–14—"However, when He, the Spirit of truth has come, He will guide you into all truth; for He will not speak on His own authority, but whatever He hears He will speak; and tell you things to come. He will glorify Me, for He will take of what is Mine and declare it to you."
6. Matt. 11:28–30—"Come to Me, all you who labor and are heavy laden, and I will give you rest. Take My yoke upon you and learn from Me, for I am gentle and lowly in heart, and you will find rest for your souls. For My yoke is easy and My burden is light."
7. Ps. 16:11—"You will show me the path of life; in Your presence is fullness of joy; At Your right hand are pleasures forevermore."
8. Ps. 26:2–3—"Examine me, O LORD, and prove me; try my mind and my heart. For Your lovingkindness is before my eyes, and I have walked in Your truth."

203. Do Not Refuse the Blessings I Have for You by Entertaining Evil

Hear Me, My child, and know My heart for you is to bless you and lead you in all spiritual blessings and provision. My heart for you is that you eat of the good of the land.

Yes, it is true that there are many difficult and challenging things coming over the earth and mankind. But did I not say to you, "When you see these things, fear not, but look up for your redemption draws near"? Indeed, there is darkness in the world. But hear Me, look up to Me, and My light will shine upon you and dispel the darkness around you. I will make a path and I will make a way for you even where it appears no path exists. I will make a path.

You must look up to Me and listen to Me. Be patient and steadfast in your faith. For I have answers to your questions. I have provisions for your needs. I have plans for you and those plans are for you to walk in victory. Do not focus on the darkness or entertain evil. Do not negate—do not refuse the blessing I have for you by entertaining evil.

Again I say to you, look up to Me, and My light will cover you. My light will protect you. My light will guide you in this present world. I will show you the way to walk. I will lead you safely home. Look up to Me.

Selected Scripture Reading

1. Jer. 29:11–14—"'For I know the thoughts that I think toward you,' says the LORD, 'thoughts of peace and not of evil, to give you a future and a hope. Then you will call upon Me and go and pray to Me, and I will listen to you. And you will seek Me and find Me, when you search for Me with all your heart. I will be found by you,' says the LORD, 'and I will bring you back from your captivity; I will gather you from all the nations and from all the places where I have driven you,' says the LORD, 'and I will bring you to the place from which I cause you to be carried away captive.'"
2. Ps. 119:64–68—"The earth, O LORD, is full of Your mercy; teach me Your statutes. You have dealt well with Your servant, O LORD, according to Your Word. Teach me good judgment and knowledge, for I believe Your commandments. Before I was afflicted, I went astray, but now I keep Your word. You are good, and do good; teach me Your Statutes."
3. Heb. 12:1–6—"Therefore ... let us lay aside every weight, and the sin which so easily ensnares us, and let us run with endurance the race that is set before us, looking unto Jesus, the author and finisher of our faith ... My son, do not despise the chastening of the LORD nor be discouraged when you are rebuked by Him; for whom the LORD loves He chastens."

204. Live My Word and You Will Not Be Taken In by Lawlessness and Deceptions

Take heed and be alert, My children—do not be taken in by the deceptions of these times. For many will come and say they are the Christ. They will say, "Follow us. We have what you need."

But I say to you, My little ones—I say to you who look up to Me—follow Me in grace and humility and walk in freedom. You will be kept safe because your heart is in Me.

Understand the enemy of your souls is enticing mankind into lawlessness and rebellion to ensnare many into deception. Do not be deceived. I say to you, study My Word. Know My heart. Understand My instructions to you. Live My word, and you will not be taken in by lawlessness and deception. You will receive My grace to overcome.

Follow Me in humble obedience, and I will receive you in triumphant glory.

Selected Scripture Reading

1. Prov. 6:16–19—"These six things the LORD hates, Yes, seven are an abomination to Him: A proud look, A lying tongue, Hands that shed innocent blood, A heart that devises wicked plans, Feet that are swift in running to evil, A false witness who speaks lies, And one who sows discord among brethren."
2. Ps. 40:12—"For innumerable evils have surrounded me; My iniquities have overtaken me, so that I am not able to look up." See 2 Cor. 7:9–10.
3. 1 Sam. 15:23a—"For rebellion is as the sin of witchcraft, and stubbornness is as iniquity and idolatry." See Ps. 81 especially vv. 8–16.
4. Ps. 130:3–4—"If You, LORD, should mark iniquities, O Lord, who could stand? But there is forgiveness with You, That You may be feared."
5. Rom. 13:1–7 (Voice)—"It is important that all of us submit to the authorities who have charge over us because God establishes all authority in heaven and on the earth. Therefore, a person who rebels against authority rebels against the order He established, and people like that can expect to face certain judgment ... But don't just submit for the sake of avoiding punishment; submit and abide by the laws because your conscience leads you to do the right thing." See 1 Peter 2:13, Titus 3:1–8, Heb. 13:17; Prov. 3:19–26.
6. Matt. 24:3–14; 2 Thess. 2:1–12; 2 Tim. 3:1–9; 2 Tim. 4:3—These indicate that before Christ returns, there will be social confusion and

chaos with great deceptions, violence, and lawlessness. God's people are to reflect His goodness and love while standing uncompromisingly for truth.

205. I Am the Resurrection

I desire for My people—I desire for you—to know and understand how much I love you. You are created in My likeness. You are a spiritual being and you have the freedom to choose, to decide what you will believe and whom you will serve—good or evil.

My love calls out to you. Open your hearts. Open your eyes. Open your ears. Hear, see, and understand what is placed before you, and choose life that you may live.

My plans for you are good; they are to give you a hope and resurrection to walk in newness of life. Throw away the old sinful, wicked ways and walk in the resurrection life with Me.

I am the resurrection and the life. Believe in Me. Walk in Me and you shall live. I am the resurrection.

Selected Scripture Reading

1. Ps. 117 (Voice)—"Praise the Eternal, all nations, Raise your voices, all people. For His unfailing love is great, and it is intended for us, and His faithfulness to His promises knows no end. Praise the Eternal."
2. Ex. 3:13–15—In this exchange between Moses and God at the burning bush, God told Moses He had heard His people's cries and was sending Moses to rescue them from slavery in Egypt. Moses requested that God give him His name so he could tell the people who had sent him. This is a most interesting passage; God was saying that He had existed forever and was the Creator, the ultimate, preeminent power. He described Himself as "I AM, the Eternal One, the LORD God of your fathers, the God of Abraham, the God of Isaac, the God of Jacob, and LORD Jehovah." He reminded them that He had made a covenant with their ancestors (Gen. 12:1–3) by which all nations would be blessed. Deuteronomy 7:7–8 clarifies that it was because of God's love that He works throughout history to speak with and watch over His people.

3. Jer. 31:31–34; Ezek. 11:19; 2 Cor. 5:17; Gal. 6:15; Heb. 8:7–13—Because of God's love for all His people though they were unfaithful to Him, He made a new covenant with Israel and Judah to write His teachings on their hearts and minds. They would still need to willingly love and follow Him, but His Holy Spirit would empower them.
4. Isa. 42:1; Jer. 16:19; Hos. 2:2; Mal. 1:11; Matt. 12:18–21; Acts 2:39, 13:44–49, 26:22–23, 28:28; Rom. 9:23–26; Eph. 3:1–9; Col. 1:2–23—These are verses that confirm God's love and empowerment for deliverance from sin were for all people.
5. Rom. 6:1–23–4—"Therefore we were buried with Him through baptism into death, that just as Christ was raised from the dead by the glory of the Father, even so we also should walk in newness of life ... the gift of God is eternal life in Christ Jesus, our Lord."

206. Both Male and Female

I have created you in My likeness, both male and female. You are created in the likeness of God. To women, I have given a special grace and calling. You are created to love even through great personal difficulty and pain. My love gives you grace to reach out and give My love to your children, to your family, and to your neighbors.

To both male and female I say, do not let the enemy steal from you the destiny I have placed in your hearts. This is a destiny to rise above every challenge, a destiny to create and build, a destiny to know My will and plans for you, and to see them through to completion. This is a destiny and a calling to bring health and restoration to your loved ones.

In this season of both perilous times and dramatic restoration, your part—the part women as well as men are called to do—is critical. Do not underestimate your purpose and calling. Rise up, My bride. Look up. Your redemption draws nigh. Male and female I have created you. See your calling to be complete in Me.

Selected Scripture Reading

1. Gen. 1:26–27 (Voice)—"Now let us conceive a new creation—humanity—made in Our image, fashioned according to Our

likeness ... God did just that. He created humanity in His image, created them male and female."
2. Prov. 31:10–31 (Voice)—"Who can find a truly excellent woman? [one who is superior in all that she is and all that she does] Her worth far exceeds that of rubies and expensive jewelry. She inspires trust, and her husband's heart is safe with her, and because of her, he has every good thing ... Delight attends her work and guides her fingers ... She wraps herself in strength [carries herself with confidence] ... She reaches out to the poor and extends mercy to those in need ... Clothed in strength and dignity, [with nothing to fear], she smiles [when she thinks] about the future. She conducts her conversations with wisdom, and the teaching of kindness is ever her concern. She conducts the activities of her household, and never does she indulge in laziness. Her children rise up and bless her. Her husband, too, joins in the praise ... Charm can be deceptive and physical beauty will not last, but a woman who reveres the Eternal should be praised above all others." See Eph. 5.
3. Judg. 4:4–6—"And Deborah, a prophetess, the wife of Lapidot, judged Israel at that time ... And she sent and called Barak ... and said to him, 'Has not the LORD God of Israel commanded ...?'"
4. Acts 21:8–9—"Philip, the evangelist, who was one of the seven [deacons] ... this man had four virgin daughters who prophesied." See Gal. 3:28.
5. Rom. 16:1–2—"I commend to you Phoebe our sister, who is a servant [*Strong's* no. 1249, *diakonos*: teacher, pastor, deacon, minister, servant] of the church in Cenchrea that you may receive her in the Lord in a manner worthy of the saints."

207. Set Yourselves Apart to Honor Me

My people are not prepared for My coming. They lie, steal, and fight among themselves, not recognizing their sin and their condition. Come out from the world, My people. Consecrate yourselves. Set yourselves apart to honor Me and to honor that which I have prepared for you.

I have prepared garments of white—garments of purity and righteousness—for you. Put on purity. Put on righteousness. Live in the garments My Son shed His blood to give you.

Walk worthily before Me, My beloved, and you shall be prepared. Seek Me first in all your days upon the earth and I will be found of you. Prepare your heart. Prepare your life to be ready when the time comes.

Selected Scripture Reading

1. Hos. 14:9 (Voice)—"The wise will understand these things; the perceptive will know them. For everything the Eternal One does is right, and the righteous follow His ways. But those who turn against Him will stumble along His path." See Prov. 9.
2. 2 Chron. 29—King Ahaz was an example of a spiritually blind leader who promoted idolatry and wickedness even in Jerusalem. After he died, his son, Hezekiah, (ca. 726 BC) became king. Though just twenty-five years old, Hezekiah "did what was right in the sight of the LORD." Verses 5–10 teach that disobedience to God's instructions results in trouble and that the way back is repentance, cleaning up your life, and sanctification.
3. Ps. 101—In this psalm, David promised to be faithful to God; it can be a model prayer for us. There are phrases such as "I will seek to live a life of integrity, I will refuse to look on any sordid thing, and I will rid my heart of all perversion; I will not flirt with any evil" (Voice). See Ps. 63:6–7.
4. Matt. 24:38–25:46—In Matthew 24, Jesus predicted the destruction of the Jewish temple, which happened in AD 70. He spoke about the signs of the times—what things to watch for that give an indication of the imminent coming of the Son of Man and when the end of the age or God's final judgment against the unrepentant would occur. Jesus emphasized watchfulness and preparedness in verses 36–44.

    This concept is further developed in the subsequent verses and continues through Matthew 25 with the parables of the faithful servant and the evil servant, the wise and foolish virgins, and the talents. We read the "Son of Man will judge the nations" in Matthew 25:31–44. See Heb. 13:20–21 for a prayer of sanctification.
5. Rev. 3:4–5—The church in Sardis is representative of spiritually "dead" believers; they are warned to strengthen their faith. It concludes with "He who overcomes shall be clothed in white garments, and I will not blot out his name from the Book of Life."

208. In Times of Great Spiritual Conflict

I speak clearly to you, My children, to bless you, to help you know and understand the way you are to walk. You are to walk by My Spirit. It is not by the flesh—it is not by worldly knowledge or worldly wisdom that you will overcome the trials and challenges of this hour.

Walk by My Spirit, setting your heart on pursuing the kingdom of God. This is the only way to overcome in these times of great spiritual conflict and confusion. Will you look to Me? Will you follow My teaching? Will you set your heart on the kingdom of God and My righteousness?

I am speaking to you clearly because I want you to understand the choice that is before you. Do not choose the path of carnality. Do not choose the path of seeking earthly treasures or pleasures. Do not choose the path of pride or fear. Do not choose the path of foolishness and lusts. Do not walk in rebellion.

My children, my children, know that I have made a way for you to overcome every temptation and every trial. Cry out to Me, and I will deliver you. Seek Me first, and My light will show you the path of righteousness. Remain in My righteousness, and you shall be safe. Your destiny is secure in Me.

Selected Scripture Reading

1. Zech. 4:6b—"'Not by might nor by power, but by My Spirit,' says the LORD of hosts."
2. Ps. 51:10–13—"Create in me a clean heart, O God, and renew a steadfast spirit within me. Do not cast me away from Your presence and do not take your Holy Spirit from me. Restore to me the joy of Your salvation, and uphold me by Your generous Spirit. Then I will teach transgressors Your ways, and sinners shall be converted to You."
3. Isa. 30:1—"'Woe to the rebellious children,' says the LORD, 'who take counsel but not of Me, and who devise plans, but not of My Spirit.'"
4. Matt. 5:38–48, Rom. 12:9–21; 1 Thess. 5:15—These verses challenge us to the point of breaking both pride and fear and then instruct us to exercise God's patience and wisdom. In Matthew 5, Jesus was

speaking to the Jews—a people who for the greater part of their existence had been conquered and ruled by a series of other nations: Babylonians, Persians, Greeks, Egyptians, Syrians, and Romans.

5. Gal. 5:16–25—"I say then: Walk in the Spirit, and you shall not fulfil the lust of the flesh … Now the works of the flesh are evident, which are adultery, fornication, uncleanness, lewdness, idolatry, sorcery, hatred, contentions, jealousies, outbursts of wrath, selfish ambitions, dissensions, heresies, envy, murders, drunkenness, revelries, and the like … those who practice such things will not inherit the Kingdom of God. But the fruit of the Spirit is love, joy, peace, longsuffering, kindness, goodness, faithfulness, gentleness, self-control … And those who are Christ's have crucified the flesh with its passions and desires. If we live in the Spirit, let us also walk in the Spirit."

209. Fear Not

I am the Lord your God. Nothing is too great for Me. I created the universe and all that is in it. I know the hearts of mankind.

I say unto you, My little ones. I say to you who seek Me and come before Me. Fear not because I am with you. Fear not the pestilence. Fear not the wars or rumors of wars. Fear not evil. Fear not man, who has the power to destroy the flesh, because in the end, he too must face Me and account for his ways and deeds.

Fear the Lord your God, and put your trust in Him for He is the one who shall comfort and deliver you. Have I not told you that you are my treasure and that I delight in you? Have I not told you that you are My bride and you are pure and spotless before Me?

Rejoice and fear not. Trust Me to do a good work in your life. I am your shield. I am your strength. I am your deliverer. Come to Me and be saved.

Selected Scripture Reading

1. Eccl. 12:1 (Voice)—"My advice to you is to remember your Creator, God, while you are young: before life gets hard and the injustice of old age comes upon you."

2. 1 Chron. 28:9—The chapter begins with King David assembling all his leaders and government officials. Addressing them publicly, David told them that God had chosen his son, Solomon, to succeed him as king and build the temple of the Lord (vv. 5–6). Then King David explained to Solomon his (Solomon's) responsibility in this assignment: "As for you, my son Solomon, know the God of your father, and serve Him with a loyal heart and with a willing mind; for the LORD searches all hearts and understands all the intent of the thoughts. If you seek Him, He will be found by you; but if you forsake Him, He will cast you off forever."
3. Ps. 148—This is a most beautiful and poetic psalm in which all creation praises almighty God. The heavens, angels, sun, moon, stars, fire, hail, snow, clouds, and winds speak in unison. And all creatures on the earth—all peoples too—by their very existence are testimony to the greatness and majesty of God. Verse 5 (Voice) reads, "Let all things join together in a concert of praise to the name of the Eternal, for He gave the command and they were created."
4. "Fear Not"—Bible Gateway records 170 results for "fear not." Some of the other words that may be tagged with fear are worry, anxiety, apprehension, distress, upset, agitated, despair, downhearted, troubled, fretful, uneasy, perturbed, dismayed, and afraid.
5. Prov. 29:25—"The fear of man brings a snare, But whoever trusts in the LORD shall be safe." See Pss. 56:3, 94:19, 91:1–16; Prov. 12:25; Isa. 41:10; Zeph. 3:17; Matt. 6:34; Mark 5:36; 1 John 4:18; Phil. 4:6–7; 2 Tim. 1:7; Rom. 8:38–39; Rev. 1:17.

210. The Coming Beauty

Look and see the coming beauty of My bride. She is elegant, pure, and shines brightly with My love. She stands uprightly, and nothing can shake her. Her strong foundations are built on the rock of Jesus Christ.

By My Spirit, she discerns truth from error. By My Spirit, she walks in the grace I give her—grace to overcome and be victorious. Oh hear Me, My people: align yourselves by My Holy Spirit and receive from Me what I have to give to My bride at this time in history.

I have an inner strength and beauty to give you. Do not look on the things of the world and be blinded and deceived. Look to Me, for I give you eternal beauty. See the salvation and power of God. Look and see, My bride.

Selected Scripture Reading

1. Ps. 27:4—"One thing I have desired of the LORD, that will I seek: that I may dwell in the house of the LORD all the days of my life, to behold the beauty of the LORD, and to inquire in His temple."
2. Zech. 12:10—"And I will pour on the house of David and on the inhabitants of Jerusalem the Spirit of grace and supplication; then they will look on Me whom they pierced. Yes, they will mourn for Him as one mourns for his only son, and grieve for Him as one grieves for a firstborn."
3. Ps. 149:1–9—"Praise the LORD! Sing to the LORD a new song. And His praise in the assembly of saints ... For the LORD takes pleasure in His people; He will beautify the humble with salvation. Let the saints be joyful in glory; let them sing aloud on their beds. Let the high praises of God be in their mouth, and a two-edged sword in their hand. [For an explanation of what that sword is, see Heb. 4:12.] ... This honor have all His saints. Praise the Lord!"
4. 2 Peter and Eph.—The authors of these books gave their lives to speak of Jesus of Nazareth being the long-awaited Messiah. The apostles Paul and Peter remind the believers of the basic foundational truths of the gospel of Christ and then admonish us that we must be diligent in living out God's teachings. We are assured that God has given us spiritual grace and wisdom to be fruitful if we will be faithful. Also noteworthy are the warnings about spiritual warfare and destructive doctrines indicating that wise and genuine spiritual discernment is essential to maintaining the church's integrity.
5. 1 Peter 3:3–4—"Do not let your adornment be merely outward—arranging the hair, wearing gold, or putting on fine apparel—rather let it be the hidden person of the heart, with the incorruptible beauty of a gentle and quiet spirit, which is very precious in the sight of God."
6. Rev. 3:5–6—"He who overcomes shall be clothed in white garments, and I will not blot out his name from the Book of Life; but I will confess his name before My Father and His angels. He who has an ear, let him hear what the Spirit says to the churches."

7. Ps. 17:15—"As for me, I will see Your face in righteousness; I shall be satisfied when I awake in Your likeness."

211. Sorrow Shall Be Turned into Rejoicing

Even in times of great distress, pain, and sorrow, My precious little ones find peace and comfort under My wings. I carry them through and above every sorrow, every pain, and every disappointment. I watch over you carefully. I am protecting you even in the midst of hard and difficult days and nights.

I hear the cry of your heart. Know that I am with you and that soon, your sorrow shall be turned into rejoicing, for I will redeem all things; I will make all things new.

Take comfort, My little ones, knowing I love you and have given My life for you that you may have eternal life and overcome every pain, every distress, and every trial in this life.

Come under My wings and receive grace and power to rise up into the heavenlies with Me. I am your God. I am your heavenly Father.

Selected Scripture Reading

1. Ps. 71:1–24—This is a psalm to read from time to time because life has a way of crushing, smothering, and depleting us of our natural, carnal inner strength. Our enemies maybe real people, circumstances, spiritual and emotional challenges, or even our own wrong attitudes. Regardless of the cause, Psalm 71 has a lot to say about how our relationship with God in the midst of the trial affects the outcome.

    Twice we are told that God's promises to the sincere are for the old as well as the young (vv. 9, 18). Many times, we are reminded of the goodness and promises of God as in the prayerful verses: "In You, O LORD I put my trust; Let me never be put the shame. Deliver me in Your righteousness, and cause me to escape; Incline Your ear to me, and save me. Be my strong refuge, To which I may resort continually; You have given the commandment to save me."

    The word *continually* tells us that we can keep calling out and running to Him for help. Verses 19–21 suggest God may use our

hardships and difficulties to refine our faith, develop our character, and become a foundation for future blessings. Verse 24 concludes with the attitude of thankfulness recognizing through all of life, God is there as our righteous advocate.
2. Ps. 27:10–11—"When my father and my mother forsake me, Then the LORD will take care of me. Teach me Your way, O LORD, And lead me in a smooth path, because of my enemies." See Pss. 68:5, 82:3–4, 146:9. Psalm 10 begins as a lament about how difficult it can be to find God in times of trouble and then acknowledges that in the end, God will execute righteous judgment. See 2 Peter 3:9.
3. Ps. 36:7—"How precious is Your lovingkindness, O God! Therefore the children of men put their trust under the shadow of Your wings." See Ex. 19:4; Ruth 2:12; Ps. 17:8; Mal. 4:2.

212. My Plans and Purposes for You

I love you dearly, My child. Know that My plans and purposes for you are to give you a hope and peace even in the midst of trials, difficulties, and persecutions. For I will build your faith. I will perfect your hope in salvation. You will know Me. You will see Me.

I am your loving Father, who sustains you with living bread and living water. Give your heart wholly—give your heart completely to Me that I may sanctify and bless you with My peace and holiness.

Watch for Me and see Me as I create the likeness of Christ in you.

Selected Scripture Reading

1. Deut. 31:34–32:7—God gave the words to Moses to write a song that was to be taught throughout the generations. This song reminds Israel and the Gentiles too (32:43) that God knows our hearts and will work throughout history to lead us, teach us, and build up our faith in Him.

   The apostle Paul quoted Deuteronomy 32:43 in Romans 15:10 as he encourages Jewish believers and Gentile Christians to respect one another and glorify God together. In recounting Israel's history, the song speaks of how the Lord chose Israel and blessed it; then in verse 15, we read, "But Jeshurun grew fat and kicked ... Then he forsook God who made him, And scornfully esteemed the Rock of his salvation." From this verse, we may conclude that there are potential dangers and temptations with prosperity—when everything is going well for us. The point here is to always be alert to the possibility of taking our relationship with God for granted and gradually forsaking His teachings.

2. Isa. 64:8—"But now, O LORD, You are our Father; We are the clay, and You our potter; and all we are the work of Your hands." See Rom. 8:15; 1 Peter 1:17.

3. Matt. 6—Jesus warned against being a religious hypocrite—someone who trusted in religious activities, self-righteousness, or an organization, heritage, or doctrine rather than in God. Verses 1, 5, 16–19, and 24 indicate that pride and self-aggrandizement are nefarious motives for the hypocrite's good works and achievement.

Jesus instructs us instead to humbly serve others (v. 3). Assuring His followers that God knew what they needed even before they asked, Jesus gave them an example of praying to God—the Lord's Prayer. Succinctly stated in verses 9–15, we are given some principles for building our faith and perfecting our hope in God's salvation.

Verses 25–34 alert us to what will tear down our faith and destroy our hope—worry and complaining. Matthew 6:33 summarizes the chapter: "But seek first the kingdom of God and His righteousness, and all these things shall be added to you."
4. Phil. 3:8–11—"I count all things loss for the excellence of the knowledge of Christ."

213. I Have a Covenant with Those Whose Hearts Belong to Me

The coming battle—the coming conflict—will separate My children from the children of the world. In the past season, the lines have been unclear; but soon, that will not be so.

For I am calling to My people: come up higher and know your God. Walk with Me and know My voice to your heart. Purify yourselves and make ready for the marriage supper of the Lamb because I have a covenant with those whose hearts belong to Me.

I have a covenant with you to watch over you. I have a covenant with you to protect you. I have a covenant to prepare you and make you ready for the wedding day.

Do not fear anything that may happen in this world. Trust Me to carry you through to complete redemption. You are My beloved bride, and I have a covenant with you.

Selected Scripture Reading

1. Jer. 31:31–33—"Behold, the days are coming, says the LORD, when I will make a new covenant with the house of Israel and with the house of Judah—not according to the covenant that I made with their fathers in the day that I took them by the hand to lead them out of the land of Egypt … But this is the covenant that I will make with the house of Israel after those days, says the LORD: I will put My law in their minds, and write it on their hearts; and I will be their God, and they shall be My people." See Heb. 8:7–13.
2. Ps. 111:1–10; 2 Cor. 3:6; Eph. 4:1–6:24—*Webster's* definition of *covenant* includes, "in theology, the promises of God to man, usually carrying with them conditions to be fulfilled by man, as recorded

in the Bible." In Psalm 111, we read, "He will ever be mindful of His covenant and He has sent redemption to His people; He has commanded His covenant forever."

These are examples of the covenants in the Bible.

- with Noah and his family to preserve them during the flood (Gen. 6:18–20)
- with Abram and his descendants to give them land (Gen. 15:9–21)
- with Abram to give him descendants and prosperity (Gen. 17:2–21)
- with the House of Jacob for establishing a priesthood (Ex. 19:5–6)
- the Mosaic covenant with Israel that was broken by the golden calf incident (Ex. 34:10–26)
- In Joshua 24, Joshua assembled the people, reviewed God's promises of blessing for obedience to the covenant, and called them to put away their idolatry and only follow God—the people made a commitment.
- Messianic covenant (Isa. 42:1–9)—God's covenant with His Servant, the Messiah, to give Him for a covenant of the people that in Isaiah 55:1–6 was expanded to include the Gentile nations.

3. 1 Thess. 5:23–24—"Now may the God of peace Himself sanctify you completely; and may your whole spirit, soul, and body be preserved blameless at the coming of our Lord Jesus Christ. He who calls you is faithful, who also will do it." See Rev. 2:7.

214. Have Confidence in My Love for You

Be alert, My little one, for your enemy, the devil, is looking for those he may separate from Me and devour with deceptions. Do not fall prey to his cunning strategies. Guard your heart with purity and My righteousness. Stay close to Me, and do not let your heart and mind wander in the world's ways and lust-filled deceptions.

Stay close to Me, My little one, and have confidence in My love for you. Keep your eyes on Me and your heart grounded in My love and truth. You will be safe in My arms.

Be alert and wise, My little one. Be safe in Me.

Selected Scripture Reading

1. Isa. 43:2–3—"When you pass through the waters, I will be with you; And through the rivers, they shall not overflow you. When you walk through the fire, you shall not be burned, Nor shall the flame scorch you. For I am the LORD your God, The Holy One of Israel, your Savior." See Ps. 1 and 1 Peter 1:3–9.
2. Prov. 4:23 (Voice)—"Above all else, watch over your heart; diligently guard it because from a sincere and pure heart come the good and noble things of life."
3. Gen. 3:1; 1 Chron. 21:1; Isa. 14:12–21; Zech. 3:1; Matt. 4:3, 13:38–39; Luke 4:13; John 13:2; 2 Cor. 2:11, 11:3; Eph. 6:12; 1 Thess. 3:5; 2 Thess. 2:8–9; 1 Peter 5:5–9; 2 Cor. 11:14; Heb. 2:14; Rev. 20:10—These are some of the many scriptures that acknowledge the existence of a wicked spiritual force that works to deceive, wound, and destroy mankind.
4. Zephaniah—There began a decline in the natural and spiritual condition of Israel with the introduction of worshipping false gods during the reign of Solomon. (1 Kings 11) Around . 975 BC, the nation was divided with the northern part being called Israel and the southern part Judah. Most of the kings of Israel and Judah were corrupt, ungodly leaders. The people wandered in idolatry, materialism, immorality, greed, and confused complacency.

    During the reign of King Josiah of Judah, the prophet Zephaniah called the people to repentance and warned them that their sins would result in national disaster. Although Josiah led a spiritual revival with reforms, it did not penetrate the culture sufficiently, and about forty years later, the Babylonians conquered Judah. There are imminent and future references to the day of the Lord, which speak a lesson to all generations and nations. Zephaniah 3:8–20 assures us that there will be a faithful remnant God will rejoice over and give an amazing restoration.
5. Rom. 11:1–36—"Even so then, at this present time there is a remnant according to the election of grace." See Romans 12–15:13 on how the remnant are to conduct their lives.

6. Phil. 4:4–9—In these verses, the apostle Paul gave a summary of what it takes to retain the divine confidence and peace that comes from God.

215. Choose Life That You May Live

To do the work I desire to do in your heart and life, you must cooperate with My Holy Spirit. That is why My Word instructs you to crucify the works of the flesh, put away all carnality, and come before Me with a humble desire to learn and obey.

Follow Me and I will lead you into abundant life. My desire is for you to live a rich, spiritual life full of love, peace, and joy—blessed in every way—enjoying the fruit of your labors.

See the choices set before you and choose life that you may live. Crucify the lusts of the flesh, and turn away from selfishness and pride for My Spirit is here to work among you and do a great work in these last days.

My bride shall be altogether lovely and beautiful. I delight in her purity of heart. I delight in her desire to be Mine.

Selected Scripture Reading

1. Psalms—There is no better way to learn how to cooperate with God's Holy Spirit than to read, study, pray, and sing the book of Psalms. If we set our hearts to know Him, the rich word pictures, honest and heartfelt prayers, seeing history through God's perspective, and eternal truths will nourish our spirits and souls.

   These 150 spiritual songs and poems are the praise hymnal of God's people throughout history. In 1 Chronicles 16:4–6 and 23:5 is the record that King David assigned 4,000 of the 38,000 Levites to sing praises to the Lord using stringed instruments, cymbals, and trumpets.

   While the predominant themes are praise and prayer, almost every topic is covered in some measure in the Psalms. As they were sung down through the generations, they reminded the people of who they were, who God is, and what His plans are for those who love and follow Him. The messages are timeless.

The broader picture of life given in these poetic songs also reveals details about God's promised Messiah. We see Christ as King in Psalms 2, 45, 72, 110, and 132:11. We see Christ as the suffering Messiah in Psalms 22, 41, 55:12–14, and 69:20–21. Comparing Psalm 16:10, Matthew 16:21, and the apostle Paul's sermon at Antioch (Acts 13:16–39), we understand that the resurrection of the Messiah is foretold in Psalm 16:10. The ascension of the Messiah is described in Psalm 68:18, recorded in Mark 16:19, and further explained in Ephesians 4, especially verse 8.
2. Every day, we make many choices. The Bible challenges us to use wisdom and not follow a self-indulgent lifestyle. The descriptive phrase "crucify the flesh" depicts the emotional struggle that may ensue as we choose self-control over self-centeredness. See Prov. 16:32; Rom. 6:1–23, 13:14; Gal. 5:16–24; Col. 3:5; 1 Peter 2:11; 4:1–11.
3. Ps. 100:1–5—"Serve the LORD with gladness; come before His presence with singing ... Be thankful to Him, and bless His name. For the Lord is good; His mercy is everlasting, and His truth endures to all generations."

216. Remember

Think and consider, My chosen—My precious bride—for there are various paths that lie before you. You must consider and evaluate the choices.

Some choices are easy to make because the outcome is clear. You understand the right path to take. You have assurance in your heart, "This is the way. Walk in it."

There are other times, however, when it is unclear to you if you should go or which way to go. Quiet your soul and remember My love for you. Remember the goodness of your God. I do not leave you or forsake you. Remember and trust Me.

Wait upon Me. Remember My words to you, and let faith increase in your heart. The faith in your heart will direct you, and by My Spirit, you will know the path to walk. Remember, I am with you.

Selected Scripture Reading

1. Deut. 30:15–20—"See, I have set before you today life and good, death and evil, in that I command you today to love the LORD your God, to walk in His ways ... that you may live ... But if your heart turns away so that you do not hear, and are drawn away, and worship other gods and serve them, I announce to you today that you shall surely perish ... therefore choose life, that both you and your descendants may live; that you may love the LORD your God, that you may obey His voice ... for He is your life and the length of your days." See Isa. 30:21.
2. Ps. 119:59—"I thought about my ways, and turned my feet to Your testimonies."
3. Josh. 1:8–9 (ONMB)—"This book of the Torah (Teaching) will not depart out of your mouth, but you will meditate on it day and night, so you can observe to do according to all that is written in it, for then you will act wisely in all your Ways, and then you will have good success. Have I not commanded you? Be strong! Be of good courage! Do not tremble! Do not be dismayed! For the LORD your God is with you wherever you go."
4. 2 Tim. 3:16–17—"All Scripture is given by inspiration of God, and is profitable for doctrine, for reproof, for correction, for instruction in righteousness, that the man of God may be complete thoroughly equipped for every good work." See 1 Tim. 4:15–16.
5. Ps. 131:2—"Surely I have calmed and quieted my soul, like a weaned child with his mother; like a weaned child is my soul within me."
6. Prov. 3:5–6—"Trust in the LORD with all your heart, and lean not on your own understanding; in all your ways acknowledge Him, and He shall direct your paths."

217. And You Will See

By My Word and by My Spirit, I speak to you. Hear and understand. Know what I am saying and you will be strengthened. You will see beyond the confusion. You will see beyond the chaos and destruction. You will see through the deceptions.

Hear and know My Word. Live by My Spirit and you will stand. You will live victoriously as you walk in My love, My truth, and My wisdom. Know My Word and put it in your heart so My Spirit may give you discernment. These are perilous times, and you must have discernment to see through the strategies of the enemy.

I am restoring My people. I am restoring your vision and understanding. Be wise, My little ones, and you will see. By My Word and by My Spirit, says the Lord your God, you will see.

Selected Scripture Reading

1. Isa. 40:8—"The grass withers, the flower fades, but the word of our God stands forever." See Luke 21:33.
2. Ps. 119:11—"Your word I have hidden in my heart, that I might not sin against You."
3. John 5:39—"You search the Scriptures, for in them you think you have eternal life; and these are they which testify of Me." See Isa. 7:14, 9:6–7; Mal. 1:11; Acts 18:24–28.
4. Rom. 15:4—"For whatever things were written before were written for our learning, that we, through the patience and comfort of the Scriptures might have hope." See Isa. 2:3.
5. Zech. 4:6—"'... not by might nor by power, but by My Spirit,' says the LORD of hosts."
6. John 6:63—"It is the Spirit who gives life; the flesh profits nothing. The words that I speak to you are spirit, and they are life." See Isa. 61; Luke 4:16.
7. Ps. 119:104—"Through Your precepts I get understanding; therefore I hate every false way."
8. Hag. 2:4—"'Be strong, all you people of the land,' says the LORD, 'and work; for I am with you,' says the LORD of hosts."
9. 2 Cor. 3:2–3—"You are our epistle written in our hearts, known and read by all men; clearly you are an epistle of Christ ... written not with ink but by the Spirit of the living God, not on tablets of stone but on tablets of flesh, that is, of the heart." See Ps. 40:8.
10. Prov. 29:18 (Voice)—"Where there is no vision from God, the people run wild, but those who adhere to God's instruction know genuine happiness."

11. Matt. 5:8—"Blessed are the pure in heart, for they shall see God." See Ps. 15.
12. James 3:17–18—"But the wisdom that is from above is first pure, then peaceable, gentle, willing to yield, full of mercy and good fruits, without partiality and without hypocrisy. Now the fruit of righteousness is sown in peace by those who make peace."

218. Have Courage

I am calling to you, says the Lord your God. I desire for you to walk in the peace and safety I have for you. I am your safe place. I am your security.

Know that I love you. Know that I am here to protect you from the destroyer. The thief comes to rob, steal, and destroy all that is good and pure. I cannot help you unless you stop following the ways of the thief.

Know that I am here to lead and guide you into all righteousness, peace, and joy. Forsake the ways of the wicked one, and do not be deceived by the lusts that war against your salvation.

I am here to help you. I am here to bring you restoration. Fear not. Have courage and come to Me. I am your safe place. In Me, you will find the peace and joy your heart desires.

Selected Scripture Reading

1. Ps. 20:7—"Some trust in chariots, and some in horses; But we will remember the name of the LORD our God."
2. Ps. 4:8—"I will both lie down in peace, and sleep; For You alone, O LORD, make me dwell in safety."
3. Ps. 5—This is a prayer for guidance in the midst of attacks and difficulties. The psalmist begins by declaring that he is crying out to almighty God and will look to Him and nowhere else for help. In verses 4–6, the one praying acknowledges that he understands God doesn't tolerate any wickedness. Pride, boasting, lying, violence, flattery, deceit, and rebellion are specifically mentioned. In essence, the psalmist says, "I know You, O God, are a God of righteousness and I want to choose the path—I want to make decisions—that pleases You. Please make Your way straight before me—make Your way clear for me to understand."

The psalmist recognizes that he has enemies who are focused on his destruction through deception and outright violence. We may not face such direct threats on our physical lives, but wickedness itself is a formidable spiritual enemy that comes in many alluring and deceptive disguises. We need God's guidance and salvation to show us and empower us into peace and safety.

4. Ps. 78:40–42—"How often they provoked Him in the wilderness, And grieved Him in the desert! Yes, again and again they tempted God, And limited the Holy One of Israel." We might ask, "How can we limit God?" First, we are assured of the strength, power, and majesty of our eternal heavenly Father. Then in verse 5 begins the history of Israel. We read about all the ways God provided for and protected them and yet they focused on their issues and complained and accused God. Verse 56 (Voice) reads, "Even after all this they disobeyed the Most High God and tested His patience and did not live by His commands." We enter His rest by trust and faith. See Deut. 1:34–35; Ps. 95:10; Heb. 4:1–5.

219. Restoration Is a Process

Be patient, My child. Restoration is a process that takes time. You must have faith and vision to see into the future. Old strongholds and ungodly ways of thinking and doing must be identified, forsaken, and torn down.

I am restoring My bride to be altogether lovely and adorned with the beauty of grace, love, and truth. She is majestic and filled with the glory and power of Christ. She is fully committed and devoted to Me.

Have faith to see the restoration of My church. Be patient and full of My love and grace as I work among you and in your midst to do this work of restoration. Look and see what I am doing in your hearts.

Selected Scripture Reading

1. Isa. 61:1–11 (NIV)—"The Spirit of the Sovereign LORD is on me, because the LORD has anointed me to preach good news to the poor. He has sent me to bind up the brokenhearted, to proclaim freedom for the captives and release for the prisoners, to proclaim the

year of the LORD'S favor and the day of vengeance of our God, to comfort all who mourn, and provide for those who grieve in Zion—to bestow on them a crown of beauty instead of ashes, the oil of gladness instead of mourning, and a garment of praise ... They will rebuild the ancient ruins and restore the places long devastated ... For I the LORD, love justice ... I delight greatly in the LORD; my soul rejoices in my God for He has clothed me with garments of salvation and arrayed me in a robe of righteousness, as a bridegroom adorns his head like a priest and as a bride adorns herself with her jewels ... so the Sovereign LORD will make righteousness and praise spring up before all nations." See Luke 4:16–21.
2. Rom. 15:1–13 (NIV)—"We who are strong ought to bear with the failings of the weak and not to please ourselves. Each of us should please his neighbor for his good, to build him up. For even Christ did not please himself ... May the God who gives endurance and encouragement give you a spirit of unity among yourselves as you follow Christ Jesus, so that with one heart and mouth you may glorify the God and Father of our Lord Jesus Christ. Accept one another, then, just as Christ accepted you, in order to bring praise to God. For I tell you that Christ has become a servant of the Jews on behalf of God's truth, to confirm the promises made to the patriarchs so that the Gentiles may glorify God for his mercy, as it is written." See 2 Sam. 22:50; Ps. 18:49; Deut. 32:43; Ps. 117:1; Isa. 11:10.
3. Heb. 10:35–36—"Therefore do not cast away your confidence which has great reward. For you have need of endurance so that, after you have done the will of God, you may receive the promise."

220. Build Eternal Treasures with Great Joy

For many years, My people have not been quick to come to Me first for understanding and wisdom concerning strategies to solve problems, design projects, or even build lasting relationships on strong foundations.

Now you are in a season of reaping what you have sown, a season of harvesting the fruit of doing things your way, without My counsel, without My Spirit. The peoples of the nations have been building many towers to their glory because their hearts are full of pride and deception.

Do you not see? Do you not understand? I am your Creator, and I call you to a higher standard. I call you to come into relationship with Me. Seek Me and know Me. Give your heart and life to Me; I will fill you with My love, counsel, and grace so you can see with wisdom and understanding. Then you shall know how to choose the good and refuse what is foolish and wicked. Then you shall know how and what to do and say and with whom and when to come together in unity to work.

Repent now. Confess your sins and the sins of your nation. There is a season of difficulty coming over all the earth. All that can be shaken will be shaken. Many towers, false gods, and carnal foundations will be exposed and destroyed.

Come up. Come up to a higher way. Come up and be saved from destruction. Come up and receive My love, grace, and wisdom to build eternal treasures with great joy.

Selected Scripture Reading

1. Ps. 73:24–25—"You will guide me with Your counsel, And afterward receive me to glory."
2. Isa. 9:6—"For unto us a Child is born, Unto us a Son is given; And the government will be upon His shoulder. And His name will be called Wonderful, Counselor."
3. Isa. 11:2—"The Spirit of the LORD shall rest upon Him, The Spirit of wisdom and understanding, The Spirit of counsel and might, The Spirit of knowledge and of the fear of the LORD." Compare with Isa. 61:1–11; Luke 4:16–21.
4. Ps. 143:10—"Teach me how to do Your will, for You are my God." Jesus said that the Holy Spirit will be our teacher and guide us in all things (John 14:26). He also said that the Holy Spirit would help us know when and what to say (Luke 12:12). Speaking on the subject of the Holy Spirit as teacher, the apostle Paul said that we human beings have no natural understanding of all the good things God has prepared for those who love Him; that only through God's Spirit can we comprehend and experience the gifts that come from God. He stated that a person who has yielded himself to learning from God would patiently examine all things with the help of God's Spirit and His truth (1 Cor. 2:7–15). Voice is a good translation for these verses in 1 Corinthians.

5. Isa. 30:1—This verse illustrates what God thinks of those who in rebellion do their own thing. See Isa. 2:15 and 30:25. What do you think the towers represent?

221. Peoples and Nations, Come

In these last days, says the Lord, shall I not speak to the hearts of all mankind a warning and a testimony to the power and glory of God? My Son is returning soon to the earth, this time to be revealed to all the peoples and nations as King of Kings and Lord of Lords. He will complete the redemption of those who know Him as Savior.

I speak to you, all peoples and nations of the earth—I speak to your hearts. Recognize and acknowledge the witness of My Holy Spirit as I speak to your hearts. I shall speak to you when the waves of the sea roar. I shall speak to you when the mountains and valleys shake and when the idols you have chased after come tumbling down. I shall call you in a still, small voice to come to Me. Follow Me and you will live. Obey My words. Trust in Me and you will find eternal peace and safety.

I call to you, peoples and nations. Come together and acknowledge I am the Lord your God—Creator and Savior of all. Who among you will forsake evil and choose good? Now is the time to choose if you will love your Creator.

Selected Scripture Reading

1. Ps. 47:8—"God reigns over the nations; God sits on His holy throne." See Isa. 26:1–3.
2. Ps. 33:8—"Let all the earth fear the LORD; Let all the inhabitants of the world stand in awe of Him." Psalm 33 continues by confirming His sovereignty in creation and throughout history. We are reminded God's eye is upon both individuals and nations.
3. Prov. 14:34 (Voice)—"Living according to God's instructions makes a nation great, but sin colors those who commit it with disgrace." See Prov. 29:18.
4. Pss. 9, 72; Isa. 5, 30; Jer. 11:17, 12:17, 45:4; Amos 9:8; Zeph. 3:8; Matt. 25:31–46; Acts 10:34–48; 2 Cor. 5:10—These passages indicate that

nations and individuals alike are held accountable by God. See John 5:22–47.
5. Jer. 23:22; Ezek. 13:1–5; Lam. 2:14; 2 Peter 1:19–21—These define a major task of preaching, teaching, and ministering is encouraging people to follow God's commands and ways. 1 Corinthians 13 lists the attributes of love that qualify one to preach, teach, and minister in God's name.
6. Mark 7:1–23—In these verses, Jesus taught that our preconceived ideas and our trust in ceremonialism and pleasant traditions can cause us to reject God's words and Spirit and even to miss what He is doing in our midst.
7. John 1:49—"Nathanael answered and said to Him, 'Rabbi, You are the Son of God! You are the King of Israel!'" See Dan. 7:14; Zech. 9:9; Matt. 21:1–11; 1 Cor. 15:20–28.
8. John 18:37—"Jesus answered, 'You say rightly that I am a king. For this cause I was born, and for this cause I have come into the world, that I should bear witness to the truth. Everyone who is of the truth hears My voice.'" See Rev. 19:11–16.

222. Drink of the Living Waters

I speak words of life to you, My people, that you may live. My words are living waters to you. Take them in and drink of Me.

For the living waters I give to you will indeed bring you salvation, peace, and great joy. I will satisfy your thirst for truth and understanding. The water I give to you will reveal My love for you.

Come and drink of the living waters. My words in you will become living waters that flow out from you and bring healing, joy, and peace to all who will receive them.

Open your eyes and see. The words of life that I give to you are living waters.

Selected Scripture Reading

1. Hos. 55:1–56:8—"Ho! Everyone who thirsts, Come to the waters; And you who have no money, Come, buy, and eat ... Incline your ear and come

to Me. Hear, and your soul shall live; And I will make an everlasting covenant with you—The sure mercies of David ... For as the rain comes down ... So shall My word be that goes forth from My mouth; It shall not return to Me void, But it shall accomplish what I please."

By these verses and chapter 56, we understand that the call to come drink of the living waters—the words of almighty God—are for all people everywhere. Verse 7b reads, "For My house shall be called a house of prayer for all nations."

2. John 4:5–26—This is the story of the Samaritan woman who met Jesus at Jacob's well. After asking the woman to give him a drink, Jesus opened the conversation about water. Samaritans were despised by Jews, and the woman asked him why He would ask her for water. Jesus spoke to her about the living water that would quench her spiritual thirst for truth and relationship with God.

3. John 7:37–39—It was a long-standing custom during the Feast of Tabernacles to have a daily water pouring ceremony commemorating the story of the water from the rock in Exodus 17. In this ceremony, the priests recited Isaiah 12:3: "Therefore with joy you will draw water From the wells of salvation."

During the last day of the Feast of Tabernacles, Jesus said, "If anyone thirsts, let him come to Me and drink. He who believes in Me, as the Scripture has said, out of his heart will flow rivers of living water." Verse 39 reveals Jesus was using the phrase "living water" to speak of the Holy Spirit.

4. Rev. 7:14–17—"These are the ones who come out of the great tribulation, and washed their robes and made them white in the blood of the Lamb. Therefore they are before the throne of God ... And He who sits on the throne will dwell among them. They shall not hunger anymore nor thirst anymore ... for the Lamb who is in the midst of throne will shepherd them and lead them to living fountains of waters."

223. I Am Here to Comfort You

Listen. Listen. Listen to My Holy Spirit as I speak to your heart. My Spirit will teach you and direct you in the things you need to know and understand.

I have made a way for you. I have made provision for you to walk through and overcome even in the perilous days of the end times. It is by My Word and by My Spirit that you will know in your heart what to believe, whom to trust, where to go, what to do, and when to speak. My Spirit will direct you when to speak and what to say.

Do not be impulsive or act in the flesh. I cannot bless that. Submit yourself completely to Me, and allow Me to fill your innermost being with My love and peace. Do not be moved or fearful because of unfolding events in the world. Stay close to Me and listen to My voice. I am here to comfort you.

Selected Scripture Reading

1. Nehemiah—Read and study the book of Nehemiah to learn how God moved upon, directed, and guided a Jewish captive servant named Nehemiah to govern and oversee a massive project of relocating exiled Jewish people from Babylon to the decimated and charred remains of the city of Jerusalem ca. 444 BC. This was a multifaceted and complicated task because he had to plan and direct the rebuilding of the stone and mortar walls of the city and he had to renew and restore the people's understanding and faith in their God.

    Nehemiah was motivated by a divine compassion combined with focused prayer and dedication. He resisted temptations to be distracted from his assigned task even when attacked by naysayers. He was skilled and knowledgeable; he gave priority to following God's principles.

    In Nehemiah's story are multiple parallel lessons for New Testament believers to apply to their lives while giving an understanding of what it takes for spiritual restoration. In Nehemiah 9, the congregation of thousands made a public confession of the works and faithfulness of God, their sins and those of their nation, of God's covenant and mercies, and the renewing of their commitment to the covenant with God.

2. Prov. 2:1–22—Synonyms of impulsivity or acting in the flesh may be indiscretion, rashness, imprudence, presumption or thoughtless—all of which signal a lack of self-control and wisdom.

3. John 14:26–27 (Voice)—"The Father is sending a great Helper, the Holy Spirit, in My name to teach you everything and to remind you of all I have said to you. My peace is the legacy I leave to you. I don't give gifts like those of this world. Do not let your heart be troubled or fearful." See 2 Cor. 9:8; Phil. 4:19.
4. 2 Cor. 1:3—"Bless be the God and Father of our Lord Jesus Christ, the Father of mercies and God of all comfort, who comforts us in all our tribulation, that we may be able to comfort those who are in any trouble, with the comfort with which we ourselves are comforted by God."

224. Your Fulfilled Redemption Is Drawing Near

Look up, My beloved, for your fulfilled redemption is drawing near. Have I not said to you that I am returning to you and will take you home to My Father? There you will be with Me forever.

Know and consider this: the great, fiery trials coming upon the earth will expose wickedness. But these hardships shall reveal the glory of God in My people who know Me and are called by My name. The light of God in you shall shine and dispel the darkness.

Do not be afraid. Do not be fearful. Understand that the testing of your faith will strengthen you. I am calling My people to come up higher and know Me more intimately.

For I am preparing you to return home with Me. Rejoice, My beloved. Rejoice. Hold fast to your faith.

Selected Scripture Reading

1. Ps. 111:9—"He has sent redemption to His people; He has commanded His covenant forever: Holy and awesome is His name."
2. Dan. 7:13–14—"I was watching in the night visions, and behold, One like the Son of Man, coming with the clouds of heaven! He came to the Ancient of Days, and they brought Him near before Him, Then to Him was given dominion and glory and a kingdom. That all peoples, nations, and languages should serve Him. His dominion is

an everlasting dominion, which shall not pass away, and His kingdom the one which shall not be destroyed."
3. Acts 1:9–11—"Now when He had spoken these things, while they watched, He was taken up, and a cloud received Him out of their sight. And while they looked steadfastly toward heaven as He went up behold, two men stood by them in white apparel. Who also said, 'Men of Galilee, why do you stand gazing up into heaven? This same Jesus, who was taken up from you into heaven, will so come in like manner as you saw Him go into heaven.'"
4. Eph. 4:30—"And do not grieve the Holy Spirit of God, by whom you were sealed for the day of redemption." See 1 Peter 1:6–7; Titus 2:11–15.
5. Luke 21:28—"Now when these things begin to happen, look up and lift up your heads, because your redemption draws near." See Rom. 8:18–25.
6. John 14:3—"And if I go and prepare a place for you, I will come again and receive you to Myself; that where I am, there you may be also."
7. Rev. 21:3—"And I heard a loud voice from heaven saying, 'Behold, the tabernacle of God is with men, and He will dwell with them, and they shall be His people. God Himself will be with them and be their God.'"

225. Every One of My Children

I have a call upon the life of every one of My children. Will you answer My call? Will you listen with your heart and hear what I am saying to you? Let your heart—let your spirit be open to My love for you so you can hear what I am saying to you.

Sift out—separate from the attitudes and beliefs that cause you to hate and be angry, even fearful. Instead, reach out to Me with love and faith and you will hear My voice to your heart.

Do not give up. Persevere, always trusting Me to do a good work in your life knowing that I will take loving care of you. You will learn to grow in grace, peace, mercy, and wisdom.

Thus, you will walk in the destiny and purposes I have for you. The nature of Christ will be formed in you, and the glory of God will shine forth from you. Your destiny shall be revealed.

226. My Prayer to You, O My God

Early in the morning will I seek You, O my God, for You are my God, and my heart cries out to You. You cover me with Your wings, and I rest in Your shadow. In You, I hide from my enemies. In You, I seek refuge from the storms of this life.

Though I cannot understand all that happens, I trust in You. You are faithful to me. You are trustworthy and dependable. I shall not fear. Hold me close to You, O my God. Fill me with Your Spirit that I may walk in Your counsel and anointing. I seek Your presence in my heart that I may know You.

I know and feel Your love for me, my Lord and my King. In Jesus Christ, You have given Yourself for me, and by Your Holy Spirit, You are my companion and comforter.

How I love You, O my God. Let not this world or the enemies of my soul steal my devotion to You. Protect me from the deceitfulness of sin and the lies of deceptions.

O God, my God, You are my heart's desire, and I desire to please You and bring to You fruitfulness that is pleasing and worthy in Your sight. May my life and the meditations of my heart bring You great joy. Help me, O God, to fulfill the calling and life's work You have ordained for me.

Let Your kingdom move forward and be established on this earth. Our desire is to love You and love others more perfectly. Let those who call on the Lord God almighty and His Son, Jesus Christ, not be disappointed or ashamed.

May we lift up Your name, O Lord, that You may draw all mankind to You for salvation. In the hour of darkness and deception, shine Your brilliance of truth and salvation over all the earth.

Your kingdom come, Your will be done in earth as it is in heaven. Let there be light so Your creation may see You!

Printed in the United States
By Bookmasters